STRESS AND MENTAL HEALTH OF COLLEGE STUDENTS

STRESS AND MENTAL HEALTH OF COLLEGE STUDENTS

MERY V. LANDOW
EDITOR

Nova Science Publishers, Inc.
New York

Copyright © 2006 by Nova Science Publishers, Inc.

For permission to use material from this book please contact us:
Telephone 631-231-7269; Fax 631-231-8175
Web Site: http://www.novapublishers.com

NOTICE TO THE READER

The Publisher has taken reasonable care in the preparation of this book, but makes no expressed or implied warranty of any kind and assumes no responsibility for any errors or omissions. No liability is assumed for incidental or consequential damages in connection with or arising out of information contained in this book. The Publisher shall not be liable for any special, consequential, or exemplary damages resulting, in whole or in part, from the readers' use of, or reliance upon, this material.

This publication is designed to provide accurate and authoritative information with regard to the subject matter covered herein. It is sold with the clear understanding that the Publisher is not engaged in rendering legal or any other professional services. If legal or any other expert assistance is required, the services of a competent person should be sought. FROM A DECLARATION OF PARTICIPANTS JOINTLY ADOPTED BY A COMMITTEE OF THE AMERICAN BAR ASSOCIATION AND A COMMITTEE OF PUBLISHERS.

LIBRARY OF CONGRESS CATALOGING-IN-PUBLICATION DATA
Available upon request.

ISBN 1-59454-839-0

Published by Nova Science Publishers, Inc. ❖ New York

CONTENTS

PREFACE

College students are subject to a massive input of stresses which require successful and ever-changing coping strategies. These stresses include inside and outside pressures by the world to succeed, financial worries, concerns about uncertain futures, social problems and opportunities since college is often the meeting place for future mates,and homework and tests in multiple and complex subjects requiring preparation and focus with often conflicting priorities. Unsuccessful coping often results in anxiety, heavy drinking, depression and a host of other mental health problems.This new book presents new and important research in this important field.

The primary goal of the research presented in chapter 1 was to explore the existence or nonexistence of counterproductive stress and its antecedents in entry level Pharm.D. students. Any empirical findings that purport the existence of stress and its antecedents in these students was a seminal work in this field because of the lacuna in the extant literature on stress in health professions students. The theoretical framework for this inquiry was the psychosocial model of stress as proposed by Lazarus and Folkman (1984). Findings from this inquiry may prove to be enormously helpful in shaping future curricula changes in schools of pharmacy. These findings may also facilitate the implementation of intervention strategies and coping programs to alleviate if not eliminate unnecessary stress in pharmacy students during their professional education. Equipped with a new knowledge of stress and its antecedents, pharmacy school administrators and faculty members would be uniquely poised to be proactive versus reactive insofar as the stress levels of their students are concerned. They should be able to take appropriate actions to diminish stress levels in their students by eliminating or minimizing the impact of the significant stressors identified in this inquiry. Diminishing counterproductive stress and its causative factors would help to create a nurturing, enabling, and productive atmosphere for these professional students. Pharmacy School administrators could greatly improve the environments for the professional education they provide by assisting their students in acquiring financial aid, eliminating sources of excessive competition among students, being more supportive of their students, and by performing analyses of course requirements to ensure that learning is commensurate with the amount of student effort outside of the classroom.

The main findings from the study in chapter 2 suggest that medical knowledge has a mitigating factor upon health anxiety. From the perspective of a cognitive model of health anxiety (Salkovskis and Warwick, 1986), acquiring medical knowledge was represented as a 'critical precipitating event' which influenced the previously held beliefs about health and symptom perception. Mechanic (1972) proposed that new medical knowledge would interact with existing stress to heighten bodily sensations, making the student more aware of his/her own bodily state. Although further research would need to be carried out to investigate the notion of self-symptom monitoring, the findings of the present study would reject Mechanic's claim. From a theoretical perspective, the acquisition of medical knowledge (as a 'critical precipitating event') is a positive influence. The author of this study would suggest that the acquisition of the knowledge enables the individual to cognitively appraise and assimilate previously held unhelpful beliefs. It also allows the cycle of rumination about health concerns (i.e. worry) can be broken, as new information causes the individual to problem-solve and resolve medical dilemmas. This would be a proposed explanation to account for lower scores in health worry (AnTI). Further research is warranted to investigate these claims. This may take the form of studying meta-cognitive processes in more detail, particularly focusing upon the interaction between attention to health concerns and emotionality.

Chapter 3 reviews a study which was conducted to look into factors that affect students' performance and in particular those leading to students being under probation. A group of factors were identified. In general, the factors contributing to the poor academic achievement can be attributed to two main categories: the intrinsic (within-individual) and the extrinsic (extra-individual) factors. The first includes a large number of causes, such as: endocrinal disorders (as thyroid dysfunction and diabetes), low intelligence, emotional disorders (anxiety and depression), behavioral disorders affecting cognitive functions (as Attention Deficit Hyperactivity Disorder), speech and language disorders (Dyslexia, Autism, Dysphasia), sensory and physical disabling conditions (as hearing impairment, cerebral palsy, poliomyelitis), and psychiatric disorders (as Schizophrenia). The external factors on the other hand cover enormous number of causes as: poverty and social injustice, poor teachers' quality, inappropriate teaching programs, improper parenting style, badly chosen friends, unsuitable housing conditions, etc. These causes affect the individual's performance at school/university according to his age, for example low intelligence causes poor school performance at the kindergarten and elementary school level, while others like anxiety and depression might cause deterioration in school (or university) achievement following a good start (if the student has no other associated problem acting from the beginning). This chapter deals with the exam stress and emotional disorders that can affect the learning process negatively among the medical students in SQU. These students on probation have been admitted to the university having obtained the highest marks among their cohorts in the secondary schools, enabling them to start their medical education. Being members of the probation committee, the authors have found a large number of students with probation suffering from exam stress and emotional disorders (anxiety and depression). These two disorders can have negative effects on human behavior, like their effects on sleep (both quantitatively and qualitatively), and on cognitive functions (attention, concentration and memory), consequently these will lead to drastic impairments in the learning process.

The university context is a locus for developmentally appropriate change and challenge in the life of college students. College communities are also ideal forums for skill-based mental health interventions Chapter 4 presents an epidemiologic assessment of the prevalence of stress, depression and related psychological states among college students. It also examines the central stressor domains that impact the lives of college students as well as the short and longer term biopsychosocial consequences from chronic stress. Furthermore, it provides an integration of the various conceptual frameworks which link stress, depression and mental health. This will be enhanced by a diagrammatic representation or modeling of these relationships. The final section of the chapter presents avenues for promising prevention intervention and research. Recently collected data on stress management courses and interventions developed and implemented on a large public university campus are presented along with recommendations for settings and theoretical frameworks for future programmatic and research efforts.

The focus of chapter 5 is on student stressors in higher education which are not confined to those of traditional college age. Working adult students experience unique stressors due to their multiple roles as students, providers, and employees, and institutions of higher learning have not always been adept at recognizing and responding to these pressures. This descriptive study examines adult students in two accelerated higher education programs (nursing and management) at one institution. Students in both programs were surveyed regarding the degree to which the university addresses the context (as opposed to merely the content) of the learning environment for these students. The data derived from the survey process indicates significant areas of positive feedback and other areas in which universities can better serve their adult students. The essay concludes with a reflection on the degree to which the faith identify of the institution is responsible for its student support ethos.

Chapter 6 concerns a study involving college student stress. Specifically, students' school stress, personal stress, and anxiety about communicating with their instructors was investigated. The authors expected that students with higher levels of stress and anxiety should differ in their classroom interest and communication. Interest was measured using an instrument that had three dimensions: competence (I feel I can be successful in my classes), impact (I believe I can make a difference in my classes), and meaningfulness (My classes are relevant to me). Communication with instructors was addressed by measuring five motives students have for communicating with their instructors: relational (I want to get to know my instructors better), functional (I need to get information that is relevant to my class), participation (I want to appear involved in the class), excuse-making (I need to explain my work to my teacher), and sycophancy (to give the impression that I think the instructor is an effective teacher). Students' level of stress and anxiety were related to their classroom interest and their motives for communicating with their instructors. Students who felt competent reported lower amounts of anxiety and pressure concerning their peers, but also reported higher amounts of worry and pressure from school. Students who were interested because the class was meaningful to them reported higher levels of pressure from school. Students who communicated more for the functional motive reported higher amounts of pressure from school, but also reported lower levels of anxiety. Students who communicated for the sycophancy motive but not the functional motive, reported lower levels of worry, and more pressure concerning their peers.

The number of programs that are designed to meet the educational needs of older, nontraditional students is growing rapidly. Understanding the needs of these older, nontraditional, working college students are important considerations for both universities and employers. Chapter 7 examines two studies which were conducted to assess the impact of attending a weekend program for nontraditional students. The findings revealed the expected stress as the result of time constraints but also highlighted the positive aspects of continuing one's education. Recommendations are put forth for colleges and universities that offer or intend to offer programs for the adult non-traditional learner. The recommendations address stress sources caused by family work roles, course requirements and university policies and procedures.

Chapter 8 is a further exploration of the relationship between optimism, perceived stress, and subsequent adjustment among college students. Unlike studies, which have typically focused on how inherent predispositions increase vulnerability to stress related illnesses, the current study focused on how acquired predispositions (dispositional optimism) influence appraisal of stress, and ultimately adjustment. Also, results from a study of 259 college undergraduates are discussed. Participants completed a measure of optimism at the beginning of the semester and then measures of stress and adjustment just before midterm break. Results indicated that optimism or outlook to life was a significant predictor of respondents' perceived stress, as well as, their levels of depression, anxiety, and overall college adjustment. Further analyses showed that optimism accounted for significant proportions of the variance in the dependent factors or measures of adjustment. Implications of these findings are discussed.

The goal of the review in chapter 9 was to explore and contrast the relative impacts of events both meeting and not meeting DSM-IV criteria as a "traumatic event" in terms of both positive and negative outcomes. Self-report data was collected from 104 participants who were classified into two groups based on whether or not the event that caused them the most subjective distress met DSM-IV criterion A1 for PTSD. These groups were compared with regard to PTSD symptoms, level of depressive symptoms, and level of perceived trauma-related growth. Interestingly, the groups scored similarly on all measures, indicating that college students perceive themselves as experiencing similar outcomes, both positive and negative, in response to negative life events that do and do not meet the DSM-IV's criteria as representing a "traumatic event." Finally, a positive relationship was found between the amount of distress produced by the various events and the amount of posttraumatic growth experienced by participants. These findings imply that the trauma literature needs to pay greater heed to events that may not meet the relatively rigid criteria set forth by the DSM-IV but may nonetheless potentially produce both significant distress and the opportunity for positive life change in experiencing individuals.

The college student experience, although often exciting, empowering, and invigorating, can also be stressful, anxiety producing, and lonely (e.g., Kohn and Frazer, 1986; Miller and Rice, 1993). Many colleges and universities have an infrastructure in place to assist students who experience mental health problems, including counseling centers and personnel who provide mental health services and make referrals for students to specialized mental health providers (e.g., psychiatrists) (Stone and Archer, 1990; Tyrrell, 1997). Unfortunately, most mental health services that are offered on college campuses seem treatment-oriented in nature; they are deliberately created to assist students who have already developed at least some level of psychological dysfunction. The authors of chapter 10 propose that preventative interventions can be developed on college campuses to help individuals develop proactive behaviors and coping strategies to avoid mental health problems, and that these interventions can be focused at either the individual level, by instructing students on ways to develop strong study and time management skills, establish social supports, and maximize their academic success, or at the institutional level, by offering structural resources to help facilitate student success and mental wellness. The purpose of this chapter will be to discuss prevalent mental health problems among college students and the causes and consequences of these problems, to outline some of these individual- and institutional-level preventative mental health interventions and to encourage administrators and faculty to promote psychological wellness rather than simply treat fully manifested psychopathology. The benefits of such preventative approaches relative to standard treatment-oriented approaches are shown.

The aim of chapter 11 is to show how the psychosemiosis offers an epistemic key to understand in psychotherapy the dilemma between the human body and mind. This work is essentially based on a series of seven qualitative case studies of the psychoanalytic psychotherapy with university students having borderline personality disorder. The cases were examined by means of the symbolization-reflectiveness model which includes a coding method of signs for the study of therapeutic interaction. Psychotherapy progresses so that the patient internalizes by symbolization-reflectiveness the therapeutic interaction to his/her internal psychic structure: the originally physical observation is transformed into the psychic experience which leads to a functioning coherent body-mind continuum. In psychotherapy adopted proper symbolic function means that the mind disentangles itself from the chains of immediate experience. The healthy functioning mind is essentially a dialogic organ with two dimensions: in horizontal axis with significant others and in vertical axis with the body.

Chapter 12 focuses on body image issues and eating disorders, both of which can have serious and wide ranging effects on the individual. These may include, but are not limited to; depression, suicide attempts, anxiety disorders, secondary health problems, and increased risk of onset of obesity (Johnson, Cohen, Kasen, and Brook, 2002; Pomeroy and Mitchell, 2002; Stice, Cameron, Killen, Hayward, and Barr Taylor, 1999); and substance abuse problems including increased tobacco (Lenz, 2004) and alcohol consumption (Anderson, Martens, and Cimini, 2005). Patients with eating disorders also have the highest rate of suicide attempts and mortality of all psychiatric disorders (Newman et al., 1996). There is a high reported prevalence of body dissatisfaction, dieting and eating disorders in college and university students, and it has been suggested that one third of women who develop clinical eating disorders do so in college (Winzelberg et al., 2000). However it is still not clear whether body image issues and eating disorders these are established before tertiary education (Vohs, Heatherton et al., 2001) or are developed as a result of the transition to college, and the different social and environmental pressures that are associated with the college environment (Compas, Wagner, Slavin, and Vannatta, 1986). This chapter will investigate the prevalence of and risk factors for body dissatisfaction, disordered eating behaviors and eating disorders among college males and females. Preventive initiatives are also reviewed.

In: Stress and Mental Health of College Students
Editor: Mery V. Landow, pp. 1-28

ISBN 1-59454-839-0
© 2006 Nova Science Publishers, Inc.

Chapter 1

MEASURING AND UNDERSTANDING STRESS IN PHARMACY STUDENTS

Arjun Pratim Dutta,[1] Michael A. Pyles and Patrick Miederhoff
Pacific University, Forest Grove, OR
Virginia Commonwealth University, Richmond, VA.

ABSTRACT

Pharmacy students undergo rigorous training before they are licensed to practice their profession. The pharmacy education process is similar to medical education and, as such, is a strenuous endeavor. However, very little is known about the impact of the education and the training process on pharmacy students. It has been noted in the literature that the education process of health professions students (e.g., medical, dental, nursing, and allied health) brings forth considerable amount of dysfunctional stress in its students (Bjorkesten et al. 1983, a, b; Lloyd and Musser, 1985; Lloyd and Gartell, 1983).
A recent study (Henning, Ey, and Shaw, 1998) compared medical, pharmacy, and dental students in terms of their levels of stress and found pharmacy students to be the most stressed. According to the researchers, some students even evinced distress levels that were similar to psychiatric patients. The result of the above mentioned study, and the evidence gathered from the research conducted in other health professions students, suggests the need for a study that exclusively deals with the phenomenon of stress and its causative factors on pharmacy students.

The primary goal of this research was to explore the existence or nonexistence of counterproductive stress and its antecedents in entry level Pharm.D. students. Any empirical findings that purport the existence of stress and its antecedents in these students is a seminal work in this field because of the lacuna in the extant literature on stress in health professions students. The theoretical framework for this inquiry is the psychosocial model of stress as proposed by Lazarus and Folkman (1984). The instrument that was used for this inquiry is the DSP (Derogatis and Fleming, 1998). The instrument has been tested and found to be reliable and valid (Derogatis and Fleming, 1997).

---

[1] The Primary author was at the School of Pharmacy, Howard University, Washington DC at the time of submission of the book chapter.

Four schools of pharmacy were selected to participate in the study. These schools were not randomly selected. It was a convenience sample based on the availability of the schools to participate in the survey. Contacts at these schools provided the survey instrument to the students. Each contact was given the same time frame to administer and return the instrument. This ensured that the data were collected in the same time period. In light of the literature reviewed, six research hypotheses were presented and tested. In addition, several antecedent variables to stress that have been identified in the literature were also examined. Multiple regression analyses were performed to identify exogenous variables that were significant in explaining the variation in total stress scores for the sample. An exploratory Factor Analysis was performed to confirm the factors of stress previously identified by Derogatis (1987).

Although pharmacy students resembled the general population in terms of overall stress scores, we did find evidence of high levels of stress in some of these students. Minority students were found to be significantly less stressed than their majority counterparts. Gender, marital status, prior degree, and type of school did not significantly contribute to an increase in overall stress score. Financial burden, unsupportive nature of faculty, absence of a counseling service, excessive study load, English not being the first language, and not being a minority student were found to be significant stressors for this sample of pharmacy students. Students reporting the above mentioned stressors were also found to be at greater risk in experiencing high or excess levels of stress. The relative risk for experiencing high or excess levels of stress as a result of being exposed to the rigorous curricula in health professions schools has not been previously studied or reported.

Findings from this inquiry may prove to be enormously helpful in shaping future curricula changes in schools of pharmacy. These findings may also facilitate the implementation of intervention strategies and coping programs to alleviate if not eliminate unnecessary stress in pharmacy students during their professional education. Equipped with a new knowledge of stress and its antecedents, pharmacy school administrators and faculty members would be uniquely poised to be proactive versus reactive insofar as the stress levels of their students are concerned. They should be able to take appropriate actions to diminish stress levels in their students by eliminating or minimizing the impact of the significant stressors identified in this inquiry. Diminishing counterproductive stress and its causative factors would help to create a nurturing, enabling, and productive atmosphere for these professional students. Pharmacy School administrators could greatly improve the environments for the professional education they provide by assisting their students in acquiring financial aid, eliminating sources of excessive competition among students, being more supportive of their students, and by performing analyses of course requirements to ensure that learning is commensurate with the amount of student effort outside of the classroom.

INTRODUCTION

Pharmacy students undergo rigorous training before they are licensed to practice their profession. The pharmacy education process is similar to medical education and, as such, is a strenuous endeavor. Very little, is however, known about the impact of the education and the training process on pharmacy students. It has been noted in the literature that the education process of health professions students (e.g., medical, dental, nursing, and allied health) brings forth considerable amounts of dysfunctional stress in its students. This fact has not been well-documented in the case of pharmacy students, despite the similarity in the education process to medical students. The purpose of this research is to document the existence or non-existence of counterproductive stress in pharmacy students. It may well be possible that pharmacy students are overtly stressed. Currently, no studies have documented the existence of stress in pharmacy students alone. There also exists a need to document the evidence of perceived stress in pharmacy students across a variety of settings. It has been suggested by some comparative studies that there may exist some amount of stress in pharmacy students. These studies have used pharmacy students as a comparison group for other health professions students (e.g., medical, dental, and nursing), in whom the levels and sources of stress have been well documented. These studies have demonstrated the need to study the existence of stress independently in pharmacy students. Health professions students have been studied in great detail in terms of the existence of stress, sources of stress, and psychiatric impairments as a result of stress. It seems plausible, therefore, that pharmacy students, who are but a part of health professions students, are subject to the same mental rigors as other health professions students. Hence, by simple syllogism, it seems important and logical to study the existence of stress in pharmacy students.

STATEMENT OF THE PROBLEM

Researchers investigating stress in health professions students, save pharmacy, have suggested the existence of dysfunctional stress among these students. The effects of stress seem to be the most adverse for medical students, followed by dental students, nursing students and students of allied health. There is, however, a lack of empirical evidence with regard to the understanding of stress and how it affects pharmacy students. There is also a lacuna in our understanding of the education process of pharmacy students, its nuances, and the association between it and discernible levels of stress in pharmacy students. It seems that without reliable and valid empirical findings it is not possible to improve upon the education process to make it less stressful-assuming that it is.

Purpose

The literature reveals that health professions students experience varying levels of stress. The purpose of this research inquiry is to document the existence or non-existence of stress and its sources in a specific group of health professions students - pharmacy students. A recent study (Henning, Ey, and Shaw, 1998) compared medical, pharmacy, and dental students in terms of their levels of stress and found pharmacy students to be most distressed. According to the researchers, some students even evinced distress levels that were similar to psychiatric patients. The result of the study, by Henning et al. (1998) and the evidence gathered from the research conducted in other health professions students, suggests the need for a study that exclusively deals with the phenomenon of stress and its effects on pharmacy students. The purpose of this inquiry was to provide a basis for understanding and measuring stress in pharmacy students.

Significance

The primary concern of this inquiry was to explore the existence of stress in pharmacy students across schools of pharmacy. Any empirical finding that purports the existence of stress in pharmacy students would be considered a seminal work in this field, due to the paucity of empirical findings in the extant literature. This investigation makes a significant contribution to the literature by providing empirical evidence as to the existence of stress and delineates the significant stressors afflicting pharmacy students. Our study found pharmacy students to be experiencing discernible levels of stress and outlines the stressors that were responsible for precipitating such stress levels. Such findings have not been noted previously in pharmacy students and as such are a significant contribution to the literature in general, and health professions students in particular.

THEORETICAL FRAMEWORK

Definition of "Stress"

The concept of stress is relatively new. It was in the late 1930s that Hans Selye (1936) first outlined the concept of stress. Antecedents to Selye's work can be traced back to Hippocrates, Bernard, and Cannon. Selye's model of stress was essentially a bio-chemical concept. He theorized that stress was a result of any non-specific demand made upon an organism. Further research by Lacey (1967) and Mason (1971) raised some doubts about Selye's physiological theory of stress. In spite of these doubts, Selye's stress theory held sway.

The psychological concept of stress was brought forth by Grinker and Speigel (1945), and Janis (1958). Psychological concepts of stress became widely known in the 1950s. The above-mentioned researchers were the first to propose that stress was not just a physiological phenomenon but also a psychological process. Until the works of Grinker et al., and Janis, the psychological attributes of stress were mostly un-researched and unknown. Lazarus (1966) was the stress researcher instrumental in popularizing the psychological attribute of stress. In fact, it was Lazarus who first spoke about coping with stress. The post Lazarus period saw a paradigm shift. Evidence of the paradigm shift could be seen in the works of Scotch and Levine (1970) and McGrath (1970), who had begun to explore the social causes of stress and the result of the interaction of the environment and the human psyche. Our present understanding of stress as a multidimensional concept is the result of the earlier works of researchers such as those mentioned above. The most widely accepted theory today is the one provided by Folkman and Lazarus (1984). They state stress to be "a particular relationship between the person and the environment that is appraised by the person as taxing or exceeding his or her resources and endangering his or her well-being" (Lazarus and Folkman, 1984, p.19). As a result of Folkman and Lazarus's work, stress was believed to be primarily a cognizance of a feeling of unease by the person undergoing stress. The level of cognition and the appraisal of stress were deemed to be different from person to person. This feeling of discomfort could be physical, mental, and/or social. In summary, stress has evolved from being merely a physiological strain to a more abstract (psychosocial) but, nevertheless, cognizable stimulus. The theoretical framework for this inquiry is a psychosocial model of stress as proposed by Lazarus and Folkman.

Measures of Stress

Out of the vast array of instruments and scales that are available for the measurement of stress, we selected four for an in-depth discussion. Selection of these instruments was based on the underlying theoretical construct of the instrument, the relevancy, or the applicability of the instrument, the ease of administration, and the normative sample that the instrument had been tested upon. The four instruments are the Derogatis Stress Profile (DSP), the Personal Views Survey II (PVS II), also known as the Hardiness Attitude Survey, the Stress Schedule (SS), and the Weekly Stress Inventory (WSI).

The PVS II is a 45-item rating-scale type questionnaire that takes 10 minutes to complete. It is designed to measure the hardiness of an individual and, according to its author, the hardier or mentally strong an individual is, the less is the perceived stress. The SS is a 60 item scale that takes 15 minutes to complete. It measures stress as an interaction between the person and his or her environment. It, however, does not take into account specific crisis events while measuring perceived stress. The WSI is an 87 item inventory that measures the physical and psychological aspect of stress on a weekly basis. No information on how long it takes to complete the instrument has been reported in the literature. The DSP is a 77 item self report inventory that takes about 15 minutes to complete. Its theoretical roots can be traced back to the psychosocial model of stress proposed by Folkman and Lazarus (1984).

After comparing these four instruments, a choice was made to use the DSP for this inquiry. The criteria for the selection of the DSP included its consistency with the theoretical framework for this inquiry, its ease of administration and interpretation, the frequency of prior usage of the instrument in health professions student populations, and the relatively low costs associated with administering it.

The DSP is based on the psychosocial model of stress proposed by Folkman and Lazarus (1984). The DSP has been found to be a very reliable and valid measure of stress (Derogatis and Fleming, 1997). The DSP has been previously used to measure stress in a population of dental and nursing students (1997).

Stress in Health Profession Students

Researchers in the area of stress in health profession students have suggested the existence of dysfunctional stress among these students (Kohl 1951; Richman et al., 1992; Sheenan et al., 1990; Swarkzy, 1998; Tyrell 1997). The effects of stress seem to be the most adverse for medical students, followed by dental students, nursing students, and students of allied health (Kellner, Wiggins, and Pathak, 1986; Lyons et al. 1997; Henning et al. 1998). Some of these studies have examined differences in stress experienced by the above mentioned student groups by making comparisons among them and by comparing them to law students and the general student populations. There is however, a lack of empirical evidence with regard to the understanding of stress and how it affects pharmacy students. In most cases, the literature on stress in health profession students has generally consisted of studies that: i) Documented stress in a student sub-group; ii) Attempted to identify the sources of stress or stressors, and iii) Provided evidence of psychological and psychiatric symptoms in various student sub-groups, and comparisons within sub-groups or other student disciplines.

The following section delineates a basic understanding of the term stress, followed by the three genres of empirical findings with regard to stress as found in the literature on 'stress in health profession students,' the gaps in the literature, and consequences of these gaps for health profession students.

Following an extensive literature review, key articles were identified that document stress, the causes of stress or "stressors," and psychiatric symptoms as a result of counterproductive stress in the disciplines of medicine, dentistry, nursing, and allied health. The earliest studies, circa 1936, involving stress in health profession students have been credited to medicine. Strecker and colleagues (1936) first noted the deleterious effects of stress in medical education. They realized that such mental strain proved to be detrimental to the health of the students during their training and that it was often a hindrance to their education. Other authors (Kohl 1951; Brosin 1948; and Wyler 1945) reported similar findings. These authors were of the opinion that a good portion of medical students suffered from personality mal-adjustments and, in some cases, severe neuroses. These were the first of many reports of empirical findings about stress in medical students that would go on to suggest that medical students were suffering from stress and stress related effects. More recently, studies (Richman et al., 1992; Silver and Glicken, 1990; Sheenan et al., 1990) reported that there was a high incidence and severity of medical student abuse. In general, medical students in these studies reported being victims of such abuse and that the abuse hindered their ability to learn and grow as physicians.

Evidence of stress in dental students was first noted by Moore (1962). Moore's study was followed by others (Davis et al., 1989; Grandy et al., 1984; Lloyd and Mussler, 1985; Newton et al., 1994; Wexler, 1978; Rubenstein et al., 1989; Sachs, Zullo, and Close, 1981) that documented evidence of stress in dental students. In all cases, these studies emphasized that dental education had reached a point where it was strenuous to students, and that further research was needed to identify the sources of stress in dental students. One study provided empirical evidence that a significant portion (about 3.5%) of withdrawals from dental school was a direct result of perceived stress due to the dental school environment (Grandy et al., 1984). It was evident from the Grandy study that dental students also suffered from psychosocial stress that was manifested as a result of their interaction with the dental school environment and the teaching process.

The literature involving nurse education followed closely behind dentistry, with studies involving stress appearing in the literature around 1976 (Garret, 1976). The fact that Swarkzy (1998) reported that nursing students were experiencing levels of stress in dealing with the education process continue to support the belief that stress in nurse education is prevalent. A study by Carter (1982), however, came to the conclusion that nurse education was not as stressful as it was perceived to be. She found it to be less stressful than an education in liberal arts.

Allied health literature also seems replete with evidence of stress in its students (Grevin, 1996; Graham and Babola, 1998; O'meara et al., 1994; Stewart, 1990; Tyrell 1997). The students in allied health range from laboratory technicians and patient counselors to paramedics and physical/occupational therapists. It can be concluded from many of the studies involving allied health students that like nursing students, allied health students appear to experience stress during their studies. The nature of the stress reported by allied health students appears to be related to the students' inability to cope with the learning environment.

The common message put forth through these articles was that education and training in the professions of health are strenuous and, as such, it causes significant amounts of counterproductive stress in students.

Considering the abundance of empirical research findings regarding stress in certain populations of health profession students, one could reasonably expect to find similar studies that have examined stress in pharmacy students in particular. However, there is a significant gap in the literature on stress in health profession students, insofar as pharmacy students are concerned. However, there is some documentation of stress in practicing pharmacists (Curtiss et al., 1978; Wolfgang, 1988; Wolfgang and Ortmeier, 1993) and pharmacy faculty members (Wolfgang, 1993) in the literature. Perhaps the dearth of empirical findings related to stress in pharmacy students is a consequence of researchers not thinking that pharmacy education could be stressful, or the failure to consider the link between future stress in the practice of pharmacy and the pharmacy education process.

Stressors

The literature also seems to be extensive in its enumeration of the stressors afflicting health profession students. However, a similar gap exists here with respect to pharmacy students, who have not been studied at all. Table 1 lists the stressors that have been identified in the literature for health profession students (medicine, dentistry, and allied health).

Psychiatric Symptoms

The literature involving medical and dental students has also noted psychiatric impairments in their respective students while pursuing their education. A study involving demographic and social characteristics of university students seeking help from a psychiatrist found that medical and dental students were significantly over-represented in the student population (Omahony, et al., 1980). The psychiatric ailments reported by the students range from nightmares, hallucinations, suicidal thoughts, phobias, anxiety reactions, depression, obsessive-compulsive neuroses, and *hypochondriasis* (Adsett, 1968; Hendrie, 1990; Lloyd and Musser, 1989). Researchers studying the impact of stress on nursing and allied health students recognized the adverse impact nursing education had on these students and made recommendations on how to alleviate such emotional and mental impairments (Mese and Spano, 1989).

Although researchers do not think the education process alone, to be responsible for such alarming levels of stress in health profession students, they do believe it to be a significant cause in precipitating high, or even in some cases psychiatric, levels of distress in students. Given the similar nature of the training process of medical students and pharmacy students, there seems ample reason to believe that similar distress may be present in pharmacy students as well. However, as seen previously, pharmacy education simply does not have enough studies documenting psychological distress. It seems that pharmacy educators have failed to notice the fact that there may be stress in pharmacy students, which eventually may turn into distress.

Table 1. Stressors Commonly Present in Health Professions Students

Stressors	Medical	Dental	Nursing / Allied Health
Academic Overload: Large volume of material to be studied, and constant pressure of maintaining good grades	√	√	√
Strained Relationship with the Faculty	√	√	√
Orientation to medical school environment: This was a very significant stressor for new students	√	NA	NA
Poor quality of teaching	√	√	No
Lack of perceived relevance of medical/dental education to everyday practice	√	√	NA
Working with cadavers	√	NA	NA
Relationship with patients: students found it difficult to remain impersonal with patients or discuss sensitive issues with them	√	√	√
Competition among peers	√	√	No
Lack of leisure time	√	√	√
Less time to spend with family	√	√	No
Financing a health professions education	√	√	√
First two years of health professions education	√	√	No
Manual skills required of a dentist	NA	√	NA
Administrative duties required of nursing students	NA	NA	√
Perceived lack of proper clinical knowledge	√	√	√
Role conflict with physicians	NA	NA	√
Frequent examinations	√	√	√
Grades in school	√	√	√

√ = Present
NA= Not applicable
No= Not identified as a stressor in the literature

Comparative Studies

Finally, the literature enumerates studies that deal with comparisons made among two or more groups of health profession students. The first of these was the study by Sekas and Wile (1980) that compared M.D.-Ph.D., M.D., and Ph.D. students. This study was an effort to document the incidence and prevalence of stress associated illness among M.D.-Ph.D. students. It was found that the M.D.-Ph.D. students were more stressed than either the M.D. or the Ph.D. students. In general, medical students have been found to be the most stressed, followed by students in dentistry, nursing, and allied health (Bjorksten, Sutherland, and Miller, 1983; Lyons, et al., 1997). Some of the excerpts were: "compared with the other students, medical students complained more intensely about almost all problem areas on the survey instrument" (Bjorksten et al. 1983a, p.763). In another study, the same authors compared 181 dental students to 1,202 health science students (allied health, medicine, nursing, pharmacy, and biomedical graduate students) (Bjorksten et al. 1983b). Here the authors noted that "compared with other health professions students, dental students have the same spectrum of perceived problems but to a somewhat lesser degree" (Bjorksten et al. 1983b p.15). Heins et al. (1983; 1984) conducted studies comparing perceived stress in medical, law, and graduate students. Contrary to the hypothesis and belief that medical students are more stressed; law students reported the highest stress levels. Moreover, in a study Lyons et al. (1997), compared nursing, allied health, and medical students to find that female nursing and allied health students were significantly more depressed than female medical students. They also found a significant relationship between anxiety and test grades.

Based on the extensive literature search, only one study (Henning, et al., 1998) could be found that dealt with stress in pharmacy students, albeit as a comparison to other health profession students.

The Henning study (1998) compared medical, dental, and pharmacy students with respect to "psychological distress," "perfectionism," and "impostor phenomenon." A separate analysis was provided for each of the student sub-groups. The results of this study are especially salient in light of stress in pharmacy students. Henning, et al. found that "pharmacy students were at the greatest risk for psychological distress, with half the students reporting distress levels similar to those reported by psychiatric populations" (Henning, et al., 1998). The authors emphasized the need to corroborate their findings about pharmacy students to see if it was an isolated, university specific incident, or a generalizable phenomenon. This was the only study that reported the existence of stress in pharmacy students (in the BS program) at such alarming levels. Gauging from the Henning study, it seems that there is a growing need for further exploration of perceived stress and the consequences to such stress in pharmacy students.

The following research hypotheses were generated after a review of literature on stress in health professions students. A list of predictor variables causing stress in pharmacy students separate from the hypothesized variables was also generated and tested using regression analysis. This was followed by an exploratory factor analysis to replicate the findings of Derogatis in our sample of pharmacy students.

Research Hypotheses

In light of the literature reviewed, six research hypotheses were posited.

1. H_1 Pharmacy students exhibit discernible levels of stress during their second professional year of training.
2. H_2 Female pharmacy students exhibit higher levels of stress than their male counterparts during their second professional year of training.
3. H_3 Minority pharmacy students exhibit higher levels of stress during their second professional year of training.
4. H_4 Married pharmacy students exhibit lower levels of stress than their unmarried counterparts during their second professional year of training.
5. H_5 Pharmacy students with a baccalaureate degree exhibit lower levels of stress during their second professional year of training.

6. H_6 Pharmacy students in private schools of pharmacy exhibit lower levels of stress during their second professional year of training than those in public schools of pharmacy.

METHODS

A total of four schools of pharmacy were used to generate the sample of pharmacy students for this inquiry. To maintain anonymity of the schools and the results of the analyses, the schools were designated as A, B, C and D. Two are private schools (C and D) and two are public or state funded schools (A, B). A and B are mid-Atlantic public schools of pharmacy, C is a southeastern private school of pharmacy, and D is a mid-western private school of pharmacy. Each of the schools offers the entry-level Doctor of Pharmacy degree. All four schools have received accreditation from the American Association of Colleges of Pharmacy (AACP). The AACP accreditation ensures that all four schools meet AACP standards in terms of their curricula and academic requirements. The four schools were similar with respect to the required credit hours per semester both in terms of year of study as well as the total number of credit hours required for the entire Pharm.D. program.

Entry level Pharm.D. students in the second year of study in each school were administered the stress instrument chosen for use in this inquiry. Each student in the sample was asked to complete the Derogatis Stress Profile (DSP) and return it to collaborators at each of the schools of pharmacy included in the study. Table 2 provides information about each of the four schools, including its location, type of institution, and the approximate number of students that are admitted each year.

Table 2. Sample of Pharmacy Students

NAME	Location	Type of Institution	Size of Class*
School A	MidAtlantic	Public	92
School B	MidAtlantic	Public	66
School C	Southeastern	Private	80
School D	Midwestern	Private	84

* Class Size refers to the number of students in the second year.

Based on the information provided by each school, the sample for this inquiry consisted of 314 students in their second year of study at each of four schools of pharmacy in the United States. The literature on medical and dental students has revealed that, when present, stress is more likely to be discerned during the pre-clinical years (the first two years) as a result of the course requirements during those years (Gaensbauer et al. 1980). However, while this is true for medical and dental students, currently there is no empirical evidence in support of this fact for pharmacy students. According to AACP requirements, all accredited schools must provide both didactic and clinical components. Most schools require their students to complete three "pre-clinical" years and a minimum of one year of clinical experiences before graduation. Our present inquiry restricted itself to the second year of pharmacy school.

It is our belief that measuring stress during the second year provides a more realistic estimate of perceived stress in these students. For most schools of pharmacy the second year is the most intense academically. Moreover, it is in the second year that the students are exposed to clinical coursework, which is probably the most difficult part of their coursework. The first year will be an adjustment to the professional learning environment for most students. By the third year students will be more accustomed to the rigors of pharmacy school and we believe, less likely to experience excess stress. Surveying a single year allows us the opportunity to spend more time on measures that will likely lead to a higher response rate and less time managing the sample itself. This being an empirical investigation, we need to ensure a high response rate to draw some valid conclusions.

The literature on health professions students has enumerated a list of stressors or causes of stress as identified by medical, dental, and nursing students. For the most part, there emerged a common set of stressors for these health professions students. As noted in the literature review, no work has been done with regard to stressors in pharmacy students. Based on our review of the literature, we elicited information from this sample of pharmacy students in an attempt to identify stressors common to all health professions students as well as those that may be unique to pharmacy students. A multiple regression analysis using the General Linear Model (GLM) was performed with the TSS as the dependent variable in order to determine the significance of various common and unique stressors on the TSS for pharmacy students. The variables were entered through the stepwise procedure. SPSS 8.0 for Windows was used to analyze the data.

Following a multiple regression, a logistic regression was also performed. A logistic regression enabled us to examine the strength of association of a particular explanatory variable relative to and in the presence of other explanatory variables. It also helped us interpret the predictor variables in terms of the relative risk or the odds of precipitating excess levels of stress in pharmacy students. The dichotomous variable, STRES, was created to denote excess (denoted by 1) or normal (denoted by 0) levels of stress. Excess and normal levels of stress were categorized in accordance with the DSP's scoring manual (TSS >= 56 => Excess Stress). In the logistic regression model, STRES was the dependent variable, while the significant antecedents to stress (stressors) as identified by the multiple regression models were the independent variables. The logistic regression enabled us to identify particular stressors that may contribute to the likelihood of excess stress among second year pharmacy students.

An exploratory factor analysis using the principle component method and varimax rotation was also performed to identify factors associated with stress in pharmacy students. Factor analysis is a powerful tool that is often used by researchers during the development of an instrument meant to identify and confirm important factors for a particular phenomenon. In previous studies involving the DSP, including the original study by the authors (Derogatis and Fleming. 1997), the original four stress factors that were conceived by the authors have been confirmed by factor analysis (Derogatis, 1984; 1987). The use of factor analysis in this instance is two-fold. First, it was used as a means of replicating the findings of Derogatis in our sample of pharmacy students. This has not been done heretofore. Secondly, performing factor analysis in the present sample of pharmacy students helped determine whether there are additional factors of stress for pharmacy students that have not been reported for other health professions students.

RESULTS

Following the collection of the survey questionnaires from the four participating schools, the data were analyzed with SPSS, 8.0. A total of 283 (90%) completed survey questionnaires were returned from the four schools. The sample consists of second year Pharm. D. students from four schools of pharmacy as described in Table 3 below.

Table 3. Response rates for the four schools of Pharmacy

NAME	Size of Second Yr. Class	N Returned	Percent Return
School A (Public)	92	84	91
School B (Public)	66	66	100
School C (Private)	80	80	100
School D (Private)	84	53	63
Total	314	283	90

As Table 3 indicates, two of the schools, B and C, had 100% return rates. Overall, the four schools of pharmacy had a rate of return for completed questionnaires of 90%. For the purposes of our research inquiry, the collection of the responses can be considered as self-completed questionnaires that were administered 'in person,' by a contact person at each school. Tables 4, 5, and 6 describe the variables used in this inquiry.

Table 4. Gender, Race, Marital Status of the respondents (Valid n=283)

Variables	Value	Responses	Percent	Missing
Gender	Females (0)	205	72.4	
	Males (1)	74	26.1	4
	Total	279	98.6	
Race	White (0)	227	80.2	
	African American (1)	29	10.2	
	Asian / Pacific Islander (2)	15	5.3	6
	Others (3)	6	2.1	
	Total	277	97.9	
Marital Status	Single (0)	214	75.6	
	Married (1)	53	18.7	8
	Divorced (2)	8	2.8	
	Total	275	97.2	

Table 5. *Quantitative Variables* (Valid n=276)

Variable	Missing	Minimum	Maximum	Mean	Median	Std. Dev
Age	7	20.0	45.0	24.5	23.0	4.23
GPA	12	2.0	4.0	3.2	3.2	0.47
Number of children living with the respondent	6	0	6	NA	0	0.58
Number of exams, tests, or quizzes	6	0	5	2.5	2.0	0.99
Number of Minutes to commute to school*	6	2	75	19.9	15.0	16.5
Number of hours worked in addition to going to pharmacy school	6	0	55.0	8.03	7.0	8.95

*Does not represent On Campus students; who were asked to report (0) for this variable.

Table 6. Qualitative Variables (Valid n=283)

Variable	% Yes (0)	% No (1)	Valid	Missing
Financial Burden	73.1	26.9	279	4
English as first language	88.1	11.9	278	5
Supportive Faculty	66.9	33.1	278	5
School has a counseling service	88.5	11.5	279	4
Have you used counseling service	18.7	81.3	278	5
Excessive study load	73.1	26.9	279	4
Too much competition	63.4	36.6	279	4
Prior Bachelor's Degree	40.9	59.1	279	4
Medical School on same campus	53.0	47.0	283	0

Total Stress Score (TSS) is a continuous variable that represents the stress level of the respondent. It has been calculated using guidelines published by the author of the DSP (Derogatis and Fleming, 1997). The TSS is the dependent variable for the statistical test ANOVA that was used to test the hypotheses and multiple regression models. The mean TSS for the entire sample was 51, indicating that second year pharmacy students in this sample were experiencing stress levels that were slightly higher than the mean of 50 reported by the author of the DSP for the normative sample (Derogatis and Fleming, 1997). The mean TSS for our sample of pharmacy students was, however, still within normal levels of the DSP (TSS less than equal to 55). [The normative sample described by Derogatis and Fleming (1997) consisted of 1,000 community respondents]. School D had the highest TSS among the four schools with a mean of 52.5, followed by School A (51.6), School B (51.4) and School C (49.2). Mean TSS for schools A, B, and D were greater than the sample mean (51). Only School C recorded a mean TSS below the sample mean. The following figure illustrates the TSS across the four schools.

Derogatis (1997) has also categorized the TSS into ranges that are indicative of the psychological state of the respondent. A TSS of 50 to 55 on the DSP indicates "Normal Stress Levels." A score of 56-62 indicates "Excess or High Stress Levels" in a respondent. Finally, Derogatis reports that a TSS greater than or equal to 63 is generally exhibited by patients with various psychiatric symptoms such as depression and mental disorders. Derogatis refers to the TSS scores greater than or equal to 63 as the "clinical range." Respondents in that range are deemed to be suffering from psychiatric levels of distress. In our sample, 9% of the students were found to have DSP scores in the clinical range, and 16% of the students were found to have scores in the high to excess stress range of the DSP (Derogatis and Fleming, 1997). Henning (1998), using the Brief Symptom Inventory (BSI) created by Derogatis and Spencer, had found that 50% of the pharmacy students in his study experienced stress levels in the clinical range. The percentage of students from our sample of second year pharmacy students, in the various stress categories of the DSP, was similar to the percentage of the normalized sample in these DSP categories (See Table 9).

It can then be said that our sample of second year pharmacy students is representative of the normal population in terms of distribution of stress. A more detailed comparison (Chi-Square) of the distribution of our sample in the various stress categories to Derogatis's normalized population is provided in the discussion section (pg. 158).

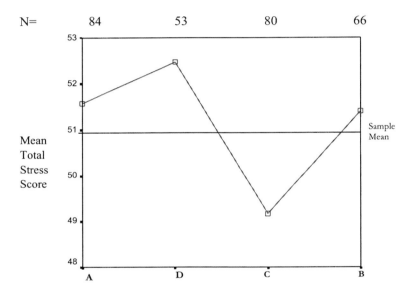

Schools of Pharmacy in the Sample
Figure 1. TSS across the four schools (Valid n=283)

The mean TSS (51) of our sample of pharmacy students, in spite of being slightly higher than the normalized mean (50), was still within normal levels of stress (50-55) reported by Derogatis (1997). Table 7 illustrates the distribution of our sample of second year pharmacy students across the four categories of TSS identified by Derogatis.

Confirmation of Hypothesis I was believed to be instrumental in providing empirical evidence as to the presence of discernible levels of stress in pharmacy students. Although, in our sample, we found evidence of some amount of stress in the pharmacy students, analysis of the data from our inquiry revealed that our sample of pharmacy students resembled the normative population on which the DSP was validated in terms of overall stress levels.

Table 7. TSS Percent Distribution of the sample (Valid n=283)

TSS	DSP Stress Range	Total n = 283	A n = 84	B n = 66	C n = 54	D n = 80	Normative Sample Of the DSP n = 1000
<50	Below Normal Levels	44	48	41	50	32	50
50-55	Normal Stress Levels	31	28	35	31	38	20
56-62	High to Excess Stress	16	18	9	16	19	19
>63	Stress Levels generally exhibited by Psychiatric Populations	9	6	15	3	11	10

The literature on stress in health professions students has long borne the evidence that female students, minority students, and unmarried students exhibit higher levels of stress than males. These findings formed the basis of hypotheses II, III, and IV. Our analysis of the data did not support hypotheses II, III, and IV. One of our findings was, in fact, contrary to the literature. We found minority pharmacy students in our sample to be less stressed than their Caucasian counterparts. This specific finding was, however, true as per the Henning study. Our test of Hypothesis V was undertaken to confirm our belief that students with a baccalaureate degree would exhibit lower levels of stress than their peers without one. It was our belief that students with a prior degree were likely to be more mature and, hence, less prone to stress in pharmacy school. Our analysis of the data, however, did not support hypothesis V. Our test of Hypothesis VI attempted to find out whether students in a public school of pharmacy, as opposed to a private school of pharmacy, have higher levels of stress. It was our belief that the type of school (public or private) has a bearing on the emphasis a school puts into teaching vis-à-vis research and, hence, may have an effect on the stress levels of its students. This hypothesis was also not supported by the analysis of our data. Thus our analysis of the data supported effects in two out of the six areas in the posited hypotheses. The following table summarizes the fore tested hypotheses.

Table 8. Summary of the Hypotheses

		Independent t-test	Multiple Factor ANOVA	(.05 significance)
Hypothesis	Variable	1-sided p-value	2-sided p-value	Hypothesis Supported
H1	Stress DSP mean	0.010589022	NA	YES
H1	Stress DSP distribution	6.20006E-05	NA	YES
H2	Gender (Female > Male)	NA	0.328	NO
H3	Race (Minority > White)	NA	0.020	Opposite Supported
H4	Status (Single > Married)	NA	0.644	NO
H5	Degree (None > Bach.)	NA	0.680	NO
H6	Type (Public > Private)	NA	0.254	NO

Multiple regression analysis found five out of the 19-predictor variables of stress or stressors to be significant in precipitating stress in pharmacy students. Table 9 delineates the results of the multiple regression analyses.

A logistic regression with multiple independent variables was also performed to identify those stressors that contribute to the likelihood of second year pharmacy students experiencing high/excess levels of stress as opposed to normal levels of stress. The logistic regression will also enable us to predict the relative risk (RR) of pharmacy students in suffering from excess or above normal levels of stress. A dichotomous variable representing high/excess stress (STRES) was created to facilitate the multiple logistic regression analysis. According to Derogatis and Fleming (1997) a Total Stress Score (TSS) of 56 and higher on the DSP is considered to be "Excess or Above Normal Levels of Stress." Based on the author's classification of stress scores in the DSP, the variable STRES was coded 0 if the TSS <=55 and 1 if the TSS was>=56. The independent variables for the multiple logistic regression analysis were those that were found to be statistically significant or near significant ($p< 0.07$) in the multiple regression analysis (A logistic regression with all 19 predictor variables did not produce any additional significant stressors than those mentioned in table 29.). The relative risk of students suffering from excess levels of stress in relation to the significant antecedents to STRES was also presented. (RR = exp (Beta) or e^{Beta} where exp is the base of the natural logarithm (2.718) and Beta is the regression coefficient). Table 10 presents the results of the multiple logistic regression analysis.

Table 9. Multiple regression results (Valid n=283

Dependent Variable = Total Stress Score

Independent Variables	Standardized Beta	Std. Error	t	Sig. (2 tailed)
Constant		5.005	9.53	.000
Financial Burden[†]	-.134	1.013	-2.29	.023
English is the first language[†]	.142	1.948	1.77	.078
Faculty Supportive [†]	.238	.947	4.07	.000
School has counseling service[†]	.189	1.411	3.25	.001
Student used counseling service[†]	-.089	1.168	-1.54	.125
Excessive Study Load[†]	-.264	1.033	-4.45	.000
Too much competition[†]	-.048	.978	.781	.436
Prior Degree[†]	-.017	.987	.266	.791
Gender (Females = 0, Males = 1)	-.065	1.01	-1.11	.268
Minority (White = 0, Rest = 1)	-.251	1.625	-3.15	.002
Married (Unmarried=0, married = 1)	-.053	1.081	-.787	.432
Age	.089	.134	1.24	.215
GPA	.038	.961	.642	.522
Number of Children	-.100	.837	-1.57	.116
Number of Exams	.045	.443	-.762	.447
Commuting time to School	.108	.030	1.722	.086
Second Job	.032	.050	.544	.587
Type of Institution (Public=0)	-.091	.948	-1.47	.142
Medical School in the same campus[†*]	-	-	-	-

$R^2 = 0.250$ [†] "Yes" = 0 "No" = 1

* The variable medical school in the same campus was coincidentally the same as the variable Type of Institution. Thus it has the same values as the latter variable. The regression model thus allowed only one variable to stay in the regression equation, it was not statistically significant.

Table 10. Multiple Logistic Regression Results (n=283)

Dependent Variable = STRESS

Variable	Beta	Relative Risk	df	Sig.
Constant	-1.157	0.0314	1	.0000
Financial Burden[†]	-.565	0.568	1	.145
English is first language[†]	2.35	10.58	1	.019
Faculty Supportive [†]	.817	2.26	1	.009
School has a counseling service[†]	.503	1.65	1	. 280
Excessive Study load[†]	-1.48	0.228	1	.002
Minority (White = 0, Rest = 1)	-3.18	0.042	1	.002
Commuting Time to School	.011	1.01	1	.233

-2 Log L Chi-Square 39.36 (7 df, p= .000) [†] "Yes" = 0 "No" = 1
[^]Hosmer –Lemeshow Goodness of Fit = 0.26

[†] *The variables Financial burden, English is the first language, Supportive faculty, School has a counseling service, Excessive Workload are all dichotomous, where 0 = Yes and 1 = No. The variable commuting time to school is a continuous variable.*

[^] *The Hosmer Lemeshow Goodness of Fit statistic when greater that 0.05 indicates that there is no difference between the observed and predicted values of the dependent variable and hence is an acceptable model.*

As can be seen in table 10,, four of the seven predictor variables were found to be statistically significant in contributing to the increased likelihood of second year pharmacy students in our sample experiencing high or excess levels of stress.

Factor analysis is quintessentially a statistical procedure that determines which items of a scale or questionnaire combine to generate a given factor. It allows the researcher to see whether or not some of the items group together in a logical way, as for example items that measure the same underlying theoretical concept. The dimensions of a scale are represented by a hypothesis matrix that reveals how scale items "hang together". In other words, this hypothesis matrix demonstrates how the scale items correlate with one another as factors and the relationship of the factors. If the hypothesis is correct, the matrix usually can be reproduced from scores obtained from a representative sample (Derogatis, 1987). Empirical tests to confirm the hypothesized matrix are usually conducted by factor analysis. Factor analysis (FA) is often used to explain the theorized multidimensional structure of the instrument. In the case of the DSP, Derogatis had performed a factor analysis of the instrument based on a sample of 867 respondents. The analysis was conducted at the level of the 11 primary stress dimensions of the DSP (Derogatis, 1987). After performing a FA of the DSP using this sample of 867 persons, Derogatis reported a total of 4 factors that accounted for 70% of the variance in the matrix structure. Derogatis (1987) used a principal components method to achieve the initial extraction, followed by a varimax rotation of the component matrix. A selection criterion of Eigen values of 0.90 or greater resulted in 4 factors for Derogatis's sample of 867 individuals, on which the factor analysis was based. Principal component extraction is a statistical process of identifying latent variables that can account for mathematical patterns of co-variation among items of a scale. A varimax rotation clarifies the factor solutions by spreading the variations across factors more equally. An Eigen-value is the total variance explained by each factor and indicates how well the factor explains the common variance. In this inquiry, we performed a factor analysis on our sample of pharmacy students consistent with that of Derogatis. The following table shows the results of the initial extraction with an un-rotated factor solution.

Table 11. Percentage Variance in Original Factor Solution (Valid n = 283)

Total Variance Explained

Component	Initial Eigenvalues			Extraction Sums of Squared Loadings		
	Total	% of Variance	Cumulative %	Total	% of Variance	Cumulative %
1	6.213	56.484	56.484	6.213	56.484	56.484
2	.788	7.166	63.650	.788	7.166	63.650
3	.651	5.919	69.569	.651	5.919	69.569
4	.603	5.483	75.052	.603	5.483	75.052
5	.527	4.791	79.843			
6	.469	4.263	84.106			
7	.430	3.912	88.019			
8	.386	3.505	91.523			
9	.335	3.049	94.572			
10	.320	2.911	97.483			
11	.277	2.517	100.000			

Extraction Method: Principal Component Analysis.

As in the case with Derogatis (1997), our factor analysis yielded 4 factors that explained 75% of the variance in the TSS. The factor analysis on the normative sample by Derogatis had also yielded four factors that accounted for 70% of the variance. The original factors hypothesized by Derogatis were Personality Mediators, Emotional Response, and Environment. However, the factor analysis originally described by Derogatis (1987) yielded four factors. Derogatis had argued that even though factor analysis rarely matches the hypothesized number of factors because of sampling variation, it was possible that the fourth factor (Health Environment) was orthogonal to the other dimensions in the Environment Factor and, hence, emerged as a separate factor (Derogatis, 1986). He did, state however, that the surprise emergence of the dimension of health issues as an independent factor may also be due to psychometric anomalies that arise due to the use of a psychometric scale such as the DSP itself. The inclusion of a fourth factor in our sample confirms Derogatis's supposition that health environment was indeed a separate factor and not a part of the Environment Factor.

CONCLUSION

This inquiry is a seminal work in providing empirical evidence of stress and its sources in pharmacy students. Although pharmacy students resembled the general population in terms of overall stress scores, some of these students were experiencing high levels of stress. We have also been able to identify potential stressors that are responsible for stress in pharmacy school. The relative risk to a student in experiencing high or excess levels of stress as a result of the significant stressors has also been noted. This, heretofore, has not been studied in health professions students. Findings from this inquiry may prove to be enormously helpful in shaping future curricula changes in schools of pharmacy. Findings from this inquiry may also facilitate the implementation of intervention strategies and coping programs that have the potential to alleviate unnecessary stress (perceived financial burden of pharmacy education and excessive competition to name a few) in pharmacy students during their professional education. Equipped with a new knowledge of stress and its antecedents, pharmacy school administrators and faculty members should be uniquely poised to be proactive versus reactive insofar as the stress levels of their students are concerned. They should be able to take appropriate actions to diminish stress levels in their students by eliminating or minimizing the impact of such significant stressors such as unsupportive nature of faculty and excessive study load. Diminishing counterproductive stress and its causative factors would help to create a nurturing, enabling, and productive atmosphere for these professional students.

It is important that future research be conducted to overcome many of the limitations of this study. The goal of future studies should be to take this empirical investigation to the next level. Similar studies should aim for a larger sample of students from more schools of pharmacy from across the U.S. It is important that this study gets replicated using a larger, national sample to provide more empirical evidence of the presence of stress in pharmacy students and its consequences. Future research should also focus on the long-term effect of pharmacy education on the students. Following a student cohort through their progress in pharmacy school is an option. The students can be measured for their stress levels at the beginning of pharmacy school and then again when they are ready to graduate. Alternatively, measuring the stress levels of students at the beginning and then again at the end of a scholastic year may also be a way to gather valuable information on the effects of stress through a scholastic year. If required, an intervention program aimed to reduce stress in pharmacy students can also be designed and tested. Such a program could note the effect of counseling or stress management class. The most preferable future study is one that incorporates a design to measure stress in pharmacy students and that attempts to control for as many of the factors that jeopardize the validity of the findings in this regard as possible. It can be a cross-sectional design study that looks at stress across four years in all the students within randomly selected public and private schools of pharmacy.

It is important that the significant stressors identified in this inquiry be further assessed for their impact on the stress levels of pharmacy students. It is apparent from the logistic regression that relationship with the faculty plays a vital role in students' perception of stress. Similarly, study load, the financial burden of pharmacy education, absence of counseling services, and English being the second language are antecedents to excess levels of stress for pharmacy students that should be further explored. Pharmacy school administrators should pay attention to these stressors and think of ways to alleviate them to provide a more conducive learning environment for students. Moreover, other stressors that may pertain to pharmacy students should also be explored as an addendum to the stressors listed in this inquiry. Whether reducing the stressors (either by intervention or redesigning curricula) affecting pharmacy students result in an alleviation of stress may also be the focus of future inquires.

Finally, as more meaningful empirical findings related to understanding and measuring stress emerge, the broader literature on stress in health professions students in general will be significantly enhanced. It will then be possible to enumerate the steps required to foster and sustain optimal learning environments for all health professions students, and, perhaps for all students.

REFERENCES

Achord, C., and Mc Carry, P. (1974). The impact of attrition on the self concept and anxiety level of nursing students. Journal of Education and Research, 13(3), 3-36.

Admi, H. (1997). Nursing student stress. Journal of Nursing Education, 36(7), 323-327.

Adsett, C. (1968). Psychological health of medical students. Journal of Medical Education, 43, 729-734.

Alexander, D., and Haldane, J. (1979). Medical Education: A student's perspective. Medical Education, 13, 336-341.

Amaranto, E. (1978). Factors affecting the growth of student mental health service. Journal of Medical Education, 53, 849-850.

Antonovsky, A. (1987). Unraveling the mystery of health. San-Francisco: Jossey-Bass.

Arnstein, R. (1986). Emotional problems of medical students. American Journal of Psychiatry, 143(11), 1422-1423.

Appley, M., and Trumbell, R. (1986). Development of the stress concept. In M. Appley and R. Trumbel (Eds.), Dynamics of Stress. (pp. 25-40). New York: Plenum Press.

Austin, G., and Maher, M. (1973). Women in dentistry. Journal of Dental Education, 37, 11-17.

Baldwin, H., and Knutson, T. (1979). Communication apprehension in pharmacy students. American Journal of Pharmaceutical Education, 43, 91-93.

Beck, D., and Srivastava, R. (1997). Perceived levels of sources and stress in university schools. Journal of Nursing Education, 36(4), 180-186.

Berger, B., and Baldwin, H, and McCroskey, J. (1983). Communication apprehension in pharmacy students. American Journal of Pharmaceutical Education, 47, 95-101.

Berger, B., and McCroskey, J. (1982). Reducing communication apprehension in pharmacy students. American Journal of Pharmaceutical Education, 46, 132-137.

Biggers, T. (1983). Nursing Education. Technical Report. (Eric Document Reproduction Service No. ED292138).

Bjorksten, O., and Miller, M. (1983). Perceptions of dental students problems. Journal of American College of Dentists, 50, 10-15.

Bjorksten, O., Sutherland, S., and Miller, C. (1983). Identification of medical students problems. Journal of Medical Education, 58, 759-767.

Boyle, B., and Coombs, R. (1971). Emotional stress and medical training. Journal of Medical Education, 46, 882-886.

Bradley, I., Clark, C., and Eisner, D. (1989). The student survey of problems in the academic environment in Canadian dental facilities. Journal of Dental Education, 53, 126-131.

Brantley, J., Jones, S., and Boudreux, A. (1997) In C. Zalaquett and R. Wood (Eds.), Evaluating Stress. (pp. 65-80). London: Scarecrow Press.

Brook, J. (1983). Depressive mood in male college students. Archives of General Psychiatry, 40, 665-669.

Brosin, H. (1948). Psychiatric experiments with selection. Social Science Review, 4, 461-468.

Buam, A., Singer, J., and Baum, D. (1981). Stress and the environment. Journal of Social Issues, 37, 4-35.

Burstein, A., Loucks, S., Kobos, J., Johnson, G., Talbert, R., and Stanton, B. (1980). A longitudinal study of personality characteristics of medical students. Journal of Medical Education, 55, 786-787.

Cannon, W. (1929). Bodily changes in pain hunger and fear. New York: Appleton.

Carter, E. (1982). Stress in nursing students. Nurse Outlook, 30(4), 248-252.

Carmel, S. (1987). Perceptions of medical school stressors. Journal of Human Stress, 13(1), 39-44.

Carraway, C. (1987). Nurse burnout- Literature review. (Doctoral dissertation, University of South Carolina, 1987). Dissertation Abstracts International 45, 534B.

Carmack, C., Amaral, M., Boudreux, E., Brantley, P., Franks, G., and McKnight, G. (1995). Exercise as a component of the physical and psychological rehabilitation of haemodylasis patients. International Journal of Rehabilitation and Health, 1, 13-23.

Chalmers, B. (1981). A selective review of stress. Current Psychological Reviews, 1, 325-344.

Clark, D., and Zeldow, P. (1998). Vicissitudes of depressed mood during four years of medical school. Journal of American Medical Association, 260(17), 2521-2529.

Clark, E., and Reicker, P. (1986). Gender differences in relationships and stress of medical and law students. Journal of Medical Education, 61, 33-40.

Coburn, D., and Jovias, A. (1975). Perceived sources of stress among first year medical students. Journal of Medical Education, 50, 589-593.

Coombs, F., and Fawzy, F. (1982). The effect of marital status in medical school. American Journal of Psychiatry, 139(11), 1490-1493.

Coombs, R., and Perrel, K. (1990). Primary prevention of emotional impairment among medical trainees. Academic Medicine, 65, 576-581.

Cox, T. (1985). The nature and measurement of stress. Ergoeconomics, 28(8), 1155-1163.

Cox, T., and Mackay, C. (1981). A transactional approach to occupational stress. In L. Corlett and P. Richardson (Eds.). Stress, work design and productivity. (pp. 91-113). New York: Wiley.

Cox, T. (1978). Stress. New York: McMillan Press.

Curtiss, F., Hammel, R., Heinen, S., and Johnson, C. (1978). The importance of education and practice factors in determining stress among young pharmacy practitioners. American Journal of Pharmaceutical Education, 42, 104-111.

Davis, R., and Fricke, N. (1977). Crisis in nursing students. Nursing Forum, 16(1), 56-70.

Davis, E., Tedesco, L., and Meir, S. (1989). Dental student stress, burnout, and memory. Journal of Dental Education, 53(9), 193-195.

Davidson, V. (1978). Coping styles of women medical students. Journal of Medical Education, 53, 902-907.

Deary, J. (1994). Need medical education be stressful? Medical Education, 28, 55-57.

Derogatis, L. (1987). The Derogatis Stress profile. In G.Fava and T. Wise. (Eds.), Research paradigms in psychosomatic medicine. (pp. 30-54). NY: Basel-Krager.

Derogatis, L., and Fleming (1997). The Derogatis Stress Profile: A theory driven approach to stress measurement. In C. Zalaquett and R. Wood (Eds.), Evaluating stress. (pp. 113-140). London: Scarecrow Press.

Derogatis, L., Gergopopulas, L., and Saudek, C. (1986, June). Psychological factors. Paper presented at the 46th Annual meeting of the American Diabetes Association, Anaheim, CA.

Dickstein, L., and Stephenson, J. (1990). Psychiatric impairment in medical students. Academic Medicine, 65, 588-593.

Dobkin, P., Phil, R., and Breault, C. (1991). Validation of the Derogatis stress profile using laboratory and real world data. Psychotherapy and Psychosomatics, 56, 185-196.

Edwards, M., and Zimet, C. (1976). Problems and concerns among medical students. Journal of Medical Education, 51, 619-625.

Eron, L. (1955). Effect of medical education on medical students' attitudes. Journal of Medical Education, 30(10), 559-566.

Everly, J., Lamport, N., and Poff, D. (1994). Perceived stressors in occupational therapy students. American Journal of Occupational Therapy, 48(11), 1022-1028.

Firth, J. (1986). Levels and sources of stress in medical students. British Medical Journal, 292, 1177-1181.

Folse, L. (1985). The relationship between stress and attitudes towards leisure. Journal of Medical Education, 60(8), 610-617.

Foorman, S., and Lloyd, C. (1986). The relationship between social support and psychiatric symptoms in medical students. The Journal of Nervous and Mental Disease, 174(4), 229-239.

Funkestein, D. (1968). The learning and personal development of medical students. Journal of Medical Education, 43, 883-896.

Gaensbauer, T., and Mizner, G. (1980). Developmental stresses in medical education. Psychiatry, 43, 61-70.

Garbee, W., Zucker, S., and Selby, G. (1980). Perceived sources of stress among dental students. Journal of American Dental Association, 100, 853-856.

Garret, A. (1976). Conceptual framework. Journal of Nursing Education, 15(6), 9-21.

Gaughran, F., and Dineens, C. (1997). Stress in medical students. Israel Medical Journal, 90(5), 184-185.

George, J., Whitworth, D., and Lundeen, T. (1987). Correlates of dental student stress. Journal of Dental Education, 51, 481-485.

Goldstein, M. (1975). Preventive efforts for women medical students. Journal of Medical. Education, 50, 289-291.

Goldstein, M. (1979). Sources of stress among first year dental students. Journal of Dental Education, 43(12), 625-629.

Gottheil, E., Thornton, C., Conly, S., and Cornelison, F. (1969). Stress, satisfaction, and performance. Journal of Medical Education, 44, 272-277.

Graham, C., and Babola, K. (1998). Needs assessment of non-traditional students in physical and occupational therapy. Journal of Allied Health, 27(4), 196-220.

Grandy, T., and Westerman, G. (1988). Stress symptoms among third year dental students. Journal of Dental Education, 52(5), 245-249.

Grandy, T., Westerman, G., and Combs, C. (1989). Perceptions of stress among third year dental students. Journal of Dental Education, 53(12), 719-721.

Grandy, T., Westerman, G., Mitchell, R., and Lupo, J. (1984). Stress among first year dental students. Journal of Dental Education, 48(10), 560-562.

Grevin, F. (1996). Post traumatic stress disorders in urban paramedics. Psychiatric Reports, 79(2), 483-495.

Grinker, R.R., and Speigel, J.P. (1945). Men under stress. New York: McGraw-Hill.

Harper, S., and Anderson, R. (1994). Stress and family health, Contemporary Family Therapy, 15, 169-178.

Harvey, V., and McMurray, N. (1997). Student's perceptions of nursing. Journal of Nursing Education, 36(8), 383-389.

Heins, M., Fahey, S., and Henderson, H. (1983). Law students and medical students a comparison. Journal of Legal Education, 33, 511-525.

Heins, M., and Nickols, S. (1984). Perceived stress in medical, law and dental students. Journal of Medical Education, 59, 169-179.

Henning, K., Ey, S., and Shaw, D. (1998). Perfectionism, impostor phenomenon, and psychological adjustment in medical, dental, nursing, and pharmacy students. Medical Education, 32, 456-464.

Hendrie, H., Clair, D., and Fadul, P. (1990). A study of anxiety. The Journal of Nervous and Mental Disease, 178(3), 204-207.

Heubner, L., Royer, J., and Moore, J. (1981). The assessment and remediation of dysfunctional stress in medical school. Journal of Medical Education, 56, 547-558.

Hilberman, E., Konac, J., and Hunter, R. (1975). Support groups of women in medical school. Journal of Medical Education, 50, 867-870.

Hohaus, L., and Berah, E. (1985). Impairment of doctors. Medical Education, 19, 431-436

Howard, C. (1986). Methods for reducing stress. Journal of Dental Education, 50(9), 542-544.

Howard, C., Graham, L., and Wycoff, S. (1986). A comparison of methods for reducing stress among dental students. Journal of Dental Education, 50(9), 542-545.

Hurwitz, A., and Eadie, R. (1977). Psychological impact on nursing students. Nursing Research, 26(2), 112-120.

Huxam, G., Lipton, A., and Hamilton, D. (1985). Does medical training affect personality? Medical Education, 19, 118-122.

Ironside, W. (1965). The incidence of psychiatric illness in a group of New Zealand medical students. Paper presented at the third conference of the Australian and New Zealand student health association, Dunedin, New Zealand.

Janis, I.L. (1958). Psychological Stress New York: John Willey and Sons.

Jones, D. (1978). The need for a comprehensive counseling service for nursing students. Journal of Advanced Nursing, 3(4), 359-368.

Jones, M., and Johnston, D. (1997). Distress, stress and coping in first-year student nurses. Journal of Advanced Nursing, 26(3), 475-482.

Kay, J. (1990). Traumatic deidealization and the future of medicine. Journal of American Medical Association, 263(4), 572-573.

Kelly, J. (1982). Stress management training in medical school. Journal of Medical Education, 57, 91-101.

Keenan, A. (1985). Stressful events in professionals. Journal of Occupational Behavior, 6, 151-156.

Kellner, R., Wiggins, R., and Pathak, D. (1986). Distress in medical and law students. Comprehensive Psychiatry, 27(3), 220-223.

Kensington, K (1967). The med student. Yale Journal of Biological Medicine, 39, 346-358.

Kilpatrick, D., Dubbin, W., and Marcotte, D. (1974). Personality, stress of the medical education process. Psychological Reports, 34, 1215-1223.

Kohl, R. (1951). The psychiatrist as an advisor and therapist for medical students. American Journal of Psychiatry, 108, 198-203.

Kris, K. (1986). Distress precipitated by psychiatric training. American Journal of Psychiatry, 143(11), 1432-1435.

Lacey, J. (1967). Somatic response patterning and stress. In M. Appley and R. Trumbell (Eds.), Psychological Stress. (pp. 14-42). New York: Appelton-Crofts.

Lazarus, R., and Folkman, S. (1984). Stress appraisal and coping. New York: Springer Company.

Lazarus, RS. (1966). Psychological stress and coping process. New York: McGraw Hill.

Lebenthal, A. (1996). Student abuse in medical school. Journal of American Medical Association, 32(3), 229-238.

LeFevre, C., and Goolishian, H. (1964). Marital Status and medical school performance. Journal of Medical Education, 39, 377-381.

Leif, H., Young, K., Spuriel, V., and Lief, V. (1960). A psychodynamic study of medical students and their adaptation problems. Journal of Medical Education, 35(7), 697-704.

Levine, S., and Scotch, N. (1970). Models of stress. In N. Scotch and S. Levine. (Eds.), (pp. 70-80). Social Stress. New York: Aldine Publishers.

Levin, R., and Walker, A. (1984). Needs assessment of first year and second year medical students. Journal of Medical Education, 59, 908-911.

Linn, B., and Zeppa, R. (1984). Stress in junior medical students. Journal of Medical Education, 59, 7-12.

Lloyd, C. (1983). Sex differences in medical students. The Journal of Nervous and Mental Disease, 171(9), 535-542.

Lloyd, C., and Gartell, N. (1981). Sex differences in medical student mental health. American Journal of Psychiatry, 138(10), 1346-1351.

Lloyd, C., and Gartell, N. (1983). A further assessment of medical school stress. Journal of Medical Education, 58, 964-967.

Lloyd, C., and Gartell, N. (1984). Psychiatric symptoms in medical students. Comprehensive Psychiatry, 25(6), 552-565.

Lloyd, C., and Musser, L. (1985). Stress in dental students. Journal of American College of Dentists, 52(2), 11-19.

Lloyd, C., and Musser, L. (1989). Psychiatric symptoms in dental students. The Journal of Nervous and Mental Disease, 177(2), 61-69.

Lorenski, S. (1965). The need for a counseling service in dental school. Journal of California Dental Association, 41, 520-521.

Lucas, J. (1976). Psychological problems of students. British Medical Journal, 45, 1431-1433.

Lyons, K.J., Young, BE., Haas, PS., Hojat, M., and Bross, TM. (1997). A study of cognitive and noncognitive predictors of academic success in nursing, allied health and medical students. Annual Forum Paper. (ERIC Document Reproduction Service No. ED410899).

Maddi, S. (1987). Hardiness training at Bell telephone. In J. Opaz. (Ed.), Health promotion evaluation. (pp. 30-45). Madison, WI: National Wellness Institute.

Maddux, J., and Hoppe, S. (1986). Psychoactive substance use among medical students. American Journal of Psychiatry, 143(2), 187-191.

Mahat, G. (1998). Stress and coping. Nursing Forum, 33(1), 11-29.

Marshall, R. (1978). Measuring the medical school environment. Journal of Medical Education, 53, 100-104.

Martinez, P. (1977). Assessment of negative effects of dental education. Journal of Dental Education, 41(1), 30-31.

Mason, J.W. (1971). A revaluation of the concept of nonspecificity. Journal of Psychology Research, 8, 323-333.

McGrath, J. (1970). Introduction to Social Stress. In J. McGrath and H. Holt (Eds.), Social and Psychological factors in stress. (pp. 23-50). New York: Reinhart Inc.

McKay, S. (1978). A review of student stress in nursing education program. Nursing Forum, 17(4), 9-21.

McMurray, J., Fitzgerald, G., and Bean, S. (1980). Stress and support systems in preclinical medical students. Journal of Medical Education, 55, 216-217.

Mcinnis, W., and Murphy, H. (1987). Identifying dental student disatissfiers using Delphi technique. Journal of Dental Education, 51(9), 540-541.

Mechanic, D. (1962). Students under Stress. Glencoe, Ill: Erlbaum.

Mese, J., and Spano, M. (1989). Retention through intervention. (ERIC Document Reproduction Service No. ED305987).

Mikhail, A. (1981). Stress: A psychophysiological conception. Journal of Human Stress, 34, 9-15.

Mitchell, R., Matthews, J., Grandy, T., and Lupo, J. (1983). A question of stress among first-year medical students. Journal of Medical Education, 58, 368-371.

Moore, J. (1962). Attitudes associated with dental school. Journal of American College of Dentists, 29, 140-164.

Musser, L., and Lloyd, C. (1985). The relationship of marital status to stress among dental students. Journal of Dental Education, 49(8), 573-579.

Neissen, L. (1992). Women dentists. Journal of Dental Education, 56(8), 555-561.

Newton, J.T., Baghaienaini, F., Goodwin, S.R., Invest, J., Lubbock, M., and Marouf-Saghakhaneh, N. (1994). Stress in dental school: A survey of students. Dental Update, 21(4), 162-164.

Notman, M., Salt, P., and Nadelson, C. (1984). Stress and adaptation in medical students. Comprehensive Psychiatry, 25(3), 355-366.

O'Mahony, P., and O'Brien, S. (1980). Demographic and social characteristics of university students attending a psychiatrist. British Journal of Psychiatry, 137, 547-550.

O'Meara, S., Kostas, T., Markland, F., and Previty, J. (1994). Perceived stress in physical therapy. Journal of Physical Therapy Education, 8(2) 71-75.

Ortmeirer, B., Wolfgang, A., and Martin, B. (1991). Career commitment and perceived stress. American Journal of Pharmaceutical Education, 55, 138-142.

O'Shea, R., Corah, N., and Ayer, W. (1984). Sources of dentists' stress. Journal of American Dental Association, 109, 48-51.

Parkerson, G., Broadhead, W., and Chiu-Kit, J. (1990). The health status and life satisfaction of first year students. Academic Medicine, 65, 586-588.

Pasnau, R., and Stoessel, P. (1994). Mental health service for medical students. Medical Education, 28, 33-39.

Perricone, P. (1974). Social concern in medical students. Journal of Medical Education, 49, 541-546.

Pitts, F., Winkour, G., and Stewart, M. (1961). Psychiatric syndromes and responses to stress in medical students. American Journal of Psychiatry, 118, 333-340.

Raskin, M. (1972). Psychiatric crises of medical students. Journal of Medical Education, 47, 211-215.

Richman, J., Flaherty, J., Rospenda, K., and Christensen, M. (1992). Mental health consequences and correlates of medical student abuse. Journal of American Medical Association, 267(5), 692-694.

Rosenberg, P. (1971). Students' perception and concerns. Journal of Medical Education, 46, 211-218.

Rosenberg, D., and Silver, H. (1984). Medical student abuse. Journal of American Medical Association, 251(6), 739-742.

Rosenberg, H., and Thomson, N. (1976). Attitudes towards women dental students. Journal of Dental Education, 40(10), 677-681.

Rubenstein, L., May, T., Sonn, M., and Batts, V. (1989). Physical health and stress in entering dental students. Journal of Dental Education, 53(9), 544-547.

Sachs, R., Zullo, T., and Close, J. (1981). Concerns of entering Dental students. Journal of Dental Education, 45(3), 133-137.

Sacks, M., Frosh, W., and Kesselman, M. (1980). Psychiatric problems in third year medical students. American Journal of Psychiatry, 137(7), 823-825.

Salmons, P. (1983). Psychiatric illness in medical students. British Journal of Psychiatry, 143, 505-508.

Saslow, G. (1956). Psychiatric problems of medical students. Journal of Medical Education, 31(1), 27-33.

Scott, T., and Howard, N. (1970). Models of stress. In N. Scotch and S. Levine. (Eds.), (pp. 50-65). Social Stress. New York: Aldine Publishers.

Schwartz, A., Swartzburg, M., Lieb, J., and Slaby, A. (1978). Medical school and the process of disillusionment. Medical Education, 12, 182-185.

Schwartz, R. (1984). A comprehensive stress reduction program for dental students. Journal of Dental Education, 48(4), 203-207.

Sekas, G., and Wile, M. (1980). Stress related illness comparing M.D.-Ph.D., M.D., and Ph.D. Students. Journal of Medical Education, 55, 440-446.

Selye, H. (1936). A syndrome produced by diverse nocuous agents. Nature, 13, 31-32.

Selye, H. (1956). The stress of life. New York: McGraw-Hill.

Sheier, M., and Carver, C. (1985). Optimism, coping and health. Health Psychology, 4, 219-247.

Sheehan, K., Sheehan, D., White, K., Leibowitz, A., and Baldwin, D. (1990). A pilot study of medical student abuse. Journal of American Medical Association, 263(4), 533-537.

Sheets, J. (1993). Personal and behavioral variables related to perceived stress. Teaching and Learning in Medicine, 5(2), 90-95.

Silver, H. (1982). Medical students and medical school. Journal of American Medical Association, 247(3), 309-310.

Silver, H., and Glicken, A. (1990). Medical student abuse. Journal of American Medical Association, 263(4), 527-531.

Smith, M., Messer, S., and Fincham, J. (1991). A longitudinal study of attitude change in pharmacy students. American Journal of Pharmaceutical Education, 55, 30-35.

Snow, L. (1969). Observations of the psychotherapy in medical students. American Journal of Psychotherapy, 23, 293-302.

Sobol, E. (1978). Nursing students response to strain. Nursing Research, 27(4), 238-244.

Speilberger, C., Gorush, R., Lushene, R., Vagg, P., and Jacobs, G. (1983). The relation between stress and disease: Manual for strait test anxiety inventory. New York: Consulting Psychologists Press.

Steenbarger, B., and Greenberg, R. (1990). Sex roles, stress and distress. Sex Roles, 22, 59-68.

Strayhorn, G. (1980). Perceived stress of black and white medical students. Journal of Medical Education, 55, 618-625.

Strecker, EA., Appel, K., Palmer, H., and Braceland, F.J. (1937). Psychiatric studies in medical education. American Journal of Psychiatry, 93, 1197-1229.

Stewart, M. (1990). Attrition of health professionals. Canadian Journal of Higher Education, 22(3), 43-63.

Stewart, S., and Betson, C. (1995) Stress and vulnerability in medical students. Medical Education, 29(2), 119-127.

Stewart, S., and Betson, C. (1997). Predicting stress in first year students. Medical Education, 31(3), 163-168.

Sturdevant, J., George, J., and Lundeen, T. (1987). An interactional view of dental student stress. Journal of Dental Education, 51, 246-249.

Swarzky, J. (1998). Understanding nursing students. Nursing Education Today, 18(2), 108-115.

Tedesco, L. (1986). A psychosocial perspective on the dental education experience. Journal of Dental Education, 50(10), 601-605.

Thomas, C. (1976). What becomes of the medical students? The Johns Hopkins Medical Journal, 138, 185-195.

Tichy, A., and Means, S. (1990). Stress coping methods and physical activity among student nurses. Community College Quarterly of Research and Practice, 14(4), 273-283.

Tisdelle, D., and Hansen, D. (1984). Stress management training for dental students. Journal of Dental Education, 48(4), 196-202.

Tyrell, J. (1997). Mental health and student health professionals. British Journal of Occupational Therapy, 60(9), 389-394.

Vitalino, P., Roland, D., and Russo, J. (1988). A biopsychosocial model of medical student distress. Journal of Behavioral Medicine, 11(4), 311-331.

Vitalino, P., Roland, D., and Russo, J. (1989). Medical student distress. The Journal of Nervous and Mental Disease, 177(2), 70-77.

Vitalino, P., Russo, J., and Carr, J. (1984). Medical school pressures. The Journal of Nervous and Mental Disease, 172, 730-737.

Waldman, H. (1983). Minority dental students. Journal of American College of Dentists, 50(3), 18-23.

Webb, E., Cambell, D., Schwartz, R., and Sechrest, L. (1966). Unobtrusive Measures. New York: Rand McNally.

Wernner, E., and Smith, S. (1982). Vulnerable but invincible. New York: McGraw-Hill.

Westerman, G., and Grandy, T. (1993). Perceived sources of stress in dental students. Journal of Dental Education, 57(3), 225-231.

Wexler, M. (1978). Mental health and dental education. Journal of Dental Education, 42(2), 74-77.

Whittemore, P., Burstein, A., Loucks, S., and Scoenfeld, L. (1985). A longitudinal study of personality changes in medical students. Journal of Medical Education, 60, 404-405.

Williams, R. (1993). The concerns of beginning nursing students. Nursing and Health Care, 14(4), 178-184.

Wolf, T. (1994). Stress coping and health. Medical Education, 28, 8-17.

Wolf, T., Bruno, A., and Butler, J. (1992). Perceived mistreatment of graduating dental students. Journal of Dental Education, 56(5), 312-315.

Wolf, T., Faucett, J., Randall, H., and Balson, P. (1988). Graduating medical students rating of stresses. Journal of Medical Education, 63, 636-641.

Wolf, T., and Kissling, G. (1984). Changes in life style characteristics. Journal of Medical Education, 59, 808-813.

Wolfgang, A. (1988). Job stress in the health professions. Behavioral Medicine, 42, 43-47.

Wolfgang, A. (1993). Job stress and dissatisfaction among pharmacy faculty members. American Journal of Pharmaceutical. Education, 57, 215-221.

Wolfgang, A., and Ortmeier, B. (1993). Career commitments, plans and job related stress. American Journal of Pharmaceutical Education, 57, 25-29.

Woods, S., and Natterson, J. (1966). Medical student's disease. Journal of Medical Education, 41, 785-790.

Wyler, C. (1945). Neurotic problems in a student practice. Lancet, 65, 104-106.

Yap, A.U., and Bhole, J. (1996). A cross-cultural comparison of perceived sources of stress in dental students. Journal of Dental Education, 60(5), 459-464.

Zalaquett, C., and Wood, R. (1997). (Eds.). Evaluating Stress. London: The Scarecrow Press Inc.

Zeldow, P., and Daughtery, S. (1987). The stability and attitudinal correlates of caring in medical students. Medical Education, 21, 353-357.

Zeldow, P., Daughtery, S., and Lekas, L. (1987). Personality changes in medical students. Journal of Medical Education, 62, 992-995.

Zocolillo, M., and Murphy, G. (1986). Depression among medical students. Journal of Affective Disorders, 11, 91-96.

In: Stress and Mental Health of College Students
Editor: Mery V. Landow, pp. 29-62

ISBN 1-59454-839-0
© 2006 Nova Science Publishers, Inc.

Chapter 2

MEDICAL STUDENTS' DISEASE: HEALTH ANXIETY AND WORRY IN MEDICAL STUDENTS

Gurminder Singh[2]

Guy's, King's and St. Thomas' School of Medicine, London, UK

INTRODUCTION

Human suffering is a universal phenomenon. We all experience suffering in the form of health problems at one time or another and, in some instances, we also experience anxiety about the significance and possible outcome of the problem. The occurrence of health anxiety can be appropriate and is sometimes of direct survival value. An absence of anxiety when there is a significant threat to one's health can be damaging. For example, not responding quickly to symptoms of a heart attack may heighten the severity of the condition, or even lead to death, which may have been avoided.

In common with other forms of anxiety, health anxiety is normative, appropriate, universal and functional – but like these other forms, excessive or inappropriate anxiety about one's health can be unadaptive and distressing. Severe, or clinically significant health anxiety (often termed *hypochondriasis*) can be distinguished from non-clinical presentations by the degree of fear and conviction about having a serious illness, the level of distress experienced, and/or impairment in social, occupational or other important areas of functioning (see Appendix A – for DSM IV criteria).

The term *hypochondria* dates back to approximately 350 BC (Asmundson et al. 2001), however the first contemporary description of the condition was probably cited in 1863 by Forbes Winslow in his book entitled, *Obscure Diseases of the Brain and Mind*:

> That psychosomatic disease termed hypochondriasis, which manifests itself principally in a morbid anxiety as to health, and is in its primitive nature essentially a diseased concentration

---

[2] Correspondence author address: Gurminder Singh Guy's, King's and St. Thomas' School of Medicine, Psychology Unit. 5th Floor Thomas Guy House, Guy's Campus, London, SE1 9RT., Tel.: 00 44 786 168 580100 44 1332 515 376, E-mail: doctorsingh@doctors.org.uk.

of physical sensibility, resulting from slight bodily ailments, which eventually assume to the distempered and deluded imagination a grave significant character. (Cited in Ladee, 1966, p.13).

It was, nonetheless, another two decades before psychopathologists began describing hypochondriasis as a distinct clinical syndrome, and another half century or more before diagnostic definitions were formalised. Yet despite the emergence in the literature, the concept was not unanimously welcomed by the clinical community at large. Stanley Rachman (2001), describes the critical movement as directed primarily at a concept that encapsulated the phenomenon of health anxiety in a negative and even pejorative sense. It implied that health anxiety is often psychopathological, and worse, that it is an exaggeration bordering on malingering. Furthermore, the concept was frequently negative in its implication that hypochondriasis is a sign of weakness; and it was too often disapproving and demeaning.

A COGNITIVE MODEL OF HEALTH ANXIETY

It was not until the introduction of cognitive frameworks for understanding anxiety disorders in general, that the concept of hypochondriasis received renewed interest from the clinical community. The 1986 paper by Salkovskis and Warwick was a landmark contribution to the literature. It proposed (from a cognitive-behavioural perspective) that the central mechanism operating in people suffering from persistent health anxiety and hypochondriasis is a relatively enduring tendency to misinterpret bodily symptoms, bodily variations and other health-relevant information as evidence of serious physical illness (Salkovskis and Warwick, 1986; Warwick and Salkovskis, 1990). The impact of misinterpretations (cognitive appraisals) is constituent upon the interaction of four factors:

1. *Probability* – the perceived likelihood of illness
2. *Awefulness* – perceived cost, suffering and burden of the illness
3. *Coping* – perceived ability to cope with the illness
4. *Rescue* – perception of the extent to which external factors will help
(e.g. effectiveness of medical help)

The model suggests that these misinterpretations regarding health related signs and symptoms can arise from negative assumptions (beliefs) about health. These assumptions in turn originate from a wide variety of sources, including previous experience of illness, later episodes of illness (critical precipitating incident), and information in the mass media (Salkovskis and Warwick, 2001). Furthermore, many of the assumptions learned are likely to be universal and/ or shared by many others of similar cultural backgrounds.

Once misinterpretations arise, a number of factors have been posited as contributing to the maintenance of health anxiety:
1. *Cognitive* – selectively attending to bodily processes (e.g. heart rate) or illness related information (e.g. media), catastrophising.
2. *Physiological* – autonomic symptoms of anxiety are misinterpreted as symptoms of illness.

3. *Behavioural* – checking of the body, avoidance (e.g. physical exertion),safety-seeking (e.g. reassurance).

An overview of the cognitive model is shown in Fig.1.

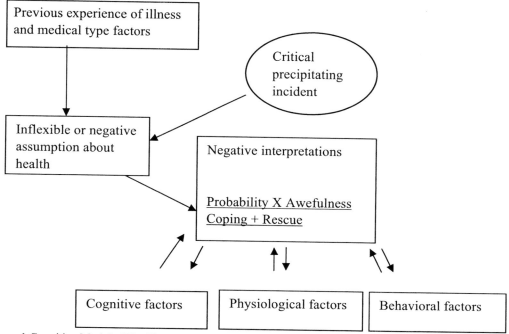

Figure 1.Cognitive Model of Health Anxiety

PREVIOUS RESEARCH

Research over the past decade within the area of health anxiety and hypochondriasis has focused largely on descriptive studies and on the development of methods of assessment and treatment. Studies have investigated the impact of the condition on social and work functioning (Barsky et al, 1990; Noyes et al, 1993), gender differences (Gumbiner and Flowers, 1997), cross-cultural differences (Gureje et al. 1997), co-morbidity (Noyes et al., 1994) and personality dimensions (Cox et al., 2000).

Although these studies have contributed to the general knowledge-base relating to health anxiety, they have not provided further insights into the mechanisms governing the aetiological basis of the condition. However, some studies have shed light upon an important area of health anxiety which has growing interest and concern: the acquisition of medical knowledge.

It seems that recent developments in technology and growing support for the 'user movements' (i.e. patients becoming more involved with the provision of services), has allowed patients the accessibility and resources to tap into a range of health related information. Where practitioners once were viewed as the sole purveyors of expert medical information, television and the internet now allow patient's to enter a physician's office equipped with sophisticated and potentially demanding expectations (Shorter, 1995). For example, the press coverage that accompanied the publication of a New England Journal of

Medicine paper regarding findings that chronic heartburn predicted esophageal cancer (Lagergren et al., 1999) prompted thousands of heartburn sufferers to seek medical attention (Brody, 1999). This suggests that self-referral was not a consequence of changes in symptomology, but initiated by the influence of medical knowledge (through the media) upon cognitive and emotional responses to heart-burn episodes.

New information about illness can be understood cognitively in Salkovskis and Warwick's (1986) model as representing a 'critical precipitating incident' which influences the previously held beliefs (assumptions) about health and in turn influences symptom perception.

Unfortunately, empirical research investigating the impact of new health-related information upon health anxiety is lacking. Exposing patients with hypochondriasis to medical information in the context of research is methodologically arduous, and potentially damaging. However, situations in which the normal attribution processes to health symptoms become disrupted as a consequence of special kinds of learning, have allowed such investigations to occur. One refers to the case of the medical student.

Mechanic (1972) proposed that medical school exposes students to continuing stress resulting from the rapid pace, examinations, anxieties in dealing with new clinical experiences and the like. Students, thus, are emotionally aroused with some frequency, and like others in the population, they experience a high prevalence of transient symptoms. The exposure to specific knowledge about disease provides the student with a new framework for identifying and giving meaning to previously neglected bodily feelings. Diffuse and ambiguous symptoms regarded as normal in the past may be re-conceptualised within the context of newly acquired knowledge of disease. Existing social stress may heighten bodily sensations through autonomic activation, making the student more aware of his bodily state and motivating him to account for what he is experiencing. The new information that the student may have about possible disease and the similarity between the symptoms of a particular condition and his own symptoms establishes a link that he would have more difficulty making if he were less informed. Furthermore, the student, in the process of acquiring new medical information may begin to pay greater attention to his own bodily experiences and may also attempt to imagine how certain symptoms feel. This tendency to give attention to bodily feelings may assist the development of health anxiety.

During the last 40 years, literature searches have revealed 5 main studies investigating health anxiety in medical students. These are summarised in Table 1.

The early studies carried out in the 1960's suggested that between 70-80% of medical students experienced groundless fears and symptoms relating to illness. This has been termed medical student's disease (Woods, Natterson and Silverman, 1966), medical studentitis and nosophobia (Hunter, Lohrenz and Schwartzman, 1964). The term 'nosophobia' however, first came into circulation during the second world war and was described by Ryle (1941) in the Guy's Hospital Gazette:

Nosophobia may take the form of unreasoning fear of a certain disease, especially in the neurotic or psychotic. It may be engendered by unexplained symptoms, erroneous medical diagnosis, or failure of the physician to reassure the patient.

Table 1. Health Anxiety and Medical Students: Previous Research

Authors	No. of participants	Controls	Assessment	Outcome
Hunter et al. health anx (1964)	None		Case records and consulations with tutors	70%
Woods et al. and (1966)	33 (random)	None	Interview	78.8% health
Kellner et al. (1986)	60	60	Illness Behav Q Illness Attitudes Scale	ns
Howes and Salkovskis (1998)	148 (clinical)	110 (all yrs)	Whitley Index Short Health Anx Invent	ns
Moss-Morris and sig Petrie (2001)	92 (1st) 85 (3rd)		82 (3rd)	MSD Scale* Whitley Index Health Concern Scale

* MSD Scale – Medical Student's Disease Perception Scale
Medical Student's Disease Distress Scale

These early studies were criticised for lacking controls, small sample sizes (Howes, 1999) and attributed the findings to selective attention biases by clinical staff (i.e. students who perceived themselves to have concerns about health were more memorable), and also for employing less stringent diagnostic criteria (Howes and Salkovskis, 1998). Furthermore, Mechanic (1972) describes the studies as being 'descriptive' rather than 'explanatory' in their ideas concerning the initial attribution, or aetiology of the illness. For example, the primary study conducted by Hunter, Lohrenz and Schwartzman (1964) suggested that the crucial mechanism operating in medical student's disease appears to be 'projective or introjective identification occurring pari passa with an occupationally reinforced hypercathexis of mind and body function' (taken from the abstract). Although, interestingly defined in psychoanalytic terms, operationally the mechanism appears to lack the empirical framework for testing such hypotheses (an important requisite for establishing theory).

Although these germinal studies are flawed in their methodology, they highlight some noteworthy findings that continue to be investigated. Firstly, medical student's disease (MSD) is short-lived, and secondly, the phenomenon occurs with relatively equal frequency throughout the four years of training (Woods, Natterson and Silverman, 1966). No studies to date have researched the latter claim in a controlled manner, and is one of the key areas of investigation for this project. With regard to the notion that MSD is short lived, the authors of the study implicate 'reassurance' (from physicians) as quintessential to the process of mitigating health anxiety. However, as we know from research following the 1960's studies, reassurance-seeking in people from persistent health anxiety may be counter-productive (Salkovskis and Warwick, 1986).

Thefirst controlled study matched medical students with law students (60 in each group) for age and sex (Kellner, Wiggins and Pathak, 1986). Responses to questionnaires assessing hypochondriacal concerns were compared. The findings suggested that medical students attended to their health and somatic symptoms more, but there were no significant differences in the prevalence of hypochondriacal tendencies. Howes (1999) has indicated that selecting control participants from a highly selected sample (law students) may not allow for a good comparison group. However, in their own study (Howes and Salkovskis, 1998) recruiting participants from a diverse student population as controls also resulted in non-significant findings.

How does one account for the dissonant findings between the former 1960's studies and the non-significant results obtained in the later studies? Moss-Morris and Petrie (2001) believe that there are two reasons to account for the non-significant findings. Firstly, both of the studies (Howes and Salkovskis, 1998; Kellner Wiggins and Pathak, 1986) measured medical student's disease using diagnostically orientated questionnaires, that are commonly utilised with clinical populations – *Illness Attitudes Scale*, and are more sensitive to fears regarding serious health concerns, rather than mild forms of anxiety. The second reason suggested for the aforementioned studies relates to the sample population – i.e. only medical students in their third, or clinical years of training were selected in the studies.

The Moss-Morris and Petrie (2001) study has been pivotal in advancing research regarding health anxiety in the medical student population into the 21st Century. The study investigated medical students' disease by comparing 92 (1st yr) and 85 (3rd yr) medical students with 82 law students using specially designed questionnaires to measure the cognitive experience (Medical Students' Disease Perception Scale) and emotional experience (Medical Students' Disease Distress Scale) of health anxiety. Additionally, specific questionnaires were also administered to measure excessive or hypochondriacal anxiety, similar to those used in previous studies (e.g. Whitley Index – a version of the Illness Attitudes Scale).

With demographic factors controlled, the results suggested that both first and third year medical students scored significantly higher than law students on the Medical Students' Disease Perception Scale. However, only first year medical students scored higher on Medical Students' Distress Scale and on the Whitley Index. Based upon these findings the authors have stated that medical students' disease appears to emerge right at the beginning of the course (1st year), when students are exposed to new information concerning health and illness. In the Salkovskis and Warwick model (1986), this would equate with a 'critical precipitating incident'. By the third year the anxiety component of medical students' disease is no longer significant, although the cognitive component remains. Furthermore, it is suggested that by this stage (3rd year), students have sufficient experience of the process or have developed coping strategies in order to lessen the emotional impact.

Although the discussions surrounding the findings certainly provide logical explanations to account for the results, there are 3 major limitations. Firstly, the authors suggest that the perceptual process of medical students' disease may be separated from the emotional response. The questionnaires: Medical Students' Disease Perception Scale and Medical Students' Disease Distress Scale have been developed to measure these components respectively. However, the validity of these measures is highly questionable, particularly as the majority of items (3 out of 5) in the Distress Scale elicit responses in the participant specifically concerning *worry*. The current research on the concept of worry indicates that worry is primarily a verbal-linguistic attempt to avoid future aversive events (Borkovec, 1994). In other words it is largely a problem-solving cognitive activity, and although has 'negatively affect-laden' components Borkovec et al. (1983), the direct association between emotionality is tentative. Essentially, the Medical Students' Distress Scale is contaminated with cognitive items and would benefit from testing its validity with standardised questionnaires involving the emotional aspects of anxiety.

A second criticism of the Moss-Morris and Petrie (2001) study is directed at making assumptions relating to first year medical students without comparing the students with a *first* year control population. It is possible that the findings of the emergence of health anxiety during the first year, may not be directly associated with medical knowledge per se, and in fact could be prevalent among most first year students. Recent research has shown that university students in general (N= 482) have significantly poorer health compared with population norms (Roberts et al. 2000) and it is possible that anxiety relating to illness is not unique to medical students in the early stages of higher education, as most students are initially exposed to health-related information.

Thirdly, the study recruited law students as the comparison group. As a highly selected sample they may not be truly reflective of the non-medical population.

FURTHER RESEARCH

As more medical knowledge and information is available to the general public through various sources, it is important for research to provide the means to understand the mechanisms by which anxiety regarding health becomes manifested.

This research proposes to investigate the impact of newly acquired information upon previous knowledge by comparing medical students across all four years (increasing knowledge) with non-medical students, in order to test the hypothesis (Woods, Natterson and Silverman, 1966) that health anxiety is an enduring phenomenon. It attempts to avoid limitations by previous studies by recruiting a large number of participants and across a variety of non-medical students (as controls).

This research aims to further the knowledge-base on health anxiety by investigating the association/influence of *worry* in this area. As mentioned previously, worry is regarded mainly as a problem-solving mental activity in order to mitigate a catastrophic event. In the cognitive model of health anxiety, worry about health may be seen as a manifestation of a hypervigilant strategy adopted by the individual so that early signs of illness may be detected, or may be a superstitious strategy intended to ward off dangers of positive thinking (Wells and Hackmann, 1993).

This proposed research intends to investigate social worry, meta-worry (worry about worry) and also health worry alongside health anxiety. It will not only provide further insights into the cognitive aspects of health anxiety, but will also add to the knowledge base concerning the psychological health of medical students.

The following hypotheses are proposed for this study:

1. No significant differences in 1st year scores between controls and medics (no exposure to information).

2. Health anxiety increases in medics over years 1-3 (pre-clinical) as students are exposed to health related information.
3. Health anxiety *declines* in year 4 as clinical knowledge counteracts pre-clinical unhelpful beliefs, or:
4. (4) Health anxiety *increases* in year 4 as clinical experience confirms pre-clinical unhelpful beliefs and as clinical experience involves exposure to emotionally-laden information directly with patients.
5. (5) No significant differences in health anxiety (in controls) over the 4 years of study since participant is not exposed to medical knowledge.

METHODOLOGY

Design

The association between health anxiety, worry and other variables (e.g demographic) in medical students was investigated using a cross-sectional, between subjects designed study. Independent variables consisted of medical (experimental), or non-medical group (control) and dependent variables were self-report measures pertaining to health anxiety and worry.

Data analysis was carried out using SPSS (V.10.1) and employed parametric tests for group comparison (ANOVA, *t*-test), and correlations (Pearson moment coefficient). Further analysis was conducted on statements obtained from open-ended questions using content analysis.

Participants

The total sample (n=1239) was drawn from the undergraduate student body at Guys, Kings' and St. Thomas' School of Medicine and Kings College, London.

The experimental groups consisted of medical student participants ranging from pre-clinical (years 1 and 2) to clinical level (years 3 and 4). The control group cohorts were also drawn from years 1-4, and were selected based upon their involvement with a non-medically related course of study. The heads of faculties relating to 4 different academic disciplines as part of the control groups were initially approached (Law, English, Chemistry, Computer Science) and invited to participate in the study, by allowing their students the option of filling out the questionnaires. Two out of the four faculty heads consented (Law and English).

Table 2 provides a breakdown of the participant population according to year of study and group.

Participants from medical groups (years 1, 3 and 4) were significantly older than controls (see Table 3), and consisted of a higher proportion of male students (see Table 4). In terms of ethnicity, the mean percentage of white participants across the 4 medical groups was 54% compared to an Asian mean percentage of 39%. Across the control groups, however, the difference was much larger with a higher percentage of white participants (74%) compared to the Asian population (20%). The percentages for each group can be observed in Table 4.

Table 2. Sample Construction

| Year of study | Number of participants (n) | | |
	Medical students	Controls	Total
1st YEAR	263	204	467
2nd YEAR	272	84	356
3rd YEAR	105	132	237
4th YEAR	114	65	179

Table 3. Age Differences between Medical Students and Controls.

| Participants | Medical Students | | Controls | | | |
	mean	(SD)	mean	(SD)	t value*	two-tailed probability
1st Year	19.62	(2.34)	18.45	(0.82)	6.81	0.001
2nd Year	20.19	(2.06)	19.82	(1.89)	1.45	0.148(ns)
3rd Year	21.81	(2.33)	20.90	(3.09)	2.50	0.013
4th Year	22.57	(1.37)	22.05	(1.61)	2.31	0.022

* t-test

Table 4. Gender and Ethnicity Profile of Total Sample

| Participants | Gender (%) | | Ethnicity (%) | | | |
	Male	Female	White	Asian	Black	Other
1st Year						
-Medical Students	32	68	48	39	4	9
-Controls	28	72	75	20	1	4
2nd Year						
-Medical Students	34	66	52	39	2	7
-Controls	26	74	73	21	0	6
3rd Year						
-Medical Students	45	55	65	35	0	0
-Controls	23	77	72	21	2	5
4th Year						
-Medical Students	44	56	52	42	0	6
-Controls	54	46	74	18	0	8

PROCEDURE

Data was collected from the participants pertaining to each group during the month of October 2001, which represents the beginning of the year of study. After seeking both ethical approval and permission from the relevant lecturers/professors or heads of faculties, the principal researcher addressed the participants during the end of their lectures and following a brief synopsis of the study, invited students to participate. Self-report questionnaires were distributed to consenting participants and collected shortly afterwards. During the period of administration the principal researcher was on hand to answer any queries and to provide assistance with the questionnaire.

This procedure was consistently adhered to across both the experimental and control groups.

MEASURES

The research instrument employed (Health Perception Questionnaire) was an inventory consisting of selected questionnaires, which were either (1) self-designed (demographic), (2) standardized measures used in clinical or research, or (3) open-ended questions.

A draft copy of the questionnaire was initially piloted with 10 participants (medical students) and refined accordingly (i.e. clarifying potentially ambiguous wording). The final questionnaire was also administered to 5 participants (medical students) at time one (beginning of October) and time two (end of October) in order to determine the test-retest reliability. All participants at this piloting and testing stage of the questionnaire were not included as participants relating to the study.

This Health Perception Questionnaire (see Appendix B for copy) was constructed in order to measure, or elicit information relating to the following key variables:

Demographic

A range of socio-demographic information was elicited relating to *year of study, age, course, gender, nationality,* and *marital status.* A further two items were included which replicated the Moss-Morris and Petrie (2001) study; *ethnicity* and *self-report visits to the GP.*

Health Anxiety

A standardized questionnaire was selected for detecting health anxiety rather than using a structured interview, simply because it was quicker to administer and did not require interviewing/clinical skills in assessment.

A summary of the health anxiety questionnaires commonly employed for clinical and research assessment are depicted in Table 5. The table indicates which of the core features (according to DSM-IV criteria) of hypochondriasis is assessed with each instrument. These core features have been organised into four different dimensions: illness fears, illness beliefs, safety behaviours, and disruptive effects. Furthermore, the table provides a succinct summary of each instrument's psychometric properties.

Although it is not the purpose of this project to provide a critical review of each of these instruments (see Stewart and Watt, 2001 for review), a number of key features were important in the selection criteria for this project and were suitably found in the Health Anxiety Questionnaire (HAQ). The HAQ (Lucock and Morley, 1996) was developed based on a cognitive-behavioural model of health anxiety. Earlier health anxiety measures were developed with clinical psychiatric samples, however, the HAQ was developed was developed with medical as well as psychiatric groups and was intended to tap a range of severity of health anxiety.

Table 5. Summary of Health Anxiety Questionnaires

Instrument	Core features assessed				Examples of psychometric properties
	IF	IB	SB	DE	
Whiteley Index	√	√			Cronbach's alpha: 0.78; test-retest r: 0.90 (4 wks); concurrent validity with Structured Diagnostic Interview for Hypochondriasis: Sensitivity: 0.87, Specificity: 0.72
Illness Attitude Scale	√	√	√	√	Cronbach's alpha: 0.87 (Illness Behaviour scale), 0.96 (Health Anxiety scale); test-retest rs for 9 subscales: 0.75-1.00 (1-4 wks); concurrent validity with Structured Diagnostic Interview for Hypochondriasis; Sensitivity: 0.79, Specificity: 0.84 (Health Anxiety scale)
Illness Behaviour Questionnaire	√	√			Test-retest rs for 7 subscales: 0.67-0.87 (1-12 wks); convergent validity with friends'/relatives' ratings: rs = 0.50-0.78
Health Anxiety Questionnaire	√		√	√	Cronbach's alpha: 0.92; test-retest r: 0.87 (6 wks, lay sample) and 0.95 (4-7 wks outpatient psychiatric sample); discriminative validity relative to trait anxiety and depression in distinguishing DSM-III-R hypochondriasis from anxiety disorders

IF = Illness fears; IB = Illness beliefs; SB = Safety behaviours; DE = Disruptive effects

Twenty-two items were initially chosen to reflect important aspects of health anxiety as identified by research and theory on the cognitive-behavioural model. Fourteen of these initial items were derived from the Illness Attitude Scale (Kellner, 1986) and the remaining items were developed from discussions with patients presenting with persistent health anxiety. One of the 22 items was dropped from the scale due to its item redundancy. Each of the remaining 21 items are rated on a 4-point Likert scale, with anchors ranging from *not at all or rarely* (0 points) to *most of the time* (3 points).

Lucock and Morley (1996) conducted three studies in developing and evaluating the HAQ. These consisted of a large sample of 284 individuals including lay participants, student nurses, medical outpatients, and clinical psychology patients from an anxiety disorders clinic. The analysis revealed four clusters of items: fear of illness and death; interference with life; reassurance-seeking behaviours; health worry and preoccupation. Factor analysis of items in which four factors were extracted with eigenvalues greater than 1 indicated that health worry and preoccupation, and interference with life loaded on the same factor. The fourth factor appeared to be largely redundant.

In summary, the following elements of the HAQ were highlighted as key features sufficient for the purpose of this project:

1. Good reliability and validity (see Table 5).
2. Based upon a cognitive-behavioural model of health anxiety.
3. Identifies individuals who are relatively unresponsive to routine medical
4. reassurance (Lucock, White, Peake and Morley, 1998).
5. Not limited to psychiatric sample.
6. Easy to administer (less than 30 items) and score (no reverse scoring).

Worry

A worry questionnaire was included for two main reasons. Firstly, it supplemented the research into health anxiety by adding another dimension of psychological well-being (i.e. worry) that had not previously been studied in the medical student population. Secondly, it provided a means of comparing the psychological and psychometric properties of the HAQ against a measure of worry, in order to identify degrees of overlap between the two concepts.

Within clinical psychology, the empirical study of the concept of worry has began to germinate, particularly as it is being implicated as a key factor in anxiety disorders (e.g. Generalised Anxiety Disorder). This study proposes to add to the literature by investigating two main facets of worry (health worry and meta-worry) in a large sample.

Although a number of measures are available (e.g. Penn State Worry Questionnaire, Worry Domain Questionnaire, Meta-Cognitions Questionnaire), a questionnaire was selected based upon the following criteria: (1) easy to administer, (2) health worry sub-scale, (3) acceptable/good reliability, (4) based upon a cognitive model. The Anxious Thoughts Inventory (Wells, 1994) fulfilled the requirements.

The Anxious Thoughts Inventory (AnTI) is a 22-item questionnaire measure of three dimensions of worry. These dimensions and corresponding sub-scales are: social worry, health worry, and meta-worry. The three sub-scales are replicable and reflect measures of worry content and process. Social and health sub-scales assess purely content dimensions, while the meta-worry sub-scale assesses worry about worry (content) and process characteristics such as the involuntary and uncontrollable nature of worrying. The scale and sub-scales have good psychometric properties with alpha's of 0.84 (social worry), 0.81 (health worry), 0.75 (meta-worry), and also a combined test-retest of 0.80 (after six weeks).

MSD-Perception

The MSD (Medical Students Disease) Perception questionnaire was included, in order to replicate the study by Moss-Morris and Petrie (2001) and compare the findings of this present study to the results obtained their own. The MSD questionnaire is a 5 item Likert scale that is reported in the above study to have an internal reliability of 0.78 (alpha).

Stress Management

A final component of the inventory involved the addition of two open-ended questions that required participants to respond freely to the following statements:

1. Do you find the course you are studying stressful? If so, what are the features associated with the course that you think cause you to experience stress?
2. What would help you to manage the stress which is encountered as a result of the course? e.g. changes to the curriculum or other support systems.

These open-ended questions were included to allow data to be collected qualitatively (and analysed differently from the rest of the questionnaire), and also to provide an opportunity of understanding psychological stress from the participants perspective rather than researcher led.

RESULTS

Data Analysis

Data was analysed using the Statistical Package for the Social Sciences (SPSS). A flow chart depicting the stages of data analysis is shown in Figure 2. below, and provides a framework for presenting the results of the study.

Parametric tests were employed as the first line of inferential statistics. Greene and D'Oliveira (1982) suggest that three criteria are prerequisites for stringent use of parametric tests: homogeneity of variance, normal distribution, and scores measured on an interval scale (not necessarily based on a 'natural' interval scale). However, they also remark that parametric tests are reasonably 'robust' as far as these criteria are concerned.

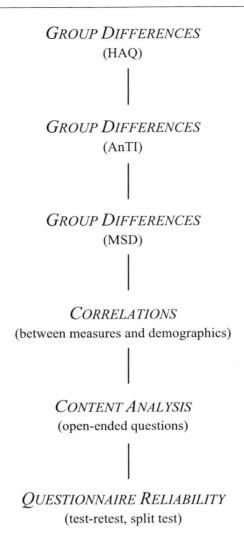

GROUP DIFFERENCES
(HAQ)

GROUP DIFFERENCES
(AnTI)

GROUP DIFFERENCES
(MSD)

CORRELATIONS
(between measures and demographics)

CONTENT ANALYSIS
(open-ended questions)

QUESTIONNAIRE RELIABILITY
(test-retest, split test)

Figure 2: Stages of Data Analysis

Before applying parametric tests in this study, the data was checked for homogeniety of variance by using the Levene Test, and normal distribution was checked using the Kolmogorov-Smirnov test with Lilliefors correction. The users guide for SPSS (p.191) cautions the researcher that, it is important to remember that whenever the sample size is large, almost any goodness-of-fit test will result in rejection of the null hypothesis. It is almost impossible to find data that are *exactly* normally distributed. For most statistical tests it is sufficient that the data are approximately normally distributed. Although plotting a histogram is a means of visually assessing normal distribution, it is sometimes difficult to mentally superimpose a normal distribution on the data values. For this reason a Q-Q normal probablity plot was used as an additional means of assessment. In this type of plot the data points cluster around a straight line if the sample is normally distributed, and represents matching between 'observed' values and 'expected' values.

One example is included in the appendix (B) which demonstrates the procedure that was followed for all the data that was subject to parametric analysis. Data that did not conform to the overall requirements of the parametric criteria was analysed using non-parametric techniques and tests.

GROUP DIFFERENCES

Health Anxiety

Scores from 21 items of the HAQ questionnaire were totalled for each participant and are summarised as group mean scores and presented as a line graph below (see Graph 1).

Participants	Medics		Controls	
	Mean	(SD)	Mean	(SD)
1st YEAR	13.35	(7.25)	14.60	(8.61)
2nd YEAR	12.06	(7.21)	14.19	(9.76)
3rd YEAR	12.24	(9.31)	13.73	(8.35)
4th YEAR	8.90	(5.45)	15.45	(8.75)

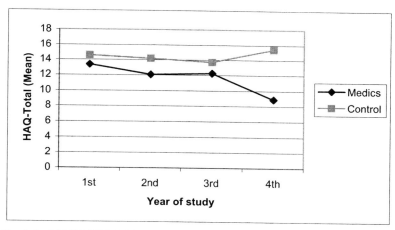

Graph 1. MEAN HAQ SCORES FOR MEDICS and CONTROLS

The results show that the medical students group (medics) mean scores for HAQ (total) were lower compared to the control groups (controls) in each year of study. Unrelated t tests indicated that significant differences existed (at the $p < 0.001$ level) between the medics and controls in year 4 only (see Table 6). Effect sizes were either small (< 0.30) or large (> 0.8) depending upon the year of study.

Further analysis using one way Anlaysis of Variance (ANOVA) demonstrated highly significant differences across the medical groups (years 1-4), with probablility at or below 0.001 (see Table 7). However, no significant differences were found between the four control groups (years 1-4).

Table 6. Effect Sizes and t-Test Values for Mean HAQ Scores Between Medics and Controls

Participants	Medics Mean	Control Mean	Mean difference	Effect size	Levene's Test Probability	t-Test score	Significance (two-tailed)
1ST YEAR	13.35	14.60	1.25	0.16	0.001 (not equal)	-1.675	0.095 (ns)
2ND YEAR	12.06	14.19	2.13	0.27	0.041 (not equal)	-1.855	0.066 (ns)
3RD YEAR	12.24	13.73	1.49	0.17	0.703 (not equal)	-1.302	0.194 (ns)
4TH YEAR	8.90	15.45	6.55	*0.87**	0.001 (not equal)	-5.456	*0.001*

* With an effect size (d) of 0.8, at probability p <0.01, power = 99 (see Appendix D for calculations)

Table 7. One-way ANOVA (Unrelated) Scores

Participants	F ratios	Significance
MEDICAL STUDENTS (1-4 years)	9.843	*0.001*
CONTROLS (1-4 years)	0.614	0.606 (ns)

Subsequent to the ANOVA's post hoc multiple comparisons were carried out on the HAQ scores pertaining to the medical groups, using the Bonferroni test (a simple modified least-significant-difference test). The results (see Table 8) indicate no significant differences between any of the first 3 years of study, and highly significant differences (at p<0.001, p<0.004) between all years when compared with the 4th year medics.

Table 8. Post Hoc Multiple Comparisons Using Bonferroni Test

| | Significance | | | |
	1st Year Medics	2nd Year Medics	3rd Year Medics	4th Year Medics
1st Year Medics	-	ns	ns	*0.001*
2nd Year Medics	ns	-	ns	*0.001*
3rd Year Medics	ns	ns	-	*0.004*
4th Year Medics	*0.001*	*0.001*	*0.004*	-

Evaluations using unrelated t-tests were also conducted to determine variance due to demographic factors. The results demonstrated no significant differences in HAQ scores (means) between males and females in any of the medics or controls. Similarly, no significant differences were found between Law and English students in the controls group.

However, when considering ethnicity there appeared to a general trend of higher HAQ scores in the Asian participants across all 4 medical groups (see Graph 2), with significant differences between the two major groups (White and Asian students) at p<0.01, for years 2 and 4. No such trends or differences were reported across the control groups. Table 9 provides an overview of the results.

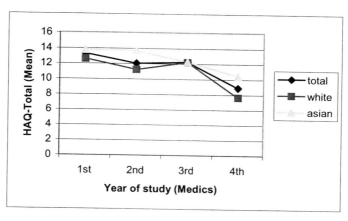

Graph 2. Mean HAQ Scores amongst White and Asian Medics

Table 9. HAQ Score Differences in Ethnicity amonst Medics and Controls using *t*-Tests

Participants	*White* Mean (SD)	*Asian* Mean (SD)	Levene's Test probability	*t* Test score	Significance (two-tailed)
1st Year					
-Medics	12.62	13.82	-	-1.245	0.215 (ns)
-Controls	14.18	15.70	-	-0.690	0.336 (ns)
2nd Year					
-Medics	11.23	13.68	-	-2.626	*0.008*
-Controls	13.80	13.00	-	-0.390	0.698 (ns)
3rd Year					
-Medics	12.22	12.27	-	-0.026	0.979 (ns)
-Controls	14.33	12.71	-	0.892	0.377 (ns)
4th Year					
-Medics	7.66	10.46	-	-2.645	*0.009*
-Controls	15.35	15.50	-	-0.062	0.951 (ns)

SUMMARY

The main findings relating to health anxiety (using HAQ measures) were:

1. Participants from the control groups experienced more health anxiety compared to participants from medical groups across all 4 years of study. However, this was found to be significant in year 4 only ($p < 0.001$).

2. As a general trend health anxiety declined from years 1-4 in the medical student population, although only year 4 scores were significantly lower compared to years 1-3 ($p < 0.004$). No such trends were found in the controls.

3. Differences in HAQ scores pertaining to gender, year of study (English, Law) and ethnicity were not significant across all 4 years in the controls.
4. Similarly, no significant differences were found in the medics relating to gender, however, significantly higher HAQ scores were found in the Asian participants compared to the White participants in years 2 and 4 (p<0.009).

Hypothesis	Supported by Results
(1) No significant differences in 1st year scores between controls andmedics (no exposure to information).	√
(2) Health anxiety increases in medics over years 1-3 (pre-clinical) as students are exposed to health related information.	X
(3) Health anxiety *declines* in year 4 as clinical knowledge counteracts pre-clinical unhelpful beliefs.	√
(4) Health anxiety *increases* in year 4 as clinical experience confirms pre-clinical unhelpful beliefs and as clinical experience involves exposure to emotionally-laden information directly with patients.	X
(5) No significant differences in health anxiety (in controls) over the years of study since participant is not exposed to medical knowledge.	√

GROUP DIFFERENCES

Worry

Mean worry scores (as measured by AnTI) for each medic and control group are depicted in Graph 3. The results indicate that medical students worry less than controls across all years of study. These differences are significant when analysed using t-tests (see Table 10) and reflect power values between 56 and 85, with small to medium effect sizes.

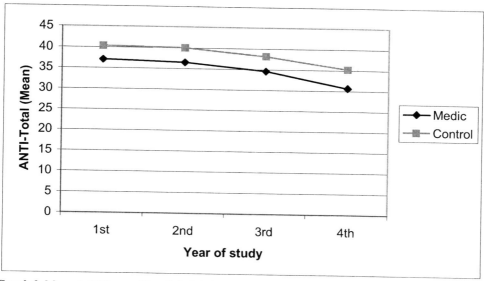

Graph 3. Mean AnTI Scores (Total) for Medics and Controls

Similar profiles to the AnTI total scores were obtained for each of the AnTI sub-scales (meta-worry, health worry and social worry). Medical student scores were lower for each year compared with controls, and the general trend demonstrates a decrease in worry scores for all three sub-scales from years 1-4 (particularly with respect to social worry. The profiles and corresponding mean scores are shown in Graph 4 and Table 11.

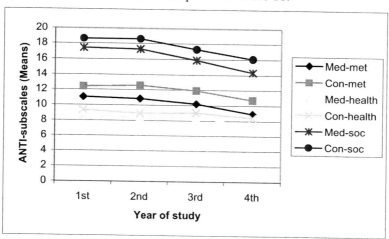

Graph 4. Profile of Mean AnTI Sub-Scale Scores

Table 10 Effect Sizes and *t*-Test Values for Mean AnTI Scores between Medics and Controls

Participants	Medics Mean (SD)	Controls Mean (SD)	Mean difference	Effect size	(Power)*	Levene's Test probability	t Test score	Significance (two-tailed)
1st Year	37.05 (10.50)	40.38 (11.12)	3.33	0.31	(85)	0.221 (equal)	-.3.316	*0.001*
2nd Year	36.47 (9.59)	40.13 (13.89)	3.66	0.64	(64)	0.0001 (not equal)	-2.255	*0.026*
3rd Year	34.58 (9.81)	38.23 (12.82)	3.65	0.31	(56)	0.058 (equal)	-2.407	*0.017*
4th Year	30.65 (8.61)	35.20 (11.37)	4.55	0.46	(71)	0.013 (not equal)	-2.802	*0.006*

* Significance criterion = 0.05; two-tailed; (Cohen, 1988)

Table 11. Mean AnTI Sub-Scale Scores for Medics and Controls

Participants	AnTi sub-scales		
	Meta Worry Mean (SD)	*Health Worry* Mean (SD)	*Social Worry* Mean (SD)
1st Year			
-Medics	11.04 (3.77)	8.59 (2.60)	17.42 (5.63)
-Controls	12.41 (4.52)	9.35 (3.31)	18.62 (5.72)
2nd Year			
-Medics	10.84 (3.73)	8.38 (2.41)	17.26 (5.30)
-Controls	12.57 (5.25)	8.96 (3.38)	18.60 (7.04)
3rd Year			
-Medics	10.22 (3.57)	8.45 (2.53)	15.91 (5.03)
-Controls	11.92 (4.60)	9.05 (3.12)	17.26 (6.61)
4th Year			
-Medics	8.92 (2.77)	7.38 (2.21)	14.35 (4.95)
-Controls	10.72 (4.06)	8.42 (3.15)	16.06 (5.94)

GROUP DIFFERENCES

MSD – Perception

Mean scores on the MSD- Perception scale were calculated for both the medics and controls (see Graph 5 below). The findings indicate that the scores *generally* increased over years 1-4 in both the medics and controls, with medics tending to demonstrate greater 'Medical Students Disease' than the controls in years 2 and 3. These differences were significant at $p<0.012$ and $p<0.003$ respectively, although effect sizes were small (see Table 12).

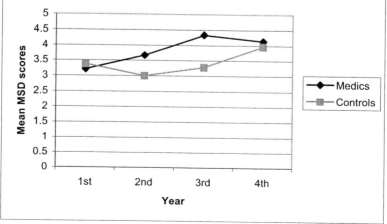

Graph 5 Mean Msd Scores For Medics And Controls

Table 12. Effect Sizes and *t*-Test Values for Mean MSD Scores between Medics and Controls

Participants	Medics Mean (SD)	Controls Mean (SD)	Mean difference	Effect size	(Power)*	Levene's Test probability	*t* Test score	Significance (two-tailed)
1st Year	3.21 (2.16)	3.38 (2.45)	0.17	0.07	(-)	0.062 (equal)	-0.788	0.431 (ns)
2nd Year	3.67 (2.13)	3.00 (2.16)	0.67	0.31	(64)	0.949 (equal)	2.521	*0.012*
3rd Year	4.34 (2.60)	3.28 (2.87)	1.06	0.38	(56-80)	0.720 (equal)	2.952	*0.003*
4th Year	4.15 (2.16)	3.97 (2.21)	0.18	0.08	(-)	0.847 (equal)	0.532	0.596 (ns)

* Significance criteria = 0.05, two-tailed, (Cohen, 1988)

CORRELATIONS

The next stage of analysis involved correlating the health anxiety questionnaire (HAQ) with the AnTI (including sub-scales), MSD-Perception measure and also two demographic variables; age and number of GP visits in the last 6 months.

The total sample (n=1239) was subjected to a parametric correlation test (Pearson Moment r), and the results together with power values are presented in Table 13.

The correlation findings can be summarized as follows:

1. HAQ/ AnTI – Strong correlations were found between the HAQ and the AnTI scales (all $p < 0.01$) with greatest correlation between the HAQ and health worry sub-scale ($r = 0.71$; power >99). Least correlation was obtained between HAQ and the social worry AnTI sub-scale (medium effect size), although significance was $p < 0.01$ with a power of >99.

2. MSD – Correlated highly with HAQ ($r = 0.44$), followed by AnTI health worry (r 0.36), meta-worry ($r = 0.21$) and finally social worry ($r = 0.12$). All correlations were at the $p < 0.01$ significance level, although power for the social worry sub-scale score was low.

3. AGE – The results indicate that as age increases, students' health anxieties and worries across the different domains decrease. The correlations with HAQ and AnTI scores were at the $p < 0.01$ level (except health worry – $p < 0.05$). The MSD scores however, demonstrated a positive correlation ($r = 0.06$) at the $p < 0.05$ significance level.

Table 13. Correlations between HAQ, AnTI, AGE and GP Visits using Pearson Product Moment r (N=1239)

		HAQ Total	MSD	AnTI Total	AnTI Meta	AnTI Health	AnTI Social	AGE	GP Visits
HAQ Total	Pearson r	-	0.44**	0.53**	0.46**	0.71**	0.35**	-0.07**	0.23**
	Power		>99	>99	>99	>99	>99	<72	>99
MSD	Pearson r	0.44**	-	0.23**	0.21**	0.36**	0.12**	0.08**	0.06*
	Power	>99		>99	>99	>99	>72	<72	<72
AnTI Total	Pearson r	0.53**	0.23**	-	0.90**	0.70**	0.92**	-0.13**	0.14**
	Power	>99	>99		>99	>99	>99	72	72
AnTI Meta	Pearson r	0.46**	0.21**	0.90**	-	0.54**	0.75**	-0.09**	0.11**
	Power	>99	>99	>99		>99	>99	<72	72
AnTI Health	Pearson r	0.71**	0.36**	0.70**	0.54**	-	0.46**	-0.06	0.21**
	Power	>99	>99	>99	>99		>99	<89	>99
AnTI Social	Pearson r	0.35**	0.12**	0.92**	0.75**	0.46**	-	-0.16**	0.08**
	Power	>99	>72	>99	>99	>99		<72	<72
AGE	Pearson r	-0.07**	0.08**	-0.13**	-0.09**	-0.06	-0.16**	-	-0.07**
	Power	<72	<72	72	<72	<89	<72		<89
GP Visits	Pearson r	0.23**	0.06*	0.14**	0.11**	0.21**	0.08**	-0.07**	-
	Power	>99	<89	72	72	>99	<72	<89	

** Correlation is significant at the 0.01 level (2-tailed)
* Correlation is significant at the 0.05 level (2-tailed)
Power tables from Cohen (1988) – p.90-93.
GP Visits – This measure correlated negatively with age (r = -0.07) at the p<0.05 level, indicating that younger students tended to visit their GP more often than older students.
The GP visits measure correlated positively (at p<0.01) with all measures on the HAQ and AnTI, although the size of the correlations was small and generally low in power.
Low correlations were obtained between the MSD scale and GP visits. Significance was at the P<0.05 level.

CONTENT ANALYSIS

Responses relating to the two open-ended questions used in the questionnaire were analyzed using content analysis. It was chosen because it is a research method that uses a set of procedures to make valid inferences from text (Weber, 1990). Compared with other data-generating and analysis techniques, content analysis has several advantages, one of which is that content analysis studies can utilize both qualitative and quantitative operations on texts. It therefore combines what are thought to be antithetical modes of analysis.

The basic methodology associated with content analysis involves, firstly, breaking down textual responses into smaller thematic units and segments. Categories are then defined as part of a 'coding frame' into which the units are 'coded'. In this study, which essentially sought to determine what features of the course students found stressful, and how they managed the stress, the responses were slotted into one of the categories shown below.

Question 1: 'What are the features associated with the course which you think cause you to experience stress?'

Categories:
1. Workload
2. Timetable
3. Teaching/training
4. Personal ability/skills
5. Exams/assessment
6. Practical difficulties
7. Other

Question 2: 'What would help you to manage the stress which is encountered as a result of the course? e.g. changes to the curriculum or other support systems.'

Categories:
1. Physical exercise/sport
2. Distraction/relaxation
3. Socialising
4. Practical support
5. Better organisation (either personal, or course)
6. Seek advice/counselling
7. Other

Graphs 6 and 7 represent the percentage distribution of responses within each category for medics and controls respectively (relating to question 1).

	work	t/table	teach	personal	exams	practical	other
1st med	48.3	8	4.9	13.7	8.7	3.8	12.5
2nd med	41.5	4	5.5	6.3	19.5	2.6	20.6
3rd med	23.8	6.7	4.8	12.4	17.1	6.7	28.6
4th med	21.1	6.1	7.9	7.9	29.8	3.5	23.7

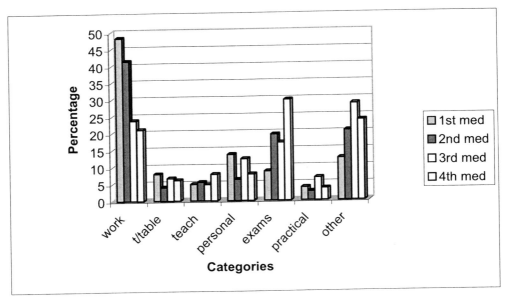

Graph 6. Percentage Distribution Scores For Medics (Q.1)

It can be observed (Graph 6) that workload, personal ability and exams represent the three largest stressors for medical students (excluding 'other'). Workload stress is particularly high for the pre-clinical years and decreases across the years. In comparison, exam and assessment stress increases from 9% to 30% from years 1-4.

	work	t/table	teach	personal	exams	practical	other
1st control	55.4	1	2	12.3	2	4.4	23
2nd control	56	1.2	3.6	16.7	2.4	1.2	19
3rd control	52.3	0	1.5	8.3	5.3	4.5	28
4th control	35.4	1.5	1.5	9.2	4.6	3.1	44.6

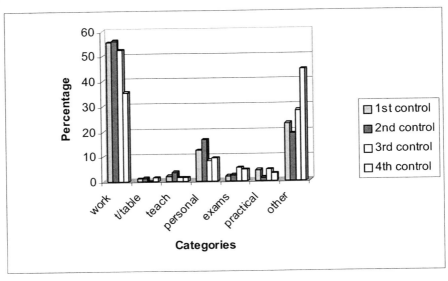

Graph 7. Percentage Distribution Scores For Controls (Q.1)

Similar profiles are obtained for the controls, except that exams and assessment stress does not appear to be a source of difficulty for this cohort of students.

Graphs 8 and 9 represent comments relating to changes perceived to be stress mitigators either to the course or personal lifestyle.

	sport	distract	social	practical	organise	counsel	other
1st med	3.4	5.3	2.7	3.4	59.7	5.7	19.8
2nd med	2.9	3.3	1.5	2.2	51.8	3.7	34.6
3rd med	3.8	2.9	0	5.7	40	2.9	44.8
4th med	3.5	0.9	0	4.4	52.6	4.4	34.2

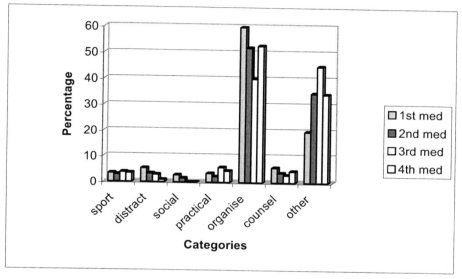

Graph 8. Percentage Distribution Scores For Medics (Q.2)

The greatest suggestion made involved changes in the organisation of the course (e.g. timetables) and also improvements in personal mangement and organisation. The graph depicts the overwhelming support for this intervention (40-60%)

	sport	distract	social	practical	organise	counsel	other
1st control	3.4	6.9	1	2.5	53.4	3.4	29.4
2nd control	2.4	11.9	1.2	2.4	52.4	3.6	26.2
3rd control	3	2.3	1.5	8.3	44.7	3.8	36.4
4th control	4.6	3.1	1.5	1.5	46.2	1.5	41.5

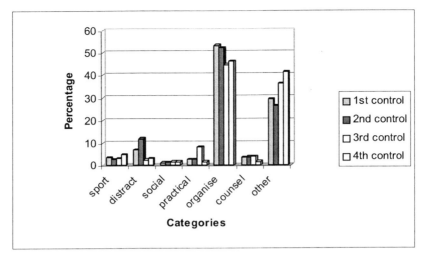

Graph 9. Percentage Distribution Scores For Controls (Q.2)

Again similar results were obtained from the control group, although other strategies were suggested (e.g. distraction and relaxation) more so than the medics.

QUESTIONNAIRE RELIABILITY

Internal Reliability

ANTI
Social worry: 1, 2, 8, 9, 12, 14, 17, 18, 20
Health worry: 4, 5, 7, 10, 15, 19
Meta-worry: 3, 6, 11, 13, 16, 21, 22

HAQ
Health worry and preoccupation: 1, 4, 6, 7, 8, 9, 11, 18
Fear of illness and death: 2, 3, 10, 14, 15, 16, 17
Reassurance seeking behaviour: 5, 12, 13
Interference with life: 19, 20, 21

	1st Yr Med	2nd Yr Med	3rd Yr Med	4th Yr Med	1st Yr Con	2nd Yr Con	3rd Yr Con	4th Yr Med	*Average alpha*
Anti									
Social	0.896	0.864	0.878	0.908	0.883	0.932	0.858	0.897	**0.890**
Health	0.744	0.708	0.748	0.813	0.815	0.853	0.806	0.836	**0.790**
Meta	0.817	0.796	0.840	0.821	0.839	0.879	0.870	0.851	**0.839**
Haq									
Hwp	0.774	0.649	0.821	0.719	0.800	0.856	0.772	0.754	**0.768**
Fid	0.761	0.738	0.821	0.699	0.833	0.854	0.774	0.820	**0.787**
Rsb	0.240	0.413	0.620	0.412	0.416	0.440	0.383	0.237	**0.395**
Iwl	0.708	0.757	0.843	0.715	0.699	0.882	0.859	0.677	**0.768**

Even though each of the standardised questionnaires used in this study have had their internal reliabilities calculated, they must be calculated once more as the internal reliability varies depending upon the size and composition of the sample used. The split-half reliabilities of each individual cluster from each questionnaire have been calculated above. All of the questionnaires used demonstrated satisfactory/high internal reliabilities as indicated by the Cronbach's Alpha values except the reassurance seeking behaviour component of the Health Anxiety Questionnaire. Having calculated the internal reliabilities with all possible combinations of item deletion, the reassurance seeking behaviour component still failed to demonstrate satisfactory internal reliability. This component will not be included in individual cluster statistical analysis due to it's low internal reliability.

TEST-RETEST RELIABILITY

The final questionnaire was administered to 5 participants (medical students) at time one (beginning of October) and time two (end of October) in order to determine the test-retest reliability. All participants at this piloting and testing stage of the questionnaire were not included as participants relating to the study.

The outcome varied from 79.7% to 100.0%. The average test-retest reliability was 93.57%.

CONCLUSION

The results of this study have highlighted a number of key points that shed further light on health anxiety in the medical student population, which will be elaborated upon in this section.

The main findings suggest that medical students have lower health anxiety (measured using the HAQ), compared to control students across all 4 years of study. However, this difference is only significant in year 4. Furthermore, as a generally trend, health anxiety (again measured by HAQ) reduces over years 1-4, and statistically speaking indicates that it is not a stable phenomenon. In terms of demographics, Asian students tended to exhibit more health anxiety compared to the mainstream White population, although significant differences could only be accounted for in years 2 and 4 of the medical group.

Worry (as measured by the AnTI) demonstrated a similar profile to that of HAQ, with lower scores compared to controls and significant differences across all 4 years rather than year 4 alone. High correlations were also obtained between the HAQ and AnTI measures, although lower correlations were obtained between both of these measures and MSD-perception.

Mean group scores on the MSD were significant between medics and controls in years 2 and 3, and scores generally increased across years 1-4, rather than diminishing as demonstrated by the health anxiety and worry profiles.

Further analyses indicated that younger students tended to be more health anxious compared to the older students, and also visited their GP more often.

Finally, both medics and controls described workload and lack of personal ability to be their greatest source of stress on the course, and for medics, exam pressure was an additional factor. All students suggested that improving the organisation (e.g. timetables) on the course would mitigate their stress, and/or acquiring the skills to improve their personal management of workload would be beneficial.

INTERPRETATION OF FINDINGS

These findings clearly challenge a number of ideas previously held in the research literature. They do not support the suggestion by Woods, Natterson and Silverman (1966) that health anxiety ('medical students' disease') is a phenomenon that occurs with relatively equal frequency throughout the four years of training. The results from this study would propose that health anxiety actually *decreases* over the four years, particularly in the final year of study. Although both 3rd and 4th year medics are technically categorised as clinical year students, in fact only the fourth year students in this study would have relevant clinical experience (1 years worth) as the sampling took place at the beginning of the academic year rather than the end. The results therefore saliently support the hypothesis that exposing medical students to clinical knowledge decreases their health anxiety, on the basis that clinical information *counteracts* rather than *confirms*, previously un-helpful health related beliefs.

Furthermore, it can be argued that it is the influence of medical knowledge on the health anxiety of medical students, since no significant differences were found across the 4 years of study in the control population. Previous studies were unable to investigate the significant differences *across* groups (years 1-4) rather than *between* groups (medics and controls).

Another challenge to the literature relates to the idea that "medical students' disease appears to emerge right at the beginning of the programme, when students are introduced to certain illnesses as clinical concepts presented in the "basic sciences" (Moss-Morris and Petrie, 2001). The implication is that medical knowledge is the key factor to account for high levels of health anxiety in the medical student population, however without the recruitment of a 1st year control group the assumptions have gone unchallenged.

The present study partly replicated the Moss-Morris and Petrie (2001) study by including one of their measures (MSD-Perception) and found that the scores actually *increased,* rather than decreased from years 1-4. Secondly, the present study used a 1st year control group and supported the hypothesis that no significant differences would be found between the medics and the controls on both the MSD-perception measure or the HAQ. In light of these results, it is proposed that it is not the acquisition of medical knowledge per se, at the beginning of the course that gives rise to health anxiety (otherwise medics would have scored higher), but rather the notion of transition and adjustment to a new course and university that heightens psychological distress. This also would account for the fact that 1st year students worry more in their first year in terms of their health and social life (AnTI measures), and report more visits to their GP than students in years 1-3.

This study did however, support previous findings (Moss-Morris and Petrie, 2001) that associated ethnicity with health anxiety. The medical student sample in this present study provided a rich source of participants from an Asian background, representing between 35-

42% of the group profile across the 4 medical years, and between 18-21% in the controls. Mean HAQ scores were higher in the Asian participants (across the 4 years) compared to the White population. This pattern, however was not observed in the Asian control population and suggests that the phenomenon is specific to factors associated with either Asian students who study medicine, or the influence of a medical course upon Asian students in general.

Although several hypotheses have been supported or refuted the study has also shown findings that are difficult to explicate without further investigation. One example, relates to the mean HAQ scores for the 4th year control group. In line with the general trend of the HAQ scores and the highly correlated AnTI scores, one would expect the 4th year (control) mean HAQ scores to decrease rather than *increase*. Additionally, the profile of the MSD-perception scores is inconsistent with previous findings and also in comparison to the HAQ scores. According to the hypotheses discussed earlier, lower scores for the medical students would have been expected compared to the controls.

The study also demonstrated new findings in association with medical students. Firstly, it has indicated that health anxiety and worry are closely related (highly correlated), and also shown that close associations exist between the three sub-scales of the AnTI.

Secondly, an investigation into the stress associated with studying medicine revealed that workload, exam pressure and perceived lack of personal ability were the main stressors.

IMPLICATIONS OF THE STUDY

The main findings from this study suggest that medical knowledge has a mitigating factor upon health anxiety. From the perspective of a cognitive model of health anxiety (Salkovskis and Warwick, 1986), acquiring medical knowledge was represented as a 'critical precipitating event' which influenced the previously held beliefs about health and symptom perception. Mechanic (1972) proposed that new medical knowledge would interact with existing stress to heighten bodily sensations, making the student more aware of his/her own bodily state. Although further research would need to be carried out to investigate the notion of self-symptom monitoring, the findings of the present study would reject Mechanic's claim. From a theoretical perspective, the acquisition of medical knowledge (as a 'critical precipitating event') is a positive influence. The author of this study would suggest that the acquisition of the knowledge enables the individual to cognitively appraise and assimilate previously held unhelpful beliefs. It also allows the cycle of rumination about health concerns (i.e. worry) can be broken, as new information causes the individual to problem-solve and resolve medical dilemmas. This would be a proposed explanation to account for lower scores in health worry (AnTI). Further research is warranted to investigate these claims. This may take the form of studying meta-cognitive processes in more detail, particularly focusing upon the interaction between attention to health concerns and emotionality.

However, caution must be taken when generalising the findings, and conclusions should be tentatively drawn since the study is confined to a non-clinical population. The mechanisms by which medical students process medical information may be substantially different to the manner in which a member of the general public will assimilate the knowledge. For example, we can not assume that the latter person will have a satisfactory understanding of the fundamental principles of medical science by which to understand the more complex processes involved with their own health conditions or concerns. The medical student however, will have acquired a systematic understanding of the medical base under guidance and tutoring, instilling confidence when exposed to medical information.

Future research is needed to investigate the findings of this study with a clinical population, and a control group that is representative of the general population rather than academically biased. The findings of this proposed study would have important implications for medical education and health anxiety. It would provide empirical evidence to confirm or refute the claims of this study that exposing individuals to medical knowledge is a positive factor to their psychological well-being concerning health anxiety.

The design of this study could include experimental conditions involving different forms of medical information (e.g. Internet sources, text-books, health-centre leaflets) and specify the conditions under which anxiety is mitigated.

LIMITATIONS OF STUDY

This study has both strengths and weaknesses. It has furthered the research in medical students' disease by improving upon previously flawed studies, and has furthered the theoretical knowledge base. This has been achieved by recruiting a large population (n = 1239), across 4 years of study involving both medics and controls (more than one non-medical cohort). The questionnaires used were appropriate to the model of health anxiety studied (cognitive), involved standardised (quantitative) and open-ended questions (qualitative), and analysed data with additional data reflecting effect sizes and power analysis.

However, the study was also limited on a number of accounts and suggestions are made for improvement. Firstly, more equal numbers of students could have been recruited from the medical and control groups. Although this did not pose a problem in terms of analysis, since statistics are able to accommodate such differences, it would have however, been ideal to have more control subjects.

Secondly, there is a distinction made in this study regarding pre-clinical (years 1-3) and clinical medical (year 4). In reality the distinction is not as pure, since pre-clinical study at GKT involves minor exposure to clinical populations ('practice of medicine').

Thirdly, improvements could have been made to the manner in which the open-ended questions were analyzed. The content analysis methodology was adhered to stringently, however it appears from the results that many responses made by participants have been coded under 'other' and consequently, it is difficult to ascertain from the graphs what 'other' actually represents. In future either the categories should be designed more carefully to accommodate and define the 'other' responses, or a methodology should be used which requires the participant to categorise their own data (e.g. Q-methodology).

REFERENCES

Asmundson, G. J. G., Taylor, S., Serperi, S., and Cox, B. J. (2001). Health anxiety: classification and clinical features.In G. J. G. Asmundson, S. Taylor and B. Cox (Eds.), *Health anxiety: clinical and research perspectives on hypochondriasis and related conditions* (pp.3-21). Chichester: John Wiley and Sons. (1994). *Diagnostic and Statistical Manual of Mental Disorders*, Revised, 4th edn. Washington, DC: American Psychiatric Association.

Barsky, A. J., Wyshak, G., Klerman, G. L., and Latham, K. S. (1990). The prevalence of hypochondriasis in medical outpatients. *Social Psychiatry and Psychiatric Epidemiology*, 25, 89-94.

Borkovec, T. D. (1994). The nature, functions, and origins of worry. In C. L. Davey, F. Tallis (Eds.). *Worrying: perspectives on theory, assessment and treatment.*Chichester: John Wiley and Sons.

Borkovec, T. D., Robinson, E., Pruzinsky, T. and Depree, J. A. (1983). Preliminary exploration of worry: some characteristics and processes. *Behaviour Research and Therapy*, 21, 9-16.

Brody, J.E. (1999, April 27). Chronic heartburn, an ominous warning. *The New York Times*, p. D6.

Cohen, J. (1988). *Statistical power analysis for the behavioural sciences.* London: LEA.

Cox, B.J., Borger, S.C., Asmundson, G.J.G., and Taylor, S. (2000). Dimensions of hypochondriasis and the five-factor model of personality. *Personality and Individual Differences.*

Escobar, J. I. (1995). Transcultural aspects of dissociative and somatoform disorders. *The Psychiatric Clinics of North America*, 18, 555-569.

Greene, J., and d'Oliveira, M. (1982). *Learning to use statistical tests in psychology.* Milton Keynes: Open University Press.

Gumbiner, J., and Flowers, J. (1977). Sex differences on the MMPI-1 and MMPI-2 *Psychological Reports,* 81, 479-482.

Gureje, O., Ustun, T.B, and Simon, G.E. (1997). The syndrome of hypochondriasis: A cross-national study in primary care. *Psychological Medicine*, 27, 1001-1010.

Hunter, R. C. A., Lohrenz, J. G., and Schwartzman, A. E. (1964). Nosophobia and hypochondriasis in medical students. *Journal of Nervous and Mental Diseases*, 130, 147-152.

Howes, O. D. (1999). Hypochondriasis. *StudentBMJ*, 7, 410-412.

Howes, O. D., and Salkovskis, P. M. (1998). Health anxiety in medical students. *The Lancet*, 351, 1332.

Kellner, R. Wiggens, R. G., and Pathak, D. (1986). Hypochondriacal fears and beliefs in medical and law students. *Archives of General Psychiatry*, 43, 487-489.

Kumar, P., and Clark, M. (2000). *Clinical Medicine*. London: Saunders.

Ladee, G. A.(1966). *Hypochondriacal syndromes.* Amsterdam: Elsevier.

Lagergren, J., Bergstrom, R., Lindgren, A., and Nyren, O. (1999). Symptomatic gastroesophageal reflux as a risk factor for esophageal adenocarcinoma. *New England Journal of Medicine*, 340, 825-831.

Lucock, M.P., and Morley, S. (1996). The health anxiety questionnaire. *British Journal of Health psychology*, 1, 137-150.

Lucock, M.P., White, C., Peake, M.D., and Morley, S. (1998). Biased perception and recall of reassurance in medical outpatients. *British Journal of Health Psychology*, 3, 273-243.

McManus, I.C., Richards, P., Winder, B.C., and Sproston, K.A. (1996). Final examination performance of medical students from ethnic minorities. *Medical Education*, 30,3, 195-200.

Mechanic, D. (1972). Social psychologic factors affecting the presentation of bodily complaints. *New England Journal of Medicine*, 1132-1139.

Moss-Morris, R., and Petrie, K. J. (2001). Redefining medical students' disease to reduce morbidity. *Medical Education*, 35, 1-5.

Noyes, R. Jr., Kathol, R.G., Fisher, M.M., Phillips, B.M., Suelzer, M.T, and Holt, C.S. (1993). The validity of DSM-III-R hypochondriasis. *Archives of General Psychiatry,*50, 961-970.

Noyes, R. Jr., Kathol, R.G., Fisher, M.M., Phillips, B.M., Suelzer, M.T, and Woodman, C.L. (1994). Psychiatric comorbidity among patients with hypochondriasis. *General Hospital Psychiatry*, 16, 78-87.

Rachman, S. (2001). Preface. In G. J. G. Asmundson, S. Taylor and B. Cox (Eds.), *Health anxiety: clinical and research perspectives on hypochondriasis and related conditions*. Chichester: John Wiley and Sons.

Roberts, R., Golding, J., Towell, T., Reid, S., Woodford, S., Vetere, A., and Weinreb, I. (2000). Mental and physical health in students: The role of economic circumstances. *British Journal of Health Psychology, 5, 289-257*.

Ryle, J. A. (1941). Nosophobia. *Guy's Hospital Gazette,* 55:76-82.

Salkovskis, P. M., and Warwick, H. M. C. (1986). Morbid preoccupations, health anxiety and reassurance: A cognitive behavioural approach to hypochondriasis. *Behaviour Research and Therapy*, 24, 597-602.

Salkovskis, P. M., and Warwick, H. M. C. (2001). Making sense of hypochondriasis:A cognitive model of health anxiety. .In G. J. G. Asmundson, S. Taylor and B. Cox (Eds.), *Health anxiety: clinical and research perspectives on hypochondriasis and related conditions* (pp.3-21). Chichester: John Wiley and Sons.

Shorter, E. (1995). Sucker-punched again! Physicians meet the disease-of-the-month syndrome. *Journal of Psychosomatic Research,* 39, 115-118.

SPSS (1993). *SPSS for Windows Base System Users Guide v.6.0*. Chicago:SPSS.

Stewart, S.H.., and Watt, M.C. (2000). Illness attitudes scale dimensions and their association with anxiety-related constructs in a non-clinical population. *Behaviour Research and Therapy*, 38, 83-99.

Warwick, H. M. C., and Salkovskis, P. M. (1990). Hypochondriasis. *Behaviour Research and Therapy*, 28, 105-117.

Wells, A. (1994). A multidimensional measure of worry: development and preliminary validation of the Anxious Thoughts Inventory. *Anxiety Stress and Coping*, 6, 289-299.

Wells, A., and Hackmann, A. (1993). Imagery and core beliefs in health anxiety: content and origins. *Behavioural and Cognitive Psychotherapy*, 21, 265-273.

Woods, S. M., Natterson, J., and Silverman, J. (1966). Medical students' disease: hypochondriasis in medical education. *Journal of Medical Education*, 41, 785-90.

In: Stress and Mental Health of College Students
Editor: Mery V. Landow, pp. 63-89

ISBN 1-59454-839-0
© 2006 Nova Science Publishers, Inc.

Chapter 3

EXAM PRESSURE, EMOTIONAL DISORDERS AND ON PROBATION MEDICAL STUDENTS

Marwan Al-Sharbati and Ali A. Al-Jabri[3]

College of Medicine and Health Sciences, Sultan Qaboos University, Muscat, Oman

ABSTRACT

Medical students are placed under probation if they did not perform well in a particular semester, so that remedial actions can be sought to get them back into a normal academic progress. Those who do not improve for four consecutive semesters will be asked to leave the Medical School. Between 10-15% of medical students, in the College of Medicine and Health Sciences, Sultan Qaboos University (SQU), are usually placed on probation every semester. A study was conducted to look into factors that affect students' performance and in particular those leading to students being under probation. A group of factors were identified. In general, the factors contributing to the poor academic achievement can be attributed to two main categories: the intrinsic (within-individual) and the extrinsic (extra-individual) factors. The first includes a large number of causes, such as: endocrinal disorders (as thyroid dysfunction and diabetes), low intelligence, emotional disorders (anxiety and depression), behavioral disorders affecting cognitive functions (as Attention Deficit Hyperactivity Disorder), speech and language disorders (Dyslexia, Autism, Dysphasia), sensory and physical disabling conditions (as hearing impairment, cerebral palsy, poliomyelitis), and psychiatric disorders (as Schizophrenia). The external factors on the other hand cover enormous number of causes as: poverty and social injustice, poor teachers' quality, inappropriate teaching programs, improper parenting style, badly chosen friends, unsuitable housing conditions, etc. These causes affect the individual's performance at school/university according to his age, for example low intelligence causes poor school performance at the kindergarten and elementary school level, while others like anxiety and depression might cause deterioration in school (or university) achievement following a good start (if the student has no other associated problem acting from the beginning).

---

[3] Correspondence author address:Dr. Ali A. Al-Jabri,Office of the Assistant Dean for Academic Affairs, College of Medicine and Health Sciences, Sultan Qaboos University, P.O. Box 35, Al Khod, Muscat123, Sultanate of Oman. Tel: 00968-2415186 Tel: 00968-2415170 Fax: 00968-2413419, e.mail: aaljabri@squ.edu.om

We are dealing in this chapter with the exam stress and emotional disorders that can affect the learning process negatively among the medical students in SQU. These students on probation have been admitted to the university having obtained the highest marks among their cohorts in the secondary schools, enabling them to start their medical education. Being members of the probation committee, we have found a large number of the students with probation suffering from exam stress and emotional disorders (anxiety and depression). These two disorders can have negative effects on human behavior, like their effects on sleep (both quantitatively and qualitatively), and on cognitive functions (attention, concentration and memory), consequently these will lead to drastic impairments in the learning process.

During the routine meeting of the committee with these students individually, those who require additional evaluation of their emotional status have been given a chance to be seen in the consultation clinic of the Department of Behavioral Medicine in SQU Hospital, in which detailed history, clinical and mental assessment together with the needed investigation are done, to be followed by an appropriate treatment and follow up. In order to improve the students' performance, and to abort such a tragedy, many lines must be adopted; including better relationships with the academic advisors, who can inform the student about the points of his/her weaknesses and strengths; help them to choose the relevant courses; and to alleviate the negative effects of stress which leads to unnecessary anxious and depressive states that may accompany them during their studies, by positively reinforcing them and make them more confident. Moreover, regular visits to the "Student Counseling and Advise Center" at SQU is of vital importance to find solutions for the social and personal problems, for those having disturbed progress in their studies. Finally, and as a last step, the student must be referred by that center to the psychiatrist when he/she does need such an intervention.

INTRODUCTION

There is a large competition for medical education all over the world and especially in the developing countries as there is a shortage of physicians in all different specialties. The demand for medical graduates in Oman is high and compared to other professions; medical doctors are automatically employed by the government hospitals directly after graduation. Although there are a reasonable number of medical schools in the Arab world, there is still a shortage of doctors there, and the Gulf States (Oman, Saudi Arabia, Kuwait, Bahrain, UAE, and Qatar) are not an exception to the rule.

Oman is a country that occupies Southeastern corner of the Arabian Peninsula and covers an area of about 309,500 sq km. In 1997 Oman had an estimated population of 2,283,324, giving it an average density of 7 persons per sq km (19 per sq mi). The population has grown steadily, doubling between 1960 and 1993. In 1997 the growth rate was relatively high approaching 3.5 percent. Oman has a very young population, with about 44% of them under the age of 18 (World Population Prospects, 2002).

Health for all has been endorsed as a national policy at the highest official level. The principal thrusts of the national health policies are that health care is the right of every individual; improving the quality of health services in general and basic health services in particular. The Sultanate has made great strides in developing its health services, leading to striking improvements in the country's public health. The quality of Oman's health care has been praised by international organisations such as the World Health Organisation, UNICEF and the United Nations Development Fund.

Oman has one national medical school and two newly opened private medical schools. Sultan Qaboos University (SQU) is the only national university in Oman, with student population of approximately 11,000. The medical school at SQU has a student's population of approximately 900. Although the medical school has a relatively short history - opened in 1986, the school has an excellent reputation, both in the regional as well as on international levels. Students from SQU-medical school travel all over the world for 3 months period, during their 6th year, for their clinical elective training. From the students' evaluation reports during their elective training, which are received from top medical schools in the USA, Europe, Asia and Africa; SQU medical students showed a high motivational status to learn, with excellent medical skills, knowledge and behavior that are evaluated with high appreciation and praise from the above mentioned medical schools. This good reputation of our medical school has created a big competition for seats to study medicine not only from Omani students but also from other neighboring Gulf State students.

1.1 The Medical Curriculum

Students, from all over Oman, compete for admission to the medical School, and only the top 100-120 students, representing the "cream" of the country, will be able to enroll in the medical college every year. Students must obtain straight "As" in scientific subjects required for the study of medicine, such as chemistry, biology, physics and mathematics. As in many medical schools, the medical curriculum in the College of Medicine and Health Sciences (COM and HS) is quite heavy. The duration of the study of medicine at the COM and HS is seven years, divided into two programs, a B.Sc. Health Sciences and an MD program.

1.2 B.Sc. Health Sciences Program

This is a four-year, 8-semesters program, in general and basic medical sciences. The B.Sc. Health Sciences degree is awarded to students after successful completion of 120 credit hours at the end of semester 8. Students who wish to obtain the MD degree have to complete all course requirements for B.Sc. in Health Sciences before entering the clinical years. Students may wish to leave the College of Medicine after obtaining the B.Sc. Health Sciences degree.

1.3 The MD Program

This is a three-year (years 5-7) clinical program in which the knowledge acquired during the basic medical sciences is applied to the clinical practice of medicine. Upon completion of this stage a Medical Doctor (MD) degree is awarded. A ten-week Elective Placement Program held in the sixth year is essential to obtain the MD degree at Sultan Qaboos University. The program provides students with an opportunity to gain more experience and skills working in a different environment. Students travel to various destinations all over the world for their electives. This program is sponsored by the University and different organizations, locally and around the world. The final phase of the Clinical Program consists of one-year (year 8) supervised on-the-job training. At the end of this internship period a certificate of satisfactory completion must be obtained before progressing to special training in residency programs of the Oman Medical Specialty Board. During the internship the trainees devote an equal amount of time to the four major disciplines: Pediatrics, Obstetrics and Gynecology, Medicine and Surgery. Most of the internship rotations involve changing from one hospital to another within the country during the year. One of the four rotations must be in a peripheral hospital (e.g. Sultan Qaboos Hospital in Salalah, Buraimi Hospital, Rustaq Hospital, Nizwa Hospital, Ibri Hospital, and others), which is considered a very beneficial experience of the breadth and depth of health care of the country.

Due to the heavy curriculum, together with the different internal and/or external factors constituting the psychosocial stressors, some medical students face difficulties in coping with the medical curriculum, hence leading to students being placed on probation.

THE PROBATION SYSTEM IN SQU

A Student who achieves a Grade Point Average (GPA) as described below will be placed on probation. This is an academic status assigned to students who are earning enough grades below 'C' to jeopardize their prospects of graduating. It is a constructive measure to reduce the student's course load to a manageable level until the academic difficulty is resolved. Probation status is determined by the GPA, with semester and cumulative standards as described below: Although not formally on probation, a student will be advised to take corrective and remedial action on his/her own behalf when the current semester GPA is 1.00 or more, but below 2.00 although the cumulative GPA remains above 2.00. This is known as the pre-probation period. In such a case the student must have a documented interview with his/her advisor before registering for the next semester, in order to be guided for suitable preventive and corrective measures. These may include one or more of the following procedures: reduction of the course load; postponement of a course to the subsequent semester, language or study skills courses; referral to different University services (e.g. Student Affairs, Health Clinic…etc) for assistance, guidance and treatment.

A student is placed on probation and required to take remedial action when a) the cumulative GPA falls below 2.00 or b) the cumulative GPA is 2.00 or above but the current semester GPA falls below 1.00 or c) the cumulative GPA is 2.00 or above but the semester GPA has been below 2.00 for 2 consecutive semesters. In such cases the student is required to reduce his/her course load to 12 credits or less (from a maximum of 18 credits). A student on probation must return to normal status within three consecutive semesters. A summer semester counts as one of the three semesters if a student registers for a full load (6 credits or more) in that session. A student who completes two consecutive semesters on probation will be notified by a warning notice reminding him/her of the final remaining semester within which to achieve a cumulative GPA of 2.00. A student who fails to fulfill this condition will be required to formally withdraw from the University. Students on probation for a second semester must inform their parents or guardians and obtain a signed agreement in order to register.

2.1. Factors that Lead to Poor Student's Performance at SQU

A study was conducted to look into factors that affect students' performance and in particular leading to students being under probation. Table 1 shows the number of students, from different cohorts, on probation during the Fall 2004 semester. It is clear that male students are more represented (78.3%) than females. All students on probation were interviewed by the Academic Committee for Students on Probation in the College. As members of this Committee we have identified a group of factors that contribute to the low academic performance of students. Table 2 summaries those factors. Poor English language and ineffective advising system are among the important factors for student's weak performance. Moreover, emotional disorders are clearly essential for students' poor academic progress as observed for many students on probation.

In general, the factors contributing to the poor academic achievement can be attributed to two main categories: the intrinsic (within-individual) and the extrinsic (extra-individual) factors. The first includes a large number of causes, such as: endocrinal disorders (as thyroid dysfunction and diabetes), low intelligence, emotional disorders (anxiety and depression), behavioral disorders affecting cognitive functions (as Attention Deficit Hyperactivity Disorder), speech and language disorders (Dyslexia, Autism, Dysphasia), sensory and physical disabling conditions (as hearing impairment, cerebral palsy, poliomyelitis), and psychiatric disorders (as Schizophrenia). The external factors on the other hand cover enormous number of causes as: poverty and social injustice, poor teachers' quality, improper advising system, inappropriate teaching programs, improper parenting style, badly chosen friends, unsuitable housing conditions, etc., other causes (both internal and external) are listed in table 2. These causes affect the individual's performance at school/university according to his/her age, for example low intelligence causes poor school performance at the kindergarten and elementary school level, while others like anxiety and depression might cause deterioration in school (or university) achievement following a good start (if the student has no other associated problem acting from the beginning).

In this chapter we discuss those factors and solutions to help students overcome the probation periods and perform well in future examinations and in their study at the medical school.

STRESS

Stress is inevitable in our existence, we face it at home, school, work, and in our social lives. It is a fact of life, and without stress life would be very boring! But on the other hand, too much stress becomes "distress"! And this can become a serious illness, if it persists for a long time, especially if it is not treated properly. A person who feels ongoing and untreated stress may go on to develop psychiatric disorders as anxiety disorder, which in turn can lead to a depressive illness (Post, 1992). These two disorders can lead to many health problems, which might proof fatal at the end (as the case with heart attacks and suicide).

Table 1. Preclinical students on probation during the Fall semester 2004, from different cohorts.

Cohort	Males	Females	Total	Type of probation				
				0	1	2	3	4
1998	3	0	3	0	1	0	2	0
1999	6	1	7	0	4	2	1	0
2000	11	1	12	3	3	4	1	1
2001	18	1	19	1	8	9	1	0
2002	12	6	18	4	8	4	2	0
2003	15	9	24	22	2	0	0	0
Total	65 (78.3%)	18 (21.7%)	83	30	26	19	7	1

N=83, All pre-clinical students under probation= 12.5% (83/662)
Probation "0" indicates first semester of cumulative GPA >2, or semester GPA of >1. Probations 1, 2, 3 and 4 indicate that the students GPA continue not to improve over the subsequent semesters.

Table 2. Factors identified that led to students' poor performance and therefore being placed on probation.

External factors:

1. Poor English Language.
2. Ineffective advising system:
   -Advisors not available during registration periods.
   -Advisors are not familiar with University Regulations and therefore do not know how to advice students.
   -Some advisors can only sign the student registration form without giving student enough time to discuss problems.
   -Advisors are too busy to see students.
   -On line registration.
3. Inefficient counseling system:
   -Family and social problems.
   -Family pressure to do medicine.
   -Time management.
   -Accommodation problems.
4. Probation system itself.
5. No remedial system (for example student's Teaching Assistants, etc.).
6. Other problems identified:
   -Difficulty in understanding subjects, too heavy load curriculum.
   -Selecting easy electives that have nothing to do with studying medicine in order to get out of probation.
   -Absentees from classes because of being with a different new cohort.
   -Cultural shock..

Table 2. (cont.)

Internal factors:

1. Emotional disorders
   - Exam pressure and stress
   - Anxiety and depression
   - Others (see text)
2. Problems attributed to students themselves
   - Generally weak students because of being unmotivated and not working hard enough
   - Students' interest in Medicine is not uniform
   - Students' capacity to do medicine is not uniformly appropriate
   - Students' maturity not always at par

Other behavioral and emotional problems consequent to stress include aggression and anger (Sutherland and Cooper, 2003). Stress is an everyday life event; it is a process, not a diagnosis. The level and extent of stress a person may feel depends a great deal on his/her attitude to a particular situation. An event, which may be extremely stressful for one person, may not be so for another. Stress is not always a bad thing! Indeed without some (optimal) stress, people would not get a lot done. That extra burst of adrenaline that helps you finish your final paper, perform well in sports, or meet any challenge, this is the positive aspect of stress.

However, when the term 'stress' is used in a clinical sense, it refers to a situation that causes discomfort and distress for a person, so that it points to the negative aspect of stress. As a clinical problem, stress occurs when the demands made on a person exceed (or he/she feels they exceed) their ability to cope with these demands.

3.1 Definition of Stress

Stress is a ubiquitous term, with no collectively accepted definition (Norman and Malla, 1993). However, the word stress, of Latin origin, has been a part of the English language since at least the fourteenth century. Its earliest meanings included "hardship, straits, adversity, affliction" as well as the process of using force or pressure on another. The use of the term continued to be broadened to include meanings such as "strain upon endurance" and even more specifically, "strain upon a bodily organ or mental power" (Simon, 1989). This plurality of definition continued to date, extends across both common usage and scientific literature depending on the adopted point of view. Some of these definitions are general, for example, Hans Selye (1956), a Canadian endocrinologist defined stress as: "The nonspecific response of the body to any demand", while others defined stress with more details like: "Stress is the mental or physical reaction which arises when there is a perceived imbalance between the demands placed on a person, on one hand, and their abilities and the support available to them on the other hand. Both over and under-demand can be stressful". These two definitions do not specify any positive or negative reaction to the "demand", however other definitions take into consideration the bad body reaction caused by that demand, for example: "Stress is any physical or psychological event that has a potential threat to physical or emotional well being of an individual". Another definition stated more clearly the negative effects of stress, "The adverse reaction people have to excessive pressures or other types of demand placed upon them". Finally, the following definition concerns the body changes consequent to the demand, event or change: "The term stress relates to a psycho-physiological response that is triggered by a reaction to a change, actual or anticipated, in the environment or within the person."

3.2 Susceptibility to Stress

The susceptibility of an individual to develop stress is likely to be a function of a variety of factors. It has been found that the concordance of psychiatric disorders is greater among monozygotic than among dizygotic twins, which is an indication that genetics almost certainly plays an important role in determining vulnerability to most major psychiatric disorders, including stress (Caspi et al., 2003; Egan et al., 2001; Merikangans and Risch, 2003; Gelder et al., 1999). However one must keep in mind that not every one who inherit the gene will exhibit the illness (England et.al., 1987). In addition, the non-genetic factors may play a role in predisposing the individual to illness later in life, including stress, by acting via physiological mechanisms. Among these factors are: intra-uterine injuries, infection and unbalanced diet (Wender et al., 1986), or exposure to drugs (Bowers et al., 1990). It has been hypothesized that early psychological trauma may affect physiology and induce chronic biological vulnerability to certain psychiatric illness (Breier et al. 1988), who found that neuro-endocrine alterations in the hypothalamic-pituitary-adrenal axis were associated with poorer quality of childhood home life and adaptation after parental loss in those adults with psychopathology compared with those without psychiatric illness, who also suffer from early loss. Moreover, affliction of an individual by a psychiatric disorder makes him/her more prone to recurrences of illness. Post (1992) stated that sensitization to psychosocial stressors and to episode occurrence affects physiology at the level of gene expression, making individuals more vulnerable to subsequent stressors and episodes of illness. Among other factors leading to increased vulnerability to stress, is less specific experience with stressful situations, which results in lowered abilities to cope with stresses (Weinman, 1987). Finally, susceptibility has been thought to be a function of the absence of protective psych-social buffers, as social support network (Rutter 1985) or cognitive strategies for coping (Monroe and Simons, 1991; Stewart et al., 1995).

For many reasons, the university students – particularly in medical schools - are more prone to develop stress. One study showed that the majority (57%) of the first year medical students scored high in the General Health Questionnaire that measures psycho-emotional distress (Ko et al., 1999). Stress was more strongly related to symptoms in women, suggesting that they may have a greater susceptibility to surrounding stress, and to somatic illness stress (Sandanger et al., 2004). The encountered stress among the medical students can lead to poor academic performance, especially during the first year (Grover and Smith 1981; Ko et al., 1999). This can be attributed to many causes; first of all, the changes in the style of study from secondary school are enormous, the university study being more demanding and less spoon-feeding than the secondary school. This will result in the university adaptation difficulties that lead to dropping out of the students (Ionescu and Bosse, 2004). Secondly, a large number of the medical students usually changes their residence, this migration might provoke stress, as the student will live far away from his normal home environment, losing the warm family relationships and its support that acts as a buffer against stress on one hand; and living with strange students on the other hand, this leads to insecurity and loneliness (Helman, 1990). Thirdly, many students come from rural and suburban areas, in which the life is still very primitive and conservative, compared with the modern, multicultural society of the capital (Muscat), this great difference in both conditions result in poor adaptation and cultural shock or bereavement (Eisenbruch, 1988).

3.3 Causes of Stress

All the above definitions of stress acknowledged that there is a demand, pressure, change or event that provoke a body reaction, which is called "stressor" or "psycho-social stressors". This can be external (from the environment), or internal (from the human being). A variety of environmental factors can contribute to a person feeling 'stressed', like: work problems, family disharmony, study difficulties, exams, routine and boring lifestyles...etc. The internal stressor is like acquiring different diseases (acute or chronic).

Stress in the workplace is common and caused by different factors. At work, many problems may never be fully resolved and remain suspended. The amount of stress a person experiences is often determined by whether or not they can accept that some things in life will simply never be sorted out to their satisfaction. For instance, a person may feel stressed by the way he/she is treated by their employer, or a student by his teachers or the behavior of a colleague at work. Sometimes this stress can be resolved by dealing with the particular behavior. In many organizations, there are processes that can be followed to deal with workplace problems like harassment, victimization or unfair treatment. In many cases the problem can be resolved if the behavior is modified or changed. However, and as what has been stated before, some problems will never be fully resolved. For example, if someone is poorly qualified and given a job he/she felt entitled to, he/she may continue to feel stressed unless he/she are able to let go of that grievance and move on.

The same can be applied for the university students, especially in the medical school. Joining the medical school, for example, creates a change in both the environment and in students' class and study routines. Until students become acclimated to the new medical school environment and to the basic processes and methods required for the study of medicine, stress may interfere with their learning experiences, and consequently causes poor academic achievement, reaching the level of failure (Maville and Huerta, 1997). In the university again, exams are one of the most stressful and worrying experiences we usually endure and inflict on others. Students may worry that they will be disgraced and embarrassed if they fail, about how their families and friends will react. The prevalence of perceived stress seems to be high among medical students, which tends to affect not only their academic performances (McMichael and Hetzel, 1975) but also other aspects of health (Shaikh et al., 2004). However, a certain amount of stress and anxiety can provide valuable stimulus that gets students to study and prepare, otherwise they might not bother to put in their best effort and therefore they do not succeed to get their objectives i.e. passing the exam. The main issue is that how to get the dose right, if a student finds exams to be relaxing, or it gives pure pleasure, and then he/she must be misunderstanding something! Therefore a required level of stress and anxiety is not only normal in life, but it is necessary. The exam results are important to medical students, and they are not entirely predictable - anyone can be anxious about that, that is the nature of a normal human being. But a student needs not to become so anxious that he/she crippled by fear, this will impede the normal cognitive functions needed for study. To overcome this, a student needs to control the stress and anxiety, and not let it control him/her. Sometimes stress needs to be placed in "quarantine" when seriously stressed people get together, they can act as an amplifier and get together more frightened. As stress reaction and anxiety can be (infectious!), a student should avoid mixing with extremely anxious friends. This may be one of the best solutions. On the other hand, keeping away from those friends who take things calmly, they may help a student to calm down, too. These are the two extremes that students should avoid otherwise their academic performance will be affected adversely.

According to what is written before, there is no doubt that many medical students feel excessive stress, especially during the first few semesters of medical education. That stress reaches its peak during the pre-exam period, which is considered in our opinion, to be the major cause to put the students under probation in SQU, as we observed during the previous two semesters through the regular meetings with such students as members of the committee dealing with these students.

3.4 Stages of Stress

Hans Selye (1974) was one of the first to write about stress and its effect on the body. He described the stages of stress, called the General Adaptation Syndrome (GAS). These stages we go through when we encounter a stressor, whether the stress is good or bad, big or small:

1. Alarm Reaction: starts by recognition of a stressor, and evaluation whether it is a threat or not. If it is a threat we gear up to deal with it. Stress affects different people in different ways. What you may evaluate as a threat, someone else won't. And, what is stressful today may not be stressful tomorrow.
2. Resistance Stage: deal with the stressor appropriately.
3. The final stage is either exhaustion or recovery. Exhaustion occurs if the stress was too big, too much, or when we use improper and poor coping skills, Exhaustion can lead to disastrous outcomes including death! Recovery on the other hand occurs when the stress is not too much and we use good coping skills. We bounce back to receive new stresses.

3.5 Body Changes in Stress

Our body system has its own set of battalion to fight stress, facilitated by a series of physiological changes. The Selye's basic notion of a generalized stress response in that "both physical and emotional stressors set into motion central and peripheral responses to preserve homeostasis" has been well supported (Chrousos and Gold, 1992). This vital defense mechanism is achieved by triggering a series of chemical chain reactions, via stimulating the hypothalamic-pituitary-adrenal axis, which results in the release of endocrinal hormones (adrenaline, nor adrenaline and cortisol) from the adrenal glands. The increased adrenaline production causes the body to increase metabolism of proteins, fats and carbohydrates to quickly produce energy for the body to use. The pituitary gland, on the other hand, increases its production of andrenocorticotropic hormone (ACTH), which in turn stimulates the release of cortisone and cortisol hormones. These hormonal releases may inhibit the functioning of disease fighting white blood cells and suppress the immune system's response. On the other hand, the chemicals in the brain and autonomic nervous system - neurotransmitters - are also affected by stress to produce adrenaline and nor adrenaline to prepare the body to defeat stress. Other brain neurotransmitters which have a very powerful influence on the mood, include serotonin, dopamine, adrenaline, noradrenaline etc., these hormones and neurotransmitters play a vital role to cope up stress in the short term, by providing of energy from the metabolism of glucose and fat, and increasing the supply of oxygen to muscles by the rise in the number of red blood cells in the circulation and increased blood flow to muscles with reduced blood flow to skin and gut, resulting in digestion slowing, constipation and discomfort...etc. Thus a state of physiological arousal is established (Sutherland and Cooper, 2003). However, in chronic cases these chemicals undermine our health, causes blood clotting – and hence heart attacks and cerebro-vascular accidents, and increases blood cholesterol level, thereby enhance the risk of many diseases including heart diseases, weaken the immune system and lead to increased susceptibility to many infectious diseases like cold and flu.

Other changes in the body, include reduction of the number of white blood cells and decrease in the natural - killer cell activity, leading to lowered immunity with simultaneous increase in titers of antibodies to herpes simplex virus, Epstein-Barr virus and cytomegalovirus, resulted from reactivation of latent viruses (Kiecolt-Glaser and Glaser, 1991).

It is a short-term physiological tension and added mental alertness that subsides when the challenge has been met, enabling you to relax and carry on. Responses to stress can be physical, such as a headache; emotional, such as fear or sadness; and mental, such as increased anxiety. If you cannot return to the relaxed state, then the stress becomes negative. The changes in your body (increased heart rate, higher blood pressure and muscle tension) start to take their toll, often leading to mental and physical exhaustion and illness. Too much stress can cause problems and affect our health, productivity and relationships (Rawson et al. 1994).

3.6 Clinical Picture of Stress

The stress can be manifested by many symptoms, physical, psychological and social, depending on the duration of the encountered stress. The short-term stress (few days) is colored by fatigue (whether mental, physical or both) (Lewis, 1996); changes in eating habits - students awaiting an exam reported higher emotional stress and an increased tendency to eat in order to distract themselves from stress (Macht et al. 2005; Epel et al. 2004). Others may have suppressed appetite during the exam, and digestion may slow (G:\probation). Disturbed sleep patterns (Ellis and Fox, 2004), which do not remit with the resolution of the stressful event (Neylan et al., 1999). Other symptoms include: irritability, nervousness, low frustration level, boredom and anxiety. In the cardiovascular system, blood pressure elevation, extra-systoles and heartbeat acceleration may develop. There is also increased muscle tension (*http://www.stress-anxiety-depression.org/stress/neurotransmitters.html*). The cognitive disturbances consist from lack of attention, concentration, and poor memory, difficult decision-making, procrastination, feelings of persecution. The above-mentioned symptoms make the individual more susceptible to minor accidents.

The stress lasting for a few months is characterized by the appearance of colds or flues, and the person becomes more prone to illness (infection) due to the suppression of immune system (Lewis, 1996), and/or mental disorders– as anxiety (APA, 1994) and depression (Fava et al,1992).

In case of chronic stress lasting for years, the person might get gastro-intestinal problems as peptic ulcers, irritable bowel syndrome, colitis; cardio-vascular disorders as high blood pressure, stroke, coronary insufficiency and heart attacks (*http://www.stress-anxiety-depression.org/stress/neurotransmitters.html*). Also psychological manifestations might develop, for example migraine, chronic headache, backache and general aches in the body (Karasek and Theorell, 1990; Lennart, 1996). Even it has been reported that there is a relationship between stress and infertility (Eskiocak et al. 2005).

Socially speaking, stress might disrupt the social ties with others through increased argumentation, isolation from social activities, and conflicts with students.

3.6 How to Manage Stress?

The old adage, 'prevention is better than cure' is certainly true for stress management. Let's see some of the antidote to cope up stress (other than antidepressant drugs, which have many harmful side effects). To manage stress, a holistic approach is desperately required; otherwise failure might be the result of any effort to contain the negative effects of stress on the physical, psychological, emotional and social aspects.

Measures to be Adopted by the Individual

As the saying goes "to the problem of your life you are the only solution", so to give an effective response to stress, the major answer lies in the person per se, and this is called the "Individual Stress Avoidance Techniques". Studies have shown that the attitude of the person is a powerful tool to defend stress (Ko et al., 1999). There are two types of coping strategies in stress, the first one is the potentially adaptive strategy (e.g. avoidance, working through problems); while the second one – the maladaptive strategy -, as in case of excessive use of alcohol and drugs, histrionic or aggressive behavior and self mutilation behavior (Gelder et al, 1999). It has been found that there is a negative correlation between using active coping styles and positive reinterpretation as a coping strategy on one hand and distress on the other hand (Stewart et al, 1995). Healing from inside is much more effective than from outside! The person who is optimistic in his life can combat stress more effectively than the person who is not. Studies have shown that patients having a positive attitude correlate with an increased ability of the immune system in fighting disease whereas patient exhibited stress and fear takes a longer healing time (Weinman, 1987). It is also known that there is a correlation between the number of lymphocytes and the patient's level of optimism. So being optimistic in our outlook toward life can work as a wonderful medicine to lead a peaceful life.

There are many strategies that can be used to prevent, or reduce the exam stress; if they are followed, the student will feel relief from that stress. Shortly before the exam, it's too late for the student to start worrying about what he/she didn't do months ago! It is impossible to return back and do your preparation better, in other words, students cannot change the past. This idea simply breeds panic and reduces self-confidence. Students can master the present and the future, so they should concentrate on what they are able to do, rather than on bewailing what you can't. Following these steps makes the situation quite better:

1. A student should think like an examiner while he/she is studying. As he/she read through the material, they should look out for things that would make a good question. Also, they can look for connections between the different things they are learning, both within and between different subjects. Students should know that the more connections there are to each piece of information they are storing away, the easier it will be to find and recall them when needed.

2. A student should always be positive, the degree to which a student reacts or "gets stressed" depends in part on what he/she says to himself/herself about the stressor. One step in stress management is learning positive self-talk and thinking. Tries to avoid negative thinking as much as possible. Instead arguing with himself/herself, in their inner voice, about how awful everything is and how he/she feels sure will fail (if the student succeeds in convincing himself/herself that he/she must fail, he/she probably will) rather strikes up a positive dialogue. We all make mistakes and we don't always get it right first time. Congratulate yourself when plans are going well, this self-praise is of great value to encourage and support the self to proceed and progress. Be careful not to blame yourself, or under-evaluate your abilities.

3. A student should encourage himself. Give yourself a good pep talk, you're an intelligent person (no-one gets as far through the system as you already have, without being intelligent you could not pass the secondary school, with the highest marks enabling you to study medicine), and certainly intelligent enough to pass the test. You have studied and worked hard, you know a lot about each subject, and you should be able to remember enough to answer each question adequately.

4. To a remarkable extent, how you choose to think about what is happening to you, influences what will happen. If a student decides to be miserable, or a failure, he/she will be. If, on the other hand, you decide that you can be successful, and cheerful, you will manage that, equally. Avoid trapping yourself within a network of Absolute declarations you make to yourself.

5. Relaxation response: students should find out the things that help them relax and do them regularly. When busy or feeling under pressure, the things that help the student to relax are the first to be ignored! For example, a student may feel too busy to exercise but these are the things that help him/her to relax enabling them to manage their time in a more productive way, both at home and at work. There are many activities that can trigger the relaxation response, both informal: as deep breathing (Sutherland and Cooper, 2003), laughing, having a hot bath, regular exercise as walking in a calm area, jogging, swimming; listening to peaceful calm music; make some quiet time for yourself; And formal: as progressive muscle relaxation, body

inventory (while lying in bed before sleep, identify where you hurt - these are probably the places you hold stress). Meditation and yoga can be of benefit during stressful situations (as in exam) among medical students (Malathi and Damodaran 1999).

6. Lifestyle management: the adoption of a healthy lifestyle will facilitate overcoming stress. The healthy life style includes: good feeding practices by eating a balanced diet, avoiding junk food, excessive coffee, tea and stimulant gaseous drinks during the nights. Try to improve your sleep hygiene by sleeping at the same time every day to control the biological clock, in a calm, well ventilated room. That habit leads to mind and body rest. Sleep time on the other hand should be enough so that you wake rested, always keep in mind that poor sleep patterns (insufficient or unsatisfactory sleep) have been shown to have deleterious consequences on mental health, and predisposing to stress (Ellis and Fox, 2004). Added to that, doing regular exercises for 30 minutes daily, or at least every other day, you have to balance your study and play, give your body what does need on a daily basis. This will improve the quality of sleep and may increase the individual tolerance to work harder (Ashton, 1993; härmä, 1996), relieve the nasty emotions, as mild anxiety and depression (Ashton, 1993), through may be better irrigation of the brain and smoothening of tense muscles. The last result will improve the physical performance of the body as well.

7. Breaking the social isolation, by talking with others, whether friends, students or professionals, to learn that you are not alone in your suffering, and others probably have the same worries, and fears you have. Those medical students who lack to contact with others, keeping their problems to themselves have high scores in psycho-emotional stress (Ko et al., 1999). This will act as a release valve for the stress. Remove the stressor, which is definitely a possible management strategy, especially if the stressor poses a danger to you. Some students perceive their courses as posing a danger and think that the best way to manage is avoiding the stress by skipping class or not doing assignments. They would rather be ``safe'' and ``comfortable'' than to expose themselves to the discomfort of personal growth. They know what happens when they do nothing and they are comfortable with it. They have fallen into a pattern of failing and they are good at it. To develop and grow and reach your potential as a person it is necessary to take risks, to change, and to learn. Keeping in mind the say: "NO PAIN, NO GAIN." That means that you have to pay in order to obtain your objectives. In another word, the absence of stress means death during life.

8. Time management: Plan and schedule your work, your day, and your week. Do not live in chaos, as this will increase your suffering and boost destructive stress! Write down all the things you are worried about they are often not quite as bad as previously thought, this also makes it easier to form a plan of action: use a diary, make lists and put them where you can find them, put tasks in order of priority, set realistic achievable goals for yourself and reward yourself when you have achieved them (i.e. be a positive thinker). To conclude, plan your life - be prepared to make changes, remember always that disorganized thinking and behavior in life is one of the causes of stress!

9. Don't work too long at one task; take a break to combat boredom that leads to weakened attention, concentration and memory.

10. Enjoy your life, organize stations of merry, as doing short visits to relatives or friends who are comfortable to you, doing shopping for a limited time, eating a meal with a friend in a restaurant..etc, it's important to make time to have some fun! Unfortunately, medical students have little time for leisure activities, which is caused by the heavy curriculum and lack of organization (Ko et al., 1999)!

11. Break the routine of life to eliminate boredom; this can be achieved by altering the room décor, by changing the dress, by putting few flowers in front of you, modify your reading place..etc.

12. Religious beliefs and faith factor: the mere thinking that the human is not alone in the battle of life, and the belief that there is a God, who supports the person and gives the help required when requested, will relief the mental pressure, tension, and stress. The relaxation response has always existed in the context of religious teachings. The effects of religious prayers on physiology include a decrease in heart rate, metabolic rate, respiratory rate and slowing of brain waves. The stress-buffering and immune-enhancing effects of meditative prayer techniques form one of the faith factor's most powerful components (Matthews and Clark, 1998). One study has showed that 28% of the university students (medicine and law) having stress turn to religion for emotional support (Ko et al., 1999).

Measures to be Adopted by the Society

Environmental systems can create or reduce stress. The difficult environment of the medical school should be modified to create less stressful situations. The value of social support as a buffer against the effect of stress is well documented (Sutherland and Cooper, 1992). This can be done through the following mechanisms:

1. Curriculum revision: reduction in information overload in the curriculum can be an important strategy to enable undergraduates cope better with the demands of tertiary education. Usually the curriculum of the medical schools is heavy- and the SQU medical school is not an exception - which is considered as one of the factors leading to stress (Ko et al., 1999; Stewart et al., 1997).

2. Academic advisors and academicians: better mentorship through an intimate relationship between the medical students on one hand, and the academic advisors and other academicians on the other hand, is vital to reduce stress (Shaikh et al. 2004). This can be achieved through different mechanisms, as: advising the students for a better selection of the subjects after taking into consideration the student's abilities and limitations; encouraging, reassuring and supporting the students, and solving any problem that arise during study. Many obstacles may be faced in this issue: as lack of motivation from the staff side – and this can be solved by giving certain incentives to make them more motivated to perform better in this task. Also some advisers are lacking the proper knowledge and experience of advising. This has been solved in SQU medical school by organizing conferences for the advisers every semester to give them the needed information about advising. Other problems stems from the students themselves, as some of them are not stimulated to contact their advisers. Some students under probation in the medical school have never seen their

advisors! This can be managed by giving lectures and seminars to increase the students' awareness about the importance of this relationship.

3. Through our regular meeting with students under probation – as members of the committee dealing with that issue- we found that some of the students are obliged by their parents to enter the medical school against their will. Therefore we think that admission to the medical school just for having high marks is not sufficient. The assessment of the students' psychological background, motivation, willing to study medicine and their personality type before admission through an interview is mandatory. These findings suggest characteristics of vulnerable students to stress and emotional disorders (as type B personality) who might be identified early on admission and provided with additional support. Educating such students to expect an increase in concerns about environment and personal ability to manage the academic load might make these concerns less overwhelming.

4. The duty of Students' Counseling and Advising Center (SCAC) is to receive the students suffering from problems, including those under probation, to focus on the evaluation process at the core of the stress response, and to present the required psychological intervention. Through the SCAC, the students must learn that when they use avoidant coping strategies, they will expect an increase in depression and anxiety, while by using active coping and positive reinterpretation, the opposite will result (Stewart et al. 1997). The stressor can initiate cognitive distortions, which needs cognitive behavioral therapy to overcome the negative, irrational thought patterns that distort the perception and evaluation of the threatening stimulus and thus prevent adaptive coping-oriented behavior (Bruch, 1997). Therefore we can reduce or eliminate a potentially stressful situation – as in case of the exam- by learning to perceive stress differently by avoiding faulty thinking. If the student will continue to suffer from stress and study difficulties in spite of the SCAC efforts, then referral to the department of behavioral medicine will be the last line for assessment and intervention. Here also, unfortunately some students do not show motivation to visit the SCAC.

5. Health education programs or courses offered to the medical students to increase the awareness about stress, at the beginning of the study and during it, is a very important stress management procedure providing long-term protective effects as well as the short-term benefits (Michie et al., 1994).

6. Students should be made more aware of the help available, and shown that they are not alone in feeling the pressure of exams. The friends' role in providing reassurance and psychological support is influential in stress buffering (Shaikh et al. 2004), the student must know that even if performance is not as good as expected, there will be other chances, and that doing badly in exams does not reflect abilities in the whole of life. KO et al. (1999) found that the majority of the medical students (70%) when faced with a problem during the first year would turn to friends and classmates for help and emotional support. The majority of those who preferred to keep their problems to themselves had significantly higher scores for psycho-emotional stress than others. However, more social involvement of some students with their friends might be a disadvantage, due to the time limitation in the medical study. Extroverted personality is regarded as one of the most important factors, which is strongly related to first-year academic failure (McMichael and Hetzel, 1975). We have a similar

conclusion for some of our students under probation, especially those who mix with colleagues from other colleges who have fewer commitments than medical students. Probably for this reason, some studies has shown that Support groups did not facilitate academic performance (Mitchell et al., 1983). To overcome this problem, some think that promotion of time-management strategies is superior than support-building interventions (Rospenda et al., 1994).

7. The family responsibility in this concern is great, not only in supporting and encouraging the medical students, but also by avoiding their involvement in the family problems, as many students under probation revealed during our routine interview with them.

By applying the above-mentioned strategies the student can avoid the negative effects of the exam stress, leading to a better productive life with a smile on the face!

EMOTIONAL DISORDERS AND MEDICAL STUDENTS UNDER PROBATION

We mean here by emotional disorders anxiety and depression. These two disorders are so commonly encountered among our medical students under probation, either separately or more frequently in combination. It is well known in psychiatry, that comorbidity in mental disorders is high (Gelder et al., 1999). We'll consider each disorder independently.

4.1.   Anxiety

Anxiety is defined as "a characteristic, unpleasant emotion induced by the anticipation of danger or frustration which threatens the security or homeostasis of the individual or the group to which he or she belongs" (Burrows and Davies, 1984). Although there is a considerable interchange in the literature between the terms anxiety and stress (Spielberger, 1976; Lazarus, 1966), some suggest this frequently synonymous use is confusing (Endler and Parker, 1990). What differentiates anxiety from stress is that anxiety is a distressing experience of dread or foreboding, but it derives from an unknown internal stimulus inappropriate to the reality of an external stimulus or concerned with a future stimulus (Rosenbaum and Pollack, 1991).

Anxiety is a normal emotional state, experienced in subjective threatening situations. By that useful (normal) anxiety, the body will be prepared to achieve the goals via physiological changes, such as increased heart rate, blood pressure, respiration and muscle tension. On the mental state, the attention and concentration are heightened. Other changes resulting from sympathetic nervous system may appear, as tremor, polyurea and diarrhea. However, the anxiety becomes pathological when it is out of proportion, to the limit that it affects the individual's academic, social or occupational life. In this case, there will be an apprehensive expectations, increased tension, helplessness, inadequacy; and physical symptoms may also be seen e.g. palpitations, easy fatigability, trembling, restlessness, shaking voice, white skin, sweaty hands. The sleep disorder seen in patients with generalized anxiety disorder is characterized by prolonged sleep latencies and increased sleep fragmentation (Neylan et al., 1999), but they exhibit normal REM latencies and decreased REM percentage (Reynolds et al., 1983). In addition, cognitive functions disturbances may occur also as attention and concentration problems (APA, 1994). The etiology of anxiety can be explained in many ways; as there are biological, psychodynamic and learning theories; which is not our concern to deal with in this chapter.

Anxiety disorders are the most common disorders encountered in psychiatry, resulting in considerable functional impairment and distress (Hollander et al., 1999). There are many types of anxiety disorders: as panic disorders, generalized anxiety disorders, phobic disorders (as social phobia and specific phobias), obsessive – compulsive disorder and post-traumatic stress disorder. Probably the most prevalent anxiety among our students is the generalized anxiety disorder.

Anxiety can result from stress (Boudarene et al., 2002), which is an important cause of the dropout of medical students particularly during the early stages of the medical education (Grover and Smith, 1981). Many studies have shown that there is an association between psycho-social stressors and different types of anxieties (Barlow, 1988; Faravelli, 1985; Sheehan et al., 1981; Rosenbaum and Pollack, 1991). The prevalence of anxiety is high among medical students, approaching 18% (Pillay et al. 2001). Another study showed that during the study in the university, up to 20% of the symptoms-free students became anxious at a clinically significant level (Andrews and Wilding, 2004). Some researchers have found that female students are more affected by both anxiety and depression than male students (Masson et al, 2004), while others found no difference between the two sexes among medical students (Stewart et al., 1995). During study in medical school, there are many factors that can lead to the development of both anxiety and depression, such as: time limit, loss of opportunity to maintain social and recreational sources of gratification, the heavy curriculum and whether one has the endurance and ability to be successful (Stewart et al., 1995).

Anxiety has been linked with cognitive defects on a wide range of cognitive tasks (MacLeod, 1996). High test-anxious individuals have been shown to report more intrusive thoughts and lower test performance relative to low test-anxious individuals (Blankstein et al., 1989). Similarly, high test-anxious individuals have consistently scored lower in tests of free (uncued) recall of memorized material (Hembree, 1988). Therefore it is not surprising that some of our medical students under probation are suffering from anxiety disorder.

4.2.   Treatment of Anxiety

To be successful in treating anxiety on the long run, many lines must be adopted in combination.

- Pharmacotherapy: many medicines can be used effectively in treating anxious patients, including Tricyclic antidepressants (like Imipramine, Amitriptyline and Desipramine), with well-established efficacy. In our practice with the medical students, we usually use the first two drugs with very good success. Other drugs include Benzodaizepines (as Alparzolam and Clonazepam) –keeping in mind the issue of dependence and withdrawal when using these medications – for this reason we rarely prescribe them. Buspiron has proven efficacy, generally well tolerated, having delayed action compared with benzodiazepines, and is not associated with a "high" (Hollander et al., 1999).

- Cognitive Behavior Therapy (CBT) is a proven breakthrough in mental health care as shown clinically and by research. Many studies have shown that CBT has become a powerful mean to treat many psychiatric conditions including anxiety disorders. By CBT, the distorted picture of what's going on in the life and certain thinking patterns that cause the symptoms as anxiety, depression and anger are corrected. Patients with co-occurring anxiety and depression can be successfully treated with a brief cognitive-behavioral intervention. The efficacy of CBT on both the short- and long-term has been proven (Lang, 2003; Gallagher et al., 2004; Otto and Deveney, 2005).

- Different types of other psychological intervention can be used, as: psychodynamic psychotherapy (Gabbard, 1990), and supportive therapy can be used (Shaikh et al. 2004).

- Meditation and relaxation therapy: similar measures used in case of stress management can be used here also. Yoga can be of benefit in anxiety states during routine activities and prior to examination (Malathi and Damodaran 1999).

- A student try to co-operate with other colleagues, they may well be feeling the pressure too, listen to colleagues' opinions and negotiate a compromise.

- The faith factor cannot be ignored in reducing the level of anxiety and keeping the mind in a balanced, calm and peaceful attitudes.

4.3. Depression

Depression is the commonest among psychiatric disorders. It affects people of all ages, races, ethnic, or economic groups. Some people experience only one episode of depression in their whole life, but many have several recurrences. Some depressive episodes begin suddenly for no apparent reason, while others can be associated with a life situation or stress. Depression is less common in teenagers and college students at the beginning of study, compared with older adults. It has been found that upon entering medical school, students' emotional status resembles that of the general population, but the rise in depression scores and their persistence over time suggest that emotional distress during medical school is chronic and persistent rather than episodic (Rosal et al., 1997). In the United States, the lifetime risk for developing a major depressive episode approaches 6% (Cassem, 1995). The prevalence of major depression ranges from 2.6% to 5.5% in men and from 6.0% to 11.8% in women (Fava and Davidson, 1996). Such women predominance in depression has been observed by other researchers (e.g. (Dubovsky and Buzan, 1999), however, others as (Stewart et al., 1995) found no difference between the sexes. One study has shown that studying in the university can induce depression, by mid-course 9% of previously symptom-free students became depressed to a clinically significant level (Andrews and Wilding, 2004). This might be attributed to the stress and anxiety induced by the university atmosphere.

Depression can be very serious, sometimes people who are depressed cannot perform even the simplest daily activities; others go through the motions, but it is clear that they are not acting or thinking as usual. Impairment from depression and its impact on daily life activities and productivity are of profound personal, occupational and social importance.

There are many types of depressive disorders: the unipolar depression (major depressive disorder), bipolar depression (alternating depression and mania), psychotic depression, melancholia, and seasonal depression (APA, 1994). The first type – the major depressive disorder, which is the most commonly encountered depression among the medical students under probation in SQU, is characterized by one or more major depressive episodes in the absence of mania or hypomania. There seem to be biological and emotional factors that may increase the likelihood to develop a depressive disorder. Research over the past two decades strongly suggests a genetic link to depressive disorders, for that reason it is not surprising to find depression running in families (Tsuang and Faraone, 1996; Gershon, 1990), especially in bipolar disorder (Jamison, 1996). However, certain personality patterns play a role in the occurrence of depression as well, as it has been found that personality disorder is concomitantly present in 30-70% of the depressed patients (Thase, 1996), usually in cluster B (i.e. borderline, histrionic and antisocial personality disorder)(Corruble et al., 1996; APA, 1994). Other factors as psychological qualities, bad life experiences and/or environmental stressors can contribute to a depressive episode as well (Gelder et al., 1999). Examples of such factors are difficulty of handling stress, low self-esteem, and extreme pessimism about the future. On the other hand, the common stressors in the medical college life include: greater academic demands, being on his/her own in a new environment, changes in family relations, financial responsibilities, changes in social life, exposure to new people, ideas, and temptations, preparing for life after graduation, can increase the chances of becoming depressed (*http://www.stress-anxiety-depression.org/depression/college-studentdepression. html*). It has been shown that academically less successful students reported somewhat higher levels of depressive ideation and symptomatology (Stewart et al., 1995).

Anxiety is very commonly seen in depressed patients (Gelder et al., 1999), as many as 70% of cases (Rosenbaum et al., 1995). In addition, comorbidity of specific mood and anxiety disorders has been also found consistently in large studies (Weissman et al., 1996). Usually comorbidity is high in psychiatric disorders in general.

Abnormal sleep is one of the most common symptoms of depression, and it is a diagnostic criterion of depression (APA, 1994). Therefore it is not amazing to be found as a frequent complaint among our medical students under probation. The quantity and/or the quality of the sleep can be badly affected in depression. The students may suffer from severe initial insomnia, sometimes inability to sleep till early hours of the morning, late insomnia, and/or sleep fragmentation. The sleep architecture is also changed in depressed individuals, manifested by a decrease in rapid-eye-movement (REM) latency (i.e. decreased length of time between the onset of the sleep to the first REM cycle), increased REM density (increased number of REMs per unit of time during REM sleep, and difficulty entering and remaining in slow-wave sleep (McDermott et al., 1997; Rush et al., 1997). Deficiencies in sleep efficiency and slow wave sleep may explain why depressed patients sometimes feel tired even if they appear to sleep excessively. This will affect their daily activities next day due to excessive sleepiness.

Depression is associated with memory problems, which improves if depression is alleviated (Antikainen et al., 2001). Probably consequent to this and other cognitive deficits, depression has been linked to academic impairment, as manifested by examination withdrawal (Meyer de Stadelhofen, et al., 2003), missed time from class, decreased academic productivity, and significant interpersonal problems. More severe depression was related to a higher level of impairment (Heiligenstein et al., 1996). The depressed patients tend to consume alcohol, abuse drug that increase the feelings of worthlessness and hopelessness.

What makes depression a dangerous disorder is its link to suicide, which must be considered seriously, as it will lead to a catastrophic end if the patient starts to execute his thoughts. Many patients who commit suicide have given warnings to friends or family. A signal or warning may be a statement such as "I wish I were dead," "I can't take it anymore, I want out," or "My parents would be better off without me." Some people even tell a friend about a plan to kill themselves before they actually do. If a friend talks like this, take it critically! Immediately make a university official aware of what your friend has said. In the last 25 years, the rate of suicide among teenagers and young adults has increased dramatically.

What is surprising that medical students under probation in the SQU, who suffer from depression and anxiety, rarely ask for help, or consult psychiatrist, in spite of the long suffering from different depressive symptoms, extending sometimes for three or four semesters. They are usually discovered to have such problems during the routine meeting between the committee dealing with probation and these students. This should alert the university to establish health education program for the medical students, starting from the first year, going side by side of the language courses. One hour or two per week is sufficient in our opinion to make the students aware about the common psychiatric disorders that could affect their academic achievement, with special concern to depression.

4.4.   Treatment of Depression

Depression is a treatable disorder. Between 80 and 90 percent of people with depression - even the most serious forms - can be helped. Symptoms can be relieved quickly with psychological therapies, medications, or a combination of both. The most important step toward treating depression - and sometimes the most difficult - is asking for help. The earlier treatment will lead to a better prognosis, especially if there is a good compliance. Often people don't know, they are depressed, so they don't ask for - or get - the right help. College students and older adults share a problem - they often fail to recognize the symptoms of depression in themselves or in people they care about.

Talking through feelings, a student may help a friend recognize the need for professional help. By showing friendship and concern and giving uncritical support, he/she can encourage a friend to talk the parents or another trusted adult, like an academic adviser or coach, about getting treatment. The student can talk to a counselor- if he/she finds his/her friend is reluctant to ask for help - that's what a real friend will do (G:\probation). Indeed depressed college students need professional treatment.

- Psychotherapy can be used with good success in treating depression. It assists the depressed individual in several ways. First, supportive counseling helps ease the pain of depression, and addresses the feelings of hopelessness that accompany depression. Second, cognitive therapy changes the pessimistic ideas, unrealistic expectations, and overly critical self-evaluations that create depression and sustain it. Cognitive therapy helps the depressed person recognize which life problems are critical, and which are minor. It also helps him/her to develop positive life goals, and a more positive self-assessment. Third, problem-solving therapy changes the areas of the person's life that are creating significant stress, and contributing to the depression. This may require behavioral therapy to develop better coping skills, or interpersonal therapy, to help in solving relationship problems. A trained psychotherapist therapist or counselor can help them achieving these goals.

- At first look, this may seem like several different therapies being used to treat depression. However, all the above-mentioned interventions are used as part of a cognitive treatment approach. Some psychologists use the term: cognitive-behavioral therapy and others simply call this approach, cognitive therapy. In practice, both cognitive and behavioral techniques are used together.

- In the past, behavior therapy did not pay any attention to cognitions, such as perceptions, evaluations or expectations. Behavior therapy only studied behavior that could be observed and measured. But, psychology is a science, studying human thoughts, emotions and behavior. Scientific research has found that perceptions, expectations, values, attitudes, personal evaluations of self and others, fears, desires, etc. are all human experiences that affect behavior. Also, our behavior, and the behavior of others, affects all of those cognitive experiences as well. Thus, cognitive and behavioral experiences are intertwined, and must be studied, changed or eliminated, as an interactive pair.

- When needed, a physician can prescribe medications to help relieve the symptoms of depression. For many patients, a combination of psychological therapy and medication is beneficial. Many medications are proved to be of value in treatment of major depressive disorder, depending on the experience and preference of that physician. Various antidepressants cab be used with good success, as: (Tricyclics - e.g. Amitriptyline, Imipramine and Clomipramine; Tetracyclics - as Maprotiline and Amoxapine; SSRIs – e.g. Fluoxetine and Paroxetine; Serotonin-norepinephrine reuptake inhibitor - Venlafaxine; Dopamine-norepinephrine reuptake inhibitor – e.g. Pupropion; and Norepinephrine-serotonin modulator – e.g. Mirtazqpine).

- Extensive studies (Muller and Leon, 1996) have disapproved the assumption of that most patients would eventually recover from a major depressive episode. There is a 50% chance of remission of depression that has been present for 3-6 months, but there is only 5% possibility of remission within the next 6 months of a major depressive episode that has been present for 2 years (Keller et al., 1996). About 12% of patients with acute major depression do not recover after 5 years of illness; 7% have not recovered after 10 years (Keller et al., 1996; Muller and Leon, 1996).

5.   CONCLUSION

As a conclusion, we can say that although it is impossible to prevent totally students' failure in our medical school, as the case in any other medical school worldwide, but we can predict a reasonable diminution in the number of students under probation during the following semesters. This prediction is based on the policy adopted by Sultan Qaboos University and its medical school to overcome this problem, via different measures undertaken to enhance students' performance, to reduce the students' stress and to improve their emotional status. These measures include: first: the establishment of the committee (consists of seven senior academic members) to deal with the students under probation, by doing routine meetings with these students and their advisors at least once during the semester, in order to find the possible causes of their poor achievement; second: holding one work-shop per semester for the advisors with the intention of increasing their knowledge and awareness about the art of student advising and the possible causes of performance deterioration; third: through a better collaboration with the SCAC to meet and solve the students' social/psychological problems; fourth: referral of those who need psychiatric evaluation and treatment to the department of behavioral medicine in the university hospital to do the needful.

REFERENCES

American Psychiatric Association (APA). (1994). Diagnostic and statistical manual of mental disorders (4th ed), Washington, DC, APA.

Andrews B, Wilding JM. (2004). The relation of depression and anxiety to life-stress and achievement in students. Bri J Psychol 95:509-21.

Antikainen R, Hanninen T, Honkalampi K, Hintikka J, Koivumaa-Honkanen H, Tanskanen A, Viinamaki H. (2001). Mood improvement reduces memory complaints in depressed patients. Eur Arch Psychiatry Clin Neurosci. 251:6-11

Ashton D. (1993). Exercise: health benefits and risks. European Occupational Health Series No. 7, World Health Organization, Copenhagen.

Barlow DH. (1988). Anxiety and its disorders. New York, Guilford.

Blankstein, K.R., Toner, B.B. and Flett, G.L. (1989). "Test Anxiety and the Contents of Consciousness: Thought-Listing and Endorsement Measures," J Res Personality 23:269-289.

Boudarene M, Legros JJ, Timsit-Berthier M. (2002). Study of the stress response: role of anxiety, cortisol and DHEAs. Encephale. 28:139-46.

Bowers MB Jr, Mazure CM, Nelson JC, et al. (1990). Psychotogenic drug use and neuroleptic response. Schizophr Bull 16:81-85.

Breier A, Kelsoe JR, Kirwin PD, et al. (1988). Early parental loss and development of adult psychopathology. Arch Gen Psychiatry 45:987-993.

Bruch MH. (1997). Relaxation training. In: Baum A, Newman S, Weinman J, West R, McManus C (eds) Cambridge handbook of psychology, health and medicine. Cambridge University Press, Cambridge, pp 248-251.

Burrows GD and Davies B. (1984). Recognition and management of anxiety. In: GD Burrows, TR Norman and B Davies (eds), Anti-anxiety agent. Amsterdam, Elsevier Science Publishers.

Caspi A, Sugden K, Moffitt T, et al. (2003). Influence of Life Stress on Depression: Moderation by a Polymorphism in the 5-HTT Gene. Science 301:386-389.

Cassem EH. (1995). Depressive disorders in the medically ill: an overview. Psychodynamics 36:S2-S10.

Chrousos GP, Gold PW. (1992). The concept of stress and stress system disorders: overview of physical and behavioral homeostasis. JAMA 267:1244-1252.

Corruble E, Ginestet D and Guelfi JD. (1996). Comorbidity of personality disorders and unipolar major depression: a review. J Affect Disord 37:157-170.

Dubovsky SL and Buzan R. (1999). Mood disorders. In: Hales RE and Yudofsky SC (eds). Essential of clinical psychiatry based on the American Psychiatric Press. Textbook of psychiatry (3rd ed.), Washington DC, American Psychiatric Press.

Egan MF, Goldberg TE, Kolachana BS, et al. (2001). Effect of COMT Val108/158 Met genotype on frontal lobe function and risk for schizophrenia. Proceedings of the National Academy of Sciences of the United States of America 98:6917-6922.

Eisenbruch M. (1988) The mental health of refugee children and their cultural development. Int. Migration Rev. 22:282-300.

Ellis J, Fox P. (2004). Promoting mental health in students: is there a role for sleep? J R Soc Health 124:129-133.

Endler NS and Parker JDA. (1990) Stress and anxiety: conceptual and assessment issues. Stress Med. 6:243-248.

England JA, Gerhard DS, Pauls DL, et al. (1987). Bipolar affective disorders linked to DNA markers on chromosome 11. Nature 325:783-787.

Epel E, Jimenez S, Brownell K, Stroud L, Stoney C, Niaura R. (2004). Are stress eaters at risk for the metabolic syndrome?.Ann N Y Acad Sci.32:208-10.

Eskiocak S, Gozen AS, Yapar SB, Tavas F, Kilic AS, Eskiocak M. (2005). Glutathione and free sulphydryl content of seminal plasma in healthy medical students during and after exam stress. Hum Reprod. (In press).

Faravelli C. (1985). Life events preceding the onset of panic disorders. J Affect Discord, 9:103-105.

Fava M and Davidson KG. (1996). Definition and epidemiology of treatment resistant depression. Psychiatr Clin North Am. 19:179-195.

Fava M. Rosenbaum JF, McCarthy M, Pava JA, Steingard R, Fox R. (1992). Correlations between perceived stress and depressive symptoms among depressive outpatients. Stress Med. 8:73-76.

G:\probation and exam stress\Surgery Door News - Exam stress can damage health say experts.htm.

Gabbard GO. (1990). Psychdynamic psychiatry in clinical practice. Washington, DC, American Psychiatric Press.

Gallagher HM, Rabian BA, McCloskey MS. (2004). A brief group cognitive-behavioral intervention for social phobia in childhood. J Anxiety Disord. 18:459-79.

Gelder M, Mayou R, Geddes J. (1999). Psychiatry (2nd edition). Oxford university press, U.K.

Gershon ES. (1990). Genetics in manic-depressive illness. Goodwin FK and Jamison KR. New York, Oxford University Press.

Grover PL, Smith DU. (1981). Academic anxiety, locus of control, and achievement in medical school. J Med Educ.56:727-36.

Härmä M. (1996). Exercise, shiftwork and sleep. In: Kerr J, Griffiths A, Cox T (eds) Workplace health: employee exercise and fitness. Taylor Francis, London.

Heiligenstein E, Guenther G, Hsu K, Herman K. (1996). Depression and academic impairment in college students. J Am Coll Health 45:59-64.

Helman GC. (1990). Culture, health and illness. Butterworth-Heinmann. 2nd edition, Oxford, UK.

Hembree, R. (1988). "Correlates, Causes, Effects, and Treatment of Test Anxiety". Review of Educational Research 58:47-77.

Hollander E, Simon D, Gorman JM. (1999). Anxiety disorders. In: Hales RE and Yudofsky SC (eds). Essential of clinical psychiatry based on the American Psychiatric Press Textbook of psychiatry (3rd ed.). Washington DC, American Psychiatric Press.

Ionescu S, Bosse M. (2004). Psychological disorders of students and university results. Ann Med Psychol (Paris)145:133-43.

Jamison KR. (1996). Manic-depressive illness, genes, and creativity. In: Hall LL (ed). Genetics and Mental Illness: evolving issues for research and society. New York, Plenum.

Karasek R, Theorell T. (1990). Healthy work, stress, productivity and the reconstruction of working life. New York: Basic Books.

Keller MB, Hanks DL, Klein DN. (1996). Summary of the DSM IV mood disorders field trial and issue overview. Psychiatr Clin North Am. 19:1-27.

Kiecolt-Glaser JK, Glaser R. (1991). Stress and immune function in humans. In: R. Ader, DL Felten and Cohen (eds): Psychoimmunology, Academic Press, San Diego.

Ko SM, Kua EH, Fones CS. (1999). Stress and the undergraduates. Singapore Med J. 40:627-30.

Lang AJ. (2003). Brief intervention for co-occurring anxiety and depression in primary care: a pilot study. Int. J Psychiatry Med. 33:141-54.

Lazarus RS. (1966). Patterns of adjustment (3rd ed.), New York, McGraw Hill.

Lennart L. (1996). Spices of life or kiss of death? In: Cooper CL (ed): Handbook of stress, medicine and health. CRC Press, Florida (USA).

Lewis S. (1996). Personality, stress and chronic fatigue syndrome. In: Handbook of stress, medicine and health. CRC Press, Florida (USA).

Macht M, Haupt C, Ellgring H. (2005). The perceived function of eating is changed during examination stress: a field study. Eat Behav. 6:109-12.

MacLeod, C. (1996). Anxiety and Cognitive Processes. In Sarason, I.G., Pierce, G.R. et al. (eds.), Cognitive Interference: Theories, Methods, and Findings. The LEA Series in Personality and Clinical Psychology (Lawrence Erlbaum Associates, pp:47-76.

Malathi A, Damodaran A. (1999). Stress due to exams in medical students--role of yoga. Indian J Physiol Pharmacol. 43:218-24.

Masson AM, Hoyois P, Cadot M, Nahama V, Petit F, Ansseau M. (2004). Girls are more successful than boys at the university. Gender group differences in models integrating motivational and aggressive components correlated with Test-Anxiety. Encephale. 30:1-15.

Matthews DA, Clark C. (1998). The faith factor: proof of the healing power of prayer. Middlesex, England, Penguin books.

Maville J, Huerta CG. (1997). Tress and social support among Hispanic student nurses: implications for academic achievement. J Cult Divers 4:18-25.

McDermott OD, Prigerson HG, Reynolds CF III et al. (1997). Sleep in the wake of complicated grieve symptoms: an exploratory study. Biol. Psychiatry 41:710-716.

McMichael AJ, Hetzel BS. (1975). Mental health problems among university students, and their relationship to academic failure and withdrawal. Med J Aust. 1:499-504.

Merikangans KR, Risch N. (2003). Will the Genomics Revolution Revolutionize Pyschiatry? American J Pyschiatry160:625-635

Meyer de Stadelhofen F, Plancherel AC, Berthoud S, Michel L. (2003). [Psychological health of students and identification of persons at risk: avoidance of an exam as symptom of depression]. Soz Praventivmed 48:97-104.

Michie S, Sandhu S. (1994). Stress management for clinical medical students. Med Educ. 28:528-33.

Mitchell RE, Matthews JR, Grandy TG, Lupo JV. (1983). The question of stress among first-year medical students. J Med Educ. 58:367-72.

Monroe SM, Simons AD. (1991). Diathesis/stress theories in the context of life stress research: implications for the depressive disorders. Psychol Bull 110: 406-425.

Muller TL, Leon AC. (1996). Recovery, chronicity, and levels of psychopathology in major depression. Psychiatr Clin North Am. 19:85-102.

Neylan TC, Reynolds III CHF, Kupfer DJ. (1999). Sleep disorders. In: Hales RE and Yudofsky SC (eds). Essential of clinical psychiatry based on the American Psychiatric Press Textbook of psychiatry (3rd ed.). Washington DC, American Psychiatric Press.

Norman RMG and Malla AK. (1993). Stressful life events and schizophrenia. I. A review of the research. Brit J of Psychiatry 162:161-166.

Otto MW, Deveney C. (2005). Cognitive-behavioral therapy and the treatment of panic disorder: efficacy and strategies. J Clin Psychiatry 66:28-32.

Pierce, G.R. et al. (1996). Cognitive Interference: Theories, Methods, and Findings. The LEA Series in Personality and Clinical Psychology (eds.), Lawrence Erlbaum Associates, pp 47-76.

Pillay AL, Edwards SD, Sargent C, Dhlomo RM. (2001). Anxiety among university students in South Africa. Psychol Rep. 88:1182-6.

Post RM. (1992). Transudation of psychosocial stress into the neurobiology of recurrent affective disorder. Am J Psychiatry, 149:999-1010.

Rawson HE, Bloomer K, Kendall A. (1994). Stress, anxiety, depression, and physical illness in college students. J Genet Psychol. 155:321-30.

Reynolds CF, Christiansen CL, Taska LS et al. (1983). Sleep in narcolepsy and depression: does it all look alike? J Nerv Dis. 171:290-295.

Rosal MC, Ockene IS, Ockene JK, Barrett SV, Ma Y, Hebert JR. (1997). A longitudinal study of students' depression at one medical school. Acad Med. 72: 542-546.

Rosenbaum JF, Pollack MH. (1991). Anxiety. In: Cassem NH (ed). Massachusetts general hospital handbook of general hospital psychiatry (3rd ed). St. Louis, Mosby – Year book.

Rosenbaum JF, Fava M, Nierenberg AA, et al. (1995). Treatment resistant mood disorders. In: Gabbard GO (ed). Treatment of psychiatric disorders. Washington DC, American Psychiatric Press.

Rospenda KM, Halpert J, Richman JA. (1994). Effects of social support on medical students' performances. Acad Med. 69:496-500.

Rush AJ, Giles DE, Schlesser MA et al. (1997). Dexamethasone, thyrotropin-releasing hormone stimulation, rapid eye movement latency, and subtypes of depression. Boil Psychiatry 41:915-928.

Rutter M. (1985). Resilience in the face of adversity: protective factors and resistance to psychiatric disorder. Br J Psychiatry 147:598-611.

Sandanger I, Nygard JF, Sorensen T, Moum T. (2004). Is women's mental health more susceptible than men's to the influence of surrounding stress? Soc Psychiatry Psychiatr Epidemiol. 39:177-84.

Selye H. (1974). Stress without distress. Philadelphia, PA: Lippincott, p.31.

Selye H. (1956). The stress of life. New York, McGraw-Hill.

Shaikh B, Kahloon A, Kazmi M, Khalid H, Nawaz K, Khan N, Khan S. (2004). Students, stress and coping strategies: a case of Pakistani medical school. Educ Health (Abingdon). 17:346-53.

Simpson JA. (1989). Oxford English Dictionary: second edition. Oxford, England, Clarendon Press.

Sheehan DV, Sheehan KE, Minichiello WE. (1981). Age of onset of phobic disorders: a reevaluation. Compr Psychiatry, 22:544-553.

Spielberger CD. (1976). The nature and management of anxiety. In: CD Spielberger and R Diaz-Guerrero (Eds.), Cross Cultural Anxiety, New York; Wiley.

Stewart SM, Betson C, Lam TH, Marshall IB, Lee PW, Wong CM. (1997). Predicting stress in first year medical students: a longitudinal study. Med Educ.31:163-168.

Stewart SM, Betson C, Marshall I, Wong CM, Lee PW, Lam TH. (1995). Stress and vulnerability in medical students. Med Educ.29:119-27.

Sutherland V, Cooper CL. (2003). De-stressing doctors: a self-management guide. Elsevier Science Limited, Philadelphia (USA).

Sutherland VJ, Cooper CL. (1992). Job stress, satisfaction and mental health among general practitioners before and after introduction of the new contract. Brit Med J. 304:1545-1548.

Thase ME, Kuppfer DJ. (1996). Recent development in the pharmacology of mood disorders. J Consult Clin Psychol 64:646-659.

Tsuang MT, Faraone SV. (1996). The inheritance of mood disorders. In: Hall LL (ed). Genetics and Mental Illness: evolving issues for research and society. New York, Plenum.

Weinman J. (1987). An outline of Psychology as applied to medicine (2nd edition). Oxford, Butterworth-Heinmann Ltd.

Weissman MM, Bland RC, Canino GJ, et al. (1996). Cross-national epidemiology of major depression and bipolar disorder. JAMA 276:293-299.

Wender PH, Kety SS, Rosenthal D, et al. (1986). Psychiatric disorders in the biological and adoptive families of adopted individuals with affective disorders. Arch Gen Psychiatry 43:923-929.

World Population Prospects: The 2002 Revision, Population Data base, United Nations Population Database, U. N.

In: Stress and Mental Health of College Students
Editor: Mery V. Landow, pp. 91-123

ISBN 1-59454-839-0
© 2006 Nova Science Publishers, Inc.

Chapter 4

STRESS AND MENTAL HEALTH AMONG COLLEGE STUDENTS: OVERVIEW AND PROMISING PREVENTION INTERVENTIONS

Donna E. Howard, Glenn Schiraldi, Arlene Pineda and Randi Campanella

College of Health and Human Performance, University of Maryland

ABSTRACT

The university context is a locus for developmentally appropriate change and challenge in the life of college students. College communities are also ideal forums for skill-based mental health interventions This chapter presents an epidemiologic assessment of the prevalence of stress, depression and related psychological states among college students. It also examines the central stressor domains that impact the lives of college students as well as the short and longer term biopsychosocial consequences from chronic stress. Furthermore, it provides an integration of the various conceptual frameworks which link stress, depression and mental health. This will be enhanced by a diagrammatic representation or modeling of these relationships. The final section of the chapter presents avenues for promising prevention intervention and research. Recently collected data on stress management courses and interventions developed and implemented on a large public university campus are presented along with recommendations for settings and theoretical frameworks for future programmatic and research efforts.

INTRODUCTION

The Scope of the Problem: Stress Indicators Among College Students

Being a college student is an experience fraught with self-discovery, new experiences and of course, stress. In today's world, there are new sources of stress that challenge individuals everyday. This experience, however, can seem magnified in the college environment.

Academic institutions all over the United States are being asked to address more complex concerns brought forward by students who need more and more help. The health of college students and, more specifically, the mental health of college students, have increasingly gained attention as a major problem that must be addressed. Various indicators and by-products of stress have begun to emerge among college students at alarming rates. The prevalence of depression, anxiety disorders, suicidal tendencies and other stress related problems are increasing and statistics indicate that this trend is one that will not soon be reversed.

In 2003, the American College Health Association (ACHA) surveyed 19,500 college students and found that stress is the number one self-reported impediment to students' academic performance. In fact, ACHA reported that college students have named stress as the primary factor affecting their academic life since the National College Health Assessment (NCHA) was first administered in spring 2000. Today's college students are being diagnosed with more severe psychological problems than past generations. Data collected in 2004 from over 300 college and university counseling centers indicate that 85.8% of directors believe that in recent years there has been an increase in the number of center clients with severe psychological problems, and 90.6% believe that students with significant psychological disorders are a growing concern on campus (Gallagher, 2004). In addition, the number of students reporting a diagnosis of depression has increased by 3.1 percentage points over the last seven NCHA survey periods, from 10.3% in 2000, to 13.4% in 2003 (American College Health Association, 2004).

Stress and Mental Health

The demographics of stress, depression and mental health issues are difficult to break down; indeed, these outcomes do not discriminate by ethnicity, gender or age. Most of the data and information that have been collected regarding stress among college students have been based on a variety of quantitative and qualitative survey methodologies. Work has also been done with those who try to provide resources and assistance to these students, such as counselors and health services providers. Institutions such as the American College Health Association (ACHA), the National Mental Health Association (NMHA) and the Cooperative Institutional Research Program (CIRP) have provided important insights into the issues of depression and stress at both the population level and at the individual level. Overall, however, it appears that individuals entering the college environment now are both more overwhelmed and more distressed than those who came before them (Kitzrow, 2003).

The severity of mental health problems on college campuses has been rising dramatically since 1998. *The College of the Overwhelmed: The Campus Mental Health Crisis and What to Do About It* documented that within the past seven years, the likelihood that a college student will suffer from depression has doubled and the number of students who have reported thoughts of suicide has tripled (Kadison and DiGeronimo, 2004). Additionally, approximately 40% of students fit the criteria for either alcohol abuse or alcohol dependence during the previous year (Kadison and DeGeronimo, 2004). During the last decade, university and college counseling centers have reported an increase in the number of students seeking counseling services. Traditionally, these centers have been called upon to provide developmental and preventative counseling, but these roles have evolved from, simply providing information, to full-scale diagnosing and treatment (Kitzrow, 2003). In 2001, 85% of counseling center directors reported seeing students with more serious psychological problems and, according to a number of recent surveys, more than 10 percent of college students receive counseling with depression as the most reported problem (National Association of Student Personnel Administrators, (NASPA), 2004).

The Cooperative Institutional Research Program (CIRP) has administered their survey to incoming freshmen from colleges and universities across the United States for over 30 years (1966 – present). The survey is distributed to a nationally representative sample of 600 institutions, reaching approximately 300,000 students (Sax, 1997). Over the past 10 years, additional questions that are concerned with issues of mental health have been added to the survey. As stress, depression, and anxiety disorders have become more relevant to college students, it has become vital that these questions be asked. The CIRP survey that was conducted in 2000 found that 28% of freshman stated that they frequently feel overwhelmed, and 8% reported feeling depressed (Sax, 1997). The survey administered by the American College Health Association in 2000 revealed similar trends. The *Journal of the American Medical Association* provided a summary of the results, stating "that 61% of college students reported feeling hopeless, 45% said that they felt so depressed they could barely function, and 9% felt suicidal" (Voelker, 2003, p. 2005). It was also documented that, overall, women generally report more depression and stress than men do, and feel less confident about their ability to deal with that stress (Sax, 1997). Although these surveys do not focus entirely upon issues of stress, depression, and other stress related issues, they do provide invaluable information about this population that may not otherwise be available.

During the college years, depression and stress increase and emotional and physical health decline (National Mental Health Association (NMHA), 2005). The National Mental Health Association has a program that is specifically targeted towards addressing the issues that college students face. This program, call the *College Student and Depression Pilot* initiative examines stress-related disorders and their impact upon college students in great detail (National Mental Health Association (NMHA), 2005).

According to the Federal Centers for Disease Control and Prevention (CDC), 7.8% of men and 12.3% of women between the ages of 18-24 experience frequent bouts of stress, which is often a precursor for depression and other mental disorders (National Mental Health Association (NMHA), 2005). Anxiety disorders and depression are associated with one another and are the two most common mental illnesses experienced by Americans. "In 2000, close to 7% of college students reported experiencing symptoms associated with anxiety disorders within the previous year (National Mental Health Association (NMHA), 2005).

Unrelenting stress and the inability to deal with stress can also result in the development of suicidal thoughts (National Mental Health Association (NMHA), 2005). In 1998, suicide was the second leading cause of death among college students, and that trend persists today. These statistics demonstrate the severity of the problem. Thoughts of suicide are often linked to untreated depression and 95 % of college students who commit suicide are suffering from depression or another stress-related disorder (National Mental Health Association (NMHA), 2005). Oftentimes, college students are able to mask their depression and feelings of loneliness from their loved ones. In one tragic example, a student at MIT appeared to be adjusting well to college, but was hiding a deep depression. She committed suicide by burning herself to death in her dorm room just hours after a visit from her parents and sister (Sontag, 2002).

Stress and Physical Health

Depression, stress, and related mental health problems have also been identified as precursors for other physical ailments. When students are unable to effectively handle their stress, or if stress becomes a constant part of one's life, stress often manifests as physical illness. While the evidence of associations between depression and cardiovascular disease and diabetes are the strongest, data also suggest links with osteoporosis, human immunodeficiency virus infection and the acquired immunodeficiency syndrome (HIV/AIDS), stroke, and cancer (Jacobson, 2003). Jeremko (1984) observed that chronic sympathetic nervous system activation (i.e., prolonged stress) can result in headaches, asthma, hypertension, ulcers, lower back pain, and other medical conditions.

It has been suggested that even minor degrees of depression may carry substantial risk, especially with respect to cardiovascular disease (Jacobson, 2003). Additionally, researchers have begun to explore the relationship between psychosocial stress and asthma. Stress can affect immune response through the impact on behaviors, such as smoking and alcohol consumption which are adopted as ways of coping with stress.

Prospective epidemiological studies have demonstrated associations between stress, social status, and quality of social relationships- social networks, tie to friends, family, work, and community through social and religious groups – and health (Wright, Rodriguez and Cohen, 1998. p. 1066). The duration and frequency of stress are seen as important determinants of its impact on health and illness (Wright, Rodriguez and Cohen, 1998).

College stress can have very serious consequences if individuals are not equipped with the proper coping mechanisms or lack the support of vital resources to help them succeed. Even with the increased attention on stress and depression in this population, it is still difficult to say whether the true magnitude of these issues has been detected. Clearly, colleges and universities must continue to closely monitor their students and provide the guidance and assistance that is vital to the mental health of these individuals.

Today's College Students: The Millennial Generation

The majority of students in college today are members of an era termed the Millennial Generation. The first group of "Millennials" entered college in 2000 and brought with them a set of unique characteristics and core traits. While it is faulty to presume that all members of a generation share common attitudes and personality traits, because all members of a generation are influenced and affected by the collective attitudes and formative events of their birth cohort, studying generations is an effective way to track and understand the distinguishing traits of a particular group (Howe and Strauss, 2000).

Generational researchers Neil Howe and William Strauss (2003) describe Millennials as being more numerous, more affluent, better educated, and more racially and ethnically diverse than the previous three generations. Labeled the "Organization Kids" in an article in *The Atlantic Monthly* (Brooks, 2001), Millennials have proven themselves "responsible, safety-conscious, and mature" (p. 42). Furthermore, they are "extraordinarily bright, morally earnest, and incredibly industrious" (Brooks, 2001, p. 43).

As a group, Millennials have been lauded as "the next great generation" (Howe, and Strauss, 2000). They manifest positive personality traits and behavioral habits that many older adults no longer associate with youth, including a commitment to their communities, a focus on teamwork, and a respect for rules and authority. While there are many positive characteristics associated with members of this new generation, these characteristics also may lead to vulnerability. Some of the dominant traits that Millennials possess can have a negative effect on their mental health. For instance, Millennials are high achievers. Many feel constant pressure from their parents to succeed, and in their ongoing pursuit to achieve "trophy kid" status, they experience excessive stress and burnout (Howe and Strauss, 2003, p. 53). Should they fail to achieve their goals, they feel defeated and depressed. Some even experience resulting physical ailments. Newton (1998) notes, "Stress and physiological symptoms, such as headaches, insomnia, gastrointestinal problems, and weakened immune systems, were once thought to be manifestations of the middle-aged corporate world but are now the most prevalent complaints of students seeking service in our counseling center" (p. 6).

In an effort to implement interventions to prevent or reduce the amount of stress, anxiety, and depression that college students are experiencing, it is important to recognize the underlying causes of these ailments. A number of these causes will likely be out of the control of university faculty and administrators, but there are certainly measures that can be taken to ensure that the campus is intentional about providing a healthful place for students. An understanding of the primary stressors of college students will assist in efforts to create university environments that foster student success and wellbeing.

There are a number of potential reasons for the increased amount and severity of stress, depression, and other psychological problems that current college students are reporting. The following sections will examine the multiple domains of stressors impacting today's college students and some possible causes of these mental health problems.

Domains of College Student Stressors: An Overview

College students today face many challenges and adaptational requirements as they make the transition from the home environment to campus life. The long awaited, but somewhat abrupt and drastic, change from high school is stressful for some students; others experience stress in being separated from home and family (Whitman,1999; Ross, Niebling and Heckert,1999; Misra, McKean, West and Russo, 2000). The transition to college may disrupt regular contact with network members and traditional support mechanisms that have previously mediated or moderated stressful experiences (Hudd, Dumlao, Erdmann-Sager, Murray, Phan, Soukas and Yokozuka, 2000).

While opportunities abound for emotional, cognitive and social growth and development while at college, these may be stressful times for young adults. And, while some stress is necessary for personal growth to occur, excessive and/or prolonged stress can overwhelm a student and affect his or her ability to cope successfully (Whitman, 1999, Hudd, Dumlao, Erdmann-Sager, Murray, Phan, Soukas and Yokozuka, 2000). One index of excessive stress or distress among college students is their use of mental health services. Symptoms commonly reported by campus mental health experts portray a general picture of school-related stress, for example, the inability to do school work and the fear of academic failure (Morrison and O'Connor, 2004).

Rising to the expectations of the college academic environment is one domain of stressors that may not only challenge, but overwhelm students in this singular role; yet, many students also experience inter-role conflict because they are juggling multiple roles in tandem, i.e., holding a job, caring for a child or other family member (Pearlin, 1999; Pearlin, 1989). As college tuition continues to rise, commuter costs increase, aid packages dwindle, and student lifestyle spending escalate, additional strain is placed on personal finances (Collins, 2005). As a result, many students today, work full or part time while they are completing their college education.

This section will briefly discuss the primary causes of stress for college students by examining the most common student stressors. Stressors are situational demands that upset balance by requiring some personal adaptation or change; thus, affecting physical and psychological well-being and necessitating restorative action (Lazarus and Cohen, 1977).

Ross and Niebling (1999) conducted a study of college students and stress using a survey instrument created for the study. This instrument, the Student Stress Survey, included items from both the Student Stress Scale (Insel and Roth, 1985) and the Taylor Manifest Anxiety Scale (Taylor, 1953). The survey consisted of 40 items that were divided into four categories of potential sources of stress: (1) intrapersonal (e.g., change in sleeping or eating habits, change in use of alcohol or drugs, spoke in public, held a job); (2) interpersonal (e.g., roommate conflict, fight with girlfriend/boyfriend, trouble with parents); (3) academic (e.g., change in major, increased class workload, lower grade than anticipated; and (4) environmental (e.g., daily hassels such as computer problems, waited in long line, messy living conditions) (Ross and Niebling, 1999). The distribution of responses among the four domains of stressors was as follows: 38% of the stressors were intrapersonal, 28% extrapersonal, 19% interpersonal, and 15% academic (Ross and Niebling, 1999).The five most frequently listed stressors were change in sleeping habits (89%), vacations/breaks (82%), change in eating habits (74%), new responsibilities (73%), and increased class workload (73%). Financial difficulties (71%) and change in social activities (71%) were also frequently reported stressors. It is important to take into account that this data was collected during a time in which many people were planning spring break trips. This may have increased the number of responses for taking a break or vacation.

Additional intrapersonal stressors that college students experience tend to vary according to the amount of time they have been a college student. To illustrate, college seniors may experience stress and doubt when they consider whether they have been adequately prepared to secure a job and enter the working world, whereas freshman students may struggle more with issues such as their transition and adjustment to college life. For instance, research shows that first-year college students often experience homesickness (Beck, Taylor and Robbins, 2002; Kazantzis and Flett, 1998; McAndrew, 1998) and friendsickness (i.e., "preoccupation with and concern for the loss of or change in precollege friendships") (Paul and Brier, 2001, p. 77) during their first weeks away from home. Furthermore, freshmen must contend with academic and social pressures, exposure to new and diverse people and situations, and challenges to their deeply held values and worldviews. They will inevitably experience some degree of stress and cognitive dissonance when examining and reconciling their personal standards of conduct, beliefs, and identities with newfound knowledge and understanding (Reeve, 2001).

In order for freshmen to effectively deal with the many pressures of being a new college student, it is essential they feel supported in their transition to college. Research indicates that successful adjustment to college is directly correlated with academic success and retention (Heyningen, 1997); therefore, student personnel staff has an important role in ensuring that students are taught skills to help them cope with intrapersonal stressors that may otherwise interfere with their ability to be successful.

Relationship Stressors

Over the past 30 years, research has continually referenced the peer group as the largest influence on college student development (Astin, 1993; Feldman and Newcomb, 1969; Pascarella and Terenzini, 1991). According to Feldman and Newcomb (1969), peer groups have the potential to: (1) provide or withhold emotional support; (2) help students achieve independence from home and family; (3) support or impede their academic achievement; (4) give students practice in getting along with others; and, (5) support or challenge attitudes, values, and behaviors. Conversely, college students that do not feel socially integrated into the academic and social fabric of the university do not experience the above mentioned benefits. As a result, these students experience a higher level of physical and psychological ailments than students who are successful in developing meaningful relationships with their peers. In a recent study of college freshmen, researchers found that social disconnection and loneliness was associated with greater psychological stress, less positive affect, poorer sleep efficiency and quality, and elevations in circulating levels of cortisol (Pressman, Cohen, Miller, Rabin, Barker and Treanor, 2005). Similarly, empirical research indicates that people with low connectedness often experience loneliness, anxiety, jealousy, anger, depression, low self-esteem, and a host of other negative emotions (Baumeister and Leary, 1995; Lee and Robbins, 1998).These findings underscore the importance of social connectedness and its influence on college student physical and psychological health and wellbeing.

Another interpersonal stressor that affects many first-year students impacts those living in an on-campus dorm or residence hall. Students who live on-campus may struggle in their efforts to foster a civil living environment with their roommate or roommates. Millennials are more averse to having roommates than previous generations, mostly because more than 75% of incoming freshmen have never shared a room with anyone, even a sibling (Howe and Strauss, 2003). As a result of interpersonal clashes between roommates, residence hall professionals spend a great deal of time mediating roommate conflicts, counseling individual students about their uncomfortable living situations, and processing room reassignments.

It is also important to mention that for many students, college is a time of rebellion, boundary bending, and experimentation. Students will be anxious to make friends, and in an effort to fit in, they may feel pressured to engage in behaviors that have the potential to threaten their personal health and safety. These behaviors include high-risk drinking, drug use, unprotected sexual activity, and participation in activities that violate university policy. It is essential that students are educated about the potentially negative consequences of their actions. Moreover, they need to be taught how to make informed decisions and empowered to make responsible choices.

Role Strains

College students, particularly freshmen, may experience stress and role strain as they separate geographically from their parents and adjust to the changing nature of familial relationships. Today's college students are significantly closer with and more dependent on their parents than students of previous generations (Howe and Strauss, 2003). Over the past decade, higher education professionals across the country have noted a marked increase in the participation of parents in the daily decisions of their sons and daughters at the university (Carroll, 2005; Howe and Strauss, 2003; Schoenherr, 2005). This cultural change has resulted in higher education institutes having to dramatically rethink and redefine their relationship with the parents and families of college students. Many of today's college parents are so invested, emotionally and financially, in their children's well-being that they have extreme difficulty relinquishing their authoritative roles and demand to be actively engaged in campus life. Given this new expectation, university staff has termed today's parents "helicopter parents" – a comical illustration of the always hovering, ultra-protective nature of the parents of Millennial college students (Holder, 2005; Howe and Strauss, 2003).

It is likely that students who leave home for the first time to attend college will experience role strain stress as they attempt to navigate the college campus as an independent adult while still maintaining daily contact with their parents. It is important that parents provide ongoing support and remain involved in their college students' lives; but, in order for their children to experience the developmental benefits of college, parents must be willing to surrender some authority and "let go" (Coburn and Treeger, 2003).

Academic Stressors

Student's perception of having to master an extensive knowledge base within a time frame that feels inadequate is a common stressor. (Misra, McKean, West and Russo, 2000). Increased work loads coupled with new responsibilities interact with changes in sleeping and eating habits in ways that create sources of stress (Ross, Niebling and Heckert, 1999; Carveth, Geese and Moss, 1996; Abouserie, 1994; Kohn and Frazer, 1986). A major source of stress surrounds taking and studying for exams and competition over grades (Archer and Lamnin, 1985; Britton and Tesser, 1991). Studies conducted among college dropouts suggest that some experience feeling a mismatch between themselves and their college, and dropping out represents a strategy for alleviating this discordance (Falk, 1975;Whitman, 1999). Among graduate students, the uncertainty of their career choice and future prospects, due to a changing job market and surplus of credentialed professionals, creates stress. Additionally, academic demands vary by the nature of the graduate training. While some stressors are common across fields of study, including medicine, law and doctoral study, such as lack of time for social intimacy, feelings of powerlessness, inadequacy and failure qualifying and licensing exams, some are particular to the field (Whitman, 1999). The literature suggests that effective time management and leisure satisfaction may be an important factor in reducing academic stress (Misra and Mclean, 2000).

A General Accounting Office report estimated that by the time they leave school about half of college students have amassed somewhere around $20,000 in student debt, of which more than 15% is from credit cards. Thus, educational loan repayments coupled with credit card debt and projected expenditures for renting an apartment and purchasing a car may create substantial anxiety and financial burden on soon-to-be graduates (United States General Accounting Office, 2001).

Financial Strains

Over the past decade, college officials and policy makers, consumer advocacy groups and governmental bodies have grown increasingly concerned about the rising debt load of college students, particularly credit card debt. (Holub, 2001). Reports indicate that the number of college students who own a credit card and the amount of debt they have amassed has been rising ((Nellie Mae, 2000; O'Malley, 2005). Estimates indicate that well over half of all college students have bank credit cards, many owning multiple cards (Joo, Grable and Bagwell, 2003; Churaman, 1988). In a study which aimed to better understand colleges students' attitudes toward credit cards, Joo et al, (2003) found that while students are heavily involved with credit cards, they often lack basic knowledge regarding credit (annual and late fees) and budgeting. Some would say that many college students are living on the verge of financial crisis (Henry, Weber and Yarbough, 2001). Indeed, in a General Accounting Office report on College Students and Credit Cards, it was noted that financial concerns are among the most cited reasons for why many college students may decide to leave school before graduation (2001).

Without a job, even without a credit history, 18 year olds are not only eligible, in many states, to procure a credit card without parental approval, but are carefully marketed by the credit card industry (Holub, 2002; Loyal, 2002). The growth of credit cards on college campuses mirrors the saturation in the general public (Xiao, Noring and Anderson, 1995). Pre-approved mailed offers arrive at students' dorm rooms unsolicited, are part of the fillers stuffed into bags at the check-out of college bookstores, or are available from sales representatives who set up tables at collegiate sports (for which Universities are paid for their assistance in this distribution) (Loyal, 2002). These and similar practices on college campuses have been characterized as a "carnival atmosphere"; raising concerns about aggressive, unregulated sales practices (United States General Accounting Office, 2001). The stress of debt burden and late payments are compounded when the credit cardholder's credit rating is impaired, affecting future credit acquisition and potential bankruptcy (United States General Accounting Office, 2001).

Cross-Cultural Dynamics

Layered on top of these challenges are those unique to minority and international students studying at the college level. Over the past half century, American institutions of higher education have experienced change in their size, complexity and diversity among students (Whitman, 1999). There is a need to further examine stressors and the outcomes from stress among ethnic populations such as Latino and African American college students at different institutions with varying levels of diversity, as well as among international students studying at US institutions (Misra and Castillo, 2001; Kodama, McEwen, Liang and Lee, 2001.) Among the stressors that international students face in US institutions are the following: 1) unrealistic academic expectations- Many international students rank in the top percentiles at their native institutions and have expectations for similar levels of achievement in their new academic setting (Mori, 2000); 2) financial pressures- limited opportunities for financial assistance for international students at undergraduate and graduate levels, including reduced opportunities for research and graduate assistanceships; 3) language and cultural challenges-difficulties with English language proficiency and adaptation to the American culture (McEwen, Liang and Lee, 2001.)

Secular Events

Another class of stressors includes those that intrude from the larger society and represent secular forces whose impact on college students has been examined. Prime among them are the terrorist attacks of September 11, 2001 (9/11). In a study examining symptoms of Post Traumatic Stress Syndrome (PTSS) among college students following the attacks on the World Trade Towers, geographic proximity to NYC was an important predictor of PTSS with students in Albany, NY (150 miles away) showing greater levels of symptoms than students in Augusta, GA (800 miles away) who in turn showed greater levels than students in Fargo, ND (1500 miles away) (Blanchard, Rowell, Kuhn, Rogers and Wittrock, 2005) While this mirrored psychological reactions experienced by broader samples of individuals (Galea, Ahern, Resnick, Kilpatrick, Bucuvalas, Gold and Vlahov 2002; Schlenger, Caddell, Ebert, Jordan, Rourke, Wilson, Thalji, Dennis, Fairbank and Kulka, 2002), it also underscores the need for college counseling services to be aware of these residual effects so appropriate services are planned for and made available to students. Another study, carried out among a sample of college students at two Eastern Universities, suggests that even low exposure to the 9/11 attacks is associated with depressive symptoms and illness episodes (MacGeorge, Samter, Feng, Gillihan and Graves, 2004). While few students had actual personal or familial exposure to the attacks, their agility and affinity with technology probably provided channels whereby the indirect exposure was heightened, particularly as compared to the general population (MacGeorge, Samter, Feng, Gillihan, and Graves 2004).

A secondary effect of the terrorist attacks is the effect it has had on the workplace and the impact these effects have on college students' employment plans and aspirations. There are indications that some students are rethinking career plans and employment locations (Lewis, 2001). Work in urban centers, particularly major cities and in skyscrapers is seen as less appealing, while the telecommunication field and securities technology is garnering more appeal (Sealy, 2001; Sebastain, and Chaker, 2001). One study found that, among working college students, general anxiety levels are higher regarding current security measures. Soon-to-be-graduates are also concerned about the location of their future place of employment and the extent to which security measures have been undertaken by these organizations (Bosco and Harvey 2003).

Climate of Violence

A growing literature attests to the prevalence of dating violence among college students. This violence includes psychological, physical and sexual victimization (Amar, 2004). Consistent with findings from studies conducted among adolescents (Howard and Wang, 2003a; Howard and Wang, 2003b; Gray and Foshee, 1997; Gaertner and Foshee, 1999), women appear as likely as men to assault their partners physically and psychologically, yet their potential for negative outcomes from victimization are much greater than for male victims (*Fiebert and Gonzalez,*1997; Gelles, 1981; Lane and Gwartney-Gibbs, 1985). One domain of stressors having received little attention is that related to aggression in the form of bullying. A convenience sample of over 1000 undergraduate students at a northeastern public university indicated that greater than 60% observed a student being bullied by another student and almost half had seen a teacher bullying a student. Furthermore, over 6% of students reported having been bullied by another student and almost 5% had been bullied by a teacher (Chapell, Casey, De la Cruz, Ferrell, Forman, Lipkin, Newsham, Sterling and Whittaker, 2004). Based on data from a random sampling of 15,000 undergraduate students from 130 four-year colleges, it has been estimated that perhaps as many as a million college students may carry a gun or other weapon on campus on a regular basis (Miller, Hemenway and Wechsler, 1999). The issue of violence, in its many forms (including dating violence, bullying, and other forms of aggression) should receive more attention as the effects from such victimization may persist for years (Holden and Delville, 2005).

A Model for Understanding and Addressing Stress: The Biopsychosocial Framework

Numerous models have been constructed to facilitate an understanding of stress determinants and consequences (Donnelly and Long, 2003; Monroe and Simons, 1991; Richardson and Waite, 2002; Schiraldi, Spaulding and Hofford, 1998); most can be subsumed within a biopsychosocial framework (Engel, 1980). This framework recognizes the important contribution and transactional nature of three systems: biological, psychological and social. One variant of this framework is the Biopsychosocial Model of Stress (Bernard and Krupat, 1994). In keeping with this model, stress involves three components: 1) an *external component* which addresses the environmental stimuli or events that precede the appraisal of stress but are capable of eliciting a stress response (Cordon, 1977). In the stress literature, these events are often categorized as major life events, daily hassles, role strains, among other stressor domains; 2) an *internal component*, which involves a set of neurological and physiological reactions to stress, associated with Seyle's General Adaptation Syndrome (GAS) (Seyle, 1976; Seyle, 1982). Stress can also be defined as the body's response to demands of the environment (Rice, 1992). Indeed, one of the most widely accepted definitions of stress describes stress as a response elicited by a variety of external events (Selye, 1976). According to the GAS, once the appraisal of stress has occurred there is an orchestrated physiological response as the body attempts to mobilize its internal resources to deal with the impending threat. This response unfolds in three stages: Alarm, often coined the "fight or flight" stage, characterized by the activation of various neurological and physiological mechanisms associated with arousal and defense; Resistance, whereby the body attempts to deactivate these internal systems that have been stimulated and reestablish homeostasis; and Exhaustion, whereby continual arousal or overwhelming stress causes depletion of energy and other physiologic reserves, leading to vulnerability to physical and psychological illness or disease; 3) the *interaction* between the external and internal components linked through cognitive processes. This transaction between an individual and his or her environment incorporates the subjective meaning a situation holds for the individual and determines whether and to what extent an event is experienced as stressful or not. It underscores the notion of appraisal processes which antecede the experience of stress and activation of GAS (Lazarus and Folkman, 1984; Lazarus and Launier, 1978; Pearlin,

1982). Paramount in this framework is the notion that stress is a condition or feeling experienced when a person perceives that demands of a situation exceed the personal and social resources he or she is able to mobilize. After the primary appraisal that a situation will tax available resources, physiological arousal occurs. During this period there is a secondary cognitive appraisal process during which the individual evaluates his or her resources for coping. Psychological and behavioral coping then follows.

Thus, stress can be most comprehensively defined as a physical and psychological reaction to issues and events emanating from one's subjective appraisal of the environment.

The application of this model to stress and mental health among college students is diagrammed as follows:

A Biopsychosocial Model of Stress among College Students

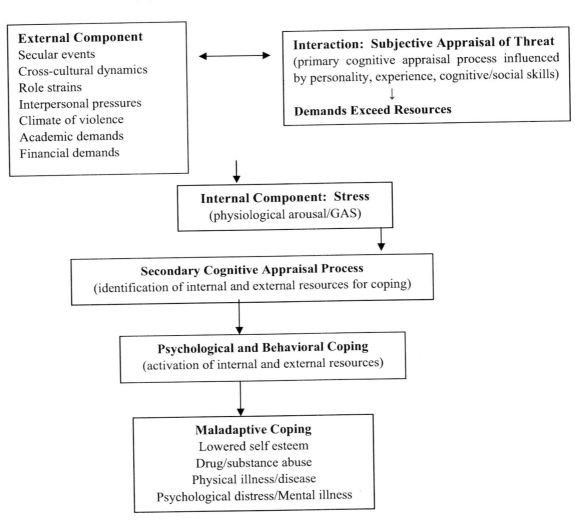

PROMISING PREVENTION INTERVENTIONS

This section will address 5 key areas related to prevention and intervention efforts:

- Pressing need for preventive efforts regarding mental health and the suitability of the college campus for such efforts
- Useful intervention framework
- Hope from previous successes
- Case studies of interventions developed via University Courses
- Future intervention possibilities

Need for Prevention in the University Setting

Five factors especially underscore the need for, and importance of, university-level classroom interventions.

- Stress-related mental illnesses are more prevalent and costly nationwide than previously assumed.

  According to the National Institutes of Mental Health National Co-morbidity Survey (Kessler, McGonagle, Zhao, Nelson, Hughes, Eshleman, Wittchen and Kencler, 1994), nearly one of two Americans will suffer a mental disorder, principally anxiety, mood, or addictive disorders. The indirect and direct costs of mental illness exceed those related to heart disease, cancer, or AIDS (SAMHSA, 1997). Furthermore, psychopathology rates have been increasing, especially in more recently born generations Kessler et al., 1994; Klerman and Weissman, 1989; Fombonne, 1998).

- Mental health is linked to physical health.

  In the Harvard Grant Study (Vaillant, 1977) it was found that mental health in college was the best predictor of physical health decades later. Mental health in college also predicted happiness, occupational and social success and enjoyment, and absence of addictions. A meta-analysis of 101 studies found that depression, anxiety, and/or anger/hostility predispose people to medical conditions ranging from cardiovascular disease to asthma, arthritis, ulcers, and headaches (Friedman and Booth-Kewley, 1987; also see reviews relating mental illness to medical disease in Baum and Posluszny, 1999; Edelmann, 1992; Friedman and Schnurr, 1995). In addition, depression is associated with physical pain (Gallagher and Cariati, 2002) and immunosuppression (Maes, Bosmans, Suy, Vandervorst, Dejonckheere and Raus, 1991, McDaniel, 1992; Kronfol, Starkman and Nair, 1991; Stein, Miller and Trestman, 1991), while the alleviation of depression appears to enhance immune system function (Kook, Mizruchin, Odnopozov, Gershon and Segev, 1995).

- Stress can cause/exacerbate mental illness, and stress-related changes in the brain are associated with anxiety (including post-traumatic stress disorder), depression, suicide, and substance abuse (McEwen, 2000).

Of particular relevance to college campuses, alcohol consumption and/or drinking-related problems have been associated with symptoms of anxiety and depression, perceived stress, and lower self-esteem (see Fenzel, 2005 for review).

- It has been argued that primary prevention, (i.e., inoculation against mental illness) is as necessary for the control/elimination of mental illnesses as preventive initiatives have been to other public health challenges (Albee and Gullotta, 1986; DeArmond and Marsh, 1984).

Accordingly, the Surgeon General has recently identified mental illness as a critical public health problem that the nation must address, and called for preventive intervention efforts (Department of Health and Human Services, 1999).

- It has also been argued (Schiraldi, Spalding and Hofford, 1998) that mobilizing educational resources on college campuses can partially address the critical need for preventing mental disorders.

College communities are ideally suited for preventive interventions. College-aged students are still in their formative years and are open to addressing mental health issues (DeArmond and Marsh, 1984). Educators, such as those in public health and/or psychology departments, can offer classes that emphasize mental *health* and *coping to improve performance,* thus avoiding the stigma sometimes associated with illness/treatment. Such interventions must not simply impart knowledge, but teach skills in order to help address the nation's growing demand/supply imbalance regarding mental health professionals.

A Useful Framework

Skill-based classroom interventions can, therefore, play an important role in the nation's efforts to prevent mental disorders. As Schiraldi and Brown (2001, p.56) have noted:

"Cognitive-behavioral interventions following the Stress Inoculation Training (SIT) model are particularly adaptable to the classroom or small group setting. Cognitive-behavioral interventions teach individuals to identify and replace their own disruptive irrational thinking habits with more realistic, adaptive patterns. In addition, individuals are helped to change or acquire lifestyle behaviors that are more conducive to mental health and coping. The SIT approach (Meichenbaum, 1985; Meichenbaum and Fitzpatrick, 1993) promotes coping through graded exposure and training, and includes three phases: a relatively short didactic component, cognitive-behavioral skills acquisition and rehearsal, and in-vivo application of these skills."

Hope from Previous Successes

Previous successes in various settings suggest that the inoculation approach might be effective for primary and secondary prevention in the college setting. For example, Lipsky, Kassinove, and Miller (1980) found that generically taught cognitive restructuring produced significant reductions in anxiety, depression, and neuroticism in adult outpatients in a community mental health setting presenting with a variety of common neurotic disturbances.

In other words, generic cognitive skills appear to effectively reduce symptoms, irrespective of diagnoses for milder disturbances.

Seligman (1995) taught cognitive restructuring and social problem solving skills to primary school children who were at risk for depression. The program was two hours per week over a 12-week period. Symptoms of depression remained lowered up to two years later. The program is being handed off to regular classroom teachers, suggesting a possible role for those who are not trained as mental health professionals.

Seligman and colleagues (Seligman, Schulman, DeRubeis and Hollon, 1999) implemented an 8-week prevention workshop to university students at risk for depression (*at risk* was defined as being in the most pessimistic quarter of explanatory style). Meeting in groups of ten once per week for two hours, the students learned skills preventively that are taught in cognitive-behavioral therapy. These included cognitive restructuring and behavioral strategies (time management, problem solving, interpersonal skills, and relaxation). Compared to controls, the workshop group had fewer self-reported depressive and anxiety symptoms, fewer episodes of generalized anxiety disorder, and fewer moderate depressive episodes. The workshop group also had significantly greater improvements in explanatory style, hopelessness, and dysfunctional attitudes, which mediated depressive symptom prevention. Explanatory style post-workshop also predicted Grade Point Average (GPA).

The above suggest the efficacy of psycho educational interventions for tertiary and secondary prevention. The question remains: Could similar interventions be designed for university students who are not identified as at-risk, thus broadening exposure of the preventive skills and eliminating possible stigmatization?

Stress and the Healthy Mind Course, University of Maryland, College Park

Given the promising results of such interventions, it was hypothesized that a cognitive-behavioral college course based on the SIT model might improve the mental health (and theoretically prevent the future development of mental disorders) in a presently healthy adult population. Schiraldi, a Ph.D. level health educator, developed and implemented a 15-week elective course, which taught skills to manage anger, prevent anxiety and depression, and build self-esteem. Taught since 1990 to adults ranging in age from 18-68, the course has significantly reduced symptoms of anxiety, depression, and hostility, and improved self-esteem (Brown and Schiraldi, 2000), with results persisting at one-month follow-up (Schiraldi and Brown, 2001). To our knowledge this was the first preventive effort to find that multiple health indicators could be improved in functioning adults through a semester's course.

The course met twice weekly for ninety-minute classes. The instructor presented principles, skills, and assignments to improve mental health and coping. Classes included lecture, group discussions, and skills practice. The practice of skills and drills was assigned as homework, and the students' experiences with these assignments were discussed in class to reinforce learning. They also kept a journal to track their experience with each assignment and their overall wellbeing and coping. The course was competency based, with students contracting for grades. That is, an "A" grade could be earned by completing all assignments, except one (to allow for anticipated discomfort with any particular assignment). Although the skills are outlined in detail elsewhere, (Schiraldi, 1990, 1996, 1997, 2000, 2001; Schiraldi and Brown, 2001a; 2002) a brief course overview is presented below.

Recognizing the interrelationship between mind and body, students contracted to develop and implement sound sleep, exercise, and eating plans, and to track their progress each day. Anger management skills were first explored. Anger is perhaps the least threatening of the topics because it is generally perceived to be triggered by external conditions. Relaxation training to reduce physical arousal was followed by introductory cognitive restructuring skills. An overview of the cognitive distortions that promote anger was followed by assignments to keep structured diaries tracking upsetting events, reactions, distortions, and rational replacement thoughts. Gestalt chair exercises encouraged calmer awareness of the complexities of anger and empathy, and written forgiveness exercises encouraged students to free themselves from the burden of bitterness without necessarily expecting reconciliation or the re-establishment of trust.

Several anxiety skills were assigned as a means of overcoming the avoidance that maintains anxious arousal. First, students were asked to record the facts and feelings regarding present worries, which have been found to significantly reduce anxiety (Borkovec, Wilkinson, Folensbee and Lerman, 1983). A second assignment addressed more distressing concerns in accordance with the following rationale. A number of studies have indicated that unresolved traumatic grief heightens the risk for enduring impairment across various domains of mental, social, and medical health, including rates of depression, suicide, anxiety disorders, substance abuse, physical pain, and mortality (for review see Prigerson, Bierhals, Kasl, Reynolds, Shear, Day, Beery, Newson and Jacobs, 1997). For example, the Adverse Childhood Experiences (ACE) Study related the current health status of more than 17,000 adults to distressing childhood experiences. It found that more than half of adults had grown up with one or more of the following, which tended not to occur in isolation: abuse of any kind, domestic violence, a substance abuser, one who is mentally ill or suicidal, or parental absence. Such experiences were strongly associated with adult depression, suicide attempts, substance use, obesity, and a range of serious medical diseases. (Anda, Fellitti, Chapman, Croft, Williamson, Santelli, Dietz and Marks, 2001; Dietz, Spitz, Anda, Williamson, McMahon, Santelli, Nordenberg, Felitti and Kendrick 1999; Felitti, 2002; Hillis, Anda, Felitti, Nordenberg and Marchbanks, 2000). Felitti (2002) reasoned, therefore, that adverse childhood experiences, arguably the most important determinant of the nation's health, are both common and destructive, and must be dealt with. Thus, students were asked to record over a four-day period the facts and feelings related to past emotional wounds. Pennebaker (1997) found this strategy to improve mood and immunocompetence in college students. In addition, students were asked to categorize worries according to their importance and controllability, as a way to stimulate active control and perspective.

It is generally agreed, with considerable support, that self-esteem is central to sound mental health and the prevention of various mental disorders, while the lack of self-esteem is associated with a variety of psychological disturbances (e.g., Beck, 1967; Brown, Schiraldi and Wrobleski, 2003; Coie,Watt, West, Hawkins, Asarnow, Markman, Ramey, Shure and Long l993; Hobfall and London, 1986; Hobfall and Walfisch, 1986; Parker, Cowen, Work and Wyman, l990; Rosenberg, 1965,1979; 1985), even in Asian cultures assumed to favor a collective orientation over individualism (Lee, 2002; Zhang, in press). Thus, it was considered important to teach several self-esteem skills.

Self-esteem was defined as a realistic, appreciative opinion of self, resting upon three pillars: (1) a sense of unconditional human worth, (2) unconditional love/acceptance, and (3) the process of actualizing potential. Using cognitive restructuring again, students identified events that threatened self-esteem, and replaced distortions that tend to undermine the sense of self-worth. In imagery, students revisited difficult periods of their lives, this time providing needed encouragement/support.

In the competency imagery strategy, students superimposed images of past mastery upon present challenges. In the cognitive rehearsal assignment, students were asked to realistically identify significant personal strengths and then note evidences for the accuracy of their observations. This exercise tends to internalize appreciation for unique strengths. As related to the third pillar, students concluded the self-esteem block by inventorying moral strengths and weaknesses, and then setting personality and character goals.

Depression prevention skills included cognitive restructuring relative to depressing events and pleasant events scheduling (Lewinsohn, Munoz, Youngren and Zeiss, 1986). The latter requires individuals to identify activities that have been pleasant in the past, then identify those that could still be pleasant, and finally make a plan to regularly engage in some of those activities. The assumption is that students under stress begin to eliminate pleasant activities that tend to keep the mood elevated. Since a pessimistic explanatory style in college has been linked to poorer adult health decades later (Peterson, Seligman, and Vaillant, 1994), participants were taught how to attribute difficult outcomes to external, specific, and temporary factors.

The course finished with relapse prevention training, where students identified high-risk situations and made a plan to cope with them using the skills they had learned in the course.

Across interventions, anxiety and depression seemed to be most responsive to change. The fact that improvements have generally been noted on various measures, even though the pre-test scores showed low symptoms of depression, anxiety, hostility/anger, and low self-esteem, suggest the promise of the SIT model for maintaining and improving mental health among mentally healthy college students, and perhaps preventing mental illness.

Wider Applications

The initial successes in teaching coping skills offers promise of dissemination through additional applications on university campuses. For example, one motivated and enterprising student was unable to enroll in the above course. Since the skills had been detailed in the aforementioned resources, she was able to take the course as an independent study, under the instructor's direction. To increase interest, she recruited her roommate and sister to form a study group under her direction. Consistent with observations that teachers usually learn more than the students, she indicated that she gained much from teaching the skills as she herself practiced them.

Similar interventions could be offered by mental health professionals and/or properly prepared faculty and peers in residential halls, classes, student health centers, counseling centers, fraternities, and sororities. For example, Deckro and colleagues (2002) taught ten cognitive and relaxation skills to college students in six sessions with resulting decreases in anxiety and stress, suggesting the potential for briefer educational interventions.

DeArmond and Marsh (1984) have cited the need for mental health professionals to work in partnership with students, including peer educators. They add: "The campus is an ideal setting in which to develop preventive strategies that may later find their way into the community-at-large" (p. 678). Such efforts might include primary and high schools, hospital-based patient and community education, and worksite health promotion.

While some might raise concerns about coping skills being taught by those who are not mental health professionals, several prominent mental health professionals encourage their involvement. For example, Price (1982, p. 42) notes that it is "within the province of educators, parents, psychologists, and health professionals to study and modify…psychological determinants" of illness. Glasser writes: "We recognize that most of the gut-level mental health work in this country is done by people without extensive training, such as parents…, teachers, etc…The major difference between therapy and common guidance that is effective is in intensity, not kind" (1975, pp. xxvii-xxviii).

Regarding the cognitive restructuring upon which so many effective interventions are based, Ellis asserts that a therapist, a teacher, or even a book "can help people replace the self-chosen thoughts that needlessly create serious emotional difficulties" (Ellis and Harper, 1975, p.x). Although his cognitive-behavioral procedures were originally developed for clinical applications, he believes that the future of such approaches "is likely to reside more in its mass applications and its educational procedures than in its use for individual and group psychotherapy" (Dryden and Ellis, 1986, pp. 261-262).

These comments seem especially relevant given the fact that mental health needs are overwhelming the present supply of mental health professionals, and this situation is expected to worsen (Albee and Gullotta, 1986; Christensen and Jacobson, 1994; NIMH, 1990). To this supply shortage, we add the fact that some are unable to afford treatment, are unaware of symptoms and treatment options, or are influenced by myths and stigma surrounding mental illness.

Integrated College-Based Programs

Muerher and Koretz (1992, p. 111) write: "With notable exceptions, universal interventions tend to be information oriented, brief, and lacking the intensity likely to significantly alter the complex processes leading to mental disorders and related problems. Although the information may be a necessary and useful first step for prevention, it is rarely sufficient for lasting behavioral change. At a minimum, effective intervention requires acquisition of knowledge and skills, motivation to use them correctly and consistently, and continual reinforcement for using them." The Stress and the Healthy Mind course attempted to address such concerns. The small-group format of this course allowed for the cultivation of a safe, motivating climate and effective skill-practice and processing.

However, from an economic perspective, the small class size of this type of intervention is also a limitation. Larger courses, while not allowing the intimate contact with students, can still play a role in primary prevention. One such course at the University of Maryland, *Controlling Stress and Tension*, has been taught to groups ranging in size from 25-200 students since the 1970's and is thought to be the first undergraduate stress management course taught at an American university (D. A. Giordano, personal communication, November 15, 1995). Largely a lecture course with some assigned homework for skill practice, this course overviews theoretical and practical issues, including the nature of stressors, the psychophysiology of the stress response, the impact of stress on mental and physical health, mental illness and treatment resources, and a variety of traditional stress management skills (detailed in Schiraldi and Brown, 2002). These skills include:

- Breath control to prevent the deleterious effects of hyperventilation
- Rudimentary cognitive restructuring and self-esteem skills
- Systematic relaxation strategies (meditation, progressive muscular relaxation, etc.)
- Moderate, regular exercise
- Meal planning
- Sleep hygiene
- Problem solving
- Interpersonal skills
- Time management
- Yoga and tai chi

While symptom reductions from such a course are less impressive, it is believed that such courses can increase motivation and prepare people for the more effective small group interventions.

CONCLUSION

Other Directions for Future Research

Another direction for preventing mental illness is to help individuals build inner strengths, which is the focus of the positive psychology movement (Seligman and Csikszentmihalyi, 2000). Toward this end, Schiraldi is implementing a University Honors Program course in resilience. This course will explore the aspects of resilient survivors and teach skills relating to the strengths of resilient coping. Resilient inner strengths identified in the research include meaning and purpose, self-esteem/efficacy, planning and problem solving skills, adaptability, optimism, morality, happiness, and social responsibility (for review see Richardson and Waite, 2002). Research will explore resulting changes in resilience, anxiety, and depression. Resilience training with adults in the workplace has already improved scores in resilience, self-esteem, internal locus of control, purpose in life, and interpersonal relationships (Waite, 2001) and offers hope that similar successes might be realized in university settings.

Finally, psycho education might be incorporated into existing drug education classes. Analyzing the data of a Centers for Disease Control survey of over 43,000 adults, Schoenborn and Horm (1993) concluded that there might be better success at reducing drug use (i.e., heavy drinking and smoking) if stress-related mental health issues, such as depression and other negative moods, were addressed in tandem with more traditional health education approaches. Interestingly, Botvin and colleagues (Botvin, Baker, Dusenbury, Botvin and Diaz, 1995) have shown that classroom teachers can help reduce drug use in seventh-grade students by teaching skills to resist social pressure, build self-esteem, manage anxiety, communicate effectively, develop relationships, and assert themselves—rather than providing much information about the health risks of drug use. They suggest that building personal competence (e.g., coping skills) might be a necessary factor in drug abuse prevention programs.

STUDENT STRESS CALENDAR

(From the ResLifePro website: http://www.residentassistant.com/reslifepro/ListofStudent ConcernsbyMonth.html)

September

- *Homesickness* - especially for freshmen.
- *Roommate conflicts* caused by personality differences, lack of understanding and unwillingness to compromise, or new experience of having to live with someone for the first time.
- *Initial adjustment to academic environment* - feelings of inadequacy and inferiority develop because of the discrepancy between high school status, grades, and initial college performance. Class size (particularly in mass lecture halls), lack of personal attention by professors, and performance expectations are also major factors.
- *Values exploration* - students are confronted with questions of conscience over conflict areas such as experimentation with alcohol, tobacco, and other drugs, morality, sexuality, race, religion and social expectations.
- *New social life adjustments* - including new freedom of not having to check with family members about what time to be in, having the opportunity to experience new areas, making your own decisions on when to conduct social activities and establishing yourself in a peer group.
- *Initial social rejections* - creates feelings of inadequacy when not immediately accepted in a peer group.
- *In-loco parentis problems* - students feel depressed because of real or perceived problems in restrictive policies and regulations of the University.
- *Campus familiarization* - includes becoming familiar with the campus, classrooms, buildings, meeting places. This is especially true on large campuses.
- *Long-distance relationships* - torn between being loyal to your significant other back in the home town and going out with new people. Can the expectations of both people involved be adequately met?
- *Inadequate feelings*, especially those of being left out, ignored, or resented, by the students who were assigned to temporary accommodations. This is especially true if the temporary area is a favorite common area for students.
- *Financial adjustment* involves adjusting to a somewhat tighter budget now that they are in school as opposed to when they were still living at home. Students who are supporting themselves have to adjust to budgeting their money, also.
- *International student adjustment problems* - experiencing a sense of confusion, vulnerability and a lack of any advocate in higher positions while trying to make a successful cultural and academic transition.

- *Family problems* seem amplified because the student may be either caught in the middle, relied on for the answer, or because they are so far away, feel helpless in helping reach a solution.
- *Adjusting to "Administrative Red Tape"* - students soon realize that it is usually a long and frustrating process when trying to find an answer to what seems to be a simple question, or trying to work something through the administrative process.

October

- *Academic stress from midterms* builds with great demand for studying and preparation. For some students this may be their first exam of the term. For many, the midterm workload pressures are followed by feelings of failure and loss of self-esteem.
- *Roommate problems* continue, but they are smaller in scope than in previous months.
- *Values exploration* continuing, especially in the area of sexuality.
- *Dating/non-dating/friendship* anxieties extremely high. Non-dating students sense a loss of self esteem because so much value seems to be placed upon dating by peers. For women and men who date, the pressure to perform sexually increases and consequently increases feelings of rejection, loneliness and guilt, and may lead to unwanted pregnancies and sexually transmitted diseases.
- *Homesickness* may still be felt by a number of students.
- *Job panic* for mid-year graduates starts with the onset of resume preparation, and off and on-campus interviewing.
- *Students decide to withdraw from school* because they realize college is not the place for them, they return home for personal reasons, or they transfer to another school.
- *Grief from not being a part of a group* develops because of underdeveloped social skills or lack of social groups.
- *Financial strain* sets in from lack of budgeting experience.
- *Homecoming blues* develop because of perceived social skill inadequacies, lack of feeling a part of social groups for social functions, and/or lack of ability/opportunity to participate in activities.
- *Graduate School Syndrome* starts to emerge for graduating seniors - signing up for graduate school exams, wondering if you will be accepted, wondering which schools to apply to and questioning whether graduate school is the right thing to do.
- *Time conflicts* between academic and social expectations emerges.
- *Adjusting to new study habits* includes not just being able to study the way they did in high school. More time and greater workload needs to be incorporated into their schedule for studying.
- *Disenchantment with school* - low reward level because students begin to realize that life at college is not as perfect as they were led to believe by family members, teachers and counselors. Old problems seem to continue and new ones are added. An external reality they had put their hopes on has failed them.

- *Advance enrollment planning* involves starting to think about what to take the following semester.
- *Room assignment planning* involves starting to think about your housing options for next semester.

November

- *Increasing thoughts/deliberation about suicide* occur from inability to cope with the pressures of academic and social expectations.
- *Academic pressure* begins to mount because of procrastination, difficulty of work assigned and lack of ability.
- *Pre-finals stress* starts to emerge as preparation begins for taking the exams.
- *Time management conflicts* continue.
- *Social apathy* causes frustration because of academic pressures.
- *Depression and anxiety* increase because of feelings that one should have adjusted to the college environment by how.
- *Economic anxieties* increase because funds from parents and summer earnings begin to run out, loans come due.
- Problems develop from *increased alcohol consumption* because students see this as an easy and acceptable way to relieve stress and from not knowing how to handle stress responsibly.
- *Pregnancies and sexually transmitted diseases* become a reality.
- *Roommate problems* may start to emerge again. This is mostly due to the pressure of school; tempers become shorter and people are less tolerant of others.
- *Deteriorating health starts to affect student performance.* Reasons include: change in weather; lack of physical exercise, sleep, proper eating habits; an increase in the use of alcohol, tobacco, and other drugs; poor stress management.
- *Students have given up making attempts to establish new friendships* beyond two or three parasitic relationships.
- *Room reassignment tensions* increase: Where will I live, who will I live with, should I move out, what do I tell my roommate?
- *Living unit tension* causes uncomfortable feelings with residents. Results from apathy, academic pressures, need for vacation from school.

- **December**
- *Increasing thought/deliberations about suicide* occur from inability to cope with the pressures of academic and social expectations.
- *Final exam pressures* including anxiety, fear and guilt increase as exams approach and papers come due. Increased use of alcohol and drugs is related.
- *Extracurricular time strains* - seasonal parties, concerts, social service projects and religious activities drain student energies.
- *Financial worries* occur with the thought of Christmas gifts and travel.

- *Pre-holiday blues* emerge, especially for those who have concerns for family members, those who have no home to visit or cannot go home, and for those who prefer not to go home because of family conflicts.
- *Friendship tensions* become high with onset of final exams.
- *Pressure increases to perform sexually* because of the approach of vacation and the extended separation.

January

- *Anxiety about second semester performance* begins because they did not go as well as expected the previous semester, and have added pressure of doing well to be able to stay in school or to keep their grades competitive with their colleagues.
- *Some students lose a loved one, friend, or significant other* by death or separation over break and find it difficult to share the happiness and joy others experience from their breaks.
- *Moving into a new environment* causes feelings of intrusion because students move into a unit where most of the friendships have been established, priorities set and expectations understood. Unfamiliarity with campus also creates some anxiety.
- *Money problems begin* because many students were unable to find jobs over the break.
- *Post-holiday depression* occurs at the beginning of the semester because students are away from the home security and positive strokes of friends and family members.
- *Some students experience unwanted weight gains* over the break with the holiday foods and "home cooking".
- *Reincorporating social and academic life* is difficult at first with not having to worry about school for an extended period.

February

- *Hourly exams* and other academic pressures approach
- Depending upon the weather, some people will experience *Cabin Fever* if the weather forces them to stay inside for a lengthy period of time. With the lack of organized activities to compensate for this, anti-social behavior sometimes occurs, such as excessive property damage, increased use of alcohol, tobacco, and other drugs and increased sexual activity and sexual assaults.
- *Vocational choice anxieties* set in with the onset of job interviews.
- *Worry of hunting for summer job begins.* This is especially high for students who were unable to work during the winter break.
- *Relationship anxieties* increase as couples experience pressure to increase commitment levels or end relationships.
- *Fall housing planning* begins with trying tentatively to decide about living arrangements for the upcoming year.

March

- *Increasing thoughts/deliberations about suicide* occur from inability to cope with the pressures of academic and social expectations.
- *Academic pressures increase* with approach of midterm exams.
- As the end of the semester approaches, *many sudents react by increasing sexual activity and/or use of alcohol, tobacco, and other drugs*. This can cause biological and behavioral problems.
- *Existential crises for seniors* - Must I leave school? Is my education worth anything? Was my major a mistake?
- *Senior job interviewing* causes increased level of anxiety.
- *Living arrangement anxieties* occur with the forcing of decisions - Should I move out? Live in the same building? Stay with the same roommate? Will a friend be left out?
- Summer job hunting will be heavy over spring break. *Worry about finding a job* or not finding one will cause severe anxiety.
- *Trying to find money to use for Spring Break* is a problem, especially when your peers are going to a place other than home and you are unable to join them. Students may also experience anxiety from not having a place to go for break periods.

April

- *Increasing thoughts/deliberations about suicide* occur from inability to cope with the pressures of academic and social expectations.
- *Academic pressures increase* with the end of the semester approaching.
- *Papers and hourly exams* approach.
- With the weather becoming nicer, there is a *fear of sexual assault*.
- *Summer job pressures continue.*
- *Senior job recruitment panic* Continues.
- *Financial strain* from spring break affects social life.
- Many students are *forced to select a major* and are not sure what field they would like to enter.
- *Social life pressures increase* during this period - formal dances, parties, concerts.
- With Spring arriving, peers may pressure students to be in a relationship. Many students go through feelings of rejection, fear of rejection, lack of self esteem, or envy towards friends who are in relationships.
- *Frustration rises from illness or depression* due to drastic weather changes. Causes colds, lethargic feelings, feelings of depression and limits their social commitments.
- As the pressures build, *students tend to become disenchanted* with many normal services and food service is the primary target. They tend to get tired of eating "the same old" institutional food.

May/June

- *Increased thoughts, deliberations about suicide* occur from inability to cope with the pressures of academic and social expectations.

- Anxiety develops because of the realization that the year is ending and a *deficiency in a number of academic areas* still exists.

- *Finals Pressures* are at a critical level with papers, take-home tests and studying. Some of the major effects of this pressure include: increased use of coffee, No-Doz and amphetamines; increase in use of alcohol, tobacco, and other drugs; increased sexual activity and sexual assaults; lack of proper diet; lack of sleep; and a lower tolerance level with friends/peers.

- *Senior job panic* sbout employment (or lack of) increases as well as trying to determine how to finance oneself until the first paycheck arrives.

- *Summer job pressures* increase for those who have not yet found one.

- *Anxiety for those couples who will be parting for the summer.* Also, the fear that their significant other will find someone else while they are separated.

- *Depression* over having to leave the friends and people that you have grown close to over the school year.

- *Anxiety of having to go home ater having been independent* the past year, especially if they are having conflicts with family members.

REFERENCES

Abouserie,R.(1994). Sources and levels of stress in relation to locus of control and self esteem in university students. Educational Psychology, 14, 323–330.

Albee, G.W. and Gulotta, T.P. (1986). Facts and fallacies about primary prevention. Journal of Primary Prevention, 6, 207-218.

Amar, A.F. (2004). Prevalence estimates of violence in the dating experiences of college women. Journal of the National Black Nurses Association, 15, 23-31.

Anda R. F., Fellitti, V.J., Chapman, D. P., Croft, J. B., Williamson, D. F., Santelli, J., Dietz, P. M., and Marks, J. S. (2001). Abused boys, battered mothers, and maleinvolvement in teen pregnancy. Pediatrics, 107 (2), E19.

Archer, J., and Lamnin, A. (1985). An investigation of personal and academic stressors in College campuses. Journal of College Student Personnel, 26, 210-215.

Astin, A. W. (1993). What matters in college: Four critical years revisited. San Francisco: Jossey-Bass.

Baum, A., and Posluszny, D. M. (1999). Health psychology: Mapping biobehavioral contributions to health and illness. Annual Review of Psychology, 50, 137-163.

Baumeister, R. F., and Leary, M. R. (1995). The need to belong: Desire for interpersonal attachments as a fundamental human motivation. Psychological Bulletin, 117, 497-529.

Beck, A. T. (1967). Depression: Clinical, experimental and theoretical aspects. New York: Hoeber.

Beck, R., Taylor, C., and Robbins, M. (2003). Missing home: Sociotropy and autonomy and their relationship to depression and homesickness in college freshmen. Anxiety, Stress, and Coping, 16, 155-166.

Bernard, L. C. and Krupat, E. (1994). Health Psychology: Biopsychosocial Factors in Health and Illness. New York: Harcourt Brace College Publishers.

Blanchard, E.B., Rowell, D., Kuhn, E., Rogers, R. and Wittrock, D. (2005). Posttraumatic stress and depressive symptoms in a college population one year after the September 11 attacks: the effect of proximity. Behavior Research and Therapy, 43,143-50.

Borkovec, T. D., Wilkinson, L., Folensbee, R., and Lerman, C. (1983). Stimulus control applications to the treatment of worry. Behavior Research and Therapy, 21, 247-251.

Bosco, S. and Harvey, D. (2003). Effects of terror attacks on employment plans and anxiety levels of college students. College Student Journal, 37, 438-447.

Botvin, G. J., Baker, E., Dusenbury, L., Botvin, E. M., and Diaz, T. (1995). Long-term follow-up results of a randomized drug abuse prevention trial in a white middle-class population. Journal of the American Medical Association, 273, 1106-1112.

Britton, B.K. and Tesser, A. (1991). Effects of time-management practices on college grades. Journal of Educational Psychology, 83, 405-410.

Brooks, D. (2001). The organization kid. The Atlantic Monthly, 287(4), 40-54.

Brown, S.L. and Schiraldi, G.R. (2000). Reducing symptoms of anxiety and depression: Combined results of a cognitive-behavioral college course. Poster session presented at the Anxiety Disorders Association of America NationalConference, Washington, DC.

Brown, S. L. and Schiraldi, G. R. (2004). Reducing subclinical symptoms of anxiety and depression: A comparison of two college courses. American Journal of Health Education,35 (3), 158-164.

Brown, S.L., Schiraldi, G.R., and Wrobleski, M. (2003). Psychological strengths as correlates of happiness and health in college students. Poster session presented at the Second International Positive Psychology Summit, Washington, DC.

Carroll, F. (2005, January 27). No escape from 'helicopter parents': Constant hovering can kick up a cloud of troubles. *Albany Times Journal.* Retrieved July 24, 2005 from *http://seattlepi.nwsource.com/lifestyle/209473_copterparents.html*

Carveth, J.A., Gesse, T., and Moss, N. (1996). Survival strategies for nurse-midwifery students. Journal of Nurse-Midwifery, 41(1), 50-54.

Chapell, M., Casey, D., DelaCruz, C., Ferrell, J., Forman, J., Lipkin, R., Newsham, M., Sterling, M., and Whittaker, S. (2004). Bullying in college by students and teachers. Adolescence, 39, 53-64.

Christensen, A. and Jacobson, N. S. (1994). Who (or what) can do psychotherapy? Psychological Science, 5(1), 8-13.

Christie, N. and Dinham, S. (1991). Institutional and external influences on social integration in the freshman year. Journal of Higher Education, 62(4), 413.

Churaman, C.V. (1988). College student use of consumer credit. Proceedings of the American Council on Consumer Interests. Columbia, Mo:ACCI. 107-113.

Coburn, K. L. and Treeger, M. L. (2003). Letting Go: A Parents' Guide to Understanding the College Years (4th ed.). New York: Harper Perennial.

Coie, J. D., Watt, N. F., West, S. G., Hawkins, J. D., Asarnow, J. R., Markman, H. J., Ramey, S. L., Shure, M. B., and Long, B. (1993). The science of prevention: A conceptual framework and some directions for a national research program. American Psychologist,48, 1013-1022.

Collins, P. (2005). Financial Issues Overwhelm Majority of College Students. TheGuardian Online. Accessed from:
http://www.theguardianonline.com/media/paper373/news/2005/05/04/News/Financial.Iss ues.Overwhelm.Majority.Of.College.Students-947367.shtml.

Cordon, I.M. (1977) Stress. California State University, Northridge. Accessed from: *http://www.csun.edu/~vcpsy00h/students/stress.htm* on July 19, 2005.

DeArmond, M. M., and Marsh, K. F. (1984). Preventive psychiatry on the college campus. Psychiatric Annals, 14, 671-678.

Deckro, G. R., Ballinger, K. M., Hoyt, M., Wilcher, M., Dusek, J., Myers, P., Greenberg, B., Rosenthal, D. S., and Benson, H. (2002). The evaluation of a mind/body intervention to reduce psychological distress and perceived stress in college students. Journal of American College Health, 50, 281-287.

Department of Health and Human Services. (1999). Mental health: A report of the Surgeon General. (DHHS Publication No. ADM 01702401653-5), Washington, DC: U.S. Government Printing Office.

Dietz, P.M., Spitz, A. M., Anda, R. F., Williamson, D. F., McMahon, P. M., Santelli, J. S., Nordenberg, D. G., Felitti, V. J., and Kendrick, J. S. (1999). Unintended pregnancy among adult women exposed to abuse or household dysfunction during their childhood. Journal of the American Medical Association, 282 (14), 1359-64.

Donnelly, T.T. and Long, B.C. (2003). Stress discourse and Western biomedical ideology: rewriting stress. Issues in Mental Health Nursing, 24, 397-408.

Dyden, W. and Ellis, A. (l988). Rational-emotive therapy. In K. Dobson (Ed.), Handbook of cognitive-behavioral therapies. New York: Guilford. 214-271.

Edelmann, R. J. (1992). Anxiety theory, research and intervention in clinical and health psychology. New York: Wiley.

Ellis, A. and Harper, R. (1975). A new guide to rational living. North Hollywood, CA: Wilshire Book.

Engel, G.L. (1980). The clinical application of the biopsychosocial model. American Journal of Psychiatry, 137, 535-544.

Falk, D. (1975). Campus environments, student stress, and campus planning. In B. Bloom (Ed.), Psychological stress in the campus community. New York: Behavioral Publications.

Feldman, K. A. and Newcomb, T. M. (1969). The Impact of College on Students. San Francisco: Jossey-Bass.

Felitti, V. J. (2002). The relation between adverse childhood experiences and adult health: Turning gold into lead. Permanente Journal, 6 (1), 1-7. Electronic version retrieved at: *www.kaiserpermanente.org/medicine/permjournal/winter02/goldtolead.html*

Fenzel, L. M. (2005). Multivariate analyses of predictors of heavy episodic drinking and drinking-related problems among college students. Journal of College Student Development, 46, (2), 126-140.

Fiebert, M.S. and Gonzalez, D.M. (1997). College women who initiate assaults on their male partners and the reasons offered for such behavior. Psychological Reports, 80, 583-590.

Finding Hope and Help: College Student and Depression Pilot Initiative Fact Sheets. (2005). Retrieved June 17, 2005 from the National Mental Health Association's Campaign for America's Mental Health website: *http://www.nmha.org/camh/college/fact_sheets.cfm*.

Fombonne, E. (1998). Increased rates of psychological disorders in youth. European Archives of Psychiatry and Clinical Neuroscience, 248 (1), 14-21.

Friedman, H. S. and Booth-Kewley, S. (1987). The "disease-prone personality": A meta-analytic view of the construct. American Psychologist, 42, 539-555.

Friedman, M. J. and Schnurr, P. P. (1995). The relationship between trauma, posttraumatic stress disorder, and physical health. In M. J. Friedman, D. S. Charney, and A. Y. Deutch (Eds.), Neurobiological and clinical consequences of stress. Philadelphia: Lipincott Raven.

Gaertner. L. and Foshee, V. (1999). Commitment and the perpetration of relationship violence. Personal Relationships, 6, 227-239.

Galea, S., Ahern J., Resnick, H., Kilpatrick, D., Bucuvalas, M., Gold, J. and Vlahov D. (2002). New England Journal of Medicine, 346, 982-989.

Gallagher, R. (2004). National survey of counseling center directors. Alexandria, VA: International Association of Counseling Services.

Gallagher, R. M. and Cariati, S. (2002). The pain-depression conundrum: Bridging the body and mind. Medscape Today Clinical Update [On-line,. Available: Medscape.com (Article No. 441743).

Gelles, R. (1981). The myth of the battered husband. In Walsh, R. and Pocs, O. eds. Marriage and Family. Duskin:Guilford.

Gibbs, N. (2005, February 21). Parents behaving badly. Times Magazine, 165(8).

Glasser, W. (1975). Reality therapy: A new approach to psychiatry. New York: Harper and Row.

Gray, H. M. and Foshee, V. (1997). Adolescent dating violence. Differences between one-sided and mutually violent profiles. Journal of Interpersonal Violence, 12, 126-142.

Henry, R.A., Weber, J.G., and Yarbough, D. (2001). Money and management practices of college students. College Student Journal, 4, 244-247.

Hillis, S. D., Anda, R. F. , Felitti, V. J., Nordenberg, D., and Marchbanks, P. A. (2000). Adverse childhood experiences and sexually transmitted diseases in men and women: a retrospective study. Pediatrics, 106 (1), E11.

Hobfoll, S. and London, P. (1986). The relationship of self-concept and social support to emotional distress among women during war. Journal of Social and Clinical Psychology, 4, 189-203.

Hobfoll, S. and Walfisch, S. (l986). Coping with a threat to life: A longitudinal study of self-concept, social support, and psychological distress. American Journal of Community Psychology, 12(1), 87-99.

Holden, G. W., and Delville, Y. (2005). Isolation and the stress of being bullied. Journal of Adolescence, 28(3), 343-357.

Holder, K. (2005, Summer). Helicopter Parents. UC Davis Magazine Online, 22(4). Retrieved July 24, 2005 from *http://wwwucdmag.ucdavis.edu/current/feature_1d.html*

Holub, T. (2003). Credit card usage and debt among college and university students. ERIC Digest. Retrieved June 24, 2005 from *http://www.ericdigests.org/20032/credit.html*.

Howard, D.E. and Wang, M. Q. (2003a). Risk profiles of adolescent girls who were victims of dating violence. Adolescence, 38(149), 1-14.

Howard, D.E. and Wang, M. Q. (2003b). Psychosocial factors associated with adolescent boys' reports of dating violence. Adolescence, 38(151), 519-533.

Howe, N., and Strauss, W. (2003). Millennials go to college: Strategies for a new generation on campus. Washington, DC: American Association of Collegiate Registrars.

Howe, N., and Strauss, W. (2000). Millennials rising: The next great generation. New York: Vintage Books.

Hudd, S.S., Dumlao, J., Erdmann-Sager, D., Murray, D., Phan, E., Soukas, N and Yokozuka. (2000). Stress at college: Effects on health habits, health status and self-esteem. College Student Journal, 34, 217-228.

Insel, P. M., and Roth, W. T. (1985). Core concepts in health. (4th ed.). Palo Alto, CA: Mayfield.

Jacobson, S. (2003). Book Review: Physical consequences of depression. The New England Journal of Medicine, 348(6), 569-570. Retrieved June 1, 2005 from journal website.

Joo, S., Grable, J.E. and Bagwell, D.C. (2003). Credit card attitudes and behaviors of college students. College Student Journal, 37, 405-420.

Kadison, R. and DiGeronimo, T. F. (2004). College of the overwhelmed: the campus mental health crisis and what to do about it. San Francisco, CA: Jossey-Bass.

Kazantzis, N. and Flett, R. (1998). Family cohesion and age as determinants of homesickness in university students. Social Behavior and Personality, 26, 195-202.

Kessler, R.C., McGonagle, K.A., Zhao, S., Nelson, C.B., Hughes, M., Eshleman, S., Wittchen, H., and Kencler, K.S. (1994). Lifetime and 12-month prevalence of DSM-III-R psychiatric disorders in the United States. Archives of General Psychiatry, 51, 8-19.

Kitzrow, M. A. (2003). The mental health needs of today's college students: challengesand recommendations. NASPA Journal, 41(1), 167-181. Retrieved June 1, 2005 from NASPA website.

Klerman, G. L. and Weissman, M. M. (1989). Increasing rates of depression. Journal of the American Medical Association, 261, 2229-2235.

Kodama, C.M., McEwen, M.K., Liang, C.T.H. and Lee, S. (2001). A Theoretical Examination of Psychosocial Issues for Asian Pacific American Students. NASPA Journal, 38(4), art1.

Kook, A. I., Mizruchin, A., Odnopozov, N., Gershon, H., and Segev, Y. (1995). Depression and immunity: The biochemical interrelationship between the central nervous system and the immune system. Biological Psychiatry, 37, 817-819.

Kronfol, Z., Starkman, M., and Nair, M. (1991). Natural killer cell activity in major depression and Cushing's syndrome. Biological Psychiatry, 29(S), 118A.

Lane, K and Gwartney-Gibbs, P. (1985). Violence in the context of dating and sex. Journal of Family Issues, 6, 45-59.

Lazarus, R.S., and Folkman, S. (1984). Stress, Appraisal and Coping. New York: Guilford.

Lazarus, R.S., and Launier, R. (1978). Stress-related transactions between person and environment. In L. A. Pervin and M. Lewis, eds. Perspectives in Interactional Psychology. New York: Plenum.

Lazarus, R. S. (1966). Psychological Stress and the Coping Process. New York: McGraw-Hill.

Lazarus, R. S. and Cohen, J. B. (1977). Environmental Stress. In I. Altman and J.F.Wohlwill (eds.), Human Behavior and Environment. (Vol. 2.). New York: Plenum.

Lee, H. J. (2002). Psychosocial variables associated with resilience among mothers-daughters dyads. Unpublished doctoral dissertation, University of Maryland.

Lee, R. M. and Robbins, S. B. (1998). The relationship between social connectedness and anxiety, self-esteem, and social identity. Journal of Counseling Psychology, 45, 338–345.

Levine, A. and Cureton, J. S. (1998). What we know about today's college students. About Campus: Enriching the student learning experience, 3(1), 4-9.

Lewinsohn, P., Munoz, R., Youngren, M., and Zeiss, A. (1986). Control your Depression. New York: Prentice Hall.

Lewis, D.E. (2001). Students graduate to uncertainty. The Boston Globe, C1-C2.

Lipsky, M.J., Kassinove, H., and Miller, N.J. (1980). Effects of rational-emotive therapy, rational role reversal, and rational-emotive imagery on the emotional adjustment of community mental health center patients. Journal of Consulting and Clinical Psychology, 48, 366-374.

Loyal, T. (2002). Don't leave college without it. Mother Jones, March/April.

MacGeorge, E.L., Samter, W., Feng, B., Gillihan, S.J. and Graves, A.R. (2004). Stress, social support, and health among college students after September 11, 2001. Journal of College Student Development, 45, 655-670.

Maes, M., Bosmans, E., Suy, E., Vandervorst, C., Dejonckheere, C., and Raus, J. (1991). Antiphospholipid antinuclear, Epstein-Barr and cytomegalovirus antibodies and soluble interleukin-2 receptors in depressive patients. Journal of Affective Disorders, 21, 133-140.

Marano, H.E. (2004). Leadership Exchange. Retrieved June 17, 2005 from National Association of Student Personnel Administrators website: www.napsa.org/membership/leader_ex_pdf/MentalHealthCrisis.pdf

McAndrew, F. T. (1998). The measurement of 'rootedness' and the prediction of attachment to hometowns in college students. Journal of Environmental Psychology, 18, 409-417.

McDaniel, J. S. (1992). Psychoimmunology: Implications for future research. Southern Medical Journal, 85, 388-396, 402.

McEwen, B. S. (2000). Allostatsis and allostatic load: Implications for neuropsychopharmacology. Neuropsychopharmacology, 22 (2), 108-124.

Meichenbaum, D. (1985). Stress inoculation training. New York: Pergamon.

Meichenbaum, D. and Fitzpatrick, D. (1993). A constructivist narrative perspective on stress and coping: Stress inoculation applications. In L. Goldberger and S. Breznitz (Eds.), Handbook of stress: Theoretical and clinical aspects (2nd ed.) New York: The Free Press. 706-723.

Miller, M., Hemenway, D., and Wechsler, H. (1999). Guns at college. Journal of American College Health; 48, 3-6.

Misra R. and McKean M. (2000). College students' academic stress and its relation to their anxiety, time management, and leisure satisfaction. American Journal of HealthStudies.

Misra, R., McKean, M., West, S., and Russo, T. (2000). Academic stress of ollege students: Comparison of student and faculty perceptions. College Student Journal, 34, 236–245.

Monroe, S.M., Simons, A.D. (1991). Diathesis-stress theories in the context of life stress research: implications for the depressive disorders. Psychological Bulletin, 110, 406-25.

Mori, S. C. (2000). Addressing the mental health concerns of international students. Journal of Counseling and Development, 78, 137–144.

Muehrer, P. and Koretz, D. S. (1992). Issues in preventive intervention research. Current Directions in Psychological Science, 1, 109-112.

National Institute of Mental Health. (1990). Mental health, United States, 1990. R.W. Manderscheid and M.A. Sonnenschein, (Eds.). (DHHS Publication No. ADM-90-1708). Washington DC: U.S. Government Printing Office.

Nellie Mae. (2000). Credit card usage continues among college students. Retrieved June 24, 2005 from *http://www.nelliemae.com/library/cc_use.html*.

Newton, F. B. (1998). The stressed student: How can we help? About Campus: Enriching the student learning experience, 3(2), 4-10.

O'Malley, M. Educating undergraduates on using credit cards. Nellie Mae. Retrieved June 16, 2005 from *http://www.nelliemae.com/library/cc_use.html*.

Parker, G. R., Cowen, E. L., Work, W. C., and Wyman, P. A. (1990). Test correlates of stress resilience among urban school children. Journal of Primary Prevention, 11(1), 19-35.

Pascarella, E. T., and Terenzini, P. T. (1991). How College Affects Students. San Francisco: Jossey-Bass.

Paul, E. L. and Brier, S. (2001). Friendsickness in the transition to college: Precollege predictors and college adjustments correlates. Journal of Counseling and Development, 79, 77-87.

Pearlin, L.I. (1989). The sociological study of stress. Journal of Health and Social Behavior, 35, 134-142.

Pearlin, L. I. (1999). Stress and mental health: A conceptual overview. In T. L. Scheid (Ed.), A handbook for the study of mental health: Social contexts, theories, and systems (pp. 161–175). New York: Cambridge University Press.

Pearlin, L. I. (1982). The social contexts of stress. In L. Goldberger and S. reznitz, eds. Handbook of Stress: Theoretical and Clinical Aspects. New York: The Free Press.

Pennebaker, J. W. (1997). Opening up: The healing power of expressing emotion. New York: Guilford.

Peterson, C., Seligman, M. E. P., and Vaillant, G. E. (1988). Pessimistic explanatory style is a risk factor for physical illness: A thirty-five-year longitudinal study. Journal of Personality and Social Psychology, 55, 23-27.

Pressman, S., Cohen, S., Miller, G. E., Rabin, B. S., Barker, A., and Treanor, J. (2005). Loneliness, social network size, and immune response to influenza vaccination in college freshman. Health Psychology, 24, 297-306.

Price, V. A. (1982) Type A behavior pattern: A model for research and practice. New York: Academic Press.

Prigerson, H. G., Bierhals, A. J., Kasl, S. V., Reynolds, C. F., Shear, M. K., Day, N., Beery, L. C., Newson, J. T., and Jacobs, S. (1997). Traumatic grief as a risk factor for mental and physical morbidity. American Journal of Psychiatry, 154 (5), 616-623.

Reeve, J. (2001). Understanding motivation and emotion (3rd ed.). Fort Worth: Harcourt College Publishers.

Rice, P. L. (1992). Stress and health. (2nd ed.). Pacific Grove, California: Brooks/Cole.

Richardson, G. E. and Waite, P. J. (2002). Mental health promotion through resilience and resiliency education. International Journal of Emergency Mental Health, 4, (1), 65-75.

Rosenberg, M. (1965). Society and the adolescent self-image. Princeton, NJ: Princeton University Press.

Rosenberg, M. (1979). Conceiving the self. New York: Basic.

Rosenberg, M. (1985). Self-concept and psychological well-being in adolescence. In R. Leahy (Ed.), The development of the self. San Diego, CA: Academic Press. 205-246.

Ross, S. E., Niebling, B. C., and Heckert, T. M. (1999). Sources of stress among college students. College Student Journal, 33, 312-18.

Sax, L. J. (1997). Health trends among college freshmen. Journal of American College Health, 45(6), 252-263. Retrieved June 1, 2005 from Academic Search Premier database. Schlenger, W.E, Caddell, J.M., Ebert, L., Jordan, B.K., Rourke, K.M., Wilson, D., Thalji, L., Dennis, J.M., Fairbank, J.A. and Kulka, R.A. (2002). Psychological reactions to terrorist attacks: findings from the National Study of Americans' Reactions to September 11. Journal of the American Medical Association, 288, 581- 588.

Schiraldi, G. R. (1990). Hope and help for depression: A practical guide. Ellicott City, Maryland: Chevron.

Schiraldi, G. R. (1996). Facts to relax by: A guide to relaxation and stress reduction. Provo, UT: Utah Valley Regional Medical Center.

Schiraldi, G. R. (1997). Conquer anxiety, worry, and nervous fatigue: A guide to greater peace. Ellicott City, Maryland: Chevron.

Schiraldi, G. R. (2000). The post-traumatic stress disorder source book: A guide to healing, recovery and growth. Los Angeles: Lowell House.

Schiraldi, G. R. (2001). The self-esteem workbook. Oakland, CA: New Harbinger.

Schiraldi, G. R. and Brown, S. L. (2001a). Primary prevention for mental health: A stress inoculation training course for functioning adults. American Journal of Health Education, 32, (5), 279-287.

Schiraldi, G. R. and Brown, S.L. (2001b). Primary prevention for mental health: Results of an exploratory cognitive-behavioral college course. Journal of Primary Prevention, 22 (1), 55-66.

Schiraldi, G.R. and Brown, S. L. (2002). Preventive mental health education for functioning adults: Stress, coping and mental health courses at the University of Maryland. International Journal of Emergency Mental Health, 4(1), 57-63.

Schiraldi, G. R. and Kerr, M. H. (2002). The anger management sourcebook. Chicago: McGraw-Hill/Contemporary.

Schiraldi, G. R., Spalding,T.W., and Hofford, C.W. (1998). Expanding health educators' roles to meet critical needs in stress management and mental health. Journal of Health Education, 29, 68-76.

Schoenborn, C. A. and Horm, J. (1993). Negative moods as correlates of smoking and heavier rinking: implications for health promotion. Advance Data from Vital and Health Statisitcs of the Centers for Disease Control and Prevention/National Center for Health Statistics, No. 236.

Schoenherr, N. (2005, July 5). Letting go as children head off to college for the first time. Washington University Record. Retrieved July 24, 2005 from ***http://news-info.wustl.edu/tips/page/normal/5426.html***

Sealy, G. (2001). How we've changed. ABCNews.com. Retrieved on June 24, 2005 from http:abcnews.go.com/selections/DALflyNews/lifechange011017.html.

Sebastain, R. and Chaker, A.M. (2001). In financial district, constant reminders. The Wall Street Journal, C1, C14.

Seligman, M.E.P. (with K. Reivich, L. Jaycox and J. Gillham). (1995). The optimistic child. New York: Houghton Mifflin.

Seligman, M.E.P. and Csikszentmihalyi, M. (2000). Positive psychology: An introduction. American Psychologist, 55, 5-14.

Seligman, M. E. P., Schulman, P., DeRubeis, R. J., and Hollon, S. D. (1999). The prevention of depression and anxiety. Prevention and Treatment [On-line serial], 2. At *http://journals.apa.org/prevention/volume2/ pre0020008a.html/*

Selye, H. (1976). Stress in health and disease. Reading, MA: Butterworth. Seyle, H. (1976). The stress of life. (2nd ed.). New York: McGraw-Hill.

Selye, H. (1982). History and present status of the stress concept. In L. Goldberger and S.Breznitz, eds. Handbook of Stress: Theoretical and Clinical Aspects. New York: The Free Press.

Selye, H. (1985). History and present status of the stress concept. In A. Monat and R.S. Lazarus, eds. Stress and Coping, 2nd ed. New York: Columbia University. Sontag, D. (2002, April 28). Who was responsible for Elizabeth Shin? [Electronic version]. The New York Times. Retrieved June 1, 2005 from Nytimes.com.

Stein, M., Miller, A. H., and Trestman, R. L. (1991). Depression, the immune system, and health and illness. Archives of General Psychiatry, 48, 171-177.

Substance Abuse and Mental Health Services Administration. (1997). Estimated costs associated with mental health disorders [E-text type]. Retrieved at: *www.samhsa.gov/ oas/srebk/costs-02.htm*

Taylor, J. A. (1953). A personality scale of manifest anxiety. Journal of Abnormal and Social Psychology, 48, 285-290.

United States General Accounting Office. (2001). Consumer Finance. College studentsand credit cards. GAO-01-773, 1-74.

Vaillant, G.E. (1977). Adaptation to life. Boston: Little Brown and Co.

Van Heyningen, J. J. (1997). Academic achievement in college students: What factors predict success? Dissertation Abstracts International Section A: Humanities and Social Sciences, 58(6-A), 2076.

Voelker, R. (2003). Mounting student depression taxing campus mental health services. The Journal of the American Medical Association, 289(16), 2055-2056. Electronic journal retrieved June 1, 2005.

Waite, P. (2001). Determining the efficacy of resiliency training in the worksite. Unpublished doctoral dissertation, University of Utah.

Whitman, N. A. (1999). Student stress: effects and solutions. Association for the Study of Higher Education. ERIC Clearinghouse on Higher Education Washington DC.

Wright, R. J., Rodriguez, M., and Cohen, S. (1998). Review of psychosocial stress and asthma: an integrated biopsychosocial approach. Thorax, 53, 1066-1074.

Xiao, J.J., Noring, F.E. and Anderson, J.G. (1995). College students' attitudes toward credit cards. Journal of Consumer Studies and Home Economics, 19, 155-174.

Zhang, L. (in press). Prediction of Chinese life satisfaction: Contribution of collective self-esteem. International Journal of Psychology.

In: Stress and Mental Health of College Students
Editor: Mery V. Landow, pp. 125-147

ISBN 1-59454-839-0
© 2006 Nova Science Publishers, Inc.

Chapter 5

MINIMIZING THE STRESS OF ACCELERATED ADULT EDUCATION: A DESCRIPTIVE STUDY

Mary T. Boylston and Anthony L. Blair
Campolo College of Graduate and Professional Studies
Eastern University, St. Davids, Pennsylvania

ABSTRACT

Student stressors in higher education are not confined to those of traditional college age. Working adult students experience unique stressors due to their multiple roles as students, providers, and employees, and institutions of higher learning have not always been adept at recognizing and responding to these pressures. This descriptive study examines adult students in two accelerated higher education programs (nursing and management) at one institution. Students in both programs were surveyed regarding the degree to which the university addresses the context (as opposed to merely the content) of the learning environment for these students. The data derived from the survey process indicates significant areas of positive feedback and other areas in which universities can better serve their adult students. The essay concludes with a reflection on the degree to which the faith identify of the institution is responsible for its student support ethos.

INTRODUCTION: REVOLUTIONS IN HIGHER EDUCATION

Within the past fifteen years Western institutions of higher education have experienced multiple, simultaneous, intertwined revolutions to a degree not experienced since the founding of the first universities in the high middle ages.[4] In that initial revolution the

---

[4] The use of the word "revolutions" here, while seemingly hyperbolic, is actually derived from another source written a full decade ago: "A revolution...has been slowly unfolding during the past several decades transforming the landscape of higher education, not only here in the United States but also throughout the world. This transformation in education is often referred to as the 'Adult Student Revolution.' Sparked by social, cultural, economic and technological factors, this sea-change is rightly called a 'revolution' since it is causing astute educators, like scientists undergoing a paradigm shift, to assume pioneering attitudes and adopt

cathedral schools morphed into degree-granting institutions with professional scholars, paying students, established curricula, and an administrative structure not entirely separate from but also not directly controlled by the Church. Later changes saw the expansion of academic disciplines beyond the *trivium* and *quadrivium*, the beginnings of state-sponsored lower and higher education, the creation and ascendance of the Doctor of Philosophy degree for professional scholars, the secularization of the academy and, most recently, the politicization and commercialization of the American university (Bok, 2003). Each of these has exerted a powerful influence on the nature and character of higher education in the early twenty-first century, yet there are other revolutions that have the potential to entirely remake and redefine higher education in the quarter century ahead. And such remaking and redefining may not necessarily be a bad thing.

As indicated, the revolutions are multiple and intertwined but may be defined as consisting of four distinct strands. The first of those strands is the large, unprecedented influx of adult students into institutions of higher learning. Adult students represented a miniscule fraction of the total enrollment in the 1980s but Richardson and King (1998) suggested that the adult learner population has soared with a 144% increase over the past 33 years, whereas the number of students younger than 25 years has reflected only a 45% increase (Anderson, 2003). The National Center for Education Statistics (NCES) reports that 39% of all postsecondary students were 25 years or older in 1999, compared with 28% in 1970. Moreover, the 1999–2000 statistics report that there was an additional increase of nontraditional students with women comprising more than half of the collegiate population (NCES, 2002). Indeed, it is appropriate to argue that while higher education programs for adult students may be yet "non-traditional," they are certainly "mainstream."

The second strand concerns the deliveries developed to provide access to these students. Even those institutions of higher learning that had adopted a congenial approach to the adult student (through re-entry programs, for example) had not necessarily made their educational offerings more accessible to those with career and family responsibilities (Fungaroli, 2000). Previous to the 1980s, "adult education" consisted largely of non-credit or non-degreed courses in job training or skills development for employment or in recreational learning (e.g. arts for the senior citizen or homemaker). In the 1980s one began to see a proliferation of for-credit programs offered through evening and weekend classes, primarily through "continuing education" or "extension" units within the colleges and universities. Finally, in the early 1990s one began to see the growth of "accelerated programs" for working adults. These programs are based on two controversial premises: that "seat time" is not, by itself, a sufficient measure of the quality of learning that takes place, and that students are more likely to succeed if the learning takes place within a consistent and supportive social network known as a "cohort." Many of these programs were and are labeled "degree completion programs" and were designed for adult students who had previously earned an associate's degree or its equivalent and need to complete their baccalaureate. A typical format consisted of creating a cohort of 10-14 students who would together take a series of five-week courses in sequence, meeting one night a week for four hours.

The third revolutionary strand involves the changes in teaching roles and instructional design as a result of these new deliveries. The new adult education programs in the 1990s

---

unprecedented methods which the influx of adult students onto college campuses demands" (Naugle, 1995, 24ff).

relied increasingly on non-professionals to teach their courses. These non-professionals were practitioners—individuals who had usually earned at least a master's degree (sometimes a doctorate) within their discipline but who preferred full-time practice in the workplace over full-time teaching or scholarship (Wachs, 1993). The utilization of practitioners as the primary instructors in these programs permitted the professional studies programs (which represented the majority of the market) to provided "just-in-time" learning. The immediacy of such learning was attractive to adult students. Further, it permitted these programs to operate with a fairly high profit margin.

The fourth and most controversial revolution was the proliferation of online programs. On the one hand, online learning is merely the latest form of "distance education," which has been in existence in various forms for quite some time. On the other hand, online learning challenges some basic assumptions of the instructional task and the learning process, assumptions that have undergirded the academy for quite some time. Therefore, while for some online learning is yet another "delivery method," for others it is a threat to traditional understandings of the primacy of the instructor in the learning process and the means by which the transmission of knowledge occurs.

All four strands have created tensions, all have been controversial, and all are still new enough to be regarded by many as unwelcome intrusions into a somewhat calcified academic culture in the West.

Faith-based institutions have responded to these revolutions in adult education more quickly than many others (Wlodkowski, 2003). This is doubtless due to both practical and ideological motives. Practically speaking, faith-based universities do not usually have either the endowment funds or public investments that other, more secular institutions enjoy, and adult professional programs have proven themselves effective profit centers for such financially strapped institutions. In an ideological sense, institutions that perceive their objectives within a comprehensive mission to redeem humanity are perhaps more likely than others to seek a broader audience for their educational services.

Of note, however, is that adult students, whether attending secular or faith-based institutions, have reported significant amount of pressures or stressors while attempting to complete a degree (O'Connor and Bevil, 1996; Sutherland, 1999). According to Kobasa (1979), "A life event is defined as stressful if it courses changes in, and demands readjustment of, an average person's normal routine" (p. 2). O'Connor asserts, "Stress has been identified as an important psychosocial factor in the educational process because it may influence both academic performance and student well-being" (p. 246). It can be argued that the addition of college or university studies to the multiple daily activities of an adult can be construed as overwhelming as the individual struggles to balance competing roles. Therefore, the combination of academic pressures and existing adult stressors may intensify and can impact academic performance and the student's ability to persist until graduation. By determining the adult student's professed items of academic importance and the concomitant levels of satisfaction derived from the institution's attempt to create an "adult-friendly" environment, faculty, staff, and administrators may acquire valuable information that can be used to provide programs and services desired by this population. Moreover, the recognition and creation of services as deemed important by the adult student may serve to minimize the stress inherent in the role of a student. Therefore, analyzing the target university's attempt to provide services to ultimately minimize these stressors are the focus of this research.

NEED FOR THE STUDY

Sissel, Hansman, and Kasworm (2001) put forth that adult students, while emerging as the new majority in higher education, may unfortunately be viewed by faculty, staff, and administrators as less important than the traditional student. There is insufficient research to identify the unique stressors of adult students; therefore, attempts to define modalities to support them through the educational process, may be insufficient (Brown and Eggert Linnemann, 1995; Hadfield, 2003; Simonite, 1997; Viechnicki, Bohlin, Milheim, 1990). Without knowledge of how to support this vital population, officials appear to make educated assumptions on what the students' needs might be; hence, conclusions may be made about creating learning environments that presume an enhanced academic experience. There is need, therefore, for additional studies of accelerated learning environments to determine the degree to which they address the unique stressors of their students.

STATEMENT OF THE PROBLEM

The hypothesis of this study is that the learning environment created for adult students in two accelerated undergraduate programs (one in Nursing, the other in Business) in an institution with significant experience in adult education adequately addresses the unique stressors of the students enrolled therein. It is assumed that this success in responding to stressors is due primarily to two factors: 1) the intentionality of design of the programs (derived from the institution's experience), and 2) the institution's faith commitment (which compels a holistic understanding of the student). This hypothesis is tested through the administration of a nationally-normed survey instrument among these two student populations and the interpretation of the data thus gathered.

DEFINITION OF TERMS

Accelerated RN to BSN Program: The Baccalaureate of Science in Nursing (BSN) is offered to Registered Nurses (RNs) in 16 to 24 months, a shorter time period than that of traditional programs. The students are more independent in achieving their goals. The courses are offered sequentially during the same time and day each week until the student has met program requirements.

Adult Learner: A college student over the age of twenty-five years and distinguished by the NCES (2002) criteria. Defined by the NCES, the "nontraditional" student will have one or all of the following characteristics: delays college enrollment after high school, attends postsecondary education part-time for at least part of the academic year, works full time, is considered financially independent, has dependents other than spouse, is a single parent, and/or does not have a high school diploma.

Faith-Based Institution: An educational institution with an explicit faith commitment that is apparent in both the content and the context of the learning environment.

Management Programs: A broad-based business program designed for students in the for-profit, not-for-profit, and public sectors. In this essay, undergraduate programs leading to a Bachelor of Arts (BA) in Organizational Management or Bachelor of Arts (BA) in Management of Information Systems and graduate Master of Business Administration (MBA) tracks in Management and Health Administration were employed as case studies.

Professional Studies: In general terms, any academic program designed to prepare students for the professions; in specific terms, any academic program designed to provide academic qualifications for existing professionals.

Registered Nurse: A member of the health care profession who has successfully completed the requirements and passed the National Council Licensure Examination for Registered Nurses (NCLEX-RN).

Stress: any noxious stimulus that affects the sympathetic nervous system.

REVIEW OF LITERATURE

The Unique Status of Adult Students in Higher Education

The NCES (2002) reports that an increase in adult students may be due to the influence of the changing employment requirements, which seem to be demanding new skills and knowledge. Interestingly, an adult student is considered "nontraditional" by institutions and faculty in higher education. However, Richardson and King (1998) purport that the "nontraditional" students or adult learners should not be treated as a homogenous group since they are more diverse than the traditional students. Thus, while this essay identifies certain unique stressors of adult students, it is important to note here that such identifications are not intended to be universal; they serve merely as generalizations to assist in the distinction between traditional and nontraditional learning environments.

In addition, Hadfield asserts that it is essential to have an appreciation for adult learners as customers of higher education as they return to college in preparation to meet new employment demands. And as the numbers of adult students proliferate, institutions are beginning to count on the revenue generated by this population (Hadfield, 2003). Presumably, administrators depend on the matriculation of "nontraditional" learners to help balance the budget and perhaps create some additional revenue for the institution to fund other programs. Furthermore, Hadfield contends that since most services in higher education focus on the traditional student, a change in culture and concomitant services would potentially benefit all students. Therefore, the goal ought to be to develop a comprehensive program to evaluate the areas of importance to adult students as they choose a higher education setting (Boylston, Peters, and Lacey, 2004).

As the adult student population rises, issues have emerged that pertain to how to recruit, educate, and retain this "nontraditional" group (Beeman, 1988; Boylston, Peters, and Lacey, 2004; Brown and Eggert Linnemann, 1995). Services in postsecondary institutions, grounded in a traditional student paradigm, often set hours in business offices, financial aid offices, bookstores, and offices of registrars that are convenient for traditional students, but completely inaccessible for the adult who has personal and professional commitments during the day (Hadfield, 2003). This pattern is shortsighted, for as Hadfield states, "Except for the quality of our academic offering, excellence in customer service is the single most important factor in determining the future of our programs for adult learners, now and for the foreseeable future" (p. 19). The lack of services may create unneeded stress for the adult learner and ultimately cause the student to drop out of the university. Furthermore, Hadfield suggests looking at the business model of customer service to attract and retain this population. Presumably, this model would include a service guarantee, formal promises made to the consumer about the services received, and the assurance of a quality educational experience (McCollough and Gremler, 1999). In addition, consistent inquiries regarding their needs and desired services can promote open communication between students and campus officials. In return, administrators can offer services that the adult student desires, thereby increasing the students' satisfaction with the educational process.

Presumably, this satisfaction data can be gleaned by periodically administering satisfaction surveys. These assessments will prospectively invite students to rate their experiences and determine whether the institution has provided the educational services needed to achieve personal and professional goals. Furthermore, students can be queried regarding their satisfaction of instructional effectiveness, registration, financial aid processes, campus climate, security, and safety. Equipped with data from a survey, administrators can strive to make changes in existing programs to enhance service and address needs of this growing population of students. El Ansari (2002) reports that student satisfaction can be an important quality indicator, with respect to teaching and learning. However, it seems that the majority of satisfaction surveys are completed at the end of the students' academic experience in the form of exit interviews. The question is then posed to the student as "Were you satisfied with your college experience?" (Elliott and Shin, 2002). This data offers a retrospective depiction of the students' experiences, thereby negating opportunities that the institution would have to create a more conducive adult-oriented environment for the responding student.

Historically, colleges and universities have provided services for the traditional student who matriculates immediately after high school (Bowl, 2001). However, with the metamorphosis of collegiate demographics there apparently has not been a concomitant change in the services that institutions of higher education offer to adult learners (Sissel, Hansman, and Kasworm, 2001). Without the benefit of accessible campus services, the "nontraditional" student may find it too difficult to achieve personal and academic goals (Zuzelo, 2001). This can ultimately affect retention (Fralick, 1993).

Characteristics of Adult Learners

Arguably, the profile of adult learners is multifaceted. Incorporating adult education theories is only one way that colleges and universities may employ to provide a holistic and meaningful educational experience. Moreover, institutions and faculty are encouraged to know the demographic data and personal distinctiveness of students who now compose the majority in their classes. The NCES (2002) characterizes 73% of undergraduates as "nontraditional" (aged 25 years or greater with part-time enrollement status). Additional defining characteristics of adult "nontraditional" students according to the NCES include an initial delay of enrolling in postsecondary education, full-time employment, perceived financial independence, support of dependents, single parenthood, or lack of high school diploma. Similarly, Horn, Peter, Rooney, and Malizio (2002) define the "nontraditional" student on a continuum based on the number of aforementioned characteristics that the individual possesses. Students can be minimally "nontraditional" to highly "nontraditional" if they have four or more of the aforesaid characteristics. According to government data collected for 1999 to 2000, 27% of all undergraduates were traditional, and 28% were highly "nontraditional", with 28% moderately "nontraditional" and 17% minimally "nontraditional" (NCES). According to the research of Horn et al. on persistence and attrition, the "nontraditional" students who enter postsecondary education seeking a degree are less likely than traditional students to attain a degree or remain enrolled after five years.

The NCES data assists in defining the "nontraditional" student; however, there are additional features that distinguish the adult student. Typically, the adult student is self-supporting, mature, and responsible (MacKinnon-Slaney, 1994). Adult students can lead lives filled with responsibilities, such as families, mortgages, and careers, and may be independent citizens. They may also be motivated to learn more readily from internal motivators, such as self-esteem, recognition or a better quality of life (O'Brien and Renner, 2000). Moreover, they can be task directed and pragmatic (Bohlin, 1994). Presumably, they cope sufficiently well with life's stressors, including child-rearing, elder care, working full-time and balancing career and education (Fairchild, 2003). In addition, they may feel compelled to return to school to update their skills for the job market (Kerka, 2001). Most adults enter higher education voluntarily (Vichnicki, Bohlin, and Milheim, 1990), whereas a vast number of adults have returned to school to cope with change in their personal lives, stretch their minds, and facilitate career change or advancement (Fishback and Polson, 1998). Moreover, adult students can present a challenge to faculty and administrators because of their personal, educational, and professional histories, along with their lack of familiarity with the university community and policies (Green, 1987). The aforementioned characteristics can assist in creating a depiction of the "nontraditional" as the higher education community attempts to recruit this population for a variety of academic programs.

Another feature that characterizes adult learners is that they appear to more effectively manage time. This may be a function of the myriad of roles that consume their lives and their ability to juggle these roles (Grupe and Connolly, 1995; Knowles, 1978; Richardson and King, 1998). Reportedly, adults are challenged to balance adult careers and family roles with college schedules (Fralick, 1993). O'Connor and Bevil (1996) argue that the balancing of all adult responsibilities while attending college can lead to stress and role overload. This can have a detrimental affect on this population's ability to persist until graduation or achieve their academic goals.

Another defining trait of adult students (in addition to their age and their level of responsibility) is their level of motivation, which Richardson and King (1998) counter-intuitively suggest may be more intrinsic than vocational. In all probability, the adult has a purpose for attending college. The reasons can be numerous, from seeking a new position to promotion in the place of employment to personal gratification. Therefore, they have a range of backgrounds and a variety of interests (Grupe and Connolly, 1995). The NCES (2002) reports that no matter how "nontraditional" the respondents were, 73% reported that personal enrichment or interest in the subject, gaining skills to advance in their jobs or career, and completing a degree or certificate were important considerations in returning to postsecondary education.

According to Fralick (1993), "programs need to be developed to increase retention. Adults will drop out if they are unsuccessful academically or unable to balance school, career, home and family" (p. 36). In response, academic programs may create course schedules conducive to adult time pressures and many provide adequate student services, as well as other programs for this population to achieve their goals. In addition, Bowl (2001) alleges that institutional and financial barriers can generate numerous stressors. With the barriers torn down by the institutions, the adult learner can focus on achieving academic goals.

Richardson and King (1998) argue that adult learners have been consistently stigmatized in terms of the ability to benefit from higher education, with faculty and administration sharing in the creation and dissemination of negative stereotypes. In addition, they have "prior life experience, which promotes a deep approach to studying in higher education" (Richardson and King, p 73). Because of this, faculty ought to address the practical and unique needs of adults. Due to the "nontraditional" heterogeneity, an attempt to meet the needs of this population can appear to be a daunting task for faculty and administration. Fishback and Polson (1998) determined that the educational process for adults can be full of emotion and the learning ought to take place in a supportive, interactive environment. Creating a milieu that addresses the uniqueness of this population may become a top priority of higher education personnel in order to recruit, retain and graduate the adult learner and minimize the stress one may face as a student.

Unique Stressors of Adult Learners

The particular stressors presented by the adult learner may pose a challenge for counselors, faculty, and advisors. According to Reed and Beaudin (1993), "Institutions of higher education need to welcome adult learners and provide processes, systems and learning environments to meet adult needs in order to survive economically in the upcoming decades" (p. 2). MacKinnon-Slaney (1994) adds that adults have concerns at home that affect their academic performance. Conversely, a disappointing grade may affect relationships at home. This may distract the student from achieving academic and personal goals. "Services for traditional college students cannot meet the needs of adult learners" (MacKinnon-Slaney, p. 269). Therefore, counseling departments can include a series of services that focus on the issues that the adult may face in order to encourage retention among this population.

An area of uniqueness explored by researchers is the fact that adults expect to immediately apply newly learned knowledge (Knowles, 1978; MacKinnon-Slaney, 1994). Theoretically, adult learners want new knowledge to be applicable and appropriate for life and work experiences. Adults want to build upon the current skills, usually focusing upon a problem or current need that must be addressed (Grupe and Connolly, 1995; Knowles, 1978). Thus, case study learning is particularly effective.

An important facet for educators to contemplate is the notion that adult learners may bring considerable knowledge to the learning process. This can potentially enhance any classroom setting (Grupe and Connolly, 1995). Hypothetically, adults can be active learners (Bohlin, Milheim, and Viechnicki, 1994). Experts concur that adults seek independence and self-direction while learning and implementing new concepts (Grupe and Connolly). This can lead to dynamic classroom discussions regarding the application of new concepts. Presumably, this can affect the quality of the class and educational experience for all beneficiaries and serves to motivate the student to stay in the program until graduation.

Creating a learning community that is open to the needs of the "nontraditional" student may assist the population in achieving its academic goals. A program that is designed to be supportive, that fits into the busy adult lifestyle, and that has a predictable structure may serve to attract and retain the "nontraditional" student (Kasworm, 2003). This can promote the student's overall success in higher education.

The stressors that the adult student may face can precipitate a physiological reaction (Selye, 1976). Hans Selye described a "fight-or-flight" response. He conceptualized three phases of his general adaptation syndrome theory. The first phase is the alarm phase, characterized by the individual's perception of a stressor. The body prepares itself for a physiological response. The second phase is the resistance stage, in which the organism or body fights the stressor. The third phase, called the exhaustion phase, occurs when the body is no longer able to fight the stressor. It is here when the individual may become ill or even death can occur.

O'Connor and Bevil (1996) researched academic outcomes and stress in full-time day and part-time evening baccalaureate nursing students. The researchers suggested the evening students' anxiety increased by mid-semester. Additionally, the participants were able to achieve academic outcomes despite the anxiety and stress. Similarly, Lee (1988) studied RNs who returned to higher education for a BSN. The research disclosed that the stress of returning to school was a deterrent to the student's success in school.

Success and Failure in Higher Education

The success and failure of adult learners in higher education can depend upon a multitude of factors. According to MacKinnon–Slaney (1994), adults must have a "robust sense of self" (p.72) in order to succeed in college. Presumably, individuals who lack a positive sense of academic self-concept may not continue their education. This is especially prevalent among women and adult learners of color (MacKinnon-Slaney, 1994). Advising implications may include support and counseling to assist the student in overcoming the multitude of hurdles and stresses that they encounter on a daily basis.

Another concern for adults is the clarification of goals, expectations, success and the meaning of education. Adult learners must commit to goals and believe that education is a pathway toward the achievement of these goals (MacKinnon-Slaney, 1994). Interestingly, success for the adult learner can be defined as "the student's subjective judgment about college achievement rather than more traditional, institutionally defined measures of college success" (Fralick, 1993, p. 30). Fralick researched college retention and found that the more academically successful students are more likely to return to complete a degree program. Consequently, the author suggests periodic satisfaction surveys be distributed to this population at regular intervals. This will help to identify the "at risk" dropout students.

Due to the complexity of adult life, there can be a number of additional factors that can lead the adult to leave postsecondary education without completing the degree program. Fairchild (2003) states, "The basic needs of the family, like food and rent or mortgage, take priority over educational outlays" (p. 12). Threats to the new role can be caused by multiple personal demands and institutional barriers. In order to combat the attrition of the adult learner or "nontraditional" student, institutions of higher education can seek to provide services that will eliminate stressors and build connections among the student, faculty, and program. This can be done with careful thought and consideration and by treating the adult learner as a unique student. Bowl (2001) admonishes, "Financial, institutional, and class-based barriers impede the progress of non-traditional students" (p. 157). These barriers seem to emerge early as the student attempts to move forward despite a commitment to education as a way to a better life. Students may be highly motivated but may remain frustrated participants unable to gain access to support and constructive advice (Bowl, 2001).

Responsiveness to the Adult Market in Higher Education

According to Havarnek and Browdin (1998), a new focus is needed to produce higher education institutions that are more responsive to students' needs by providing access to quality support services. Additionally, "colleges and universities are extraordinarily slow to change in the face of new realities that make change necessary for their continued survival" (Havernick and Browdin, 1998, p. 116). Bohlin, et al. (1994) concur: "In order to effectively teach learners with a different set of needs, motives, and backgrounds, we need a new set of techniques and instructional strategies" (p. 4). By asking the students what they value in an educational experience through qualitative and quantitative measures, a pool of data can be developed that may provide answers and solutions and direct administrators toward innovation. Interestingly, Bowl (2001) purports that institutions tend to "problematize" the nontraditional student rather than seek ways to promote success among this population.

For the adult learner, the role of student is one of multiple responsibilities and commitments that compete for their time (Kerka, 1995). Stressors such as child care, family problems, and job demands can cause withdrawal from higher education. Furthermore, Kerka asserts that the institution cannot control personal problems, but the university and faculty can influence student's satisfaction with the program through personal attention to the needs of the student. Attention to the "nontraditional" student and the creation of flexible, user-friendly models of education can serve to attract and retain the role overloaded adult (Ayer and Smith, 1998).

METHODOLOGY

To determine the effect of the campus services and their effect on minimizing academic stressors, the researchers employed the following research methodologies. A nationally-normed survey instrument was employed to compare results between two different academic departments (Nursing and Management Studies) within the same institution of higher learning. They are presented here in tandem as Survey A (Nursing) and Survey B (Management).

For each survey, the authors gained university permission to conduct the study, and the informed consent of the student after describing the research. All subjects were anonymous and data were coded to maintain confidentiality. Respondents to Survey A were invited to participate in an additional interview process, consent for which was indicated by signing one's name and providing an email address at the bottom of the consent form to be contacted at a later date. The researcher and participant discussed a mutually agreed upon time to meet. The researcher selected students for interviews until the discussions yielded a saturation of themes. An audiotape was used to capture the participant's mood or strength of feelings on raised issues. Respondents to Survey B also responded to unique questions regarding stressors in their own academic experience.

SUBJECTS

The sources of data for Survey A (Nursing) were volunteer students who were enrolled in an accelerated RN to BSN program in a relatively small faith-based institution of higher learning. All of the matriculated students in the program were recruited for the study. There was a 100 percent return for a total of 53 students. Ten of the respondents were interviewed in person.

The accelerated nursing program has been in existence for six years with steady enrollments. The university offers a twenty-month, 48-credit baccalaureate in nursing science (BSN). In accordance with the university's mission, a Bible course is mandated for graduation. Students take this course at the end of the program.

The average age of a practicing nurse is 45.2 years (AACN, 2003) as compared to the age of the studied population at the university, which is 35 years or older. The majority of the sampled BSN population was female (94.34%). The ethnicity/race of the students was Caucasian/White (58.49%), African American/Black (13.21%), and Asian (18.87%). All students were attending classes full-time with the majority (67.92%) also employed full-time.

The sources of data for the Management survey were volunteer students who were enrolled in an accelerated management program in the same faith-based institution. A total of 407 students participated in the survey; 76% of respondents completed the survey in-class and 23% online. Fifty-nine percent of respondents were female and 41% male. Sixty-two percent were between the ages of 25 and 44. The ethnicity of respondents was as follows: African American (32.90%), Asian (2.33%), Caucasian (52.85%), Hispanic (2.59%), and "Other" (3.89%).

The sources of data for Survey B (Management) were students enrolled in accelerated undergraduate and graduate programs in the Management or Business disciplines. These programs were the first offered of their delivery by any institution of higher education in the market area. Begun in 1989, they had graduated over 450 cohorts of adult students by early 2005. The average age of the students is 33 years (slightly higher for undergraduate students). The programs enjoy a wider ethnic/racial diversity in their student demographics than does the university as a whole. Nearly 95% of the students are employed full-time while maintaining a full-time, accelerated academic load.

Options for Management education include an undergraduate Organizational Management major (offered in an accelerated degree completion program format), an undergraduate Management of Information Systems major (delivered in the same format as the Organizational Management program and designed for a niche market), two tracks (Management and Health Administration) in an accelerated ("Fast-Track"®) Master's of Business Administration, and a Master of Science in NonProfit Management (delivered via a distance education/residency model). Instruction is offered in over twenty sites throughout the market area, including campuses of corporate partners. Respondents to the survey were from all five Management programs.

SURVEY INSTRUMENT

To obtain an in-depth depiction of "nontraditional" student satisfaction in the selected accelerated programs, the researcher analyzed survey responses and employed qualitative interview techniques to triangulate the data. The proposed research design called for a tool that could measure adult learners' expectations within an academic program along with the concomitant level of satisfaction with existing university services, curriculum, and personnel. To accomplish this, the Noel Levitz Adult Student Priorities Survey[TM] (ASPS), a three-part instrument, was used to gather data on student satisfaction.

The ASPS consisted of 50 items that cover a full range of college experiences as well as demographic characteristics of the respondents. Students were asked to rate each Likert-like statement on a seven-point scale ranging from one (1), not very important at all or not satisfied at all, to seven (7), very important or very satisfied. The ASPS is designed to measure students' perceptions along eight dimensions, which include academic advising effectiveness, instructional effectiveness, service excellence, registration effectiveness, campus climate, service excellence, admissions and financial aid services, and safety and security. Three summary questions were identified: levels of satisfaction with overall educational experience, levels of expectations met by the institution, and whether the respondent would enroll again in the selected baccalaureate program.

Noel-Levitz[TM] (2003) reports that the ASPS's reliability is high. For example, "Cronbach's coefficient for the importance scores was .93 and .90 on items of satisfaction, and the test-retest reliability estimate was .82 and .81 for the mean satisfaction scores" (p. 3). In addition, the validity was assessed both quantitatively and qualitatively. The quantitative assessment was .74 for importance and .67 for satisfaction ($p < .0001$). Qualitatively, the instrument validity was conducted by correlating respondents' scores on the ASPS with their interview responses on a qualitative protocol reflecting the content of the instrument. All scale correlations were significant ($p = .05$) (Noel-Levitz[TM]), thereby indicating that the instrument reflects the construct that it was designed to measure.

To triangulate the findings, an interview portion of the Nursing student survey was employed with the additional use of four prepared questions. The posed questions were as follows:

- What made you choose this program to complete your BSN?
- What services do you seek in an academic program?
- What would cause you to withdraw from this program?
- What services do you need the university to provide to keep you in the program?

The Management student survey contained two unique questions:

- Being a student was a stressful experience for me.
- My stress was lowered as a result of the support I got from my instructors, other staff members, and fellow students.

RESULTS

The findings of the Nursing Program study (Survey A) were delineated by using the Noel-Levitz Adult Student Priorities Survey™ (ASPS) and personal interviews that identified the levels of importance that accelerated RN to BSN students place on aspects of their student experience. The experiences were included in the analysis of eight inventory composite scales from the ASPS, which were identified as academic advising effectiveness, academic services, admissions and financial aid effectiveness, campus climate, instructional effectiveness, registration effectiveness, safety and security, and service excellence. Data results represent areas of importance and potential levels of satisfaction among the sampled population.

Figure 1 depicts a graphic representation of the RN to BSN students' responses to the ASPS questions. Instructional effectiveness and advising effectiveness were the highest areas of importance.

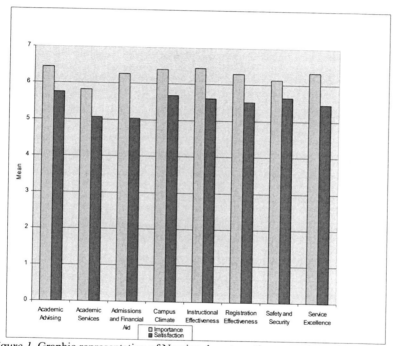

Figure 1. Graphic representation of Nursing department's composite scales.

Table 1 demonstrates a statistical summary of the participants' responses in relationship to the composite scales. Academic services were rated at the bottom of the eight scales with a higher performance gap (0.75) indicating a satisfaction with services despite the lower rating in importance (5.81).

Table 1. Nursing Survey: Institutional Means of Composite Scales

Scale	Importance	Satisfaction	Gap
Instructional Effectiveness	6.44	5.60	0.84
Academic Advising	6.43	5.74	0.69
Campus Climate	6.40	5.74	0.73
Service Excellence	6.34	5.45	0.89
Registration Effectiveness	6.29	5.51	0.78
Admissions and Financial Aid	6.26	5.51	1.22
Safety and Security	6.14	5.65	0.49
Academic Services	5.81	5.06	0.75

Specific items pertaining to university services were extrapolated from the data. Of the top ten items of importance rated by the students, five of ten focused on the relationship between the professor, advising process, and quality of the educational experience. The other more notable items of importance determined by the sampled population were as follows: (a) classroom locations are safe and secure for all students; (b) classes are scheduled at times that are convenient for me; (c) tuition paid is a worthwhile investment; and (d) I am able to complete most of my enrollment tasks in one location.

The interviews gleaned additional data for analysis. When questioned about the reasons for choosing the program, all respondents stated the convenience of the classes as important. The dominance of the convenience theme as articulated by all subjects was evident with comments such as "I like the convenience of staying in my own area." Other statements verified the need to be in close proximity to home or work. "I have a large family, a lot of responsibilities, and so forth, so it was the flexibility that was the major aspect and my primary goal" was voiced by another student.

Thirty percent mentioned the number of transfer credits accepted by the institution was instrumental in selecting the program. The more credits accepted, the fewer courses the student would have to take to complete the degree and the less time spent in class. One student purported, "I came to an open house and they would accept my high school chemistry; that was important to me."

In addition, twenty percent noted the Christian worldview and the supportive cohort model as instrumental in enrolling and staying at the university. "I like the cohort setting of going in with the same women through the whole program." Another student suggested, "I like being in a group....we really support one another."

The second question posed to the students, "What services do you seek in an academic program?" yielded additional information. Fifty percent mentioned the advising and support offered by faculty as important variables needed by the students to minimize the pressures of attending the university. According to one student, "It's hard to feel that you are out there on your own. This program does not have that...you have support." Another student volunteered, "The services that I seek in an academic program are that you have one person and have them help you or facilitate contact with other people. It's frustrating when you go to one person then you are sent to another, and then you are sent to another. I don't have time for that. Give me the person to contact and she can help with the problem."

Another theme that emerged from the data was the need for financial aid. Students clearly stated the expense of the program and their unwillingness to incur additional debt that could compromise their family financial solvency were indicators of their need for some type of financial assistance that could help them with the stresses of tuition and book fees. One student verbalized, "The family comes first."

The third question, "What would cause you to withdraw from the program?" generated two themes. Theme number one was a family crisis. According to one student, "It would take a family problem....this has been hard on my family." Theme number two emerging from the data was a "major life crisis." "It would take something cataclysmic for me to leave the program" was verbalized by a student. "Family stressors...just not having the time that you want to have spend doing the work and just being okay with that but where's the point where okay I'm not spending enough time doing school work. It's hard to balance family and family comes first" was stated by another student. "To withdraw I would have to feel totally overwhelmed with what is going on in my life, it is difficult going to school full time and working fulltime

Question number four, "What services do you need the university to provide to keep you in the program?" revealed a need for a financial aid infrastructure to complete the program. Several students commented, "I need financial aid to stay in school." Otherwise, students described the current university services were adequate to address the stressors in their situations. One student reported, "The ongoing support is already there."

Figure 2 depicts a graphic representation of the Management students' responses to the ASPS questions. As with the Nursing survey, instructional effectiveness and advising effectiveness were rated the highest areas of importance.

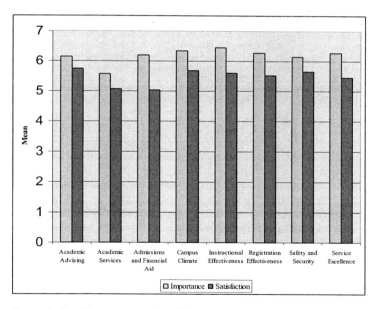

Figure 2. Graphic representation of Management programs' composite scales.

As for the Management survey, it generated no scale in which the performance gap exceeded 1.00, indicating a rather positive evaluation of program's effectiveness. Indeed, the scores for the eight scaled items exceeded national norms for the Noel-Levitz survey in every category except academic services, which is not surprising. One of the features of many adult education programs (and of the Management programs of the studied institution) is that classes are held at off-campus sites. Of the two dozen or so classroom sites utilized by these Management programs, only six are staffed. The inevitable result is occasional frustration at not being able to resolve issues with a live person at the moment those issues arise. It is important to note that the students do regard this as a stressor in their academic experience, however, and to work creatively to find ways to address it.

Table 2 demonstrates a statistical summary of the participants' responses in relationship to the composite scales. As with the Nursing survey, academic services were rated at the bottom of the eight scales in terms of both importance and performance. The performance gap of 0.99 was the highest in this survey.

Table 2. Management Survey: Institutional Means of Composite Scales

Scale	Importance	Satisfaction	Gap
Instructional Effectiveness	6.45	5.74	0.71
Academic Advising	6.15	5.36	0.79
Campus Climate	6.34	5.74	0.60
Service Excellence	6.27	5.45	0.82
Registration Effectiveness	6.28	5.71	0.57
Admissions and Financial Aid	6.19	5.35	0.84
Safety and Security	6.15	5.36	0.79
Academic Services	5.86	4.87	0.99

The two unique questions addressed how the institution explicitly addressed the issue of stress in the life of the students. Students agreed strongly that "being a student is a stressful experience for me" but also agreed that their stress was lowered as a result of the support received from instructors, other staff members, and fellow students. It appears that the structures created by the studied institution have been effective to some degree in minimizing the unique stressors of the adult student.

It is interesting and instructive that the responses to the two surveys were quite similar; this indicates a consistency from one program to another throughout the institution in addressing the learning environment of adult students. The stressors are not discipline-specific and neither are their remedies.

DISCUSSION

While research has already established that student satisfaction improves retention (Brown and Eggert Linnemann, 1995), it also contributes to academic, personal, and professional achievement (Bean and Bradley, 1986). In addition, by monitoring items of importance to students, the institution can scrutinize areas of weakness and strength, and seek to fortify areas of satisfaction. "By collecting information from students that asks not only how satisfied they are with aspects of the campus but also how important these aspects are, a college can prioritize its interventions" (Juillerat and Schreiner, 1999, p. 4). The findings of the both studies suggest the subjects identified several items of importance related to teaching and academic services needed to stay in college in an attempt to complete a degree. From the

ASPS data, students identified advising and instructional excellence as the most valued items of importance in both departments. The program advisors are typically full-time faculty or staff members who advise the entire cohort. In other words, the individual faculty member is known by all of the students in one cohort as the primary advisor who begins the relationship in orientation and ends it at graduation. Part of the workload of faculty members is to advise students. One student stated, "I can contact my advisor at any time."

Due to the nature of accelerated education, the need for quality faculty has been identified by the students as high in importance with a concomitant level of high satisfaction. Students articulated that they want knowledgeable and available instructors who are master teachers and will not repeat content and concepts. Students desire faculty who can assist them in applying newly learned knowledge (Knowles, 1978). According to one student, "Professors need to recognize that we are adult learners and that we bring experience to the program. We want this to be an additional growth experience and not repeat everything that we have already learned."

Interestingly, participants rated service excellence high in importance and relatively high in satisfaction. This scale assessed the university staffs' attitude toward students as a positive one. Staff friendliness and ability to be responsive to students' inquiries resulted in positive responses by the subjects.

Presumably, the nature of higher education can be service oriented. Students need to navigate through a complicated system to enroll, register, purchase textbooks, attend classes, and communicate with financial aid and registrar's offices. As adult learners, the majority of the sampled population are employed and have spouses and children, which adds layers of complexities and responsibilities. These multiple roles may threaten their academic success (Fairchild, 2003). The research suggests that having positive contact with staff correlates with increased satisfaction with the campus, climate, and personnel, and university. "From the perspective of adult students, access to higher education institutions sensitive to their developmental, academic, and logistical needs will maximize the outcomes from their educational investments" (Brown and Eggert Linnemann, 1995, p. 11). In addition, it is suggested that student satisfaction has a positive impact on student motivation, recruiting efforts, and fundraising (Elliott and Shin, 2002).

Registration effectiveness, an integral component of the higher education process, was rated lower in importance and higher in satisfaction. Billing and registration processes comprise this scale. At the studied institution, the students register once at the beginning of the program and there is no need for additional paperwork. Interestingly, students reported convenience as the dominant feature for enrolling in the program. With the streamlining of the registration process, the convenience of completing university formalities within the classroom generated overall satisfaction with this process.

For the Nursing population, seven of the eight composite scales had performance gap scores of less than one (1.0) and for the Management population, all eight of the composite scores had performance gap scores of less than one (1.0), indicating an overall satisfaction with the student experience and services offered by the university. Of interest, only admissions and financial aid were reflected a gap score of greater than 1.0 (1.22), indicating dissatisfaction among Nursing students with these services. The items of dissatisfaction, focused on the variety of payment plans for adult students, adequate financial aid, and admissions representatives responding to the students' needs. Further, these findings were validated by the interview responses. When questioned what services students needed in order to stay enrolled at the university, the most frequent response was the need for financial aid. With private school tuition, textbook and fees, the amount of money spent on tuition was an expressed concern for participants. Subjects' reactions corroborate the findings of Wlodkowski (2003), who suggests that the use of financial aid strengthens adult student persistence. "Adults who received financial aid were three times more likely to persist, than adults who receive no financial aid" (p. 11).

In contrast, safety and security were rated low in importance yet high in satisfaction (particularly among Nursing students, who are more likely to take classes at the main campus). The scale measured the effectiveness of security personnel and campus facilities. Presumably, the safe location of classrooms with close parking while not considered essential was well received by participants. With panic boxes for emergency use located in strategic positions in each of the parking lots, low crime statistics were reported in the surrounded vicinities. In other words, students feel safe at this institution.

Interestingly, the lowest rated (in terms of importance) of eight composite scales was academic services. The services had a concomitant high satisfaction rating and a fairly narrow performance gap, which suggested that students were satisfied with quality service and personal concern, demonstrated by faculty, staff, and administration. This was also reflected in the highly rated advising effectiveness. From data gleaned from interviews, students verbalized that the faculty and staff at this institution consider students with a customer focus since the faculty work diligently to return phone calls and e-mails within a short time frame. In addition, support personnel have been reported as accessible and responsive to student questions and concerns. According to one participant, "I think the staff are easily available and are more than willing to be helpful."

Moreover, at the participants' university, academic services available for traditional and nontraditional students and even maintain extended hours to accommodate their needs. However, given the nature of the modern university, which fosters computerized literature searches and the use of a personal laptop computer, the need to come to campus on a regular basis except for class has been minimized. One student's comment, "I have never been to the library" may reflect the nature of the university's computerized informational resources. In addition, since the university subscribes to an interlibrary loan service, which is a computerized retrieval system, students can send a request to the librarian and have articles, research studies, dissertations, or books sent to their homes. Presumably, this ease of facilitation via the Internet and campus Intranet had a positive impact on satisfaction with the university, program, and services, as reflected by data from interviews. Upon reflecting on this university's services, one participant responded, "The ongoing support is already there."

The service departments within the university have been designated as responsive and proactive. Because all books and syllabi are delivered to the students' classrooms, one week before the beginning of the next class, the student does not need to use the bookstore to purchase textbooks. With service focus on students, support staff attempt to create an environment of assistance that leads to effectively educating the student. An interviewed student commented, "I don't need the services that I needed when I was younger." Further, another interviewee suggested, "It's nice to have everything delivered to you. You do not have to run to the bookstore." Another student concurred, "It's hard to feel that you are out there on your own. This program does not have that...you have support." Lastly, a student verbalized, "I like the support."

Of the ten top rated items, delineated from eight composite scales, six implicated the value of qualified faculty. These items included the following: (a) "nearly all faculty are knowledgeable in their field;" (b) "the quality of instruction that I receive in my program is excellent;" (c) "faculty are fair and unbiased in their treatment of students;" (d) "faculty provide timely feedback about my progress;" (e) "my academic advisor is knowledgeable about requirements in my major;" and (f) "my academic advisor is accessible by telephone and email." The scores reinforced the importance of faculty knowledge, approachability, advising, and treatment of students as adult learners. Furthermore, data indicated that quality of instruction was rated as highly important and with correlated satisfaction. Since the goal of the academic process is to educate students with a quality, flexible, and effective program, students' satisfaction rating was one of high significance for the administration and university. The high ratings also provided positive feedback to the faculty, whose attention to detail was appreciated by the students. Interviewees corroborated survey results; that is, students appreciate the quality of instruction and responsive nature of the faculty to questions and concerns. One student said, "I feel that the faculty have done real well." Another student concurred, "The instructors are supportive." Lastly, one student responded, "I enrolled because I wanted a program to be all inclusive in terms of providing the best nursing related education that it can; provide a well-rounded school; and a school that has a high academic standard."

As demonstrated in the academic advising composite scale, two items involved the quality of the advising process and faculty student interactions. The importance and continued significance of advising had been implicated as one of the dominant themes of this study, and interestingly, was supported throughout the interview process. One student stated, "You have one person and have them help you or facilitate contact with other people." Another student concurred with the value of quality advisement, "Give me the person to contact and she can help with the problem." Lastly, one student stated, "I have a fabulous advisor."

As suggested by related research (Beeman, 1988), convenience emerged as another dominant theme, based on the high rating of classes being scheduled at suitable times. Presumably, this also reflected satisfaction with the predictable class schedule that remains unchanged until graduation. Designed for adult students, the classes meet the same night each week at the one location for the duration of the program. Students know where and when the classes are scheduled, up to 24 months in advance. A busy adult can plan his or her schedule based on this knowledge. Similarly, the item "I am able to complete most of my enrollment tasks in one location" was rated high in importance and satisfaction. Therefore, based on the design of an adult friendly system, the student can complete important educational transactions from registration to advisement sessions in their classroom. Participants' responses supported the theme of convenience, as highly valued, and listed it as one of the reasons for enrolling in the program.

CONCLUSIONS

Based on the findings of these studies, which sought to identify the items of importance and areas of satisfaction for the adult students, relevant implications were presented.

1. The adult students value quality academic advising and the collegial relationships that are forged with this experience. The university should continue to incorporate the use of competent and available faculty who understand the program and the needs of the adult student. This model can minimize the stress of returning to higher education.

2. The students value quality faculty. They appreciate faculty who are unbiased, approachable, knowledgeable, committed to excellence, and provide timely feedback.

3. Students are concerned with the quality of instruction and interactions with faculty as a measure of satisfaction and importance. Hiring procedures should focus on individuals who are academically and clinically qualified and are comfortable with working with the accelerated format and adult learners.

4. The institution should focus on cohort orientations to include advisement procedures, service access, technology and use of online databases. By focusing on minimizing time spent on campus, students can be assured that the university values their time.

5. The university ought to work with financial aid services to improve communication about programs, loans, scholarships, and grants. In addition, this information needs to be published in catalogs and student handbooks, posted online, and included in admissions packets.

6. External forces, such as family commitments, job responsibilities, and loss of financial aid, impact the students' ability to persist until graduation. Therefore, advisors may seek to remove institutional barriers while assisting students to identify methods to complete the degree.

7. Students look for convenience as a determining factor for enrolling in a program; therefore, the placements of cohorts and classrooms should be strategic in a dense population of potential students.

8. Students value and appreciate a safe learning environment. This aspect should be preserved.

9. Students favor the convenience of an accelerated program and camaraderie of the cohort model. Maintaining this model is suggested.

10. Despite a shortened time frame to complete assignments, students are able to perform well academically in the program and are motivated to complete the program as evidenced by interviews and high grade point averages.

Presumably, the sampled population responded positively and honestly when asked to participate in a study with specific research questions. With a high return of the ASPS, the indications are that students were ready and willing to voice their needs and suggestions on improving the entire educational process. Participants articulated what was and was not important to them in their academic experience. These data can assist in empowering faculty, staff, and administration at this institution to make changes, and to be more proactive in meeting students' needs and expectations. Additionally, these findings can help to create an academic environment conducive to preparing the adult learner to succeed in a professional environment. The focus on the adult student and program excellence may yield dividends undiscovered by the university.

SUMMARY

Stress can manifest itself in a number of physiological and psychological ways in each individual (Jacobs, 1999). By providing academic services for the burden-laden adult, the university may minimize the number or trips to campus, bookstore, registrar's office and library thereby diminishing the stress levels. In addition, with online libraries and databases, combined with technological support, the student may perform research from home and remote locations thereby decreasing the number and times on campus to complete assignments. According to one student, " I enjoy the services such as the books delivered to the classroom."

Adult students face unique stressors as they attempt to balance their life roles. Returning to school may be construed as a stressful event (Holmes and Rahe, 1967). One student commented, "If I couldn't balance it anymore I would quit the program."

Institutions that wish to establish programs designed for adult students must take these stressors into consideration when designing a supportive learning environment. As one student verbalized, "It's hard to feel that you are out there on your own. This program does not have that…you have support."

Students in the studied institution rate it highly in terms of providing that learning environment, and that satisfaction exists in two very different academic disciplines. "It's nice to have everything delivered to you…you're not running to the bookstore."

Based on the findings of these studies, further research may focus on the use a pre- and post-assessment of stress and anxiety to ascertain whether the services were instrumental in diminishing student stressors. Additionally, by treating the adult student as a customer of higher education, the university may increase the interpersonal support provided to each individual.

REFERENCES

Anderson, E. (2003). Changing U. S. demographics and American higher education. *New Directions for Higher Education, 121*, 3–12.

Ayer, S., and Smith, C. (1998). Planning flexible learning to match the needs of consumers: A national survey. *Journal of Advanced Nursing, 27*, 1032–1047.

Beeman, P. (1988). RNs' perceptions of their baccalaureate programs: Meeting their adult learning needs. *Journal of Nursing Education, 27*(8), 364–370.

Bohlin, R. M., Milheim, W. D., and Viechnicki, K. J. (1994). The development of a model for the design of motivational adult instruction in higher education. *Journal of Educational Technology Systems, 22*(1), 3–17.

Bok, D. (2003) *Universities in the marketplace: The commercialization of higher education.* Princeton: Princeton University Press, 2003.

Bowl, M. (2001). Experiencing the barriers: Nontraditional students entering higher education. *Research Papers in Education, 16*(2), 141-160.

Boylston, M. T., Peters, M. A., and Lacey, M. (2004). Adult student satisfaction in traditional and accelerated RN-to-BSN programs. *Journal of Professional Nursing, 20*(1), 23–32.

Brown, C. D., and Eggert Linnemann, R. (1995, Spring). Services for adult undergraduate students in a four-year college. *The Journal of Continuing Higher Education,* 2–13.

El Ansari, W. (2002). Student nurse satisfaction levels with their courses: Part I – effects of demographic variables. *Nurse Education Today, 22*(2), 159–170.

Elliott, K. M., and Shin, D. (2002). Student satisfaction: An alternative approach to assessing this important concept. *Journal of Higher Education, 24*(2), 197–209.

Fairchild, E. E. (2003/Summer). Multiple roles of adult learners. *New Directions for Student Services, 102,* 11-16.

Fishback, S. J., and Polson, C. J. (1998). *The cognitive development of adult undergraduate students.* In *Proceedings of the 17th annual Midwest research to practice conference in adult, continuing, and community education.* Edited by G. S. Wood, Jr. and M. M. Webber, p. 81-86. Muncie, Indiana: Ball State University (ED 424 419) Retrieved January 28, 2004, from
http://www.bsu.edu/teachers/departments/edld/conf/cognitive.html

Fralick, M. (1993). College success: A study of positive and negative attrition. *Community College review, 20*(5), 29-36.

Fungaroli, C.S. (2000) *Traditional degrees for nontraditional students.* New York: Farrar, Straus, and Giroux, 2000.

Green, C. P. (1987). Multiple role women: The real world of the mature RN learner. *Journal of Nursing Education, 26*(7), 266-271.

Grupe, F., and Connolly, F. (1995, January – February). Grownups are different: Computer training for older adult learners. *Journal of Systems Management,* 54-68.

Hadfield, J. (2003, Summer). Recruiting and retaining adult students. *New Directions for Student Services. 102,* 17-26.

Holmes, T., and Rahe, R. (1967). Social readjustment rating scale. *Journal of Psychosomatics Research, 11,* 213-218.

Horn, L., Peter, K., Rooney, K., and Malizio, A. G. (2002). *Profile of undergraduates in U. S. postsecondary institutions 1999-2000: Statistical analysis report* (NCES 97-578). Retrieved July 5, 2004, from http://nces.ed.gov/pubs2002/2002168.PDF U. S. Department of Education, NCES. Washington, DC: U. S. Government Printing Office.

Jacobs, G. D. (1999). The physiology of mind-body interactions: The stress response and the relaxation response. *The Journal of Alternative and Complementary Medicine, 7*(1), S-83-S-92.

Kasworm, C. E. (2003, Spring). From the adult students' perspective: Accelerated degree programs. *New Directions for Adult and Continuing Education, 97,* 17-27.

Kerka, S. (1995). *Adult learner retention revisited.* Washington, DC: Office of Educational Research and Improvement. (ERIC Document Reproduction Service No. ED 389880)

Kerka, S. (2001). *The balancing act of adult life.* Washington, DC: Office of Educational Research and Improvement. (ERIC Document Reproduction Service No. ED 459323)

Knowles, M. (1978). *The adult learner: A neglected species (2nd ed).* Houston, TX: Gulf Publishing Company.

Lee, E.J. (1988). Analysis of coping methods reported by returning RNs. *Journal of Nursing Education, 27*(7), 309-313.

MacKinnon-Slaney, F. (1994). The adult persistence in learning model: A road map to counseling services for adult learners. *Journal of Counseling and Development, 73*(2), 268-275.

McCollough, M. A., and Gremler, D. D. (1999). Guaranteeing student satisfaction: An exercise in treating students as customers. *Journal of Marketing Education, 21*(2), 118–130.

National Center for Education Statistics (NCES) (2002). Special analysis 2002: Nontraditional undergraduates. Retrieved January 29, 2004, from http://www.nces.ed.gov/programs/coe/2002/analyses/nontraditional/index.asp

Naugle, D. (1995). The Christian college and adult education. *Faculty Dialogue* 24 (Spring, 1995), 24ff.

O'Brien, B. S., and Renner, A. (2000). Nurses on-line: Career mobility for registered nurses. *Journal of Professional Nursing, 16*(1), 13–20.

O'Connor, P. C., and Bevil, C. A. (1996). Academic outcomes and stress in full-time day and part-time evening baccalaureate nursing students. *Journal of Nursing Education, 35*(6), 245–251.

Reed, N., and Beaudin, B. (1993). Adult students and technology in higher education: A partnership for participation. *Collegiate Microcomputer, XI*(1), 1-4.

Richardson, J. T. E., and King, E. (1998). Adult students in higher education: Burden or boon? *Journal of Higher Education*, 69(1), 65-88.

Selye, H. (1977). *The stress of life.* New York: McGraw Hill.

Sissel, P. A., Hansman, C. A., and Kasworm, C. E. (2001). The politics of neglect: Adult learners in higher education, *91*, 17–27.

Viechnicki, K. J., Bohlin, R. M., and Milheim, W. D. (1990, Fall). Instructional motivation of adult learners: An analysis of student perceptions in continuing education. *The Journal of Continuing Education,* 10-14.

Wachs, M. (1993). *The case for practitioner faculty.* Los Angeles: Graduate School of Architecture and Urban Planning.

Wlodkowsi, R. J. (2003, Spring). Accelerated learning in colleges and universities. *New Directions for Adult and Continuing Education, 97,* 5-15.

Viechnicki, K. J., Bohlin, R. M., and Milheim, W. D. (1990, Fall). Instructional motivation of adult learners: An analysis of student perceptions in continuing education. *The Journal of Continuing Education,* 10-14.

ABOUT THE AUTHOR

Matthew M. Martin (Ph.D., Kent State University, 1992) is a Professor, Communication Studies Department, West Virginia University, Morgantown, WV, 26506, (304-293-3905), *MMartin@wvu.edu.* Jacob L. Cayanus (Ed.D., West Virginia University, 2005) is an Assistant Professor at Oakland University. Keith Weber (Ed.D., West Virginia University, 1998) is an Assistant Professor at West Virginia University. Alan K. Goodboy (M.A., West Virginia University, 2004) is a doctoral student at West Virginia University.

In: Stress and Mental Health of College Students
Editor: Mery V. Landow, pp. 149-169

ISBN 1-59454-839-0
© 2006 Nova Science Publishers, Inc.

Chapter 6

COLLEGE STUDENTS' STRESS AND ITS IMPACT ON THEIR MOTIVATION AND COMMUNICATION WITH THEIR INSTRUCTORS

Matthew M. Martin, Jacob L. Cayanus, Keith Weber and Alan K. Goodboy

West Virginia University, Morgantown, West Virginia
Oakland University, Rochester, Michigan

ABSTRACT

This chapter concerns a study involving college student stress. Specifically, we investigated students' school stress, personal stress, and anxiety about communicating with their instructors. We expected that students with higher levels of stress and anxiety should differ in their classroom interest and communication. We measured interest using an instrument that has three dimensions: competence (I feel I can be successful in my classes), impact (I believe I can make a difference in my classes), and meaningfulness (My classes are relevant to me). Communication with instructors was addressed by measuring five motives students have for communicating with their instructors: relational (I want to get to know my instructors better), functional (I need to get information that is relevant to my class), participation (I want to appear involved in the class), excuse-making (I need to explain my work to my teacher), and sycophancy (to give the impression that I think the instructor is an effective teacher). Students' level of stress and anxiety were related to their classroom interest and their motives for communicating with their instructors. Students who felt competent reported lower amounts of anxiety and pressure concerning their peers, but also reported higher amounts of worry and pressure from school. Students who were interested because the class was meaningful to them reported higher levels of pressure from school. Students who communicated more for the functional motive reported higher amounts of pressure from school, but also reported lower levels of anxiety. Students who communicated for the sycophancy motive but not the functional motive, reported lower levels of worry, and more pressure concerning their peers.

INTRODUCTION

According to the transactional model of stress (Lazarus, 1981; Lazarus and Folkman, 1984), the occurrence of stress is extremely subjective based on how individuals evaluate the stressful events they encounter. Stress has commonly been researched focusing on major events that produce change (e.g., Barrett, Rose, and Klerman, 1979; Creed, 1993; Elliot and Eisdorfer, 1982; Gruen, 1993). One such event is an individual trying to adapt to the stress and pressure of college life. As Kaufman and Feldman (2004) stated, "Because college is invested with so much meaning in the larger society, to feel worthy of attending college is itself significant for how individuals identify themselves by these characteristics" (p. 470).

For many college students, new educational environments and social environments can lead to stress (Misra and Castillo, 2004). Students must deal with new demands of class work, choosing a major, and actually going to class while fitting in the new social networks they encounter. Many students also have to find time to work and deal with the stress of being away from home for the first time. This stress caused from student life can lead to higher amounts of risk taking behavior as well as depression (Pledge, Lapan, Heppner, Kivlighan, and Roehlke, 1998). According to Hughes (2005), "stress contributes to anxiety, which can in turn interfere with students' academic performance" (p. 22).

Furr, Westefeld, McConnell, and Jenkins (2001) noted that students often feel stress over grades, relationships, money, being lonely, and their parents. Concerns about academic performance (i.e. grades) are the most common form of stressor for college students (Abouserie, 1994; Furr et al., 2001; Westefeld and Furr, 1987) and not just in North America (Makaremi, 2000; Naito, Kijima, and Kitamura, 2000). Students feel a great deal of stress over grades based on self-imposed stress, stress from peers, and stress from family. Financial issues also lead to stress for college students (Andrews and Widing, 2004; Hodgson and Simoni, 1995).

While many researchers have examined the impact stress has on college students (e.g., Edwards, Hershberger, Russell, and Market, 2001; Misra, McKean, West, and Russo, 2000; Thomas and Williams, 1991; Winkelman, 1994), most of these studies focus on major life changes as the main cause of stress. While change is a frequent precursor to stress, questions have been raised concerning whether or not change itself should be the only form of stress experience studied (e.g., Turner and Wheaton, 1995; Zautra and Reich, 1983). Pressure has been proposed to be another important form of stress (Weiten, 1988).

Pressure, as described by Weiten (1988), is a subjective perception of both the expectations and demands of how an individual should behave in a certain manner. Weiten further delineated pressure into two subtypes: performance and conforming. Performance pressure refers to performing certain tasks successfully while pressure to conform involves others' expectations placed on the individual concerning thinking and behaving. As Feldman (1972) argued, "As a student progresses through college, those around him- teachers, peers, parents, and the general community within and outside the college, etc.- define and label him according to the positions he occupies in college" (p. 13).

Wieten (1988) developed the Pressure Inventory as a way to measure pressure as a type of stress. The author found that the Pressure Inventory does measure pressure and that pressure may contribute to the prediction of adaptational outcomes. This finding is important in terms of discovering ways students can cope with pressure more effectively. One of the main benefits of the Pressure Inventory is that the measure enables researchers to examine pressure which could be a way to incorporate the interpersonal aspects of stress (Weiten, 1998).

Although scant research has been conducted on pressure as a separate form of stress, based on the findings of Weiten (1988; 1998), it appears to be an important concept. Pressure affects individuals differently as it is a subjective experience. While much of the past research has focused on achievement outcomes, the focus of this project was on interest and motivation. In relation to the interpersonal aspects of stress, two questions arise: does pressure affect a student's interest in the class? And does pressure affect a students motivation to communicate in the class?

WORRYING

Worrying is a common human experience and refers to experiencing uncontrollable thoughts about possible future events that are negative (Borkovec, Ray, and Stober, 1998; Borkovec, Robinson, Pruzinsky, and Depree, 1983). These thoughts are difficult to dismiss because a worrier tends to be aware of, and cognitively rehearses, possible future danger (Mathews, 1990). The phenomenon of worrying can be characterized as both functional and dysfunctional in terms of outcomes (Gladstone and Parker, 2003). As Tallis, Davey, and Capuzzo (1994) noted, worrying leads to a plethora of cognitive, affective, and behavioral outcomes including pessimism, depression, exaggeration, and restlessness. However, worrying can occasionally serve a positive function for individuals. For instance, worrying is an important response mechanism to danger (Mathews, 1990) and can increase job performance (Perkins and Corr, 2005). Despite the specific role worrying plays in individuals' lives, there are several consistent findings.

First, worrying is a central diagnostic characteristic in general anxiety disorder (GAD). Chronic and uncontrollable worry are labeled GAD (American Psychiatric Association, 1994; Borkovec et al., 1998; Ruscio and Borkovec, 2004). Individuals with GAD allow worrying to affect their lives as they report higher amounts of severe symptoms due to worry (Ruscio and Borkovec, 2003), more negative appraisals of worry (Wells, 1995), and perceive their worrying to be more uncontrollable and less correctable (Borkovec et al., 1998; Montorio, Nuevo, Marquez, Izal, and Losada, 2003).

Second, personality and cognitive characteristics are important predictors of worrying. For instance, Pruzinsky and Borkovec (1990) reported that worriers are higher in public self-consciousness, obsession, and social anxiety. Similarly, worrying can effect communication and cause psychological discomfort in public speaking (Addison, Clay, Xie, Sawyer, and Behnke, 2003).

Third, worrying leads to a number of actual behaviors. Worriers engage more in negative daydreaming (Pruzinsky and Borkovec, 1990) and experience more problem- solving deficits (Dugas, Letarte, Rheaume, Freeston, and Ladouceur, 1995). Furthermore, worrying leads to poorer test performance (Everson, Smodlaka, and Tobias, 1994). However, as previously noted, worrying can elicit positive behaviors as well. For example, worrying has been linked to smoking cessation (Dijkstra and Brosschot, 2003).

Fourth, worrying serves a major and distinct function. Borkovec et al. (1998) asserted that worrying mainly serves as a sort of cognitive avoidance for threatening stimuli. Thoughts about possible future events and how to avoid negative outcomes is a type of cognitive preparation and avoidance of threat. Chronic worriers believe that negative events are more likely to occur in their lives (Vay and Borkovec, 1992). Worrying serves an important avoidance function for these individuals.

Fifth, worrying is distinct from other constructs such as obsession. Turner, Beidel, and Stanley (1992) explained that worrying focuses on daily experience instead of obsessive themes. They noted that worrying is usually triggered by internal or external factors, while obsessed individuals are usually unable to identify triggers. Additionally, Wells and Morrison (1994) suggested that worrying involves verbal thought while obsession involves imagery.

Based on the aforementioned research, we believed that students who worry more often would differ in their classroom communication behaviors in comparison to students who tend not to worry. Beyond current stress that students would be experiencing in their lives, their tendency to worry in general should play a role in their classroom communication behaviors. Another factor which would influence students' interest and motives for communicating with their instructors would be their state anxiety when communicating with their instructors.

STATE ANXIETY

While some may view worry and anxiety as overlapping constructs, worry can be viewed as negative thoughts while anxiety involves fear, tension, and overall uncomfortableness (Barlow, 2002; Kelly, 2004a, 2004b; Kelly and Miller, 1999). People often experience anxiety about communication. People high in anxiety talk less and are less satisfied in their communication with others. In fact, anxiety is negatively related to three essential components of learning: communication competence, communication skill, and positive affect (McCroskey and Beatty, 1999). Students that are high in anxiety have an overall negative attitude about school and fare worse in school than students low in anxiety (Hurt and Preiss, 1978; McCroskey, Booth-Butterfield, and Payne, 1989). Students high in anxiety are often apprehensive due to classroom evaluation as well as lack self-efficacy in their own interpersonal skills (Neer and Kircher, 1989). When students are worried about their success, their anxiety increases and students experience uncomfortable physical sensations (Addison, Clay, Xie, Sawyer, and Behnke, 2003; Kopecky, Sawyer, and Behnke, 2004; Smith, Sawyer, and Behnke, 2005).

Booth-Butterfield (1988a; 1988b) concluded that anxiety, or communication apprehension, is most consistent cross-situationally in formal contexts, such as the classroom. In other words, one would expect high communication apprehensives to be apprehensive in classroom activities and interactions. High communication apprehensives would talk less in class, talk less to their fellow students, and talk less to the teacher (Martin, Valencic, and Heisel, 2002; McCroskey and Sheahan, 1978). When students have less time to prepare and must complete complex tasks, they face greater anxiety (Ayres, 1988). Dobos (1996) found that high communication apprehensives had less motivation and more difficulty in participating in collaborative learning activities. This supports McCroskey's (1977) argument that communication apprehension would be a greater factor in the small classroom environment versus the large lecture class. Additionally, Beatty, Forst, and Stewart (1986) reported that high communication apprehensives talk less in public speaking classes.

Frymier and Houser (2000) argued that the relationship between an instructor and a student develops in part based on the interpersonal skills of the participants. Students high in anxiety are less competent communicators than students low in anxiety. Thus, students' levels of anxiety should be related to when and why students would communicate with their instructors. Additionally, students' level of anxiety should be related to their feelings of competence, meaningfulness, and impact.

STUDENT INTEREST

The role of interest in learning has been a topic of discussion for over the past hundred years. According to Schiefele (1991), interest can be traced back to Herbart in the 1800s who believed that interest promoted long-term storage of information and motivation for learning. Contemporary researchers view interest as a three dimensional construct consisting of a superordinate factor structure (Schraw and Dennison, 1994; Tobias, 1994). These three dimensions are meaningfulness, impact, and competence (Hidi and Baird, 1988; Mitchell, 1993; Weber, Martin, and Patterson, 2001). Meaningfulness relates to the perceived value of a task (Schiefele, 1996; 1998). The more a task has meaning to individuals, the harder they will work to complete that task. Competence refers to people's evaluation of their own abilities and previous knowledge. Individuals tend to be more interested in topics they feel competent discussing or have some prior knowledge about (Alexander, Jetton, and Kulikowich, 1995). Finally, impact signifies that the source is important to the completion of a task, and that the task makes a difference (Boscolo and Mason, 2003). The more impact individuals believe they have, the more interested they feel.

Schiefele (1996) investigated the effect of interest on text learning. He found that high-interested readers found the material more meaningful and were able to assimilate text messages more completely. Interest has also been found to be related to recall and elaboration (Schiefele and Krapp, 1996; Tobias, 1994). Alexander, Kulikowich, and Schultze (1994a) found a significant relationship between interest and recall, as well as between interest and prior knowledge. In a separate investigation, Alexander, Kulikowich, and Schultze (1994b) found that college students' interest and topic knowledge were significant predictors of their comprehension of a physics text.

The majority of the interest research has been conducted in the field of educational psychology. In fact, until recently the study of interest has been virtually ignored in the instructional communication literature. Although student interest has been referred to as a variable impacting both motivation and learning (Frymier, 1994; Gorham and Millette, 1997; Richmond and Gorham, 1996), there was a lack of empirical evidence to support this idea.

Weber and Patterson (2000) argued that the absence of interest research was mainly due to the lack of a valid measurement instrument. Researchers in educational psychology mostly use the Schraw, Bruning, and Svoboda (1995) Perceived Interest Questionnaire (PIQ) as a measure of interest. The PIQ is a highly reliable one-dimensional scale. However, Weber and Patterson questioned the content validity of the scale when they asserted that a one-dimensional scale cannot assess a multidimensional construct adequately. With this in mind, the authors suggested using the Frymier, Shulman, and Houser (1996) Learner Empowerment Scale (LES) as a more valid measure of student interest because the operationalization of the LES is similar to the conceptualization of interest.

Frymier et al. (1996), building on the work done in the field of management, set out to develop a measure of empowerment that was appropriate for an instructional setting. Thomas and Velthouse (1990) defined empowerment as intrinsic task motivation that results from performing tasks that increase feelings of self-efficacy. Furthermore, Thomas and Velthouse asserted that empowerment is a four dimensional construct. The first three dimensions (similar to interest) are termed Meaningfulness, Impact, and Feelings of Competence. The fourth dimension is Choice, which refers to the degree that individuals make their own decisions regarding tasks that they undertake. In Frymier et al.'s attempt at creating a learner empowerment measure, choice failed to emerge as a viable dimension. This led these authors to conclude that choice is not a critical aspect of learner empowerment because students are not accustomed to making choices in the classroom.

Whether or not students value choice is immaterial for the current discussion; what is of concern is the incongruity between the conceptualization of learner empowerment and its operationalization. When examining the literature in the area of learner empowerment, what instructional researchers are left with is a conceptually sound construct with a flawed operationalization. This is similar to the concern discussed previously about the definition and measurement of interest. However, when studying these two areas together (empowerment and interest) it is clear that the operationalization of the Frymier et al. (1996) LES is consistent with the conceptualization of student interest. Weber and Patterson (2000) made this argument and provided support that the LES is a valid measure of interest through the use of an exploratory factor analysis. These authors conducted a factor analysis with items from both the LES as well as those of the PIQ. The result was a three-factor solution with all of the PIQ items loading on the same factor as the Meaningfulness items from the LES. This led these authors to conclude that the PIQ was only measuring that one dimension of interest.

In studies looking at the relationship between interest (as measured by the LES) and motivation, Weber and Patterson (2000) reported positive correlations between these two constructs. Weber et al. (2001) found a similar positive relationship between interest and motivation in a sample of at-risk middle school students. These findings are consistent with those found by Frymier et al. (1996) who also found that the LES was related to immediacy, relevance, self-esteem, and both affective and behavioral learning in two separate studies.

Weber, Fornash, Corrigan, and Neupauer (2003) conducted an experiment in an attempt to validate the relationship between interest and cognitive learning by manipulating the presence of interest variables in the content of a lesson. The results indicated that students in the interest group were significantly more interested in the material, and scored higher on multiple choice tests, than the control group. Furthermore, when interest was statistically controlled for, the difference in the test scores between the two groups was not significant. These results lend support to the link between cognitive learning and interest.

Weber, Martin, and Cayanus (2005) reported on a two-part study in an attempt to shorten the original 29-item LES. The result of the first study was an 18-item version of the LES that obtained high alpha scores as a measure of internal reliability. Additionally, this shortened form of the LES performed similarly to the original longer version. In the second part of the study, the authors further validated the LES as a measure of interest by supporting the multi-dimensional nature of the scale through the use of a confirmatory factor analysis. Weber et al.

also found that students who are interested because they believe the material is meaningful and believe they can make an impact communicated with their instructors for relational and excuse making motives. Conversely, students whose interest is attributable to their feelings of competence tend to communicate with their instructors for more functional motives

We expected that students who tend to worry more overall, who are feeling stress involving their lives, and who express more anxiety about communicating with their instructors in general would differ in their interest compared to students who report worrying less and feeling less anxiety and stress. Thus, we proposed the following research question.

RQ1: What is the relationship between students' worrying, anxiety, and stress with their feelings of interest (i.e., competence, meaningfulness, and impact)?

STUDENTS' MOTIVES FOR COMMUNICATING

Schutz (1966) identified three main reasons for why people communicate with others: affection, inclusion, and control. Affection is the need to communicate with others to express caring and love. Inclusion is the need to communicate with others to participate in and maintain relationships. Control is the need to communicate with others in order to maintain power and influence others. Schutz argued that people communicate with others in order to satisfy these needs.

Building on the work of Schutz, Rubin, Perse, and Barbato (1988) were interested in why people talk, with whom people talk, and what people talk about. In doing so, they identified three other motives, in addition to affection, inclusion, and control, for why people communicate with others. These three were pleasure, relaxation, and escape. Pleasure involves the need to be excited or entertained. Relaxation deals with a need to rest or to feel less tense. Escape focuses on a need to avoid other activities and worries. Rubin et al. argued that these six motives influence how and why people communicate. However, they also made it clear that in different contexts, people will have different motives, or reasons, for communicating with others.

In the context of the college classroom, Martin, Myers, and Mottet (1999) have identified five motives students have for communicating with their instructors: relational, functional, excuse-making, participation, and sycophancy. When students communicate for *relational* purposes, they are trying to develop personal relationships with their instructors. Communication for *functional* reasons includes learning more about the material and the assignments in the course. Students also communicate to offer *excuses*, attempting to explain why work is late or missing or to challenge grading criteria. A fourth reason students have for communicating is for *participation*. Students want to demonstrate to their instructors that they are interested in the class and that they understand the material. A fifth reason is *sycophancy*, which involves getting on the instructor's good side. Students may communicate in order to make a favorable impression or to get the instructor's approval.

Students differ in why they communicate with their instructors in part due to their own personalities. Students who are competent communicators, who are both assertive and responsive, tend to talk to their instructors more overall (Myers, Martin, and Mottet, 2000a). On the other hand, students who are high in communication apprehension avoid talking to their instructors (Martin, Valencic, and Heisel, 2002). Martin et al. also reported that students with higher classroom motivation expressed communicating more often for the motives of relational and participation. When students are paying attention in the classroom and report that they are enjoying themselves, they will communicate more with their instructors for the relational, functional, participation, and sycophancy motives (Martin, Mottet, and Myers, 2005).

How instructors communicate with their students/classes also influences why students report communicating with those instructors. Students will talk to their teachers more for the relational, functional, and participation motives when they perceive their instructors as being responsive, confirming, and nonverbally immediate (Martin, Valencic, and Heisel, 2001; Myers, Martin, and Mottet, 2000a; Myers, Mottet, and Martin, 2000). Similarly, when instructors use verbal approach strategies and prosocial behavioral alteration techniques, students will be more likely to communicate with their instructors (Martin, Heisel, and Valencic, 2000; Mottet, Martin, and Myers, 2004). However, when instructors use avoidance strategies or antisocial behavioral alteration techniques, students will refrain from communicating with their instructors. But when instructors are viewed as open, are willing to talk about their lives and opinions, and maintain a positive classroom atmosphere, students are more likely to talk to their instructors (Cayanus and Martin, 2004; Cayanus, Martin, and Goodboy, 2004).

Several studies have focused on how students' motives influence their communication with their instructors. Myers, Martin, and Mottet (2002a) found that students' motives were related to their information-seeking strategies. For example, students who communicate more frequently for functional reasons were more likely to use overt strategies. Knapp and Martin (2003) reported that students who had higher motivation for communicating in class (i.e. participation) were more likely to have greater amounts of out-of-class communication with their instructors. Kelly, Duran, and Zolten (2001) found no differences in students' motives for communicating with their instructors when comparing face to face communication with the use of e-mail.

Students' motives for communicating with their instructors have also been found to be related to classroom behavior and performance. Martin et al. (1999) found that students who communicated with their instructor more often in general communicated more with their instructors to relate and participate. When students report communicating more for the relational, functional, and participation motives, they also report greater course affect and cognitive learning (Martin et al., 2000).

Previous research in the area of student motives illustrates that certain motives, in particular the functional, relational, and participation motives, are related to positive learning outcomes. Weber et al. (2005) found that when students feel they can make an impact in the classroom, find the coursework meaningful, and believe they have the necessary competence to succeed, they are more likely to communicate with their instructors.

In this study, we were interested in the role that stress plays in why students communicate with their instructors. We expected that students who tend to worry more overall, who are feeling stress involving their lives, and who express more anxiety about communicating with their instructors in general would differ in their motives compared to students who report worrying less and feeling less anxiety and stress. Thus, we proposed the following research question.

RQ2: What is the relationship between students' worrying, anxiety, and stress with their motives for communicating with their instructors?

METHOD

Participants

Participants in this study were 195 (75 women, 120 men) undergraduate students enrolled at a large Mid-Atlantic university. There were 119 first year students, 41 sophomores, 22 juniors, and 13 seniors. Approximately 36% (N = 70) of the participants currently held a job working 8.50 hours a week on average (*SD* = 12.44). Half of the participants (N = 97) received some type of scholarship to attend school and overall the participants were responsible for 34.28% (*SD* = 33.28) of their college expenses.

Procedure

Participants completed a questionnaire containing measures of student interest, worry, anxiety, stress, student motives to communicate, and demographic variables. Students were reporting on their current feelings and behaviors involving their current courses/instructors. The questionnaire was administered during the 12th week of class. This study was approved by the university's research board and participation was voluntary.

Measures

Students' motives were measured using Martin, Mottet, and Myers' (2000) Student Classroom Motives Scale. The scale contains 30 items, with a 5-item Likert-type response set ranging from *Exactly Like Me* (5) to *Not At All Like Me* (1). The items for this scale are in Figure 1. Means, standard deviations, and reliabilities obtained in this study were: relational (*M* = 13.58, *SD* = 5.44, α = .89), functional (*M* = 20.12, *SD* = 5.10, α = .82), excuse making (*M* = 15.89, *SD* = 5.25, α = .82), participatory (*M* = 15.12, *SD* = 5.38, α = .84), and sycophancy (*M* = 14.04, *SD* = 5.47, α = .85).

Interest was measured using the 18-item version of Frymier et al.'s (1996) Learner Empowerment Measure (Weber, Martin, and Cayanus, 2005). There are six items for each of the subscales: impact, competence, and meaningfulness. This measure uses a 7-point Likert scale with responses ranging from *Completely Agree* (7) to *Completely Disagree* (1). Sample items for each of the subscales are: impact (I can make an impact on the way things are run in my classes, I make a difference in the learning that goes on in my classes), competence (I believe in my ability to do well in my classes, I believe that I can achieve my goals in my classes), and meaningfulness (The work that I do in my classes is meaningful to me, The things that I learn in my class are useful). The means, standard deviations, and coefficient alphas in this study were: impact (*M* = 22.46, *SD* = 6.91, α = .82), competence (*M* = 31.38, *SD* = 6.25, α = .83), and meaningfulness (*M* = 25.90, *SD* = 6.35, α = .79).

Worry was measured using Kelly's (2004b) Three Item Worry Index. Participants rate on an 11-point scale, from *Never/Not at All* (0) to *Continuously/Very Much* (10) to the following three questions: how often do you worry, how much is worry a problem for you, and to what extent would you call yourself a worrier. The coefficient alpha for this scale was .95 (M = 14.65, SD = 7.89).

Motives	Scale Items
Relational	to learn about him/her personally so we can develop a friendship to build a personal relationship to learn more about the teacher personally because I find him/her interesting because we share common interests
Functional	to clarify the material to get assistance on the assignments/exams to learn how I can improve in the class to ask questions about the material to get academic advice to get more information on the requirements of the course
Participation	to appear involved in class because my input is vital for class discussion to demonstrate that I understand the material to demonstrate my intelligence because my classmates value my contribution to class discussions because my instructor values class participation
Excuse-Making	to explain why work is late to explain absences to explain why I do not have my work done to challenge a grade I received to explain why my work does not meet the instructor's expectations to explain the quality of my work
Sycophancy	to pretend I'm interested in the course to give the instructor the impression that I like him/her to give the impression that I think the instructor is an effective teacher to give the impression that I'm learning a lot from the instructor to give the impression that I'm interested in the course content to get special permission/privileges not granted to all students

Figure 1. Students' Motives for Communicating

Note. Students rate on a Likert-type scale, from *exactly like me* (5) to *not at all like me* (1) how each of the statements reflects their reasons for talking to their instructors.

State anxiety was measured using eight items from the Situational Communication Apprehension Measure (Richmond and McCroskey, 1998). This instrument is a Likert-type measure, with responses ranging from *Extremely Accurate* (7) to *Extremely Inaccurate* (1). Individuals reported about their feelings about communicating with their current instructors. The eight items were: I feel apprehensive, I feel uneasy, I feel self-assured (r), I feel fearful, I feel composed (r), I feel bothered, I feel flustered, and I feel good (r). The coefficient alpha for this measure was .82 (M = 26.94, SD = 8.08).

Stress was measured using the following three subscales of the Pressure Inventory - Form 3 (Weiten, 1988): school relations, peer relations, and self-imposed. Each subscale has seven items which were measured using a five-point Likert scale ranging from *A Great Deal of Pressure* (5) to *No Pressure* (1). Sample items for each of the subscales are: school relations (to get excellent grades or to improve my grades, to make important decisions about my education future), peer relations (to provide help or emotional support to friends or neighbors, to achieve greater success in the eyes of my friends), and self-imposed (to change or improve my personality, to be more efficient in my use of my personal time). The means, standard deviations, and coefficient alphas attained in this study were: school relations ($M = 23.31$, $SD = 4.71$, $\alpha = .70$), peer relations ($M = 18.66$, $SD = 5.72$, $\alpha = .78$), and self-imposed ($M = 20.29$, $SD = 5.47$, $\alpha = .71$).

RESULTS

The first research question asked if students' interest in their courses would be related to their worry, anxiety and stress. To answer this research question, a canonical correlation was conducted with the three dimensions of student interest serving as one set of variables and students' worry, anxiety, and stress serving as the second set of variables. There were two significant and interpretable roots (Wilks' $\Lambda = .72$, $F [15, 513] = 4.37$, $p < .001$): Rc1 = .46 and Rc2 = .27 that accounted for 29% of the variance (see Table 1). With root one, students who felt more competent and found their courses to be meaningful reported lower amounts of anxiety and peer stress, but also reported higher amounts of worry and school stress. This root accounted for 21% of the variance. With root two, students who were interested because the class was more meaningful but did not feel competent reported higher levels of school stress. Root two accounted for 8% of the variance.

Table 1. Canonical Correlation involving Stress Variables and Student Interest

Canonical Loadings	Root 1	Root2
Set 1: Stress Variables		
Worry	.51	.06
Anxiety	-.42	.16
School Pressure	.59	.68
Peer Pressure	-.83	.22
Self-Pressure	-.05	.22
Redundancy coefficient	[.14]	[.04]
Set 2: Student Interest		
Impact	-.24	.16
Meaningfulness	.47	.89
Competence	.83	-.57
Redundancy coefficient	[.15]	[.11]

Note. Wilks' $\Lambda = .72$, $F (15, 513) = 4.37$, $p < .001$; Rc1 = .46, Rc2 = .27

The second research question asked if students' motives for communicating with their instructors would be related to their worry, stress, and anxiety. To answer this research question, a canonical correlation was conducted with the five dimensions of student motives to communicate serving as one set of variables and worry, anxiety, and stress serving as the second set of variables. There were two significant and interpretable roots (Wilks' $\Lambda = .66$, F [25, 685] = 3.30, $p < .001$): Rc1 = .50 and Rc2 = .29 that accounted for 34% of the variance (see Table 2). With root one, students who communicated for the functional motive reported higher amounts of school stress, but also reported lower levels of anxiety. This root accounted for 25% of the variance. In root two, students who communicated more for the sycophancy motive but not the functional motive, reported lower levels of worry, but also reported more peer stress. Root two accounted for 9% of the variance.

Table 2. Canonical Correlation involving Stress Variables and Students' Motives for Communicating with their Instructors

Canonical Loadings	Root 1	Root 2
Set 1: Stress Variables		
Worry	.09	-.82
Anxiety	-.45	.19
School Pressure	.76	-.28
Peer Pressure	.23	.71
Self-Pressure	.08	.37
Redundancy coefficient	[.08]	[.08]
Set 2: Student Interest		
Relational	.12	.11
Functional	-.65	.72
Excuse Making	.34	.13
Participatory	.14	.30
Sycophancy	.05	.57
Redundancy coefficient	[.07]	[.05]

Note. Wilks' $\Lambda = .66$, F (15, 685) = 3.30, $p < .001$; Rc1 = .50, Rc2 = .29

POST HOC ANALYSIS

The Pearson correlations between the stress variables with student interest and motives are in Table 3. The strongest correlations involved school stress. The more school stress students report, the more meaningful they find their courses and the more likely they are to communicate with their instructors for all of the motives except the relational motive. Table 4 shows the correlations involving the same variables when considering the sex of the student. There are several differences of note. Female students report a positive relationship between school stress and feelings of making an impact. Male students who are experiencing school stress and self-stress are more likely to communicate for the motive of sycophancy.

Table 3. Correlations between the Stress Variables with Student Interest and Motives

	Worry	Anxiety	School Stress	Peer Stress	Self Stress
Impact	.06	.05	.14	.10	.07
Meaningfulness	.17*	.05	.30*	.02	.10
Competence	.06	-.25*	.07	-.28*	-.18*
Relational	.08	.06	.12	.25*	.20*
Functional	.19*	-.16*	.40*	.17*	.16*
Excuse-making	.03	.08	.30*	.19*	.21*
Participatory	.01	.03	.26*	.26*	.21*
Sycophancy	.03	.02	.20*	.29*	.20*

Note. (*) = significant at the $p < .01$ level.

Table 4. Correlations between the Stress Variables with Student Interest and Motives – Considering Sex of Student

	Worry		Anxiety		School Stress		Peer Stress		Self Stress	
	M	F	M	F	M	F	M	F	M	F
Impact	.05	.06	-.10	.04	.08	.23*	.05	.17	.02	.16
Meaningfulness	.22*	.03	-.09	.01	.26*	.36*	-.02	.06	.10	.09
Competence	.08	.09	-.20*	-.34*	.02	.21	-.30*	-.25*	-.19*	-.14
Relational	.15	.05	-.06	-.03	.09	.20	.25*	.27*	.19*	.26*
Functional	.12	.22*	-.18*	-.13	.35*	.48*	.21*	.09	.18*	.10
Excuse-making	-.02	.10	-.07	-.10	.26*	.37*	.13	.29*	.17	.26*
Participatory	.05	-.04	-.01	-.08	.30*	.21	.26*	.26*	.28*	.11
Sycophancy	.11	-.17	-.03	-.17	.32*	-.01	.29*	.29*	.30*	.09

Note. (*) = significant at the $p < .01$ level.

We were also interested whether or not having a job while attending college affected students' worry, anxiety, or stress. Having a job did not significantly affect worry t (129) = 1.25, $p > .05$, anxiety t (141) = -.75, $p > .05$, school stress t (130) = -.30, $p > .05$, peer stress t (139) = .56, $p > .05$, or self-stress t (140) = 1.49, $p > .05$. Additionally, we were interested to see if the percentage of students' college finances paid for by the student correlated with worry, anxiety, and stress. Worry was not associated with amount paid by the students (r = -.07, $p > .05$), while anxiety (r = -.14, $p < .05$), school stress (r = -.18, $p < .01$), peer stress (r = -.15, $p < .05$), and self-stress (r = -.12, $p < .05$) were negatively related to the percentage of living/school expenses paid by the students.

CONCLUSION

In this study, we investigated how students' stress, worry, and anxiety influenced students' interest and motives for communicating with their instructors. We expected that students higher in stress would differ in their communication versus students lower in stress. The results confirmed this expectation.

Both of the interpretable roots from the canonical correlation conducted in response to research question one indicate that students whose interest stems from the meaningfulness of the material report higher amounts of worry and stress from school. This finding is consistent with the writings of other scholars studying the interest construct who assert that interest is an affective variable that energizes learning through intrinsic means (Weber, et al., 2001). The current findings reinforce the idea that as students perceptions concerning the value or the meaningfulness of the material increases, so does the importance students place on correctly and completely assimilating new information with prior knowledge. It is quite possible, if not probable, that this increased importance manifests itself as the stress and worry reported by the participants in this study.

An unexpected finding in the current investigation is the mediating role played by the feelings of competence dimension in the relationship between interest and the negative affective states of stress and worry. Apparently, students who feel that they are well prepared to face the challenges presented to them in the instructional setting, or in other words have a greater evaluation of their own competence, report less stress as a result of peer-pressure. Not only does this finding serve to reinforce the notion that interest is an intrinsically motivating force, but also is consistent with Covington's (1984) Self-Worth Theory which asserts that students with greater appraisals of their own ability will be more likely to attempt to perform more difficult tasks. Conversely, students who hold lower appraisals of their own competence are more likely to attempt to avoid performing more difficult tasks in hopes of protecting themselves from feelings of embarrassment.

The results of the current investigation also highlight the utility of the interest construct, as well as its operationalization, in conducting instructional research. The discovery of the mediating role played by the feelings of competence dimension was only possible due to the multi-dimensional nature of the construct and measurement device utilized. Had a unidimensional measure, such as the Perceived Interest Questionnaire, been utilized the subtlety of this relationship would have been overlooked. Similarly, had a unidimensional construct, such as global motivation or affective learning, been included in this investigation rather than interest, it would have been impossible to look for such delicate relationships. It is the multidimensionality of the Learner Empowerment Scale, and its ability to uncover such subtle relationships, that sets it apart from numerous other measures used in instructional research.

Involving research question two, when students have stress about their schoolwork and feel comfortable talking to their teachers, they report communicating to their teachers for the functional motive. In other words, these students ask their teachers for clarifications, for assistance in understanding the material, for clear guidelines, and for any other type of information needed to succeed. This result supports previous findings that students high in anxiety are less likely to communicate and possibly lack the skill and motivation to communicate with their instructors (Hurt and Preiss, 1978; McCroskey and Beatty, 1999). While school stress is positively related to all five motives for communicating in the classroom, the first root of the canonical correlation indicates that having low anxiety also impacts how students communicate. Seemingly, if instructors create a classroom atmosphere and communicate in constructive ways so that students have lower anxiety about talking, students will communicate more functionally (e.g., they will talk to their teachers to learn more about the course content and requirements). When instructors are responsive, confirming, and nonverbally immediate, students are more likely to be active in their learning (Myers, Martin, and Mottet, 2000a; Myers, Mottet, and Martin, 2000).

Of future interest is to what extent functional communication reduces school stress. When students' uncertainty about their courses decreases, they feel more comfortable and confident in their ability to succeed (Avtgis, 2001). Additionally, when student uncertainty for an instructor is low, students report more similarity, liking, and communication satisfaction for that instructor (Goodboy, 2005). When students have an abundance of uncertainty about a class or instructor, it can lead to negative outcomes such as challenge behaviors because students engage in information–seeking (Simonds, 1997). If students' uncertainty about their courses is not addressed, or increases, seemingly students' stress about school would remain, or possibly even increase. Similarly, if instructors create a cold or hostile learning environment, students will feel uncomfortable communicating with their instructors (Mottet et al., 2004).

The second root of the canonical correlation involving student motives indicates that when students tend not to worry overall but do feel stress from their peers (e.g., to create more friendships, to conform to the expectations of friends, to be clever to impress others), the focus of their communication in the classroom is sycophancy, attempting to make a good impression on their instructors. In fact, these students rarely communicate with their instructors for the functional motive. Items that are used to measure sycophancy include: to pretend I'm interested in the course, to give the instructor the impression that I like him/her, and to give the impression that I'm learning a lot from the instructor. Are these students, those who report high peer stress while communicating to impress the instructor, (1) trying to be a "good" student by making prosocial and complimentary comments to the instructor so that other students view them as socially attractive or (2) attempting to make fun of or embarrass the instructor by being insolent? Sycophancy is the second most common motive, after functional, that students give for communicating with their instructors (Martin, Myers, and Mottet, 2002). More attention should be paid to what students are trying to accomplish by using sycophantic messages.

Most students are likely to feel stress about school at one time or another. When students find the material meaningful, stress is higher. Stress also motivates students to communicate more with their instructors. The stress students feel about school influences meaningfulness and their motives for communicating more than students' overall tendency to worry or their anxiety about communicating with their instructors. Since meaningfulness and several of the motives have been shown to be positively related to learning outcomes, possibly a *normal* amount of stress is not detrimental to a student's success. What is a normal amount of stress and how instructors could reduce high levels of stress that some students experience must be further explored.

REFERENCES

Abouserie, R. (1994). Sources of levels of stress in relation to locus of control and self-esteem in university students. *Educational Psychology, 14,* 323-330.

Addison, P., Clay, E., Xie, S., Sawyer, C. R., and Behnke, R. R. (2003). Worry as a function of public speaking state anxiety type. *Communication Reports, 16,* 125-131.

American Psychiatric Association (1994). *The diagnostic and statistical manual of mental disorders* (4th Ed.). Washington, DC: American Psychiatric Press.

Alexander, P. A., Jetton, T. L., and Kulikowich, J. M. (1995). Interrelationship of knowledge, interest, and recall: Assessing a model of domain learning. *Journal of Educational Psychology, 87*, 559-575.

Alexander, P. A., Kulikowich, J. M., and Schulze, S. K. (1994a). The influence of topic knowledge, domain knowledge, and interest on the comprehension of scientific exposition. *Learning and Individual Differences, 6*, 379-397.

Alexander, P. A., Kulikowich, J. M., and Schulze, S. K. (1994b). How subject-matter knowledge affects recall and interest. American Educational Research Journal, 31, 313-337.

Andrews, B., and Wilding, J. M. (2004). The relation of depression and anxiety to life-stress and achievement in students. *British Journal of Psychology, 95,* 509-521.

Ayres, J. (1988). The impact of time, complexity, and organization on self-reports of speech anxiety. *Communication Research Reports, 5*, 58-63.

Barlow, D. H. (2002). *Anxiety and its disorders: The nature and treatment of anxiety and panic* (2nd ed.). New York: Guilford Press.

Barrett, J. E., Rose, R. M., and Klerman, G. L. (1979). *Stress and mental disorder*. New York: Raven Press.

Beatty, M. J., Forst, E. C., and Stewart, R. A. (1986). Communication apprehension and motivation as predictors of public speaking duration. *Communication Education, 35*, 143-146.

Biggers, T., and Masterson, J. T. (1983). A reconceputalization of communication apprehension in terms of the emotion-eliciting qualities of communication situations. *Communication, 12,* 93-105.

Biggers, T., and Masterson, J. T. (1984). Communication apprehension as a personality trait: An emotional defense of a concept. *Communication Monographs, 51,* 381-390.

Booth-Butterfield, S. (1988a). A meta-analysis of the cross-situational consistency of communication apprehension. *Communication Research Reports, 5,* 64-70.

Booth-Butterfield, S. (1988b). Instructional interventions for reducing situational anxiety and avoidance. *Communication Education, 37*, 214-223.

Borkovec, T. D., Ray, W. J., and Stober, J. (1998). Worry: A cognitive phenomenon intimately linked to affective, physiological, and interpersonal behavioral processes. *Cognitive Therapy and Research, 22,* 561-576.

Borkovec, T. D., Robinson, E., Pruzinsky, T., and Depree, J. (1983). Preliminary explanations of worry. *Behavior Research and Therapy, 21,* 9-16.

Boscolo, P., and Mason, L. (2003). Topic knowledge, text coherence, and interest: How they interact in learning from instructional texts. *Journal of Experimental Education ,71,*126-148.

Cayanus, J. L., and Martin, M. M. (2004). An instructor self-disclosure scale. *Communication Research Reports, 21*, 252-263.

Cayanus, J. L., Martin, M. M., and Goodboy, A. K. (2004, April). *The relationships among teacher self-disclosure, student motives to communicate and teacher credibility.* Paper presented at the annual conference of the Eastern Communication Association, Boston.

Covington, M. (1984). The self-worth theory of achievement motivation: Findings and implication. *Elementary School Journal, 85,* 5-20.

Creed, F. (1993). Stress and psychosomatic disorders. In L. Goldberg and S. Breznitz (Eds.), *Handbook of stress: Theoretical and clinical aspects* (2nd ed., pp. 496-510). New York: Free Press.

Dijkstra, A., and Brosschot, J. (2003). Worry about health in smoking behaviour change. *Behavior Research and Therapy, 41,* 1081-1092.

Dobos, J. A. (1996). Collaborative learning: Effects of student expectations and communication apprehension on student motivation. *Communication Education, 45,* 118-134.

Dugas, M. J., Letarte, H., Rheaume, J., Freeston, M. H., and Ladouceur, R. (1995). Worry and problem solving: Evidence of a specific relationship. *Cognitive Therapy and Research, 19,* 109-120.

Edwards, K. J., Hershberger, P. J., Russell, R. K., and Market, R. J. (2001). Stress, negative social exchange, and health symptoms in university students. *Journal of American College Health, 50,* 75-79.

Elliot, G. R., and Eisdorfer, C. (1982). *Stress and human health: Analysis and implications of research.* New York: Springer Publishing.

Everson, H. T., Smodlaka, I., and Tobias, S. (1994). Exploring the relationship of test anxiety and metacognition on reading test performance: A cognitive analysis. *Anxiety, Stress, and Coping: An International Journal, 7,* 85-96.

Feldman, K. A. (1972). Some theoretical approaches to the study of change and stability of college students. *Review of Educational Research, 42,* 1-26.

Frymier, A. B. (1994). A model of immediacy in the classroom. *Communication Quarterly, 42,* 133-144.

Frymier, A. B., and Houser, M. (2000). The teacher-student relationship as an interpersonal relationship. *Communication Education, 49,* 207-219.

Frymier, A. B., Shulman, G. M., and Houser, M. (1996). The development of a learner empowerment measure. *Communication Education, 45,* 181-199.

Furr, S. R., Westefeld, J. S., McConnell, G. N., and Jenkins, J. M. (2001). Suicide and depression among college students: A decade later. *Professional Psychology: Research and Practice, 32,* 97-100.

Gladstone, G., and Parker, G. (2003). What's the use of worrying? Its function and its dysfunction. *Australian and New Zealand Journal of Psychiatry, 37,* 347-354.

Goodboy, A. K., and Myers, S. A. (2005, April). *Student communication satisfaction, teacher similarity, and teacher liking as a function of attributional confidence.* Paper presented at the annual meeting of the Central States Communication Association, Kansas City.

Gorham, J., and Millette, D. M. (1997). A comparative analysis of teacher and student perceptions of source motivation and demotivation in college classes. *Communication Education, 46,* 245-261.

Gruen, R. J. (1993). Stress and depression: Toward the development of integrative models. In L. Goldberg and S. Breznitz (Eds.), *Handbook of stress: Theoretical and clinical aspects* (2nd ed., pp. 550-569). New York: Free Press.

Hidi, S., and Baird, W. (1988). Strategies for increasing text-based interest and recall of expository text. *Reading Research Quarterly, 23,* 465-483.

Hodgson, C. S., and Simoni, J. M. (1995). Graduate student academic and psychological functioning. *Journal of College Student Development, 36,* 244-253.

Hughes, B. M. (2005). Study, examinations, and stress: Blood pressure assessments in college students. *Educational Review, 57,* 21-36.

Hurt, H. T., and Preiss, R. (1978). Silence isn't necessarily golden: Communication apprehension, desired social choice, and academic success among middle-school students. *Human Communication Research, 4,* 315-328.

Kaufman, P., and Feldman, K. A. (2004). Forming identities in college: A sociological approach. *Research in Higher Education, 45,* 463-496.

Kelly, L., Duran, R. L., and Zolten, J. J. (2001). The effect of reticence on college students' use of electronic mail to communicate with faculty. *Communication Education, 50,* 170-176.

Kelly, W. E. (2004a). A brief measure of general worry: The Three Item Worry Index. *North American Journal of Psychology, 6,* 219-226.

Kelly, W. E. (2004b). Examining the relationship between worry and trait anxiety. *College Student Journal, 38,* 370-373.

Kelly, W. E., and Miller, M. J. (1999). A discussion of worry with suggestions for counselors. *Counseling and Values, 44,* 55-66.

Knapp, J. L., and Martin, M. M. (2003, Nov.). *The relationship between out-of-class communication, student interest, and student motivation.* Paper presented at the annual conference of the National Communication Association, Miami.

Kopecky, C. C., Sawyer, C. R., and Behnke, R. R. (2004). Sensitivity to punishment and explanatory style as predictors of public speaking. *Communication Education, 53,* 281-285.

Lazarus, R. S. (1981). The stress and coping paradigm. In C. Eisdorfer, D. Cohen, A. Kleinman, and P. Maxim (Eds.), *Models for clinical psycholpathology* (pp. 177-214). New York: Spectrum.

Lazarus, R. S., and Folkman, S. (1984). *Stress, appraisal, and coping.* New York: Springer Publishing.

Makaremi, A. (2000). Relation of depression and anxiety to personal and academic problems among Iranian college students. *Psychological Reports, 87,* 693-698.

Martin, M. M., Heisel, A. D., and Valencic, K. M. (2000, April). *Students' motives for communicating with their instructors: Considering instructors' use of BATs.* Paper presented at the annual conference of the Eastern Communication Association, Pittsburgh.

Martin, M. M., Mottet, T. P., and Myers, S. A. (2000). Student motives for communicating with their instructors. *Psychological Reports, 87,* 830-834.

Martin, M. M., Mottet, T. P., and Myers, S. A. (2005, April). *The relationship between college students' emotional responses and their motives for communication with their instructors.* Paper presented at the annual Eastern Communication Association Convention, Pittsburgh.

Martin, M. M., Myers, S. A., and Mottet, T. P. (1999). Student motives for communicating with their instructors. *Communication Education, 48,* 155-164.

Martin, M. M., Myers, S. A., and Mottet, T. P. (2002). Students' motives for communicating with their instructors. In J. L. Chesebro and J. C. McCroskey (Eds.), *Communication for teachers (pp. 35-46).* Boston: Pearson.

Martin, M. M., Valencic, K. M., and Heisel, A. D. (2001, April). *The relationship between students' motives for communicating with their instructors and perceptions of instructor nonverbal immediacy*. Paper presented at the annual Eastern Communication Association Convention, Pittsburgh.

Martin, M. M., Valencic, K. M., and Heisel, A. D. (2002). The relationship between students' communication apprehension and their motives for communicating with their instructors. *Communication Research Reports, 19*, 1-7.

Mathews, A. (1990). Why worry? The cognitive function of anxiety. *Behavior Research and Therapy, 28*, 455-468.

McCroskey, J. C. (1977). Classroom consequences of communication apprehension. *Communication Education, 26*, 27-33.

McCroskey, J. C., and Beatty, M. J. (1999). Communication apprehension. In J. C. McCroskey, J. A. Daly, M. M. Martin, and M. J. Beatty (Eds.) *Communication and personality: Trait perspectives* (215-232). Cresskill, NJ: Hampton Press.

McCroskey, J. C., Booth-Butterfield, S., and Payne, S. K. (1989). The impact of communication apprehension on college student retention and success. *Communication Quarterly, 37*, 100-107.

McCroskey, J. C., and McCroskey, L. L. (1986). The affinity-seeking of classroom teachers. *Communication Research Reports, 3*, 158-167.

McCroskey, J. C., and Sheahan, M. E. (1978). Communication apprehension, social preference, and social behavior in a college environment. *Communication Quarterly, 26*, 41-45.

Misra, R., and Castillo, L. G. (2004). Academic stress among college students: Comparison of American and International students. *International Journal of Stress Management, 11*, 132-148.

Misra, R., McKean, M., West, S., and Russo, T. (2000). Academic stress of college students: Comparison of student and faculty perceptions. *College Student Journal, 34*, 236-245.

Mitchell, M. (1993). Situational interest: Its multifaceted structure in the secondary school mathematics classroom. *Journal of Educational Psychology, 85*, 424-436.

Montorio, I., Nuevo, R., Marquez, M., Izal, M., and Losada, A. (2003). Characterization of worry according to severity of anxiety in elderly living in the community. *Aging and Mental Health, 7*, 334-341.

Mottet, T. P., Martin, M. M., and Myers, S. A. (2004). Relationships among perceived instructor verbal approach and avoidance relational strategies and students' motives for communicating with their instructors. *Communication Education, 53*, 116-122.

Myers, S. A., Martin, M. M., and Mottet, T. P. (2002a). The relationship between student communication motives and information seeking. *Communication Research Reports, 19*, 352-361.

Myers, S. A., Martin, M. M., and Mottet, T. P. (2002b). Students' motives for communicating with their instructors: Considering instructor socio-communicative style, student socio-communicative orientation, and student gender. *Communication Education, 51*, 121-133.

Myers, S. A., Mottet, T. P., and Martin, M. M. (2000). The relationship between student communication motives and perceived instructor communicator style. *Communication Research Reports, 17*, 161-170.

Naito, M. K., Kijima, N., and Kitamura, T. (2000). Temperament and character inventory (TCI) as predictors of depression among Japanese college students. *Journal of Clinical Psychology, 56*, 1579-1585.

Neer, M. R., and Kircher, W. F. (1989). Apprehensives' perception of classroom factors influencing their class participation. *Communication Research Reports, 6,* 70-77.

Perkins, A. M., and Corr, P. J. (2005). Can worriers be winners? The association between worrying and job performance. *Personality and Individual Differences, 38,* 25-31.

Pledge, D. S., Lapan, R. T., Heppner, P. P., Kivlighan, D., and Roehlke (1998). Stability and severity of presenting problems at a university counseling center: A 6-year analysis. *Professional Psychology: Research and Practice, 29,* 386-389.

Pruzinsky, T., and Borkovec, T. D. (1990). Cognitive and personality characteristics of worriers. *Behavior Research and Therapy, 28,* 507-512.

Richmond, V. P., and Gorham, J. (1996). *Communication, learning, and affect in instruction.* Edina, MN: Burgess.

Richmond, V. P., and McCroskey, J. C. (1998*). Communication: Apprehension, avoidance, and effectiveness.* Scottsdale, AZ: Gorsuch-Scarisbrick.

Ross, J. A. (1988). Antecedents and consequences of teacher efficacy. In J. Brophy (Ed.), *Advances in research on teaching* (Vol. 7, pp. 49-74). Greenwich, CT: JAI Press.

Rubin, R. B., Perse, E. M., and Barbato, C. A. (1988). Conceptualization and measurement of interpersonal communication motives. *Human Communication Research, 14,* 602-628.

Ruscio, A. M., and Borkovec, T. D. (2004). Experience and appraisal of worry among high worriers with and without generalized anxiety disorder. *Behavior Research and Therapy, 42,* 1469-1482.

Schiefele, U. (1991). Interest, learning, and motivation. *Educational Psychologist, 26,* 299-323.

Schiefele, U. (1996). Topic interest, text representation, and quality of experience. *Contemporary Educational Psychology, 21,* 3-18.

Schiefele, U. (1998). The role of interest in motivation and learning. In S. Messick and J. McCollis (Eds.), *Intelligence and personality: Bridging the gap in theory and measurement.* Hillsdale, NJ: Lawrence Erlbaum Associates, Inc.

Schiefele, U., and Krapp, A. (1996). Topic interest and free recall of expository text. *Learning and Individual Differences, 8,* 141-160.

Schraw, G., Bruning, R., and Svoboda, C. (1995). Sources of situational interest. *Journal of Reading Behavior, 27,* 1-15.

Schraw, G., and Dennison, R. (1994). The effect of reader purpose on interest and recall. *Journal of Reading Behavior, 26,* 1-18.

Schutz, W. (1966). *The interpersonal underworld.* Palo Alto, CA: Science and Behavior Books.

Shann, M. H. (1998). Professional commitment and satisfaction among teachers in urban middle schools. *The Journal of Education Research, 92,* 67-73.

Simonds, C. J. (1997). Challenge behavior in the college classroom. *Communication Research Reports, 14,* 481-492.

Smith, C. D., Sawyer, C. R., and Behnke, R. R. (2005). Physical symptoms of discomfort associated with worry about giving a public speech. *Communication Reports, 18,* 31-41.

Tallis, R., Davey, G. C. L., and Capuzzo, N. (1994). The phenomenology of non-pathological worry: a preliminary investigation. In G. C. L. Davey and F. Tallis (Eds.), *Worrying: Perspectives on theory, assessment, and treatment* (pp. 61-89). London: Wiley.

Thomas, K. W., and Velthouse, B. A. (1990). Cognitive elements of empowerment: An "interpretive" model of intrinsic task motivation. *Academy of Management Review, 15,* 666-681.

Thomas, S. P., and Williams, R. L. (1991). Perceived stress, trait anger, modes of anger expression, and health status of college men and women. *Nursing Research, 4,* 303-307.

Tobias, S. (1994). Interest, prior knowledge, and learning. *Review of Educational Research, 64,* 37-54.

Turner, R. J., and Wheaton, B. (1995). Checklist measurement of stressful life events. In S. Cohen, R. C. Kessler, and L. U. Gordon (Eds.), *Measuring stress: A guide for health and social scientists* (pp. 29-58). New York: Oxford University Press.

Turner, S. M., Beidel, D. C., and Stanley, M. A. (1992). Are obsessional thoughts and worry different cognitive phenomena? *Clinical Psychology Review, 12,* 257-270.

Vay, M. W., and Borkovec, T. D. (1992). A catastrophizing assessment of worrisome thoughts. *Cognitive Therapy and Research, 16,* 505-520.

Weber, K., Fornash, B., Corrigan, M., and Neupauer, N. C. (2003). The effect of interest on recall: An experiment. *Communication Research Reports, 20,* 116-123.

Weber, K., Martin, M. M., and Cayanus, J. L. (2005). Student interest: A two study reexamination of the concept. *Communication Quarterly, 53,* 71-86.

Weber, K., Martin, M. M., and Patterson, B. R. (2001). Teacher behavior, student interest, and affective learning: Putting theory into practice. *Journal of Applied Communication Research, 29,* 71-90.

Weber, K., and Patterson, B. R. (2000). Student interest, empowerment and motivation. *Communication Research Reports, 17,* 22-29.

Weiten, W. (1988). Pressure as a form of stress and its relationship to psychological symptomatology. *Journal of Social and Clinical Psychology, 6,* 127-139.

Weiten, W. (1998). Pressure, major life events, and psychological symptoms. *Journal of Social Behavior and Personality, 13,* 51-69.

Wells, A. (1995). Meta-cognition and worry: A cognitive model of generalized anxiety disorder. *Behavioural and Cognitive Psychotherapy, 23,* 301-320.

Wells, A., and Morrison, A. P. (1994). Qualitative dimensions of normal worry and normal obsessions: A comparative study. *Behavior Research and Therapy, 32,* 867-870.

Westefeld, J. S., and Furr, S. R. (1987). Suicide and depression among college students. *Professional Psychology, Research and Practice, 18,* 119-123.

Winkelman, M. (1994). Culture shock and adaptation. *Journal of Counseling and Development, 73,* 121-126.

Zautra, A. J., and Reich, J. W. (1983). Life events and perceptions of life quality: Developments in a two-factor approach. *Journal of Community Psychology, 11,* 121-132.

In: Stress and Mental Health of College Students
Editor: Mery V. Landow, pp. 171-186

ISBN 1-59454-839-0
© 2006 Nova Science Publishers, Inc.

Chapter 7

FACTORS THAT INCREASE AND DECREASE STRESS FOR NONTRADITIONAL COLLEGE STUDENTS

Peter G. Kirby[5], Joan L. Biever and Christy L. Shell
Our Lady of the Lake University, San Antonio, Texas

ABSTRACT

The number of programs that are designed to meet the educational needs of older, nontraditional students is growing rapidly. The needs of these older, nontraditional, working college students are important considerations for both universities and employers. Two studies were conducted to assess the impact of attending a weekend program for nontraditional students. The findings revealed the expected stress as the result of time constraints but also highlighted the positive aspects of continuing one's education. Recommendations are put forth for colleges and universities that offer or intend to offer programs for the adult non-traditional learner. The recommendations address stress sources caused by family work roles, course requirements and university policies and procedures.

FACTORS THAT INCREASE AND DECREASE STRESS FOR NONTRADITIONAL COLLEGE STUDENTS

Educational institutions continue to see a rise in nontraditional student enrollment. The National Center for Educational Statistics (NCES, 2002) estimates that 73% of all undergraduates are in someway considered nontraditional. Further, NCES estimated, as of 1999, 39% of post secondary students were 25 years or older, compared to 28% in 1970. The number of programs that have been and are being developed to meet the educational needs of older, nontraditional students is growing rapidly. Little is known, however, about graduate

---

[5] Corresponding author: Peter G. Kirby, School of Business, Our Lady of the Lake University, 411 SW 24th Street, San Antonio, TX 78207 (e-mail) kirbp@lake.ollusa.edu)

and undergraduate students who participate in nontraditional educational programs and the impact that returning to school has on their lives.

As staying current in one's field, learning new knowledge and skills and changing careers through formal education are essential in the current economic environment of the United States, it is anticipated that the numbers of nontraditional students will continue to increase. In order to provide services tailored to meet the needs of nontraditional students, universities need to gain a better understanding of the factors that increase or decrease stresses associated with attending college.

While both traditional and nontraditional students encounter stressful events associated with education, Dill and Henley (1998) found that there are significant differences in the way traditional and nontraditional students perceive stressful events. Nontraditional students were more affected by bad teachers or classes than were traditional students; however, they were less affected by problems with peers. This may be due to differences in developmental stages and life demands (Herman and Davis, 2004). For example, with age there is an increase in the number of roles and responsibilities. The likelihood of stress in nontraditional students resulting from work, family obligation and financial issues has been well documented (Dill and Henley, 1998; Herman and Davis, 2004; Hyberlson, Hulme, Smith, and Holton, 1992). Meyers and Mobley (2004) found one of the most frequent environmental factors of stress for nontraditional students was "the feeling overwhelmed or conflicted about fulfilling all my role responsibilities" (p. 41).

While little research has examined the influence of school on family stress, the influence of work on family has been well documented (e.g., Hood, 1993; Zedeck, 1992). Greenhaus and Beutell (1985) reviewed sixteen studies examining the relationship between the individual's work role and other roles performed. Work-family conflict was defined as:

> "... a form of inter-role conflict in which the role pressures from the work and family domains are mutually incompatible in some respect. That is, participation in the work (family) role is made more difficult by virtue of participation in the family (work) role." (p. 77)

Home (1993, 1998) pointed out that while balancing multiple roles can increase feelings of confidence and self-esteem in nontraditional students, strain due to time or resource constraints is frequently experienced. Scheinkman (1998) noted that student marriages are especially vulnerable.

Several studies have looked at sources of interpersonal support for nontraditional students. Miller (1988), in a qualitative study of nontraditional female students in public relations graduate programs, discovered that respondents received minimal support from their families, male professors or male classmates. Their greatest source of support was female friends or acquaintances in their graduate program. Mallinckrodt and Leong (1992) surveyed 272 married graduate students to identify sources and types of social support that were beneficial to graduate students coping with stress. Social support moderated the effect of stress for women, with greater social support contributing to positive coping. In contrast, both graduate program and family support had direct effect on the coping of men regardless of their level of stress. Brazier (1998) found that time management, flexibility on the part of all stakeholders, and the use of a cohort model led to better coping with the conflicts between family and school responsibilities for married students in a nontraditional graduate program in education. Sanders and Nassar (1995) interviewed second career Masters in Social Work

(MSW) students and found that peer support, mentoring relationships with faculty, and a sense of autonomy and control in their lives were seen as contributing to a positive graduate school experience.

Hammer, Grigsby, and Woods (1998) included work, school, and family factors in their study of role conflict for students in a large urban university. They found that lower levels of perceived effectiveness of support services and lower levels of satisfaction with education experiences were related to high degrees of work-school conflict. Both family size (number of children) and course load (number of credit hours) were related to family-work conflicts. Family-school conflict was not significantly related to satisfaction with the education experience. Hammer et al. recommended restructuring class schedules to better accommodate working students, stress management and coping skills workshops, and teaching students how to negotiate for flexibility in work schedules.

Research has found that support systems play a significant part in a nontraditional student's adaptation to college (Hyberlson et al., 1992; San Miguel Bauman et al, 2004). Students feel "balancing my personal needs with the demands of others" to be beneficial (Meyers and Mobley, 2004). A nontraditional student's decision to return to school affects their personal and work relationships (Chao and Good, 2004). By incorporating their resources such as family, friends and teachers they are able to make their college education experience less stressful (Chao and Good, 2004). Although these environmental resources are beneficial in reducing stress, San Miguel Bauman et al. (2004) suggested there is a need for some form of campus services that would require expertise in areas such as stress management. Research by Pritchard and Wilson found that "positive emotional coping strategies and the ability to handle stress are related to higher retention" (Herman and Davis, 2004).

INITIAL STUDY

As reported by Kirby, Biever, Martinez, and Gomez (2003; 2004), we initially examined the influence of school responsibilities on family, work, and social interactions for students in a nontraditional, degree granting weekend college program for working adults. The work-family-school conflict measure used by Hammer et al. (1998) was adapted for use in that study. The Hammer et al. measure is a 41 item questionnaire with an internal consistency reliability estimate of .87. Questions dealing with work and family inter-role conflict were eliminated as were several other items deemed not necessary for this study. The Hammer et al. survey items consist solely of negative inter-role conflict. Items assessing the positive impact of school on work and family were added. This resulted in 23 items to which participants responded on a Likert scale from 1 (strongly disagree) to 5 (strongly agree). Reverse scoring procedures were utilized in assessing the direction on some of the items. Three questions were added to assess overall satisfaction with work, school, and family using a scale of 1 (very unsatisfied) to 5 (very satisfied). Finally, there were three open-ended questions requiring written responses on the impact of school on family, work and social life. Demographic information including age, race/ethnicity, educational status, marital status, number of dependents, and work status was also collected from the participants.

Surveys were completed by 566 of the approximately 1100 students enrolled in a weekend college program at a small, private university. Sixty-four percent of 530 participants who indicated their sex were women. Ages ranged from 22-55 for the 562 participants who reported this variable. Twenty-six percent were ages 22-30, 21% were 31-35, 20% were 36-40, 17% were 41-45, 10% were 46-50, and 6% were 51-55, Of the 564 participants who indicated their race/ethnicity, 41% were White, 39% were Hispanic, 14% were African-American, 2% were Asian-American, 1% were American Indian. Three percent indicated other race/ethnicity. Of the 466 participants who completed data on student status 210 or 45% were graduate students and 256 or 55% were undergraduate students. Twenty percent of the 564 participants had a partner with no children, 43% had a partner and children, 20% were single with no children, and 17% were single parents. The mean number of dependents for the entire sample was 1.08 (SD=1.148) with a range from 0-6. Five hundred twenty-two participants reported their work status. Of these, 93% worked full-time and the remaining 7% worked part-time.

Quantitative Findings. Two sets of regression analyses were completed. The first of the regression analyses were simultaneous models that directly tested the predictors' contribution to family stress. In the this analysis, ethnicity, age, family situation, number of dependents, number of WEC credit hours, and satisfaction with educational experience served as predictor variables and family stress served as the dependent variable. None of the predictors in this analysis were significant.

In the second regression analysis, family support was added as a predictor variable in accordance with hypotheses derived from factor analytic data. Thus, family support, ethnicity, age, family situation, number of dependents, number of WEC hours, and satisfaction with educational experience served as predictor variables, and family stress remained as the dependent variable. Age (beta = .117) was found to be a significant predictor of family stress with older individuals reporting lower levels of family stress, $F(7,426) = 21.744$, $p=.000$ (27% of the variance explained). Greater family support (beta=.518) was also found to be a significant predictor of lower stress.

Simultaneous multiple regression analyses was utilized in the analyses of predictors of work stress. In the first analysis, ethnicity, age, work status, number of dependents, number of WEC hours, and satisfaction with the educational experience served as predictor variables and work stress served as the dependent variable. Satisfaction with school experience (beta = .102) was also found to be a significant predictor of work stress, with more satisfied students of Weekend College reporting lower work stress levels. Work status (beta = -.482) was also found to be a significant predictor of work stress; full-time employees were found to report higher degrees of work stress, $F (6,483) = 27.006$, $p=.000$ (25% of the variance explained).

In the second analysis, support from work was added to the predictor variables. Thus, work support, ethnicity, age, work status, number of dependents, number of WEC hours, and satisfaction with educational experience served as predictor variables, and work stress served as the dependent variable. Results of these analysis reveal that participants who reported more support (beta = .454) from the workplace were found to report lower work stress. Full-time employees (beta = -.225) in this sample were found to have higher stress levels when compared to part-time employees, $F (7, 483) = 43.151$, $p= .000$ (39% of the variance explained).

Family support was added to the set of predictor variables to assess its contribution to work stress. Thus, family support, work support, ethnicity, age, work status, number of dependents, number of WEC hours, and satisfaction with educational experience served as predictor variables, and work stress served as the dependent variable. Greater work support (beta = .451) was associated with lower reported stress at work; it is noteworthy that greater family support (beta = .069) was also indicative of lower work stress but this finding was not statistically significant. Full-time employment (beta = -.224) continued to be a significant predictor of greater work-related stress in this sample, $F (8,483) = 38.271$, $p=.000$ (40% of the variance explained).

Qualitative findings. Content analysis was used to examine the responses to the open-ended questions. For impact on family, fifteen original categories were reduced to eight; twenty-six categories were reduced to eight for impact on work and eleven categories were reduced to five for impact on social life. Two categories, "no impact" and "WEC format is helpful" were found for all three questions; all other categories were found for only one question. The unique categories for each question are presented below.

The first area of interest was the influence of returning to school on family life. Not surprisingly, 185 (39.9%) reported that attending school interfered with family time or events. More surprising was the low level of concern for childcare problems, only 1.5% overall indicated this as a problem, as did 10% of those without partners, still a relatively low response. Representative comments include:

- Family life is put on hold.
- Family members must become self-sufficient while I am in school.
- I am bettering myself but less time with my family.
- Interrupted family life, no socializing, no communication.

A number of respondents (70 or 15%) indicated that they received support and cooperation from their family. This was stronger for respondents with partners (20%) than those without partners (6%). Many found that attending school enriched family life (49 or 11%). Some of the beneficial effects of attending school are illustrated by the following comments:

- My partner and I are more understanding at sharing responsibilities at home.
- Brought us closer as we all depend on each other more to make school possible.
- My husband and children miss me, but are excited about me finishing. They handle me being gone very well. They support me completely which makes it very easy for me to come to class.
- My family would like for me to spend more weekends at home, but they understand that the sacrifice we are making now will benefit us in the future.
- School has made my family life a little easier as both my wife and I attend school on the weekends. This gives us more to talk about, helps us understand one another better.

Setting-a-good-example-for-family-members, was mentioned by 30 (7%) respondents with those having children reporting this area more frequently. For example:

- Made my children more aware of the importance of school.

- Motivated my husband and children to continue their education.
- Positive role model when working on homework.
- My grown children know what it took for me to earn my degree and respect me for my efforts.
- My teenagers are excited and it has encouraged them to continue their education beyond high school.

Another benefit, better time management and coping skills, was mentioned by 21 or 5% of respondents.

- Has opened up conversations for improvement and change.
- Have applied learned materials toward my family life.
- Time is more precious, I must be more efficient when attending school.
- Improves focus on achieving more quality time and scheduling.
- I have had to use my time a lot more wisely.

The second area of interest to the researchers was the impact of attending WEC on the students' work. Respondents reported that attending school took time away from work (96 or 21%). Some felt stress, reporting that they were busy or tired at work as a result of attending school (74 or 16%). Examples of these negative impacts include:

- Adds to the stress. Work is most of the stress. School a little because I want to do extremely well in school.
- Schoolwork has become a juggling act. Must take time off from work to complete with labor intensive course.
- Can't always work overtime because I have school work.
- It makes a stressful work week in completing homework and projects.

A positive reaction was increased business knowledge, skills, understanding and confidence at work by 71 or 15% of respondents. Additionally 41 or 9% reported that they were able to apply learning gained in school to the work environment. Fifty-six (12%) reported that attending school had enhanced their careers, while 19 (4%) reported that there was an increase in respect or status at work. Examples of these positive effects include:

- Has greatly improved my knowledge and teaching skills.
- Improved my job and earning opportunities,
- Has contributed to my self-confidence and has opened my mind to different approaches to problem solving.
- It has made me more knowledgeable and I have been able to institute what I have learned to my organization.
- Better equipped to add value to my team, another dimension or perspective to enrich results.
- Have applied academics at work, helpful.
- I have more tools in my "toolbox" when dealing with issues at work.

Attending WEC had a large impact on respondents' social life. A large number (257 or 55.4%) reported that their social life had been reduced or they had no social life (our favorite response was "what social life?"). In this category 38% of single parents reported this concern as compared to 61% of all other respondents. A number of respondents (49 or 11%) reported that attending school resulted in new social opportunities while 41 or 9% reported that their social skills had improved. For example:

- Also have more tools for interacting w/ people on a social level.
- Pride in describing program to friends and colleagues.
- I have become a little bit more well rounded in conversation.
- I have met a lot of people who have similar interests and backgrounds.
- Given me more confidence.
- Actually improved because of the contact w/ other students.
- Going to school has impacted my social life by helping me in interacting w/ other people, such as networking for employment prospects.

CURRENT STUDY

Methods

Setting. The setting for the study was the Weekend College (WEC) program of a small Catholic university located in a metropolitan area in the southwest. The WEC was founded in 1979 to offer undergraduate degree completion programs for working adults. Graduate programs were added in 1983 and the undergraduate and graduate programs were later expanded to two regional campuses. The WEC degree programs are limited contact hour in nature, usually meeting seven times per semester. The first session is a one-hour course orientation with the remaining six class meetings occurring every other weekend in four-hour segments.

Participants. Thirty-nine undergraduate students and 34 graduate students completed returned questionnaires. Forty of the respondents were women and 33 were men. Thirty-four respondents were single while 39 were married or living with a partner. Twenty-eight had no dependents, 39 had dependent children, 4 had responsibility for a parent or other dependent adult, and two reported both dependent children and adults. Most of the respondents (62) worked full-time, eight were working part-time, and three were not employed. Twenty-nine respondents enrolled in the university to change careers or employers, 17 hoped to advance with their current employer, 17 were attending for their own personal growth, and 8 did not specify their reason for enrolling in the university.

Questionnaire. The purpose of this study was to identify with some specificity, the dimensions of stress that going to school induces in the nontraditional student. Participants were requested to respond as specifically as possible to the following five open-ended questions dealing with the stress they experience:

1. Have you noticed an increase or decrease in the stress levels you experience since attending WEC? If yes, please describe.

2. What aspects of WEC tend to increase your stress levels?
3. What aspects of WEC tend to decrease your stress levels?
4. What could your professors do to decrease the stress you encounter?
5. What services could the University provide to help you deal with the stress you encounter?

Procedures. Questionnaires were distributed in two locations, the main campus and at a distant location some 200 miles away. These were convenient samples. One of the researchers was teaching two undergraduate WEC classes and distributed the questionnaires during class time. Another researcher was located at the distant campus and professors in two graduate courses distributed questionnaires. The questionnaires were completed voluntarily and anonymously and were collected for review by the researchers.

FINDINGS

The responses to each question were examined using content analysis. One researcher entered the responses to each question into a spreadsheet. Separate entries were created when more than one idea was expressed within a response. Initial review of the responses to Question 1 revealed that 59 of the 73 respondents indicated that their level of stress had increased, two reported a decrease in stress and nine reported no change. The reasons stated for this increase were very similar to the responses given to Question 2. Likewise, the reasons given by the two respondents who indicated that their stress had decreased were similar to the answer given to question 3. Thus, the responses that indicated increased stress were combined with the responses to Question 2 and the responses indicated decreased stress were combined with the responses to Question 3. The responses to the remaining questions were analyzed separately.

The three researchers categorized the responses to each question according the theme(s) represented. Differences between the researchers where resolved through discussion, frequently resulting in a new category being created. Following the initial categorization, the data was sorted by category. The researchers reviewed the list of categories. Like categories were then combined. New categories were created for responses that were initially coded similarly but were judged to express different ideas during the second review. Categories that contained three or more responses will be reported below. Following the coding, the categories were re-sorted to examine frequency trends, e.g., responses primarily from graduate as opposed to undergraduate students.

Factors that increase stress. Responses to the first two questions ("Have you noticed an *increase or decrease* in the stress levels you experience since attending WEC? If yes, please describe." and "What aspects of WEC tend to increase your stress levels?") addressed the factors related to increased stress among WEC students. Not surprisingly, the most frequently mentioned factor that increased stress was course requirements. The following comments were typical of the 50 responses in this category:

- The amount of work due or required. Need to figure our how to balance classes, so as not to have two classes that req. a lot of work.

- The lack of time to truly analyze course work; dig deep into research, etc.
- Amount of homework expected for each class

The category the occurred with the next greatest frequency (16 responses) was the struggle to balance multiple roles (student, spouse, parent, worker). The following are representative of responses in this category:

- Great increase, lack of sleep, no time for personal items or chores, less time w/husband and family, less flexibility at work - all around affect.
- Increase-hard to juggle school, work, and family (not a complaint because weekend is far easier to do than night with young children).
- Absolutely an increase. It is very difficult juggling a home, family, full-time work, and attending classes, doing all class assignments and projects.
- Not enough hours in the day to meet work, family, and school obligations.

Two related categories were interference with family (6 responses), interference with work (14 responses), and interference with social life (4). The following are examples of interference with family:

- Lack of time has lead to lack of communication with my family. This leads to stress in our relationships.
- It is stressful to give spouse enough time and attention when so much weekend time is taken away from family.
- The dates often coincide with weekends I have my children.

Below are examples of interference with work:

- Increase because with full time sales position already very demanding and workloads of school coming so quick for the stretch of time we have, it is stressful.
- Distraction at work because of thinking of school assignments.

An example of interference with social life is:

- Very little time for anything else other than school

The next most frequent category was the availability of support services (12). Examples of responses in this category are:

- Unavailability of resources (access to computer, labs, library, bookstore, food service, printing, etc.). Not available during or after WEC hours.
- Offices, labs, libraries, cafeteria are sometimes closed when WEC students need them.
- Not enough available services, i.e., cafeteria, labs, etc.

Interestingly, all of the responses in this category were from students on the main campus. It may be that students on the main campus believe that more services are available to traditional students or that the remote campus, which only has weekend programs, does a better job of meeting the needs of students. A related category, costs versus services, was mentioned by three students from the main campus. An example of this category is:

- Costs--same as traditional but we don't get the same benefits.

The category of time management had eleven responses. Below are typical responses in this category:

- Being able to organize the work within my available time.
- Time management-full time work and school requires a lot of time.
- Had to do school work at 5:30 am before work. Eventually let school work slide a little in the 2nd year.

Nine responses indicated stress due to group work and team assignments. The examples below demonstrate these concerns:

- Group work-finding time to meet with other students is difficult-we all have different schedules and family commitments.
- Hard to coordinate family responsibilities with meeting times.

Three students mentioned an increase in stress related medical symptoms such as gastrointestinal problems. Finally, three responses noted that stress is an expected, and even, positive aspect of returning to school. For example:

- I truly believe that if you are committed to get an education, then stress is part of the format. If a person wants to better themselves, then they have to do whatever it takes to obtain their goals.
- Increase, it's normal, it's good stress that accompanies performance.

Factors that Decrease Stress.

Four categories emerged from the responses to Question 3 (What aspects of WEC tend to decrease your stress levels?). No differences due to location or student status (graduate or undergraduate) were noted.

The trimester format was by far the most frequently mentioned factor; it was coded 20 times as opposed to six each for the other three categories. The weekend class format may have been the reason that many of the students chose to attend WEC rather than one of the many universities in both locations that offer evening degree completion and graduate programs. The following responses are representative of this category:

- Easy to attend on weekends. Not an issue to get way from work at a certain time.
- Weeks between classes are conducive to having plenty of time to study and accomplish work.
- Being that it's the weekend it allows for more time to apply studies.
- Knowing that I can study (go to college) while working. If I had to quite my job, I would be unable to attend college.
- The fact that there are only 6 classes - no time is wasted with irrelevant information.

As mentioned in the previous section, team and group assignments were noted as one source of stress for students. Team assignments, however, were also seen as beneficial as they helped students form supportive relationships with their peers. For example:

- Meeting fellow students experiencing the same things, in the "same boat"
- Class/team involvement
- Relationships [with peers] are so strong we keep each other going.

Teaching excellence and supportive instructors were also mentioned as factors that reduced stress. Typical responses for this category include:

- The attention and understanding of the professors.
- A good professor that has engaging lectures!!!
- Instructors who understand the dynamics of WEC students
- Wonderful instructors, who listen to you and are available.

Finally, gaining new knowledge and skills is a factor that reduces stress. For example:

- I believe that there has been a decrease in the stress level due to the fact that my advanced learning is helping me solve problems that I experience at work.
- Knowing I will have more opportunities when I rejoin the workforce
- Progress toward degree, learning, good grades, feels successful.

Suggestions For Instructors

Seven categories emerged from the responses to the Question 4 (What could your *professors do* to decrease the stress you encounter?). No differences due to location or student status (graduate or undergraduate) were noted.

The most frequently coded category, modify course requirements, paralleled the stressful aspects of course requirements mentioned in response to Question 2. The following are examples of the student suggestions regarding course requirements:

- Take home test work better-you have to read and search for answers.

- Make assignments that are realistic to complete considering 99% of students attending WEC are working FT and have families.

Ten of the 23 responses in this category mentioned team and group assignments. For example:

- Assign fewer group assignments.
- Stop giving so many team projects!! Most of work in long organizations and understand this concept. We get it.

The next most frequently coded category, increased flexibility and understanding, paralleled the code "teaching excellence and supportive instructors" found for Question 3. Typical responses in this category are below:

- Not be so strict for deadlines that fall around holidays or planned family trips.
- Try to be more understanding and remember the struggles they overcame when they were in grad school.
- Acknowledge that must of us are fulltime students and taking classes in 3 months that normally are 6 months long elsewhere, because work load tends to be rough here.

Ten responses were coded as "no change needed." These responses reflected student satisfaction with the quality of instructors, for example:

- Not sure, the professors are great!
- Nothing they are doing their job.
- I think our professors overall are very good about treating us like adults.

The next most frequently occurring category, preparation and organization, reflects the students need for clear standards and requirements. Typical responses included:

- Be clear on expectations.
- More detailed information on requirements 1st day of class. I should have more information on major assignments/papers earlier.
- Give the details and material within first couple of classes.

Finally, improved communication was mentioned in six responses. Responses in this category included:

- Returning communications (e-mail/phone calls) in a timely fashion, more instructor or guidance for special projects, monitor team member contributions when using teams.
- Make sure they (professors) are available at all time and respond to e-mail immediately.
- Just be there to answer any questions at any time.

Suggestions For University

Six categories emerged from the responses to Question 5 (What services could the University provide to help you deal with the stress you encounter?). The most frequently occurring category (22 responses), increased availability of support services, was mentioned most frequently by students from the main campus. This may reflect their awareness of services that are less available on the weekend than they are during the work week. As the satellite campus has only weekend programs, the services at that campus are more available during the weekend. The following are representative of responses in this category:

- Have all areas be open in evenings and weekends, there should be rep from Weekend College around.
- Provide needed departmental support during weekend college hours (i.e., accessibility to advisors or WEC office, bookstore).
- All facilities open would be nice.

The second most frequently coded category, availability and adequacy of advisors, occurred sixteen times. Below are typical responses for this category:

- Have advisors available on class weekends.
- More knowledgeable advisors.
- Counselors who are willing to listen and comment constructively.
- Increase visibility of services that the advisors provided to students, especially the new students so they become better adjusted to the culture of the weekend program.

Making counseling services available was coded eight times. As all of these responses were from students in a graduate program in psychology on the satellite campus, it may reflect their knowledge of the effectiveness of such services. Likewise three categories mentioned by a few students, academic support (4 responses), increased course selection (4 responses), and childcare (3 responses), may reflect the specific needs of those few students.

DISCUSSION

It is evident that attending Weekend College has a substantial impact—both positive and negative—on students' lives and the amount of stress they encounter. In the initial study, results of the regression analysis highlighted the importance of support from family members and the work setting in reducing stress in the family and work settings. This is consistent with the previous findings (Mallinckrodt and Leong, 1992; Sanders and Nassar, 1995. Unlike Mallinkdrodt and Leong (1992), no gender effects were found.

The results of both studies highlight the continual need for balancing school requirements with the demands of work and family. The first study found satisfaction with school predicted work, but not family, stress. We previously (Kirby et al. 2004) contended one reason may be that the weekend only format may better accommodate the needs of working students. While both weekend and evening programs impinge upon family time, weekend only classes may interfere less with work time. The findings of the current study support this contention. The format was the most frequently mentioned aspect of WEC that reduced stress. Further, as in the first study, students reported that stress was decreased by successful completion of courses and being able to utilize newly acquired skills and knowledge in their work setting.

While attending school will almost inevitably increase time pressures and necessitate the negotiation of multiple roles, many of the factors identified as increasing stress by the participants of the current study could be mitigated by the thoughtful design and delivery of instruction and support services. For instance, the use of team or group assignment was reported as both increasing and decreasing stress. Stress was increased when students had difficulty coordinating schedules. Instructors could reduce this stress by considering location and time availability when assigning students to teams. Incorporating the use of technology, such as chat rooms, may minimize such stress. Using these technologies, however, may require specific instruction in how they may facilitate team interaction. Instructors should design group activities that facilitate the supportive nature of teams meaning that teams need to have assignments due across the trimester. A single project due at the end of the trimester does not facilitate team development and may increase stress as student delay beginning the project.

Faculty responsiveness to student's needs may also reduce their stress. For instance, faculty should communicate that they understand the stressful nature of working while attending school and respond to questions and concerns as promptly as possible. Additionally, assignments that increase skills and knowledge that can be applied in the work setting may be viewed as more valuable, thus creating less stress. Students could be encouraged to consult with their supervisors on ways to make course content more relevant to the student's work setting. Consistent with the first study, students suggested that faculty make assignments that "are realistic' meaning that they are related to their work environment.

The quality and availability of academic advising is another factor that may affect the stress felt by nontraditional students. Inaccessible or ineffective advising service can lead to greater stress and discontent. Nontraditional students who are only on campus for a limited period of time need to have to ready access to advising and other services. There is a need to create a "welcoming" environment where students can meet, interact with each other and access the academic services they need. Further, students who have limited availability need to be assisted in making the best use of their time in order to complete their degree program as efficiently as possible. Thus, advisors need to be knowledgeable resources for these students.

In the current study, students from the main campus evidenced much more discontent with university services than did students from the satellite campus. This difference in responses may have been due to actual differences in the two campuses or differing expectations. For instance, WEC college students on the main campus are aware of services that are more available to traditional students. Campuses that offer both traditional and weekend programs must take care to ensure that weekend students do not feel like "second class citizens."

Both studies revealed the obvious, there is stress related to returning to school for nontraditional students. There appears to be three major sources of stress: that caused by the interaction with school and family and work roles, that caused by the educational experience itself and that created by university policies and procedures.

The results of these studies suggest that one strategy for reducing the felt stress of nontraditional students is to increase the applicability of course content and assignments. By having students work on "real problems" it facilitates the linking of theory to their world of work providing a practical orientation to their learning. If the increasing skills and knowledge are viewed as an asset by the students' employers, it may reduce work-related stress. Likewise, the opportunity to apply learned concepts in a meaningful environment may enhance the students' learning.

A profoundly important question is how can the institution mitigate the stress created in the family by the return to school? As suggested in the earlier study, engaging family members in the educational process would be helpful. If family members understood the demands of courses and work outside the class meeting times they would be in a better position to alleviate the natural stress that occurs. Such things as having the family join in course orientations, sending a newsletter about happenings going on at school, providing social opportunities sponsored by the institution for family and students would all lead to clearer understanding of the learning demands. It would also provide opportunity to interact with other families of students who are experiencing the same problems and this would them help discover alternate methods for dealing with stress.

The institution has an obligation to actively reduce the stress created by policies and procedures. It is evident that nontraditional students need to have some special handling if they are to consider themselves an integral part of the university. Students in weekend programs housed in traditional university settings need an open and a welcoming place to go. Of great import to students is the opportunity to obtain accurate information and advising while they are on the campus. There is a need to have people on duty that can help solve a variety of problems that occur when dealing with a university: registrar problems, financial aid situations and a variety of other irritating, to the student, barriers to a positive educational experience.

Catering to the needs of nontraditional students is a positive way to help them deal with the stressors they encounter while pursuing their college education. Treating the nontraditional student as 'just another student" misses the mark. In fact, this probably causes more student stress as they feel they are secondary in importance as their unique needs are not addressed and the institutions focus is toward the traditional student body.

REFERENCES

Brazier, A. A. (1998). Nontraditional students in nontraditional graduate programs in educations: Coping with conflicts between family and career responsibilities and the institutional demands of higher education. *Dissertation Abstracts International, 54* (2-A):0383. (UMI No. AAM9824729).

Chao, R. and Good, G. E. (2004) Nontraditional Students' Perspectives on College Education: A Qualitative Study. *Journal of College Counseling, 7,* 5-12.

Dill, P. L., and Henley, T. B. (1998). Stressors of college: A comparison of traditional and nontraditional students. *Journal of Psychology, 132,* 25-32.

Greenhaus, J. H., and Beutell, N. J. (1985). Sources of conflict between work and family roles. *Academy of Management Review, 10,* 76-88.

Hammer, L. B., Grigsby, T. D., and Woods, S. (1998). The conflicting demands of work, family, and school among students at an urban university. *Journal of Psychology, 132*, 220-226.

Herman, D. A., and Davis, G. A. (2004). College student wellness: A comparison between traditional- and nontraditional-age students. *Journal of College Counseling, 7*, 32-39

Home, A. (1993).The juggling act: The multiple role woman in social work education. *Canadian Social Work Review, 10*, 141141-156.

Home, A. (1998). Predicting role conflict, overload and contagion in adult women university students with families. *Adult Education Quarterly, 48* (2), 85-98.

Hood, J. C. (1993). *Men, work, and family.* Newbury Park: SAGE.

Hyberson, D., Hulme, E., Smith, W. A., and Holton, M. A. (1992). Wellness in nontraditional-age-students. Journal of College Student Development, 33, 50-55.

Kirby, P. G., Biever, J. L., Martinez, I. G., and Gómez, J. P (2003). Nontraditional students: A qualitative study of the impact of returning to school on family, work, and social life. *National Social Science Journal, 21*(1), 42-47.

Kirby, P. G., Biever, J. L., Martinez, I., Gómez, J. P. (2004). Adults returning to school: The impact on family and work. *Journal of Psychology, 138*, 65-76

Mallinckrodt, B., and Leong, F. T. L. (1992). Social support in academic programs and family environments: Sex differences and role conflicts for graduate students. *Journal of Counseling and Development, 6*, 716-723.

Miller, D. A. (1988). Women in public relations graduate study. *Public Relations Review, 14* (3), 29-35.

Myers, J. E., and Mobley, A. K. (2004). Wellness of undergraduates: Comparisons of traditional and nontraditional students. *Journal of College Counseling, 7*, 41-49.

National Center for Education Statistics (2002). Findings from the condition of education 2002: Nontraditional undergraduates. Retrieved July 11, 2005 from http://nces.ed.gov/pubs2002/2002012.pdf

San Miguel Bauman, S., Wang, N., and DeLeon, C. W., Kafintzis, J., Zavala-Lopez, M. A., and Lindsey, M. C. (2004). Nontraditional Students' Service Needs and Social Support Resources: A Pilot Study. *Journal of College Counseling, 7*, 13-17.

Sanders, G. R., and Nassar, R. (1995). The experience of second career women MSW students. *The Jewish Social Work Forum, 31*, 49-63.

Scheinkman, M. (1998). Graduate student marriages: An organizational/interactional view. *Family Process, 27*, 351-368.

Zedeck, S. (1992). *Work, families, and organizations.* San Francisco: Jossey-Bass.

In: Stress and Mental Health of College Students
Editor: Mery V. Landow, pp. 187-201

ISBN 1-59454-839-0
© 2006 Nova Science Publishers, Inc.

Chapter 8

RELATIONSHIP BETWEEN OUTLOOK TO LIFE AND COLLEGE ADJUSTMENT: AN ANALYSIS OF THE ROLE OF OPTIMISM IN STRESS APPRAISAL AND OVERALL MENTAL HEALTH AMONG COLLEGE STUDENTS.

Sussie Eshun

Psychology Department, East Stroudsburg University
East Stroudsburg, Pennsylvania

ABSTRACT

This chapter is a further exploration of the relationship between optimism, perceived stress, and subsequent adjustment among college students. Unlike studies, which have typically focused on how inherent predispositions increase vulnerability to stress related illnesses, the current study focused on how acquired predispositions (dispositional optimism) influence appraisal of stress, and ultimately adjustment. Also, results from a study of 259 college undergraduates are discussed. Participants completed a measure of optimism at the beginning of the semester and then measures of stress and adjustment just before midterm break. Results indicated that optimism or outlook to life was a significant predictor of respondents' perceived stress, as well as, their levels of depression, anxiety, and overall college adjustment. Further analyses showed that optimism accounted for significant proportions of the variance in the dependent factors or measures of adjustment. Implications of these findings are discussed.

INTRODUCTION

Adjustment is often conceptualized as an appropriate change in an individual, which is typically in response to an alteration in his or her environment. It is composed of behaviors that help us cope with the demands of daily living. Thus adjustment reflects a response to an intrinsic and/or extrinsic change. Generally, college is one of the major adjustments that young adults encounter. It comes with mixed feelings; on one hand the young adult is excited about enjoying a sense of independence from their parents and guardians. On the other hand, he or she underestimates the demands and stressors that come with such independence. As a professor, I have worked with several college students as they struggle to make their way through this dance of change: while some students are often late to class because of poor sleeping habits, others never seem to know when their assignments are due and therefore spend a substantial portion of the semester trying to play "catch-up". Most common of all are issues related to interpersonal relationships and substance abuse, which often begin in high school and may worsen in college. If there is one word that college students use most, it is "STRESS". This chapter explores how an individual's learned dispositions, specifically their outlook to life, influences their appraisal of the demands or stressors they face, and subsequently impacts emotional well being. It focuses on how the perceptions and appraisal of experiences influence how college students cope with stress and consequently influence their vulnerability for depression, anxiety, and overall adjustment in college.

ASSESSMENT OF COLLEGE ADJUSTMENT

What is college adjustment, and how has it been assessed among college students? As mentioned earlier in this chapter, adjustment refers to coping. It reflects our ability to respond to pressures in our environment. Adjustment could be at a physical or psychological level. Physical adjustment often involves a change to meet a given condition, such as wearing light clothes and drinking more cold fluids in warm climate. On the other hand, psychological adjustment affects emotions. It includes experiences such as death of a loved one, balancing the demands of work and family, or an upcoming exam. Regardless of the circumstance, the best way to adjust to a demand is by "...seeing pressures and problems for what they are" (Rathus and Nevid, 1999, p.5)

Review of literature on adjustment among college students indicates that the topic has been studied extensively, using different measures. One assessment, tool the Student Adaptation to College Questionnaire (SACQ) by Baker and Siryk (1986), has been used quite widely for measuring successful adjustment to college (see Choi, 2002; Lapsley and Edgerton, 2002; Martin, et al, 1999). The SACQ is composed of four subscales, which measure Academic Adjustment, Social Adjustment, Personal-Emotional Adjustment, and Goal Commitment-Institution Attachment. Most studies that utilized the SACQ focused on overall adjustment, and therefore did not necessarily consider specific factors that constitute psychological well-being such as depression, anxiety, or perceived stress.

Some studies of adjustment among college students have also used measures that were not necessarily developed for college samples. The most common examples are the Symptoms Checklist-90-Revised (SCL-90-R) (Derogatis 1983), which is often used as a general assessment of distress in non-clinical samples, the Beck Depression Inventory (Beck, et al, 1961), the Satisfaction with Life Scale (Diener, et al, 1985), and the Index of Well-Being (Campbell, Converse, and Rogers, 1976). Although these assessment tools have good psychometric qualities, they may not necessarily capture experiences that are unique to college students. Other researchers have developed their own self report scales with items measuring academic, social, and mental adjustment, and required that respondents compare their overall adjustment with that of an average freshman (Aspinwall and Taylor, 1992). The latter effort is certainly an improvement over generic scales, as they zero in on unique experiences of college students.

The present study attempted to minimize some of the drawbacks mentioned earlier by including generic measures, as well as those developed uniquely for college samples. In the current study, college adjustment was assessed using the College Adjustment Scales (Anton and Reed, 1991), the Beck Depression Inventory, the Beck Anxiety Inventory, the Adult Suicide Ideation Questionnaire, and the Pennebaker Inventory on Limbic Languidness. In sum, college adjustment as measured in the current study focused on levels of depression, anxiety, suicide ideation, interpersonal and family problems, academic and career problems, substance abuse, as well as, physical symptoms.

ASSESSMENT OF OUTLOOK TO LIFE

As mentioned earlier in this chapter, the current study focused on how outlook to life and perceived stress influence adjustment to college. Outlook to life constituted respondents' levels of optimism, which has been defined as overall positive outcome expectancies (Scheier and Carver, 1985). Although previous studies looked at optimism and pessimism (i.e., generalized negative outcome expectancies), as a bidimensional concept more recent studies have focused on optimism as a unidimensional concept (Lai, 1997; Scheier and Carver, 1994). The present study thus focused on the latter, that is, optimism as a unidimensional concept.

Generally optimism and pessimism have been found to be crucial in a person's psychological and physical well being. For instance, optimism has been associated with positive health outcomes (Achat, et al, 2000; Schweizer, et al, 1999; Scheier and carver, 1992), lower stress levels as indicated by decreased levels of cortisol (Ebrecht, et al, 2004), and improved immune functioning (Segerstrom, et al, 1998; Scheier, Carver, and Bridges, 1994). Other studies have reported an important link between optimism and positive stress appraisal, and have also emphasized that stress plays a crucial role in the link between optimism and physical well-being (Segerstrom, 2005). Specifically, Segerstrom (2005) reported that the relationship between optimism and immune functioning is negative when an individual is encountering extreme stress, but positive when the stress is under control. Similarly, Bromberger and Mathews (1996) reported that the interaction between optimism-pessimism and stress was a reliable predictor of depressive symptoms in middle-aged adults. In sum, it has been documented over and over that optimism is positively correlated with better psychological adjustment among adult samples (Scheier, Carver, and Bridges, 2001; Scheier and Carver, 1992, 1985).

Researchers who focused on college samples have also found an overall positive link between optimism and subsequent adjustment. Reports have indicated that optimism is positively correlated with life satisfaction (Chang, et al, 1997) and overall college adjustment among Asian-American and Caucasian-American students (Chang 1996). Furthermore some studies have looked at the extent to which dispositional optimism predicts physical and psychological well-being in college samples. For instance, in a study of the degree to which psychological resistance factors (such as optimism) predict general health among 202 undergraduate students, Ebert, Tucker, and Roth (2002) found that optimism, sense of coherence, and neuroticism were significant predictors of psychological well-being. Yet still, more recent studies have considered the role of social support in the negative relationship between optimism and poor psychological adjustment (Brisette, Scheier, and Carver, 2002). Brisette and her colleagues (2002) reported that optimism was associated with less perceived stress, less depression, and better social support network among 89 first semester college students. All in all, research findings have also linked optimism with better physical and psychological well-being among college samples.

The purpose of the present study was to continue exploring the relationship between optimism and adjustment, using measures that were solely developed for college samples. This is important because some researchers have found younger people to be more neurotic, have more physical symptoms, and to be less optimistic compared to relatively older adult samples (Chang 2002; Ebert, et al, 2002). If optimism which is negatively related to poor psychological well-being is lower among college samples, and the latter group also has higher levels of perceived stress and subsequent depression, then it is worth studying this unique sample using diverse measures. Also, given research suggesting that life stressors play a key role in the initial episode of depression than subsequent episodes (Kendler, Thornton, and Gardner, 2001), and estimates that sixty percent of individuals with at least one depressive episode will have another one in the future (Solomon, et al, 2000), it is crucial that research on the link between optimism, stress, and psychological well-being is taken seriously to help further exploration of preventative efforts.

The current study sought to investigate the following questions:

1. Will the negative link between optimism and poor psychological and physical well being be confirmed utilizing both measures normalized for college samples as well as those which were not normalized solely for college samples?
2. Compared with perceived stress, will dispositional optimism be a better predictor for physical, psychological, and overall adjustment among this college sample?

METHODOLOGY

Participants:

Participants consisted of 259 undergraduates, who were enrolled in a General Psychology course at a medium-sized university in the north eastern region of the United States. Participants consisted of 171 females and 88 males with ages ranging from 17 to 35 and an average age of 19.61 (SD = 4.27). One hundred and eighty two (70.27%) of the sample were freshmen, twenty-eight (10.81%) were sophomores, twenty-four (9.26%) were juniors, and the remaining twenty four participants (9.26%) were seniors. One individual failed to identify their year in college. Furthermore, participants were predominantly Caucasians (224 or 86.49%), 14 (5.4%) were African-Americans, 8 (3.1%) were Asian-Americans, 4 (1.5%) were Hispanic-Americans, 4 (1.5%) described themselves as other, and the remaining 5 (1.9%)

failed to identify their race. Although the ethnic proportions are skewed, they are a reflection of the racial distribution in the particular region that the study was conducted.

MEASURES

Demographic Data

Demographic information collected included age, gender (i.e., male or female), race (i.e., Caucasian, Black or African-American, Asian or Asian-American, Hispanic, or Hispanic-American, Native American Indian, and Other), and year in college (i.e., freshman, sophomore, junior, and senior).

Independent Measures

1. Optimism

Optimism was measured using the Life Orientation Test-Revised (LOT-R) by Scheier, Carver, and Bridges, 1994. The LOT-R is a shortened version of the Life Orientation Test - LOT by Scheier and Carver. It consists of 10 items; 3 items assessing optimism, another 3 items for pessimism, and 4 filler items. Respondents are asked to indicate the degree to which they agree with each of the statements by choosing one of five options (0 = strongly disagree, 1 = disagree, 2 = neutral, 3 = agree, and 4 = strongly agree). The LOT-R has been found to be reliable with Cronbach's alpha of .86 for a college sample of 2055 students, and correlations greater than .90 between the original LOT and the LOT-R (Scheier, et al., 1994).

2. Perceived Stress

Perceived stress was assessed using a modified version of the Undergraduate Stress Questionnaire (Crandall, Preisler, and Aussprung, 1992). The Undergraduate Stress Questionnaire consists of 82 stressful events that are common to college students. It includes general events such as lack of money, death of a loved one, and car problems, as well as events unique to college samples such as problems at the registrar's office, working while in school, and trying to decide on a major. Respondents are asked to check all stressful events on the list that they have encountered in the last 2 weeks. For the current study the USQ was modified such that in addition to checking stressful event, participants were asked to indicate the intensity or severity of each stressful event that they checked on a 5-point scale ranging from 0 = not intense or severe to 5= extremely intense or severe. The latter modification is what constituted perceived stress for the present study. The USQ has been found to correlate negatively with positive mood and also with good physical well-being. Overall students have rated it as the most accurate of different tools that assess stressful life events.

Dependent Measures

1. Suicide Ideation

Suicide Ideation was assessed with 2 different instruments, the Adult Suicide Ideation Questionnaire and the Suicide Ideation sub-scale of the College Adjustment Scales, which is discussed later in this section. The Adult Suicidal Ideation Questionnaire (ASIQ) by Reynolds (1991) was used to assess participants' level of suicidal thoughts. It is a 25-item measure of suicidal ideation. Each item assesses for a specific suicidal ideation or behavior (e.g., I thought it would be better if I was not alive; I thought about what to write in a suicide note; I wondered if I had the nerve to kill myself, etc.). Respondents are asked to rate each item on a 7-point scale assessing the frequency of occurrence of such suicidal ideation within the past month. Responses ranged from 0 – "I never had this thought" to 6 – "Almost everyday". The ASIQ has been found to possess high internal consistency reliability among adult community samples and college samples, with coefficient alphas of 0.96 and 0.961 respectively (Reynolds, 1991), and 0.97 for a sample of college students in the U.S. (Eshun, 2003).

2. Depression

Depression was also assessed with 2 different instruments, the second edition of the Beck Depression Inventory (BDI-II) and the Depression sub-scale of the College Adjustment Scales, which is discussed later in this section. The BDI-II is a 21-item self-report inventory for measuring severity of depression in individuals 13 years and older. It assesses depressive symptoms according to the fourth edition of the diagnostic criteria of the Diagnostic and Statistical Manual of Mental Disorders (DSM-IV) of the American Psychiatric Association (1994), such as sadness, pessimism, fatigue, loss of interest, appetite disturbance, and feelings of worthlessness. Respondents are asked to select the statement that describes their feelings and experiences in "the past week, including today" (Beck, Steer, and Brown, 1996). Coefficient alpha of the BDI-II was .92 for outpatients and .93 for a sample of 12 college students (Beck, et al, 1996).

3. Anxiety

Anxiety was also measured using 2 different instruments, the Beck Anxiety Inventory (BAI) and the Anxiety subscale of the College Adjustment Scales, which is discussed later in this section. Like the BDI, the BAI (Beck, Epstein, Brown, and Steer 1988) is also a 21-item self-report inventory, which was originally designed to discriminate anxiety from depression in adults. The respondent is asked to rate how much he or she has been bothered by a list of 21 anxiety symptoms over the past week on a 4-point scale (Beck, and Steer, 1990). The scale ranges from 0 (not at all) to 3 ("severely – it bothered me a lot"). The BAI has been reported to have high internal consistency with correlations up to .71, and also acceptable test-retest reliability, with a correlation of .75. Although the original normative sample consisted of psychiatric outpatients, it has been used quite extensively in clinical and research settings.

4. College Adjustment

College Adjustment was assessed using the College Adjustment Scales (CAS) by Anton and Reed (1991). The CAS is a 108-item multi-dimensional inventory that assesses common psychological and developmental problems among college students. For each of the 108 items respondents are asked to select the response that best describes them on a four-point scale with 1 = "false or not at all true", 2 = "slightly true", 3 = "mainly true", and 4 = "very true". The CAS yields scores on nine scales: Anxiety (AN), Depression (DP), Suicide Ideation (SI), Substance Abuse (SA), Self Esteem (SE), Interpersonal Problems (IP), Family Problems (FP), Academic Problems (AP) and Career Problems (CP). Each of the nine sub-scales consists of 12 items with a minimum sub-scale score of 12 and a maximum of 48. Higher scores are an indication of poor adjustment and lower scores imply good adjustment. Reports of reliability and internal consistency have indicated coefficient alpha levels ranging from .80 to .92, with means of .86 (Anton and Reed, 1991). Coefficient alpha for the current sample was .95.

5. Physical Well-Being

Physical well-being was assessed with the Pennebaker Inventory of Limbic Languidness - PILL (Pennebaker, 1982). The PILL is a 54-item measure that asks the individual to report frequency of occurrence of a variety of physical symptoms in the past year. Responses are indicated on a 5-point scale ranging from "never or almost never" to "more than once a week". High scores imply poor overall physical health.

PROCEDURE

After completing relevant informed consent forms, participants completed two sets of questionnaires at separate times. They completed the Demographic Data and the LOT-R during the second and third week of a 15-week semester (Time 1), when students were just settling into school and the normal stresses that typically occur at the very beginning and end of the semester were relatively lower. The second set of assessment tools was administered six to eight week later, which was around midterm (Time 2). Time 2 measures included the ASIQ, BDI-II, BAI, CAS, PILL, and the USQ. All participants completed their surveys individually in a group (classroom) setting. No personal identification information was required. In order to link scores from Times 1 and 2, participants were assigned research identity numbers.

RESULTS

The final results were based on 238 participants, as the remaining 29 participants had missing data, which meant it was either impossible to compute total scores for a given assessment instrument, or they did were not available to complete surveys at Time 2. Component scores for each inventory or subscale was computed for each participant and then group means and standard deviations were computed and they are shown in Table 1 below.

Table 1. Means and Standard Deviations of Measures of Physical and Psychological Well-being

Variable	N	Mean	Standard Deviation
ASIQ	239	8.80	18.76
BDI-II	239	8.36	8.20
BAI	238	9.28	9.13
CAS – total score	228	62.64	36.35
CAS – Anxiety (AN)	232	10.75	8.08
CAS – Academic Problems (AP)	238	11.36	6.13
CAS – Career Problems (CP)	239	7.26	8.03
CAS – Depression (DP)	239	7.44	5.92
CAS – Family Problems (FP)	233	7.91	5.04
CAS – Interpersonal Problems (IP)	239	11.05	6.82
CAS – Substance Abuse (SA)	237	4.66	5.78
CAS – Self Esteem (SE)	237	4.66	5.04
CAS – Suicide Ideation (SI)	238	2.27	4.46
PILL	233	105.02	28.79

To investigate the question pertaining to negative link between optimism and college adjustment as well as that between perceived severity of stress and college adjustment, zero-order correlations were run between variables. As shown in Table 2 below, there were significant negative correlations between all dependent measures of college adjustment and outlook to life or optimism. Correlations ranged from 0.168 (p<.01) for CAS-Substance Abuse and CAS-Self Esteem to 0.537 and 0.535 (p<.0001) for the BDI and CAS-total scores respectively. In other words, participants who had higher scores on optimism, had lower score on the CAS or were better adjusted, while those with lower levels of optimism had high CAS scores suggesting adjustment problems. On the other hand, significant positive correlations were found between all dependent measures of college adjustment and perceived severity of stress. Correlations ranged from r = .243 (p<.01) for CAS-Substance Abuse and CAS-Self Esteem to r = .613 and r = .591 for the total CAS and BDI-II scores respectively. That is, Pearson correlations between perceived stress and adjustment scores indicated that the higher the perceived stress levels of respondents, the poorer their adjustment.

Furthermore, regression analyses were performed to examine the extent to which the dependent measures (adjustment scores) are predicted by levels of optimism and perceived stress. Table 3 below shows the r-squared, beta, and F-statistics for all of the adjustment measures utilized in this study. As presented in Table 3, optimism accounted for 31%, 30%, 29%, and 28% of the variance in CAS-Depression, CAS-Anxiety, BDI-II, and CAS-total scores respectively. Similarly, perceived stress accounted for significant proportions of the variance in all dependent scores. Specifically, perceived stress accounted for 37%, 35%, 34%, 29%, and 28% of the variance in CAS-total, BDI-II, CAS-Anxiety, BAI, and CAS-Interpersonal Problems respectively.

Table 2.Intercorrelations between Optimism, Perceived Stress, and Adjustment Scores
Table 1.Means and Standard Deviations of Measures of Physical and Psychological Well-being

	Pearson Correlations (r)	
	Optimism	Perceived Stress
Dependent Measures		
ASIQ	-.405***	273***
BDI-II	-.537***	591***
BAI	-.428***	545***
CAS – total score	-.535***	.613***
CAS – Anxiety (AN)	-.553***	.582***
CAS – Academic Problems (AP)	-.406***	.409***
CAS – Career Problems (CP)	-.329***	.322***
CAS – Depression (DP)	-.560***	.561***
CAS – Family Problems (FP)	-.222**	.469***
CAS – Interpersonal Problems (IP)	-.425***	.538***
CAS – Substance Abuse (SA)	-.168*	.243***
CAS – Self Esteem (SE)	-.372***	.243***
CAS – Suicide Ideation (SI)	-.537***	.314***
PILL	-.427***	.468***

*   p<.01
**   p<.001
*** p<.0001

Table 3.Regression Analyses of the Role of Optimism and perceived Stress in Adjustment

	Predictors					
	Optimism			Perceived Stress		
	r^2	Beta	F	r^2	Beta	F
ASIQ	.16	-.41	46.31***	.07	.27	18.77**
BDI-II	.29	-.54	95.70***	.35	.59	124.91***
BAI	.18	-.43	51.42***	.29	.55	98.19***
CAS-total	.28	-.54	90.69***	.37	.61	133.67***
CAS-Anxiety	.30	-.55	101.77***	.34	.58	115.72***
CAS-Academic Problems	.16	-.41	46.33***	.16	.41	46.72***
CAS-Career Problems	.10	-.33	28.62**	.10	.32	27.03***
CAS-Depression	.31	-.56	108.10***	.31	.56	106.77***
CAS-Family Problems	.05	-.22	12.21**	.22	.47	65.79***
CAS-Interpersonal Problems	.18	-.43	52.14***	.28	.53	90.29***
CAS-Substance Abuse	.02	-.17	6.82*	.05	.24	14.50**
CAS-Self Esteem	.02	-.17	6.82*	.05	.24	14.50**
CAS-Suicide Ideation	.14	-.33	37.84**	.09	.31	25.35***
PILL	.18	-.43	51.42***	.22	.47	63.59***

*   p<.01   **.   p<.001   ***   p<.0001

DISCUSSION

In the present study, negative correlations were found between optimism and poor college adjustment, as was measured with instruments designed specifically for the college population and those developed for adults in general. These findings confirm earlier studies of adjustment in college samples (Chang, 1996; Ebert, et al, 2002). Also, as mentioned earlier in this chapter (Segerstrom, 2005), negative correlations were found between perceived stress and college adjustment. The link between optimism and/or stress and adjustment was much stronger for psychological factors such as depression, anxiety, and suicide ideation, moderate for physical well-being, interpersonal and family problems, and relatively lower for academic and career problems. Altogether, results from the current study indicated a link between optimism, which is viewed as a dispositional factor, perceived stress, and adjustment.

Furthermore results from regression analyses specify that optimism and perceived stress independently account for significant proportions of the variance in adjustment among college students. A comparison of the two factors (i.e., optimism and perceived stress) showed that they were both significant predictors of subsequent depression and overall adjustment in this sample. Optimism accounted for 29% of BDI-II scores and 31% of the CAS-depression sub-scale, in the same vein, perceived stress accounted for 35% of BDI-II scores and again 31% of the CAS-depression scale. However, proportions of physical and psychological well-being explained by optimism and perceived stress varied for some of the dependent variables. For instance, optimism seemed to be a better predictor of suicide ideation (with proportions of 16% for ASIQ and 14% for CAS-Suicide Ideation), than perceived stress, which accounted for comparatively less of the variance in both measures of suicide ideation (i.e., 7% for ASIQ and 9% for CAS-Suicide Ideation). On the contrary, compared to optimism, perceived stress accounted for relatively more of the variance in family problems and interpersonal problems. Whereas 22% of the variance in the CAS-Family Problems was accounted for by differences in perceived stress, optimism accounted for only 5%. Similar outcomes were found for interpersonal problems, with perceived stress accounting for 28% and optimism accounting for 18% of the variance in the CAS-Interpersonal Problems scores. These differences in proportions suggest that optimism seems to be a better predictor of psychological problems related to adjustment, such as depression, suicide ideation, and anxiety, while perceived stress seems to be a better predictor for problems concerning interpersonal relationships.

Subsequent data analyses in which the two predictors were combined yielded interesting findings. As shown in Figure 1, optimism and perceived stress together explained 54% of the variations in overall college adjustment, as measured by the CAS-total score. Similarly, the two factors combined accounted for 53% of depression scores on the BDI-II and 51.5% on the CAS-Depression scale. These proportions are similar and suggest that both scales are good measures of adjustment in college samples. On the other hand, whereas optimism and perceived stress together accounted for 51% of the variance in anxiety scores assessed by the CAS-Anxiety sub-scale, they only accounted for 38% of that on the BAI. The latter percentages may imply a need to take a more critical look at the BAI as an instrument for college samples or perhaps non-clinical samples. Thus, so far, aside the fact that it is more convenient (one instrument only), the CAS seems to be a comparatively better instrument for assessing adjustment among college students.

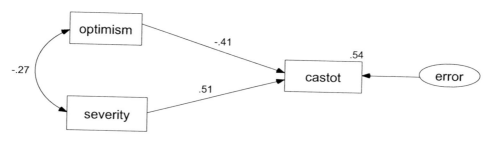

Figure 1.College Adjustment as predicted by Optimism and Perceived Severity of Stress.
Note:
    Adjusted r-squared values are at the top of variable boxes.
    Standardized beta values are on each predictor (straight) line.
    Correlations between variables are shown on the curved lines.

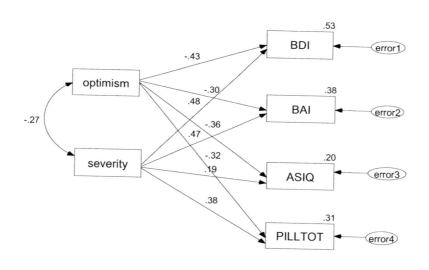

Figure 2.Depression, Anxiety, Suicide Ideation and Physical well-being as predicted by Optimism and Perceived Severity of Stress.
Note:
    Adjusted r-squared values are at the top of variable boxes.
    Standardized beta values are on each predictor (straight) line.
    Correlations between variables are shown on the curved lines.

    Another important aspect of the study was to explore how measures on the CAS compare with other commonly used measures of college adjustment, such as BDI-II, BAI, and ASIQ. Significant correlations were found between the ASIQ and the CAS-Suicide Ideation score (r = .89, p<.0001), BDI-II and the CAS-Depression score (r = .78, p<.0001), and also between the BAI and the CAS-Anxiety score (r = .70, p<.0001). Also, significant correlations existed between the total CAS score and BDI-II (r = .79, p<.0001) and PILL (r = .60, p<.0001). These correlations are of importance because they provide some more information about convergent validity for these sub-scales of the CAS and encourage use in research of non-clinical college samples.

In conclusion, results from the current study and a review of the literature on adjustment in college emphasize prior notions that optimism influences the way a person perceives and appraises their stress, and both optimism and perceived stress influence physical and psychological well-being (Segerstrom, 2005; Ebert, et al, 2002; Chang, 1996). However, it is worth noting that the relationship between optimism and adjustment may vary based on an individual's ethnic or cultural background. In studies of Asian-American college samples, they have been found to be significantly more pessimistic, but not necessarily less optimistic, compared with Caucasian-American samples (Chang, 1996; Zane, 1991). Specifically, Chang (1996) found that whereas pessimism was a significant predictor of subsequent psychological health for Caucasian Americans, lack of optimism (not pessimism) predicted subsequent psychological health in Asian Americans.

The current findings and those from previous studies have implications for working with college students. For instance if counselors are able to assess students' levels of optimism at the beginning of the semester, they may be successful in helping those with low levels of optimism by providing activities and opportunities that may help alter their negative perceptions. The latter is very important especially where the individual's low optimism or high pessimism level is somewhat irrational or based on unrealistic expectation. Perhaps college counselors could develop weekly group sessions with such individuals to help them track their academic progress and manage their stress levels. Furthermore, future research should go beyond merely exploring the relationship between optimism and adjustment and look at possible mechanisms or programs that can be put in place to help improve the quality of life, physical, and psychological well being of college students. Such preventative measures are important as they may further decrease the risk of more serious psychological problems like depression, since stress has been identified as a trigger of depression and also, a plausible explanation for why females in particular have higher levels of depression (Hammen and Mazure, 2003; Maciejewski, Prigerson, and Mazure, 2001).

The present study has some limitations that need to be mentioned. First, the sample was predominantly white. Given research findings about ethnicity and optimism/pessimism discussed earlier, it is important that caution is taken in generalizing results from studying a predominantly Caucasian group to non-Caucasian groups. Second, because all of the measures used were self-report inventories, there may be influences from social desirability, especially for the measures administered at Time 2. Some participants may have responded in a way that either made them appear strong or healthy (faking good), while others may have responded in a way that made them appear stressed and less adjusted (faking bad). Having said that though, it is worth mentioning that problems with social desirability may be minimal, given the large sample size.

REFERENCES

Achat, H., Kawachi, I., Spiro, A., Demolles, D.A., And Sparrow, D. (2000). Optimism And Depression As Predictors Of Physical And Mental Health Functioning: The Normative Aging Study. Annals Of Behavioral Medicine, 22, 127-130.

American Psychiatric Association. (1994). Diagnostic And Statistical Manual Of Mental Disorders (4th Ed.). Washington, Dc: American Psychiatric Association

Anton, W.D. And Reed, J.R. (1991). College Adjustment Scales: Professional Manual. Odessa, Fl: Psychological Assessment Resources

Aspinwall, L.G. And Taylor, S.E. (1992). Modeling Cognitive Adaptation: A Longitudinal Investigation Of The Impact Of Individual Differences And Coping On College Adjustment And Performance. Journal Of Personality And Social Psychology, 63 (6), 989-1005.

Baker, R.W. And Siryk, B. (1986). Exploratory Intervention With A Scale Measuring Adjustment To College. Journal Of Counseling Psychology, 33, 31-38.

Beck, A.T. And Steer, R.A. (1990). Manual For The Beck Anxiety Inventory. San Antonio, Tx: Psychological Corporation

Beck, A.T., Epstein, N., Brown, G., And Steer, R.A. (1988). An Inventory For Measuring Clinical Anxiety: Psychometric Properties. Journal Of Consulting And Clinical Psychology, 56, 893-897.

Beck, A.T., Steer, R.A., And Brown, G.A. (1996). Bdi-Ii Manual. San Antonio: The Psychological Corporation.

Beck, A.T., Ward, C.H., Mendelson, M., Mock, J., And Erbaugh, J. (1961). An Inventory For Measuring Depression. Archives Of General Psychiatry, 4, 561-571.

Brisette, I., Scheier, M.F., And Carver, S.C. (2002). The Role Of Social Network Development, Coping, And Psychological Adjustment During A Life Transition. Journal Of Personality And Social Psychology, 82 (1), 102-111.

Bromberger, T.T., And Mathews, K.A. (1996). A Longitudinal Study Of The Effects Of Pessimism, Trait Anxiety, And Life Stress On Depressive Symptoms In Middle-Aged Women. Psychology And Aging, 11, 207-213

Campbell, A., Converse, P.E., And Rogers, W.L. (1976). The Quality Of American Life: Perceptions, Evaluations, And Satisfactions. Beverly Hills, Ca:Sage.

Chang, E.C. (1996). Cultural Differences In Optimism, Pessimism, And Coping: Predictors Of Subsequent Adjustment In Asian American And Caucasian American College Students. Journal Of Counseling Psychology, 43, 113-123.

Chang, E.C., Maydeu-Oliveras, A., And D'zurilla, T.J. (1997). Optimism And Pessimism As Partially Independent Constructs: Relations To Positive And Negative Affectivity And Psychological Well-Being. Personality And Individual Differences, 23, 433-440.

Choi, K.H. (2002). Psychological Separation-Individuation And Adjustment To College Among Korean American Students: The Role Of Collectivism And Individualism. Journal Of Counseling Psychology, 49 (4), 468-475.

Crandall, C.S., Preisler, J.J., And Aussprung, J. (1992). Measuring Life Event Stress In Thelives Of College Students: The Undergraduate Stress Questionnaire (Usq). Journal Of Behavioral Medicine, 15, 627-662.

Deiner, E., Emmons, R.A., Larsen, R.J., And Griffin, S. (1985). The Satisfaction With Life Scale. Journal Of Personality Assessment, 49, 71-75.

Derogatis, L.R. (1983). The Scl-90r: Administration, Scoring, And Procedures Manual Ii. Baltimore, Md: Clinical Psychometric Research

Ebert, S.A., Tucker, D.C., And Roth, D.L. (2002). Psychological Resistance Factors As Predictors Of General Health Status And Physical Symptom Reporting. Psychology, Health And Medicine, 7 (3), 363-375.

Ebrecht, M., Hextall, J., Kirtley, L., Taylor, A., Dyson, M., And Weinman, J. (2004). Perceived Stress And Cortisol Levels Predict Speed Of Wound Healing In Healthy Male Adults. Psychoneuroendocrinology, 29 (6), 798-809.

Eshun, S. (2003). Sociocultural Determinants Of Suicide Ideation: A Comparison between American And Ghanaian College Samples. Suicide And Life-Threatening Behaviors, 33 (2), 165-171.

Hammen, C. And Mazure, C.M. (2003). Symposium: Understanding The Interaction Of Stress And Gender In The Prediction Of Major Depression – Introduction. Archives Of Women's Mental Health, 6, 3-4.

Kendler, K.S., Thornton, L.M., And Gardner, C.O. (2001). Genetic Risk, Number Of Previous Depressive Episodes, And Stressful Life Events In Predicting Onset Of Major Depression. American Journal Of Psychiatry, 158, 582-586.

Lai, J.C.L. (1997). Relative Predictive Power Of The Optimism Versus The Pessimism Index Of A Chinese Version Of The Life Orientation Test. Psychological Record, 47:3, 399-411.

Lapsley, D.K. And Edgerton, J. (2002). Separation-Individuation, Adult Attachment Style, And College Adjustment. Journal Of Counseling And Development, 80, 484-492.

Maciejewski, P.K., Prigerson, H.G., And Mazure, C.M. (2001). Sex Differences In Event-Related Risk For Major Depression. Psychological Medicine, 31, 593-604.

Martin, W.E., Schwartz-Kulstad, J.L., And Madson, M. (1999). Psychological Factors That Predict The College Adjustment Of First-Year Undergraduate Students: Implications For College Counselors. Journal Of College Counseling, 2, 121-133.

Pennebaker, J.W. (1982). The Psychology Of Physical Symptoms. Ny: Spring-Verlag

Rathus, S.A. And Nevid, J.S. (1999). Adjustment And Growth: The Challenges Of Life. 7th Edition. Orlando, Fl: Harcourt Brace College Publishers.

Reynolds, W.M. (1991). Development Of A Semi-Structured Clinical Interview For Suicidal Behavior In Adolescents. Psychological Assessment: A Journal Of Consulting And Clinical Psychology, 2, 382-390.

Reynolds, W.M. (1991). Adult Suicidal Ideation Questionnaire Professional Manual. Psychological Resource Inc., Florida.

Scheier, M.F. And Carver, C.S. (1985). Optimism, Coping And Health: Assessment And Implications Of Generalized Outcome Expectancies. Health Psychology, 4, 219-247.

Scheier, M.F. And Carver, C.S. (1992). Effects Of Optimism On Psychological And Physical Well-Being: Theoretical Overview And Empirical Update. Cognitive Therapy And Research, 16, 201-228.

Scheier, M.F., Carver, C.S. And Bridges, M.W. (1994). Distinguishing Optimism From Neuroticism (And Trait Anxiety, Self-Mastery, And Self-Esteem): A Reevaluation Of The Life Orientation Test. Journal Of Personality And Social Psychology, 67, 1063-1078.

Scheier, M.F., Carver, C.S. And Bridges, M.W. (2001). Optimism, Pessimism, And Psychological Well-Being. In E.C. Chang (Ed.), Optimism And Pessimism: Implications For Theory, Research, And Practice (Pp. 189-216). Washington, Dc: American Psychological Association.

Schweizer, K., Beck-Seyffer, A., And Schneider, R. (1999). Cognitive Bias Of Optimism And Its Influence On Psychological Well-Being. Psychological Reports, 84, 627-636.

Segerstrom, S.C. (2005). Optimism And Immunity: Do Positive Thoughts Always Lead To Positive Effects? Brain, Behavior And Immunity, 19 (3), 195-200.

Segerstrom, S.C., Taylor, S.E., Kemeny, M.E., And Fahey, J.L. (1998). Optimism Is Associated With Mood, Coping, And Immune Change In Response To Stress. Journal Of Personality And Social Psychology, 74, 1646-1655.

Solomon, D.A., Keller, M.B., Leon, A.C., Mueller, T.I., Lavori, P.W., And Shea, M.T. (2000).

Multiple Recurrences Of Major Depressive Disorder. American Journal Of Psychiatry, 157, 229-223.

Zane, N.W.S., Sue, S., Hu, L., And Kwon, J. (1991). Asian-American Assertion: A Social Learning Analysis Of Cultural Differences. Journal Of Counseling Psychology, 38, 63-70.

In: Stress and Mental Health of College Students
Editor: Mery V. Landow, pp. 203-224

ISBN 1-59454-839-0
© 2006 Nova Science Publishers, Inc.

Chapter 9

A Trauma by Any other Name: Examining College Students' PTSD Symptoms, Posttraumatic Growth, and Depression Following Exposure to Negative Life Events

April M. Robinson, Russell L. Kolts and Philip C. Watkins
Eastern Washington University, Cheney, Washington

ABSTRACT

The Diagnostic and Statistical Manual of Mental Disorders, fourth edition (DSM-IV; American Psychiatric Association [APA], 1994) provides criteria for Posttraumatic Stress Disorder (PTSD) that clearly define what is to be considered a "traumatic event" for purposes of diagnosis, and college students represent a population with a high frequency of exposure to events meeting this criteria. A significant body of literature has examined various impacts of such events, including negative outcomes such as PTSD and depression, as well as perceptions of personal growth, termed "posttraumatic growth." However, in our research we have frequently encountered individuals who, while endorsing experiences that the DSM-IV would categorize as "traumatic" in nature, consistently identify their "most traumatic event" as an experience that does not meet the criteria laid forth by the DSM-IV. These events are most often crises of an interpersonal (divorce, parental divorce, painful break-up), occupational (job loss, academic difficulties), or legal nature. The goal of the current research was to explore and contrast the relative impacts of events both meeting and not meeting DSM-IV criteria as a "traumatic event" in terms of both positive and negative outcomes. Self-report data was collected from 104 participants who were classified into two groups based on whether or not the event that caused them the most subjective distress met DSM-IV criterion A1 for PTSD. These groups were compared with regard to PTSD symptoms, level of depressive symptoms, and level of perceived trauma-related growth. Interestingly, the groups scored similarly on all measures, indicating that college students perceive themselves as experiencing similar outcomes, both positive and negative, in response to negative life events that do and do not meet the DSM-IV's criteria as representing a "traumatic event." Finally, a positive relationship was found between the amount of distress produced by the various events and the amount of posttraumatic growth experienced by participants. These findings imply that the trauma literature needs to pay greater heed to events that may not meet the relatively rigid criteria set forth by the DSM-IV but may nonetheless potentially produce both significant distress and the opportunity for positive life change in experiencing individuals.

INTRODUCTION

As reflected by a large volume of traumatic stress literature, there is overwhelming evidence that traumatic events cause distress which can negatively impact the lives of individuals experiencing such events (van der Kolk and McFarlane, 1996). The *Diagnostic and Statistical Manual of Mental Disorders, fourth edition* (DSM-IV) provides a specific definition of what constitutes a traumatic event, characterizing such events as involving the experiencing, witnessing, or confronting an event that involves actual or threatened death, serious injury, or a threat to the physical integrity of self or others, with the individual's response involving intense fear, helplessness, or horror (American Psychiatric Association [APA], 2000). Reactions to such events can vary from acute stress, which is present immediately following the trauma but then dissipates, to chronic stress that causes significant and enduring disruptions in the individual's functioning.

TRAUMA AND ITS EFFECTS

It is estimated that 60% of Americans will experience a life-threatening trauma during the course of their lives (Kessler et al., 1995). Additionally, college student populations in particular represent a group which has been documented as having been exposed to potentially traumatic events at rates of 80 to 84% (Vrana and Lauterbach, 1994; Hayman, 1999). Despite the frequent occurrence of such potentially traumatic events, most individuals are able to return to normal functioning following such experiences (van der Kolk and McFarlane, 1996). This response does not imply that they have forgotten the event or are not changed by it, but that the reminders and cues do not significantly impair the individual's ability to function. However, in some individuals, extreme responses to traumatic events can cause excessive distress and impairment in many aspects of the individual's life. Perhaps the most salient example of such extreme responses to traumatic experiences is posttraumatic stress disorder (PTSD). Other psychopathological responses to trauma can include major depressive disorder, panic disorder, and generalized anxiety disorder (McFarlane and Girolamo, 1996).

PTSD is characterized by the DSM-IV by the trauma criterion described above in combination with three separate symptom clusters (APA, 2000). The first and defining criterion for a PTSD diagnosis is the re-experiencing of the traumatic event. In contrast with individuals who are able to integrate the trauma into the narrative of their lives and to some extent move on, individuals with PTSD may re-experience the event to such an extent that it may seem to become a defining characteristic of the individuals' lives. This re-experiencing may occur via intrusive thoughts, images, feelings, flashbacks, dreams, or physiological reactions when cues of the event are present (APA, 2000). The second symptom criterion for a PTSD diagnosis involves the avoidance of stimuli associated with the event and the numbing of general responsiveness in response to the traumatic experience. Individuals with PTSD often spend significant time and effort attempting to avoid reliving the event in the manner described above, which paradoxically seems to prevent them from integrating the experience and moving beyond it. Avoidance symptoms may include actively avoiding thoughts, feeling, activities, places, and/or people who are reminders of the event. Also characteristic of PTSD is a general numbing of emotional responsiveness, particularly with regard to positive emotions. Numbing is reflected primarily in a restricted range of affect or feelings, and also is reflected in symptoms of social detachment and thoughts of foreshortened future. The third criterion includes symptoms of increased arousal that were not present before the traumatic experience. Individuals with PTSD experience an often broad-based disruption of arousal processes that can negatively impact both basic functions such as the individual's ability to concentrate, sleep, and regulate emotions, as well as their ability to discriminate legitimate threats from intense but non-threatening neutral stimuli (van der Kolk, 1996a, 1996b). Examples of such disruptions of arousal are exemplified in the DSM-IV symptoms of hypervigilance and exaggerated startle response (APA, 2000).

PTSD as a result of traumatic experiences has been observed in response to a wide variety of trauma types, including exposure to war, rape, natural disasters, accidents, medical procedures, and other events (Shalev, 1996). Although individuals differ in their response to such traumatic experiences, risk factors linked with both the experiencing individual and the nature of the traumatic events have been identified that contribute to a greater or lesser likelihood of PTSD development. Previous exposure to trauma during childhood greatly increases the risk for developing PTSD in response to subsequent trauma experienced in adulthood, and this is particularly true with regard to sexual abuse (Breslau et al, 1999; Udwin et al, 2000). It has been consistently observed that traumatic events involving sexual assault tend to result in higher rates of PTSD than do most other types of traumatic experiences. Prevalence rates of PTSD vary across sexual assault events with completed rapes producing the highest rates, with approximately 50% of rape survivors developing PTSD (Resnick, et al., 1993; Foa and Rothbaum, 1998; Favarvelli et al., 2004; Yehuda, 2004). In contrast, the literature provides some evidence that less individualized traumatic experiences (e.g. earthquakes and hurricanes) yield lower rates of PTSD. For example, it is estimated that 5% individuals who survive natural disasters will go on to develop PTSD at some point (Kessler, 1995).

Many researchers have interpreted the high prevalence of PTSD rates resulting from trauma such as sexual assault and war combat as being a result of the severity of such events, incorporating both the extent of threat and injury experienced by individual as well as the intensity of the fear, helplessness, or terror that he or she experienced (Resnick et al., 1993;Gilboa-Schechtman and Foa, 2001;Yehuda, 2004; Koren et al., 2005). However, the severity of a trauma is generally defined by a subjective emotional rating and therefore differs among individuals (Yehuda, 2004).

WHEN IS A TRAUMA NOT A "TRAUMA?"

The subjective interpretation of trauma severity has led researchers to explore personal characteristics that may influence individual responses to traumatic events. Foa and Rothbaum (1998) include the amount of controllability, predictability, and the intensity of fear that is evoked in the individual as contributing factors to the development of PTSD. Also identified as a factor is the individual's sense that he or she could have prevented the circumstances or changed them for the better (Urdwin, et al., 2000). Thus, the traumatic response is not completely based on event severity, but also seems highly related to the experiencing individual's personal appraisal both during and following the event. If we consider that an individual's interpretation of an event is important in predicting his or her response to a traumatic experiences, it is possible that some individuals might have "traumatic" personal reactions to events that do not include experiencing, witnessing, or being confronted by actual or threatened death, but that evoke intense fear, helplessness, or horror (Parks, Cohen, and Murch, 1996;Tedeschi and Calhoun, 1996). Such an event, while not meeting the DSM-IV's criteria as being a trauma, could potentially impact the lives of experiencing individuals in a manner no less profound than that seen in events which are regularly considered as being "traumatic."

The traumatic stress literature has explored different types of severe experiences and responses to trauma, but has generally neglected the exploration of extremely stressful life events not meeting the DSM-IV trauma criteria, and the potential for such events to provoke extreme responses. Despite this general neglect, a number of studies have highlighted the need to consider such experiences when studying the impacts of extreme events. Andrews and Wilding (2004) found that 29% of a British college sample endorsed their most stressful experience within an academic year as relationship problems, which significantly correlated with anxiety. In three different studies exploring stressful experiences within college samples, college students consistently reported "problems in romantic relationships" (14 to 19% of each sample) as being their most stressful experience within that year (Parks, Cohen, and Murch, 1996). The college samples also endorsed "academic performance problems" (6 to 15%) and "moving away to college" (7 to 14%) as being more stressful than severe traumatic events they experienced within the same year.

Such negative life experiences generally fall under the criterion for Adjustment Disorder in the DSM-IV, however the symptoms and individual interpretations may potentially be more reflective of the specific responses observed in PTSD (APA, 2000). Relationship separation or divorce are common experiences, but can impact and significantly change an individual's life with the potential for feeling helpless and fear for the future (Lester, 1994). It is conceivable that individuals who have experienced relationship difficulties could re-experience events from their relationships such as intrusive thoughts, dreams, or physiological responses when cues are provided, avoid thoughts, feelings, activities and/or people associated with their former partner, and experience increased arousal symptoms including difficulties sleeping, concentration problems, and experience excessive anger. Divorce rates have been highly correlated to suicide rates in many countries (Lester, 1994; Kondrichin and Lester, 2002). Taylor (2004) has labeled divorce as a "trauma" and recommended therapeutic methods typically used for PTSD, such as hypnosis, Eye

Movement Desensitization and Reprocessing (EMDR), and counseling groups, for therapists assisting individuals who are recovering from divorce.

Poor academic performances and adjustment to college have been explored within the context of psychological distress (Kelvin, Lucas, and Ojha, 1965; Parks, Cohen, and Murch, 1996; Andrews and Wilding, 2004). In a study of 351 college students, Andrews and Wilding (2004) observed that upon entering the university and mid-course through the first year, previously symptom free students reported clinical levels of anxiety (20%) and depression (9%). The researchers attributed the responses to feelings of entrapment or helplessness and fear of not attaining academic goals for the future. These elevated rates of both depression and anxiety have important implications for the well-being of students and suggest a need to explore the severity of the symptoms related to life stressors and related treatment possibilities.

A recent study by Gold, Marx, Soler-Baillo, and Sloan (2005) provides the only systematic comparison of the potential for stressful life events that do and do not meet DSM-IV trauma criteria to produce PTSD symptomatology. This study of 454 undergraduate students grouped participants as DSM trauma-congruent and trauma-incongruent based upon whether or not their identified event met the DSM-IV-TR Criterion A1 definition as a traumatic stressor. Groups were then compared with regard to differences in the level of PTSD symptoms that participants endorsed on the Posttraumatic Stress Diagnosis Scale (PDS; Foa, 1996). Surprisingly, the DSM trauma-incongruent group endorsed significantly higher levels of PTSD symptoms than did the group whose identified event met the DSM-IV-TR trauma criterion. This study documents the potential for negative life events that are not currently included under the DSM-IV-TR's definition of PTSD to produce significant levels of posttraumatic symptomatology, and the need for the traumatic stress literature to pay further attention to the impacts of such events.

POSTTRAUMATIC GROWTH

Despite widely documented evidence of posttraumatic psychopathology, there is also evidence that not all responses to trauma are negative and/or harmful. In fact, it appears that in many cases, traumatic experiences may actually lead to positive growth on the part of the experiencing individual (Janoff-Bulman and Berger, 2000). In addition to the negative responses mentioned previously, some individuals who experience traumatic or significantly negative life events report positive life changes or growth (Calhoun and Tedeschi, 1999). In the 1980's, psychology researchers identified a significant number of subjects who reported personal growth that they attributed to having experienced a traumatic event, which the researchers termed "posttraumatic growth" (PTG; Tedeschi, Park, and Calhoun, 1998). This construct has also been labeled "appreciation" (Janoff-Bulman and Berger, 2000), " benefit finding" (Tennen and Affleck, 1999), "perceived benefits" (McMillen, Zuravin, and Rideout, 1995), and "stress-related growth" (Park, Cohen, and Murch, 1996) in the literature that has described positive outcomes following traumatic experiences.

PTG has been defined as a "significant positive change arising from the struggle with a major life crisis" (Calhoun, Cann, Tedeschi, and McMillan, 2000, p. 521). As a result of traumatic experiences, individuals can develop "beyond their previous level of adaptation, psychological functioning, or life awareness" (Tedeschi et al., 1998, p.3). Specific domains in which individuals have reported experiencing PTG which are largely agreed upon by other researchers in the area include perceptions of self and interpersonal relationships. In addition to these two domains, Calhoun and Tedeschi (1995) have added changes in philosophies of life to their concept of growth. Moos and Schaefer (1993) have also included enhanced coping skills as a domain of positive change following trauma.

When individuals experience traumatic events, their assumptions of the world as a safe place where good things happen to good people can be shattered. "Terror characterizes the immediate aftermath of trauma, for the universe is now perceived as threatening and frightening, and their disintegrated inner world no longer provides a road map for negotiating daily life" (Janoff-Bulman and Berger, 2000, p.32). However, some research suggests that the labels that individuals apply to themselves after the event can positively impact their recovery process. Tedeschi (1999) found that PTG was higher in individuals who did not label themselves as a "victim," but rather as a "survivor" (p.322). This label may give trauma survivors the personal perception of power and strength, rather than of helplessness and depression. Survivors may report feelings of trauma-related expertise as a result of the event. In this case, they may feel that they have survived one of the worst experiences any human can endure and have prevailed. These feelings of self-efficacy can be very healthy and helpful for coping with the trauma (Tedeschi, 1999). Along with this perceived improvement in self-image, survivors can have an increase in appreciation for their own lives and for those of others. Survivors have an increased ability to create meaning out of their life through appraisals of the value and worth of life (Janoff-Bulman and Berger, 2000). Through the evaluation of value and worth, it is not uncommon for individuals who experience PTG to recognize the fragility of life and to increase their utilization of social support (Tedeschi et al., 1998).

In the domain of interpersonal relationships, some trauma survivors report an increased sense of closeness to others after the traumatic event (Tedeschi, 1999). It appears that allowing survivors to disclose their thoughts and feelings associated with the event and "allowing the trauma to have an impact, rather than avoiding the distressing aspects of it, is critical for posttraumatic growth" (Tedeschi, 1999, p.324). At least some trauma survivors seem to utilize their social support networks in order to work through the more difficult parts of the trauma, rather than avoiding contact or not discussing the event. Some survivors also report an increased ability to be compassionate and empathic to others who themselves are experiencing traumatic events (Tedeschi and Calhoun, 1995).

Calhoun and Tedeschi have suggested that individual philosophies of life are changed through PTG. As mentioned above, individuals experiencing trauma have reported an increased appreciation of life (Tedeschi and Calhoun, 1995). This enhanced appreciation of their own lives can be reflected in a variety of positive life changes, including an increase in pleasurable activities and self-care behaviors, attempting to live each day to the fullest, and shifting or changing priorities. For example, many survivors report spending more time with their families and spending less time on "inconsequential" acitivities (Tedeschi, 1999, p.324).

Trauma survivors may also perceive growth in the spiritual aspects of their lives. At first, there may be a temporary weakening of spirituality, but later survivors have reported a strengthening of spiritual beliefs due to addressing existential issues that may have arisen following the trauma (Tedeschi, 1999). This process can take the form of a "spiritual emergency," in which the individual feels that he or she must become more in touch with the metaphysical world and therefore takes on a quest to find answers to life's questions (Tedeschi et al., 1998). Other individuals may look to religion as a resource or strengthen their religious affiliations because of the event (Tedeschi and Calhoun, 1995). During the trauma, the individual may have experienced a close encounter with death. Therefore, it makes sense that trauma survivors begin to contemplate issues such as the purpose of life and acceptance of death.

The concept of wisdom has been presented as another example of possible changes in life philosophy. Wisdom can be conceptualized as the ability to integrate emotional and intellectual understanding in relation to the traumatic event, a process which does not appear to be limited by age (Tedeschi, 1999). The event may have been painful and horrifying, but it has been suggested that with gained wisdom, the survivor is will often construct a meaning around the trauma in which he or she can find truth or peace (Tedeschi et al., 1998).

In addition, Moos and Schaefer (1993) introduced the idea of enhanced coping skills to the PTG literature. They have suggested that survivors who experience growth also gain better and more adaptive coping skills that may be used in the case of another crisis. Survivors may also feel an increased sense of control over their lives due to the effectiveness of their learned coping skills.

MEASURING POSTTRAUMATIC GROWTH

Research in the area of PTG has lead to the development of pencil-and-paper assessments designed to measure growth after traumatic experiences. Tedeschi and Calhoun (1996) have developed a measure to assess growth as a multidimensional construct: the Posttraumatic Growth Inventory (PTGI). The PTGI is a 21-item questionnaire that assesses changes in three domains: perceptions of self, interpersonal relationships, and philosophies of life. In developing this measure, undergraduate college students were recruited that had experienced a negative life event within the past five years. The most frequent events experienced by the sample included bereavement, injury-producing accidents, and separation of parents, accounting for 62% of the total number of recalled events (Cohen et al., 1998).

Park et al. (1996) have also developed a measure to assess perceived benefits as a unidimensional construct: the Stress-Related Growth Scale (SRGS). The SRGS is a 50-item questionnaire similar to the PTGI. This questionnaire attempts to investigate changes in social relationships, personal resources, and coping skills in relation to a significantly stressful event (Cohen et al., 1998). To develop this measure, undergraduate college students discussed their "most stressful/upsetting event" within the past 12 months. The most frequently endorsed events were romantic relationships, academic problems, and moving away to college, accounting for 48% of total recalled events (Cohen et al., 1998).

A growing body of research has investigated PTG using both the PTGI and SGRS. Although the DSM-IV provides specific criteria for use in defining traumatic events, this definition has generally not been considered in studies of PTG, which have variously been used with populations experiencing events meeting the DSM-IV trauma criteria as well as with individuals experiencing situations that clearly do not meet this criteria.

PREDICTORS OF POSTTRAUMATIC GROWTH

In the posttraumatic growth literature, some predictors have been identified that may predispose individuals to experience growth in the wake of extreme events. Research in this area has supported the idea that some personality characteristics are more likely to facilitate the experience of PTG than are others. Affleck and Tennen (1996) found that dispositional optimism and dispositional hope were significant predictors of PTG. Dispositional optimists tend to positively interpret the events that surround them and to have expectancies for positive outcomes. Dispositional hope is different from dispositional optimism in that the individual not only expects positive outcomes, but he or she can also imagine attaining those goals (Affleck and Tennen, 1996).

Another personality characteristic that may facilitate growth following trauma is cognitive complexity (Tennen and Affleck, 1998). Affleck and Tennen (1996) define cognitive complexity as "the ability to achieve personal goals despite barriers imposed by an aversive event" (p. 910). Individuals who are more cognitively complex may have more resources to draw upon in constructing coping efforts. They may have more flexible ways of thinking, may have different self-schemas to draw upon, and may adapt more easily (Affleck and Tennen, 1998). Individuals who are more cognitively complex may also have the ability think more actively about the event and possibly find ways to make sense of the situation (Calhoun et al., 2000). Morgan and Janoff-Bulman (1994) found that positive self-complexity was strongly associated with overall adjustment following a traumatic experience. Self-complexity seems to function serve as protection from the long-term negative effects of trauma, as survivors are able to draw from their many other self-representations to receive psychological strength (Morgan and Janoff-Bulman, 1994).

In addition to dispositional optimism, dispositional hope, and cognitive complexity, PTG investigators have also examined relationships between PTG and the "Big Five" personality dimensions of neuroticism, extraversion, openness to experience, conscientiousness, and agreeableness. Tedeschi and Calhoun (1996) administered the NEO Personality Inventory (NEO; Costa and McCrae, 1985) and the Posttraumatic Growth Inventory (PTGI; Tedeschi and Calhoun, 1996) to trauma survivors and found that four of the five personality factors (extraversion, openness, agreeableness, and conscientiousness) were significantly correlated with PTG. The most significant predictor of PTG was extraversion, followed by openness to experience. Although these findings are not necessarily surprising, they do confirm that certain personality characteristics may be more related to PTG, and also raise the question of whether or not personality characteristics can transform as a result of a traumatic experience (Tennen and Affleck, 1996).

While personality characteristics and styles may predispose certain individuals to experience PTG following trauma, it is also the case that social support is linked to growth outcomes. Support derived from one's social and family networks can be important factors for facilitating growth after extreme events (Moos and Schaefer, 1993). Social resources may be helpful for modeling and influencing effective coping strategies as well in facilitating successful adjustment in response to life crises (Schaefer and Moos, 1998). Relationships that have strong foundations can represent helpful resources for individuals after a traumatic experience (Tedeschi and Calhoun, 1995). Healthy families and friendships can provide positive contexts for individuals to discuss their experiences and may assist in growth processes.

Support groups can also contribute to positive outcomes (Schaefer and Moos, 1998). It can be a very powerful experience for individuals to interact with others who have suffered a similar event and who express empathy (Tedeschi and Calhoun, 1995). Additionally, people who have endured a traumatic event and have experienced PTG can be a source of inspiration for other survivors. They can also represent a valuable resource by providing information about effective methods of coping with symptoms, life adjustments, and being a role model for individuals who have experienced traumatic events (Tedeschi and Calhoun, 1995).

PTG AND TRAUMA CHARACTERISTICS

Along with personality and social support, characteristics of the event itself can also be predictive of PTG. McFarland and Alvaro (2000) investigated self-improvement and perceived PTG in survivors and acquaintances of survivors based upon the severity of the event experienced. In the course of four studies, they used the combination of the SRGS and the PTGI to assess perceived benefits from negative life events, which were rated by the participants as being severe ("traumatic") or mild. The negative life events that were reported by the participants included bereavement, relationship problems or loss, work – school- or home-related stress, illness or injury, psychological problems, stress due to close other's problems or illness, and physical/sexual abuse. Participants were classified as being either a victim or an acquaintance of a victim who had experienced a negative life event. The participants rated the level of PTG of the victim and events considered mostly likely to facilitate growth. Victims reported higher levels of growth after experiencing traumatic events, whereas acquaintances reported observing higher levels of growth in victims experiencing mild negative events. The authors of these studies discuss inconsistent perceptions of growth as evidence to support that improvement after stressful events may reflect exaggerated perceptions of growth from the victim and derogation of their previous attitudes. Yet, despite the potential for exaggerated growth perceptions and altered preincident attitudes, this response may represent an effective coping strategy that may provide comfort for victims of particularly extreme events.

In a situation that involves the devastation of physical illness, growth is more likely to occur if the event is severe and life threatening and support from family and friends is readily available (Schaefer and Moos, 1998). However, if the illness is excessively severe or long-lasting, it may have a negative impact on the individual and deplete social resources. The relationship of PTG and disasters appears to be similar to that seen in survivors of physical illness. If the disaster is minor, it can bring friends and family closer and may facilitate growth. Yet, if the disaster is very severe, the resources of the community may be depleted and more negative outcomes are predicted (Schaefer and Moos, 1998). PTG can occur as a result of severe disasters, but when the event is severe, with a high death rate, growth will often be postponed until the community can recover. This can also be seen in communities of war and violent crimes (Schaefer and Moos, 1998). Tedeschi and Calhoun suggest that, for the individual, the event has to be challenging enough to provoke the individual to evaluate the situation and activate available resources, whereas overwhelming events that are too emotionally demanding are likely to lead to exclusively negative outcomes for the individual (Tedeschi and Calhoun, 1995).

As PTG represents a relatively new area in trauma research, there are few studies that explore predictor variables and test theoretical models. McMillen et al. (1995) investigated child sexual abuse and perceived benefits in low-income women. They used an open-ended interview format to assess PTG and found that 46.8% of the participants in the study endorsed perceiving some benefit resulting from the abuse. McMillen et al. acknowledged that the presentation of an open-ended question might have produced inflated results of reported PTG (Cohen, Hettler, and Pane, 1996).

In another study, McMillen, Smith, and Fisher (1997) compared three different events (tornado, mass shooting, plane crash) and their relationship to mental health and perceived benefits, as well as changes of perceived benefit over time. In this study, McMillen et al. used an open-ended interview format similar to that used in a previous study (McMillen et al., 1995). Participants were interviewed 4-6 weeks after the event and again three years later. Survivors of the tornado endorsed the highest levels of PTG, followed by the mass shooting, and then the plane crash. Those who reported experiencing high levels of PTG also reported higher levels of recovery from the event. Interestingly, after controlling for the severity of the traumatic event, predictors of PTG included the perception of individuals that they might die during the event and the presence of a higher number of pre-incident mental health diagnoses. Overall, the participants reported a decrease in the levels of endorsed PTG from the initial interview to the follow-up. Limitations of this study that were discussed by the authors included a single-item assessment of PTG, which limited their ability to identify various domains of PTG, as well as the sorts of perceived benefits were most useful to the participants.

THE CURRENT STUDY

The PTSD literature generally has not addressed potentially stressful experiences that do not meet the DSM-IV criteria for a trauma, but could significantly impact the experiencing individual. Gold et al. (2005) recently found that individuals identifying events that were inconsistent with the DSM-IV-TR's trauma criterion actually endorsed significantly higher levels of PTSD symptoms than did individuals experiencing events meeting this criterion. The current study sought to replicate this finding with regard to PTSD symptomatology, and to extend it into the area of posttraumatic growth. Repeatedly, participants in PTG studies have reported events which did not meet the DSM-IV trauma criteria as their most stressful or traumatic experiences (McFarland and Alvaro, 2000; Park et al., 1996; Tedeschi and Calhoun, 1996). However, while the PTG literature has examined both events meeting DSM-IV criteria as a traumatic event (e.g. bereavement, sexual assault, mass shooting) and negative experiences that do not meet this criteria (e.g. relational problems, academic problems, moving away from home), it has not distinguished between the two in terms of the relative ability of these events to produce PTG.

Finally, the PTG literature acknowledges the presence of PTSD as a negative and unpleasant reaction to traumatic experiences, but does not discuss how PTG and PTSD might be related to one another (Calhoun and Tedeschi, 1999). The literature seems to suggest that they are share a negative relationship (Aldwin and Sutton, 1998; McMillen, et al, 1997; Schaefer and Moos, 1998). While it may seem intuitive that as PTG increases, the severity and frequency of PTSD symptoms should decrease, this proposition has yet to be supported by empirical evidence.

The goals of the current study were to address these concerns by grouping college-student participants by the type of events that they had experienced (those meeting DSM-IV criteria as a traumatic event, and significantly negative life experiences not meeting this criteria) and examining whether the groups differed significantly with regard to PTG as well as to symptoms of PTSD and depression. We also sought to examine relative rates and levels of PTSD symptoms among groups in the context of traumatic events or perceived significant life stressors. Finally, the current study sought to explore the relationship between PTSD symptom level and PTG in DSM and non-DSM trauma groups.

The specific hypotheses of the current study predicted that individuals identifying experiences meeting DSM-IV criteria as a traumatic event and negative life experiences which did not meet this criteria would differ with regard to PTG. We have chosen to refer to these groups as the DSM trauma-congruent group and DSM trauma-incongruent group, respectively, to keep the language consistent with the Gold et al. (2005) study. Additionally, the DSM trauma-congruent group was expected to exhibit higher levels of PTSD symptoms than did the DSM trauma-incongruent group. Finally, the current study sought to examine potential relationships between PTSD symptoms and PTG.

METHOD

Participants

One hundred eleven undergraduate students enrolled in general psychology classes at a regional university in the inland northwest completed a questionnaire packet containing measures of traumatic experience and subsequent experiences of growth and psychopathology. For inclusion in the study, students had to endorse experiencing a traumatic or significantly negative life event. All participants were offered partial course credit in participating course in exchange for their participation. One hundred and four packets (94%) were considered for full analysis. Six participants were excluded because they did not endorse an event as causing distress on the trauma/negative life events measure, and one additional participant chose not to participate in the study after completing the demographic form. All procedures were evaluated and approved by the participating university's Institutional Review Board.

The sample of participants included predominately Caucasian, college-age individuals. Participants included 71 (64%) females and 40 (36%) males. The mean age of the sample was 21.2 with an age range of 17 to 50. Seventy-seven percent (n=85) of the sample was Caucasian, 8% (n=9) Asian, 5% (n=5) Hispanic, 1% (n=1) African-American, 1% (n=1) Native American, and 9% (n=10) endorsed "other" ethnicity or endorsed more than one ethnic group.

MEASURES

Traumatic Life Events Questionnaire (TLEQ). The TLEQ (Kubany, Leisen, Watson, Haynes, Owens, and Burns, 2000) consists of 21 items assessing whether the respondent has experienced a variety of traumatic life events, including natural disasters, military combat, motor vehicle accidents, and other situations. The TLEQ is consistent with the *DSM* posttraumatic stressor criteria A1 and A2 (APA, 2000). Respondents are offered seven fixed-choice options to indicate how often they had experienced each event, ranging as follows: never, once, twice, 3 times, 4 times, 5 times, more than 5 times. There is a section for the respondents to indicate whether they experienced intense fear, helplessness, or horror for each endorsed event. After completing the trauma history questions, respondents circle the one event that causes them the most distress. The final portion of the TLEQ provides a section for respondents to provide date/age of when the event first occurred and last time and six forced-choice options for distress ranging from no distress to extreme distress. For the purpose of this study, additional items were added to the questionnaire to assess negative life experiences that do not meet *DSM* criteria, including divorce/separation, painful breakup or stressful interpersonal situation, loss of employment, academic problems, legal difficulties, financial difficulties, and life transition for a total of 32 items (See Table 1 for additional items).

Modified PTSD Symptom Scale-Self Report Version (MPSS-SR). The MPSS-SR (Falsetti, Resnick, Resick, and Kilpatrick, 1993) is a self-report measure that assesses the severity and frequency of each PTSD symptom over the course of the past two weeks. The MPSS-SR has good internal consistency (Cronbach's alpha = .98) and convergent validity with the SCID PTSD module (Falsetti et al., 1993).

Beck Depression Inventory (BDI). The BDI (Beck, Ward, Mendelson, Mock, and Erbugh, 1961) is a widely used 21-item self-report measure of depressive symptomatology. The BDI has an internal consistency range of .73 to .92 and has favorable content, concurrent, and discriminant validity (Groth-Marnat, 1999). It is moderately correlated with the MMPI Depression Scale (.76) and is consistent with DSM-IV criteria for Major Depressive Disorder (Groth-Marnat, 1999).

Posttraumatic Growth Inventory (PTGI). The PTGI consists of 21 items comprising five subscales: Relating to Others, New Possibilities, Personal Strength, Spiritual Change, and Appreciation of Life (Tedeschi and Calhoun, 1996). The PTGI assesses posttraumatic growth as a multidimensional construct. Internal consistency for the scale was .90 with subscales ranging from .67 to .85. PTGI displays adequate test-retest reliability (.71).

Stress-Related Growth Scale (SRGS). The SRGS consists of 50 items that assess perceived growth as a unidimensional construct. The SRGS examines changes in social relationships, personal resources, and coping skills following a stressful event (Cohen, Hettler, and Pane, 1996). The SRGS demonstrates good internal reliability (Cronbach's alpha = .94) and test- retest reliability (.81) (Park, Cohen, and Murch, 1996).

Procedure

Experimenters solicited participants from general undergraduate psychology classes and read a statement to inform potential participants about the study and of scheduled times that they could participate. All participants received research participation credit in their respective classes. After arriving at the arranged time, experimenters provided a brief description of the study, discussed confidentiality, and obtained informed consent.

Participants were informed that they could withdraw from participation at any point in the procedure without penalty. Prior to filling out the questionnaires, participants were asked if they had any questions regarding the study and were asked to complete a demographics form that was kept separate from the questionnaire packet. Participants were given the questionnaire packet after the experimenters collected the demographic forms. Upon turning in the questionnaire packet, all participants were provided with a referral sheet describing available campus and community mental health resources. The measures in the packet were ordered with the BDI first, followed by the TLEQ, with measures of PTSD and PTG administered last. The posttraumatic growth measures (PTGI, SGRS) were counterbalanced with the PTSD symptom measure (MPSS-SR) to control for potential order effects. Participants were placed into 1 of 2 groups (DSM trauma-congruent, DSM trauma-incongruent) based on whether or not the event that they had endorsed as causing them the most distress met criterion A1 for PTSD in the *DSM-IV-TR* (APA, 2000).

RESULTS

Life Experiences

Table 1 presents the overall total frequencies of experienced events (939) by all participants (110) and the frequencies of the endorsed event that caused the most distress for each participant (n = 104). Nearly all participants in the sample endorsed experiencing one traumatic or negative life event that caused them distress (n = 104, 95%). In this sample, when asked to identify the one event that had caused them the most distress, 53 (48%) participants endorsed an event meeting DSM-IV trauma criteria and were placed in the DSM trauma-congruent group, 51 (46%) endorsed a stressful negative life event that did not meet this criteria and were placed in the DSM trauma-incongruent group, and 6 (6%) did not endorse any such events and were not included in the following analyses.

MEASURES OF GROWTH AND PTSD SYMPTOMATOLOGY

Total growth scores were calculated with the PTGI and SRGS by summing across all items. The maximum score available on the PTGI is 126 and for the SGRS is 100. Symptoms on the MPSS-SR were considered to be endorsed by participants if they indicated at least 1 symptom for frequency and at least a 2 for symptom severity intensity. Total symptom severity scores on the MPSS-SR were calculated by summing the frequency and severity scores across all items. For the MPSS-SR, a cutoff score of 28 has been recommended as indicative of PTSD for screening purposes (Coffey, Dansky, Falsetti, Saladin, and Brady, 1998). The BDI scores were calculated by summing all items, recommended cutoff scores for the BDI are less than 10 for normal mood fluctuations, 10-16 for mild depression, 17-29 for moderate subclinical depression, and over 29 for severe depression (Beck, Steer, and Garbin, 1988). Table 2 presents the means and standard deviations for measures of growth, depression, and PTSD symptom severity scores. As expected, the PTGI and SGRS were highly correlated (r =. 703), as were measures of PTSD and depressive symptomatology (r =.

634). Correlations are presented in Table 4. An alpha level of .05 was used for all statistical tests. Missing data on specific measures was dealt with via pairwise case deletion.

Table 1

Frequency of Negative Life Events in a College Sample (N = 104)

Type of event	Overall Event Frequency	% of All Events Endorsed (n = 939)	Frequency of "Most Distressing" Events	% of "Most Distressing" Events (n = 104)
Traumatic Events (Original TLEQ Items)				
Natural Disaster	58	6.2	0	0
Motor Vehicle Accident	26	2.8	3	2.9
"Other" kind of accident	25	2.7	1	1.0
Combat or warfare	4	0.4	1	1.0
Sudden death	70	7.5	16	15.4
Life-threatening/disabling event to loved one	50	5.3	6	5.8
Life-threatening illness	12	1.3	4	3.8
Robbery/weapon used	12	1.3	0	0
Assaulted by acquaintance/stranger	15	1.6	0	0
Witnessed severe assault or acquaintance/stranger	25	2.7	0	0
Threatened with death/serious harm	35	3.7	0	0
Growing up: witnessed family violence	19	2.0	6	5.8
Growing up: physically punished	32	3.4	2	1.9
Physically hurt by intimate partner	15	1.6	2	1.9
Before 13: sexual contact – someone 5 years older	19	2.0	4	3.8
Before 13: unwanted sexual contact	15	1.6	2	1.9
As a teen: unwanted sexual contact	18	1.9	4	3.8
As an adult: unwanted sexual contact	10	1.1	1	1.0
Sexual harassment	39	4.2	1	1.0
Stalked	29	3.1	0	0
Miscarriage	5	0.5	0	0
Abortion	6	0.6	0	0
Events Not Meeting DSM-IV Trauma Criteria				
Divorce/marital separation	22	2.3	6	5.8
Painful break-up or stressful interpersonal situation	94	10.0	17	16.3
Loss of employment	16	1.7	1	1.0
Academic problems	54	5.8	5	4.8
Legal difficulties	22	2.3	3	2.9
Financial difficulties	50	5.3	2	1.9
Life transition	87	9.3	9	8.7
"Other" stressful life experience	55	5.9	8	7.7

Table 2

Means and Standard Deviations for Symptomatology and Growth Measures

Measure	Mean	Standard Deviation
MPSS-SR	21.85	20.86
BDI	8.73	7.19
PTGI	65.32	24.46
SGRS	47.31	24.30

Event Types and Posttraumatic Growth

To examine differences between groups with regard to PTG, independent samples t-tests were calculated, using the PTGI and SGRS as dependent variables. The range of scores for the PTGI was from 25 to 121 and for the SGRS was from 2 to 93. The differences between the DSM trauma-congruent group and the DSM trauma-incongruent group were not statistically significant for either measure of PTG (PTGI, $t(98) = .277$, $p = .782$; SGRS, $t(91) = .661$, $p = .661$), however, the means for the DSM trauma-incongruent tended to be slightly higher on the growth measures than for the DSM trauma-congruent group. Table 3 presents group means and standard deviations on these measures. Sample means for the PTGI and SGRS were consistent with those seen in previous studies (Cohen et al., 1998; Parks et al., 1996; Tedeschi and Calhoun, 1996).

Table 3

DSM Trauma-Congruent and DSM Trauma-Incongruent Group Means and Standard Deviations for Symptomatology and Growth Measures

Measure	DSM Trauma-Congruent			DSM Trauma-Incongruent		
	N	Mean	Standard Deviation	N	Mean	Standard Deviation
MPSS-SR	49	18.28	20.43	42	26.00	20.93
BDI	56	7.57	6.53	47	10.11	7.76
PTGI	53	64.68	26.83	47	66.04	21.75
SGRS	50	46.28	25.24	43	48.51	23.40

EVENT TYPES AND MEASURES OF PTSD AND DEPRESSION

To examine differences between groups with regard to symptoms of PTSD and Depression, independent samples t-test were calculated with the MPSS-SR and BDI as dependent variables. No differences were seen between the DSM trauma-congruent group and the DSM trauma-incongruent group with regard to symptoms of either PTSD symptomatology (MPSS, $t(89) = 1.779$, $p = .079$) or symptoms of depression (BDI, $t(101) = 1.802$, $p = .075$). Similar to what was seen in regard to the growth measures, the means for the DSM trauma-incongruent group tended to be slightly higher on the measures of PTSD and depressive symptom measures than did the DSM trauma-congruent group.

Relationship of PTG and PTSD Symptomatology

To examine the relationship between PTG and PTSD symptomatology, Pearson product-moment correlation coefficients were calculated between measures of PTSD, depressive symptoms, and PTG. As shown in Table 4, there was no significant relationship between the MPSS-SR, BDI, and PTGI. However, a significant relationship was found between MPSS-SR and SGRS, indicating a modestly positive relationship between PTSD symptoms and a measure of post-event growth ($r = .25$, $p < .05$).

Table 4

Relationship between Posttraumatic Growth and Symptom Measures

Measure	MPSS-SR	BDI	PTGI	SRGS
Modified PTSD Symptom Scale	--	.634**	.137	.252*
Beck Depression Inventory	.634**	--	.102	.134
Posttraumatic Growth Inventory	.137	.102	--	.703*
Stress-Related Growth Scale	.252*	.134	.703*	--

* $p < .05$
** $p < .01$

CONCLUSION

The results of the current study demonstrated that events both meeting and not meeting DSM-IV criteria as a traumatic event had equal capacity to produce both posttraumatic growth and symptoms of posttraumatic stress disorder in this university sample. The results indicated no differences between groups defined by type of event that the participating individuals had labeled as most distressing on measures of PTG, PTSD symptoms, or symptoms of depression. These findings have a number of implications that are worth considering.

The finding that that PTSD and depressive symptoms did not differ between DSM trauma-congruent and DSM trauma-incongruent groups implies that individuals who experience negative life events such as divorce, job loss, legal problems, and financial crises may indeed display levels of symptoms that are similar to those experienced by individual who experience events that are more traditionally considered traumatic. The conception of "traumatic" events has traditionally hinged upon the presence of threats to the life or physical integrity of the individuals involved. While the events endorsed by the DSM trauma-incongruent group clearly did not involve such threat to life, they did involve at least the perception of a threat to the identity or lifestyles of the experiencing individuals. There is significant literature indicating that subjective cognitions following traumatic events significantly impact the likelihood of PTSD following trauma. For example, Foa and colleagues (1999) have demonstrated that a measure of the extent to which an individual experiences negative cognitions about him or herself, negative cognitions about the world, and self-blame following exposure to a trauma can successfully discriminate between individuals who do and do not develop PTSD. While the events experienced by the DSM trauma-incongruent group did not involve a threat to life, a strong case could be made that they would likely have a significant impact upon the perceptions held by experiencing individuals regarding their personal competence and responsibility as well as the malevolence of the world. Being that such perceptions seem strongly linked to PTSD symptoms, it makes sense that exposure to such events could result in posttraumatic psychopathology in individuals who make such interpretations.

While our results are not entirely consistent with those of Gold et al. (2005), who found that individuals in the DSM trauma-incongruent group actually reported higher levels of PTSD symptoms, the results clearly reiterate the point that events that are not included in the DSM-IV's definition of a trauma can potentially produce PTSD symptomatology at a comparable level to that produced by events included in this definition. It is not the purpose of this paper to suggest that the *DSM* criteria that define what constitutes a traumatic event should be broadened. Other authors have discussed this issue (Gold et al., 2005), and cases have been made for both broadening the DSM's trauma criterion (Ziksook, Chentsova-Dutton, and Shuchter, 1998) and for the contention that it is already too inclusive (McNally, 2003). The point here is that clearly there are limitations with the manner in which the DSM considers various types of stressful events, and that these limitations warrant significant consideration as the field continues to refine its classification systems.

The current results also indicated that individuals in the DSM trauma-incongruent group experienced comparable levels of posttraumatic growth as compared to their counterparts in the trauma-congruent group. This finding is consistent with previous studies in PTG that have demonstrated the occurrence of PTG in response to varied types of experiences, some of which would typically be considered traumatic and others which clearly would not (McFarland and Alvaro, 2000; Parks et al., 1996; Tedeschi and Calhoun, 1996). The objective intensity and severity of the event may not be as important for subsequent growth as may have been previously expected. Individuals regularly experience both traumatic and non-traumatic events that have the potential to cause them considerable distress, and they report their lives have benefited from such experiences. Just as negative responses to trauma seem clearly related to the subjective interpretations made by experiencing individuals, it may be that the objective characteristics of stressful events are less predictive of positive life changes in survivors than are the subject perceptions that the individual makes. Stressful events of varying sorts can be expected to prompt individuals to activate their coping resources, examine their lives, and perhaps make active choices regarding how they will live them.

It is likely that in order for such a process to take place, the individual's equilibrium must be sufficiently "shaken up" by the event. Consistent with this suggestion, the current results indicated a positive relationship between PTSD symptoms and PTG, indicating as PTSD symptoms increase so does the likelihood of perceived growth. This is consistent with trauma literature indicating that severe events may disrupt schemas of security and activate the individual's utilization of social support (Affleck and Tennen, 1998; Schaefer and Moos, 1998). This finding is also consistent with Janoff-Bulman and Berger's work with appreciation and psychological adjustment in the presence of trauma. Janoff-Bulman and Berger (2000) suggest that individuals who experience an extremely traumatic event are more likely to value and appreciate their own lives, as well as others, as a result of being confronted with issues of mortality. Regardless of the objective severity of a trauma, events which are not sufficiently stressful or significant to the individual survivor seem unlikely to provoke either PTSD or PTG. However, individuals who experience an event that they perceive as excessively stressful may be forced to restructure or reevaluate their lives in response to the event; it may be the case that stress provokes movement. A recent example can be seen in the aftermath of September 11th, 2001, in which individuals who reported experiencing "anger, fear, disgust, and contempt," also reported a range of positive emotions such as motivation to "count their blessings," and "newfound love for friends and family" (Fredrickson et al., 2003).

The current results seem particularly important when considering college populations. College-aged individuals regularly experience a variety of life transitions involving sometimes dramatic changes in roles and relationships, which could present opportunities for the sorts of negative and positive experiences assessed in the current project. The current findings validate the potential of the college years to be a time of both turmoil and meaningful personal growth, and it seems that the two experiences are strongly linked. University mental health resources should consider this, and address survivors of various life stressors in a manner that is designed not only to alleviate symptoms, but which recognizes that the symptoms themselves may signal the opportunity for significant and positive life changes. Our results also suggest that clinicians should not assume that certain types of traumatic events determine certain outcomes. The more important issue appears to be how the individual interprets these events.

There are some limitations that should be considered in interpreting the findings of the current study. First, the current study was unable to assess the recency of the event in a way that was consistent for all participants; therefore, it is possible that the current findings regarding the events that participants labeled as most distressing reflect the recency of the experienced events rather than the stress produced by them. However, previous results have shown that effects related to the impacts of events meeting and not meeting DSM Criterion A were robust even when recency effects were controlled for (Gold et al., 2005). Secondly, the results are based entirely upon self-report, retrospective data. In general, self-report measures can be less reliable and are vulnerable to demand characteristics (Groth-Marnat, 1999). Thirdly, all participants received some information prior to participation that they would be asked to disclose information about traumatic and/or negative life events and their reactions to those experiences. Providing this information may have biased the sample of individuals who chose to participate and may account for the high number of traumatic and/or negative life events endorsed by the current sample. Finally, all participants were college students with higher education than the normal population. While this group is clearly of interest in the current study, the representativeness and generalizability of these findings may thus be limited and should not be assumed to apply to other populations.

Despite these limitations, the current results offer directions for future study. Future research is needed to further explore the impacts of various types of stressful events, and further consideration needs to be given to how to describe and categorize various forms of mental illness that are related to stressful experiences. Additionally, it would be useful to further explore the relationship between PTSD and PTG. Relatively little is known about experiences of PTG in terms of onset, course, and specific factors which may facilitate such growth. We now know that personally significant negative life events have the potential to produce the meaningful life growth. Traditionally, psychology has, out of necessity, focused on the negative outcomes of trauma. In the future, we should consider the potential of stressful events to produce both negative and positive outcomes as well as specific factors which may facilitate both the minimization of posttraumatic psychopathology and the maximization of positive life change.

REFERENCES

Affleck, G., and Tennen, H. (1996). Construing benefits from adversity: Adaptational significance and dispositional underpinnings. *Journal of Personality, 64,* 899-922.

Aldwin, C. M., and Sutton, K. J. (1996). A developmental perspective on posttraumatic growth. In R. G. Tedeschi, C. L. Park, and L. G. Calhoun (Eds.) *Posttraumatic growth: Positive changes in the aftermath of crisis* (pp 43-64). Mahwah, NJ: Lawrence Erlbaum Associates.

American Psychiatric Association. (2000). Diagnostic and statistical manual of mental disorders. (4th ed. rev.). Washington, DC: Author.

Andrews, B. and Wilding, J. M. (2004). The relation of depression and anxiety to life-stress and achievement in students. *British Journal of Psychology, 95,* 509-521.

Beck, A. T., Ward, C. H., Mendelson, M., Mock, J., and Erbaugh, J. (1961). An inventory for measuring depression. *Archives of General Psychiatry, 4,* 561-571.

Beck, A. T., Steer, R. A., and Garbin, M. G. (1988). Psychometric properties of the Beck Depression Inventory; Twenty-five years of evaluation. *Clinical Psychology Review, 8,* 77-100.

Breslau, N., Chilcoat, H. D., Kessler, R. C., and Glenn G. C. (1999). Previous exposure to trauma and PTSD effects of subsequent trauma: Results from the Detroit area survey of trauma. *American Journal of Psychiatry, 156,* 902-907.

Calhoun, L. G., and Tedeschi, R. G. (1999). *Facilitating posttraumatic growth: A clinician's guide.* Mahwah, NJ: Lawrence Erlbaum Associates.

Calhoun, L. G., Cann, A., Tedeschi, R. G., and McMillan, J. (2000). A correlational test of the relationship between posttraumatic growth, religion, and cognitive processing. *Journal of Traumatic Stress, 13,* 521-527.

Coffey, S. F., Dansky, B. S., Falsetti, S. A., Saladin, M. E., and Brady, K. T. (1998). Screening for PTSD in a substance abuse sample: Psychometric properties of a modified version of the PTSD symptom scale self-report. *Journal of Traumatic Stress, 11,* 393-399.

Cohen, L. H., Hettler, T. R., and Pane, N. (1998). Assessment of Posttraumatic Growth. In R. G. Tedeschi, C. L. Park, and L. G. Calhoun (Eds.) *Posttraumatic growth: Positive changes in the aftermath of crisis* (pp 23-42). Mahwah, NJ: Lawrence Erlbaum Associates.

Costa, P. T. Jr., and McCrae, R. R. (1985). *The NEO Personality Inventory Manual.* Odessa, FL: Psychological Assessment Resources.

Falsetti, S. A., Resnick, H. S., Resick, P. A., and Kilpatrick, D. G. (1993). The modified PTSD symptom scale: A brief self-report measure of posttraumatic stress disorder. *The Behavior Therapist, 16,* 161-162.

Faravelli, C., Giugni, A., Salvatori, S., and Ricca, V. (2004). Psychopathology after rape. *American Journal of Psychiatry, 161,* 1483-1485.

Foa, E.B. (1996). *Posttraumatic stress diagnostic scale: administration, scoring, and procedures manual.* Minneapolis, MN: National Computer Systems, Inc.

Foa, E. B., and Rothbaum, B. O. (1998). *Treating the trauma of rape: Cognitive-behavioral therapy for PTSD.* New York: Guilford Press.

Foa, E.B., Tolin, D.F., Ehlers, A., Clark, D.M., and Orsillo, S.M. (1999). The posttraumatic cognitions inventory (PTCI): Development and validation. *Psychological Assessment*, 11: 303-314.

Frerickson, B. L., Tugade, M. M., Waugh, C. E., and Larkin, G. R. (2003). What good are positive emotions in crisis? A prospective study of resilience and emotions following the terrorist attacks on the United States on September 11, 2001. *Journal of Personality and Social Psychology, 84,* 365-376.

Gilboa-Schechtman, E. and Foa, E. B. (2001). Patterns of recovery from trauma: The use of intraindividual analysis. *Journal of Abnormal Psychology, 110,* 392-400.

Gold, S.D, Marx, B.P., Soler-Baillo, J.M., and Sloan, D.M. (2005). Is life stress more traumatic than traumatic stress? *Journal of Anxiety Disorders, 19*, 687-698.

Groth-Marnat, G. (1999). *Handbook of Psychological Assessment* (3rd ed.). New York: John Wiley and Sons.

Hayman, D.T. (1999). The relationship of traumatic life events and symptoms of post-traumatic stress to academic performance, and the influence of learned resourcefulness on this relationship in a nonclinical population of college students. *Dissertation Abstracts International: Section B: The Sciences and Engineering, 59* (9-B), 5084.

Herman, J. (1997). *Trauma and Recovery: The aftermath of violence-from domestic abuse to political terror.* New York: Basic.

Janoff-Bulman, R., and Berger, A. R. (2000). The other side of trauma: Towards a psychology of appreciation. In J. H. Harvey and E. D. Miller (Eds.) *Loss and trauma; General and close relationship perspectives* (pp 29-44). Philadelphia: Brunner-Routledge.

Kelvin, R. P., Lucas, C. J., and Ojha, A. B. (1965). The relation between personality, mental health and academic performance in university students. *British Journal of Social and Clinical Psychology, 4,* 244-253.

Kessler, R. C., Sonnega, A., Bromet, E., Hughes, M., and Nelson, C.B. (1995). Posttraumatic stress disorder in the national comorbidity survey. *Archives of General Psychiatry, 52,* 1048-1060.

Kondrichin, S. V. and Lester, D. (2002). Suicide in the Ukraine. *Crisis, 23,* 32-33.

Koren, D., Norman, D., Cohen, A., Berman, J., and Klein, E. M. (2005). Increased PTSD risk with combat-related injury: A matched comparison study of injured and uninjured soldiers experiencing the same combat events. *American Journal of Psychiatry, 162,* 276-282.

Lester, D. (1994). Domestic integration and suicide in 21 nations, 1950-1985. *International Journal of Comparative Sociology, 35,* 131-136.

McFarland, C., and Alvaro, C. (2000). The impact of motivation on temporal comparisons: coping with traumatic events by perceiving personal growth. *Journal of Personality and Social Psychology, 79,* 327-343.

McFarlane, A. C., and de Girolamo, G. (1996). The nature of traumatic stressors and the epidemiology of posttraumatic reactions. In B. A. van der Kolk, A. C.McFarlane, and L. Weisaeth (Eds.) *Traumatic Stress* (pp 129-154). New York: Guilford Press.

McMillen, C., Zuravin, S., and Rideout, G. (1995). Perceived benefit from child sexual abuse. *Journal of Consulting and Clinical Psychology, 63,* 1037-1043.

McMillen, J. C., Smith, E. M., and Fisher, R. H. (1997). Perceived benefit and mental health after three types of disaster. *Journal of Consulting and Clinical Psychology, 65,* 733-739.

McNally, R.J. (2003). Progress and controversy in the study of posttraumatic stress disorder. *Annual Review of Psychology, 54,* 229-252.

Moos, R. H. and Schaefer, J. A. (1993). Coping resources and processes: Current concepts and measures. In L. Goldberger and S. Breznitz (Eds.) *Handbook of stress: theoretical and clinical aspects* (pp 234-273) New York: Free Press.

Morgan, H. J., and Janoff-Bulman, R. (1994). Positive and negative self-complexity: Patterns of adjustment following traumatic versus non-traumatic life experiences. *Journal of Social and Clinical Psychology, 13,* 63-85.

Park, C. L., Cohen, L. H., and Murch, R. (1996). Assessment and prediction of stress-related growth. *Journal of Personality, 64,* 71-105.

Pitman, R. K., Altman, B., and Macklin, M. L. (1989). Prevalence of posttraumatic stress disorder in wounded Vietnam veterans. *American Journal of Psychiatry, 145,* 667-669.

Resnick, H. S., Kilpatrick, D. G., Dansky, B. S., Saunders, B. E., and Best C. L. (1993). Prevalence of civilian trauma and posttraumatic stress disorder in a representative national sample of women. *Journal of Consulting and Clinical Psychology, 61,* 984-991.

Schaefer, J. A., and Moos, R. H. (1998). The context for posttraumatic growth: Life crisis, individual and social resources, and coping. In R. G. Tedeschi, C. L. Park, and L. G. Calhoun (Eds.) *Posttraumatic growth: Positive changes in the aftermath of crisis* (pp 99-125). Mahwah, NJ: Lawrence Erlbaum Associates.

Shalev, A. Y. (1996). Stress versus traumatic stress: from acute homeostatic reactions to chronic psychopathology. In B. A. van der Kolk, A. C. McFarlane, and L. Weisaeth (Eds.) *Traumatic Stress* (pp 77-101). New York: Guilford Press.

Taylor, R. J. (2004). Therapeutic intervention of trauma and stress brought on by divorce. *Journal of Divorce and Remarriage, 41,* 129-135.

Tedeschi, R. G., and Calhoun, L. G. (1995). *Trauma and transformation: Growing in the aftermath of suffering.* Los Angeles, CA: Sage.

Tedeschi, R. G., and Calhoun, L. G. (1996). The posttraumatic growth inventory: Measuring the positive legacy of trauma. *Journal of Traumatic Stress, 9,* 455-471.

Tedeschi, R. G., Park, C. L., and Calhoun, L. G. (1998). Posttraumatic Growth: Conceptual Issues. In R. G. Tedeschi, C. L. Park, and L. G. Calhoun (Eds.) *Posttraumatic growth: Positive changes in the aftermath of crisis* (pp 1-22). Mahwah, NJ: Lawrence Erlbaum Associates.

Tedeschi, R. G. (1999). Violence transformed: Posttraumatic growth in survivors and their societies. *Aggression and Violent Behavior, 4,* 319-341.

Tennen, H., and Affleck, G. (1998). Personality and transformation in the face of adversity. In R. G. Tedeschi, C. L. Park, L. G. Calhoun (Eds.) *Posttraumatic growth: Positive changes in the aftermath of crisis* (pp 65-98). Mahwah, NJ: Lawrence Erlbaum Associates.

Udwin, O., Boyle, S., Yule, W., Bolton, D., and O'Ryan, D. (2000). Risk factors for long-term psychological effects of a disaster experienced in adolescence: Predictors of post traumatic stress disorder. *Journal of Child Psychology, 41,* 969-979.

van der Kolk, B.A. (1996a). The complexity of adaptation to trauma: Self-regulation, stimulus discrimination, and characterological development. In B. A. van der Kolk, A.C. McFarlane, and L. Weisaeth (Eds.) *Traumatic Stress: The effects of overwhelming experience on mind, body, and society* (pp 182-213). New York: Guilford Press.

van der Kolk, B.A. (1996b). The body keeps the score: Approaches to the psychobiology of posttraumatic stress disorder. In B. A. van der Kolk, A.C. McFarlane, and L. Weisaeth (Eds.) *Traumatic Stress: The effects of overwhelming experience on mind, body, and society* (pp 214-241). New York: Guilford Press.

Vrana, S., and Lauterbach, D. (1994). Prevalence of traumatic events and post-traumatic psychological symptoms in a nonclinical sample of college students. *Journal of Traumatic Stress,* 7(2), 289-302.

White, T. W. (1999). *How to identify suicidal people: A systematic approach to risk assessment.* Philadelphia: Charles Press.

Yehuda, R. (2004). Risk and resilience in posttraumatic stress disorder. *Journal of Clinical Psychiatry, 65,* 29-36.

Ziksook, S., Chentsova-Dutton, Y., and Shuchter, S.R. (1998). PTSD following bereavement. *Annals of Clinical Psychiatry, 10,* 157-163.

In: Stress and Mental Health of College Students
Editor: Mery V. Landow, pp. 225-243

ISBN 1-59454-839-0
© 2006 Nova Science Publishers, Inc.

Chapter 10

FACILITATING PREVENTATIVE MENTAL HEALTH INTERVENTIONS FOR COLLEGE STUDENTS: INSTITUTIONAL AND INDIVIDUAL STRATEGIES

Theodore W. McDonald, Mary E. Pritchard and R. Eric Landrum
Department of Psychology, Boise State University

ABSTRACT

The college student experience, although often exciting, empowering, and invigorating, can also be stressful, anxiety producing, and lonely (e.g., Kohn and Frazer, 1986; Miller and Rice, 1993). Many colleges and universities have an infrastructure in place to assist students who experience mental health problems, including counseling centers and personnel who provide mental health services and make referrals for students to specialized mental health providers (e.g., psychiatrists) (Stone and Archer, 1990; Tyrrell, 1997). Unfortunately, most mental health services that are offered on college campuses seem treatment-oriented in nature; they are deliberately created to assist students who have already developed at least some level of psychological dysfunction. We propose that preventative interventions can be developed on college campuses to help individuals develop proactive behaviors and coping strategies to avoid mental health problems, and that these interventions can be focused at either the individual level, by instructing students on ways to develop strong study and time management skills, establish social supports, and maximize their academic success, or at the institutional level, by offering structural resources to help facilitate student success and mental wellness. The purpose of this chapter will be to discuss prevalent mental health problems among college students and the causes and consequences of these problems, as well as to outline some of these individual- and institutional-level preventative mental health interventions. We show the benefits of such preventative approaches relative to standard treatment-oriented approaches, and to encourage administrators and faculty to promote psychological wellness rather than simply treat fully manifested psychopathology.

INTRODUCTION

The college student experience, although often exciting, empowering, and invigorating, can also be stressful, anxiety producing, and lonely (e.g., Kohn and Frazer, 1986; Miller and Rice, 1993). Many students beginning their college experience are overwhelmed by the higher academic standards than those found on their high school campuses, and experience a sense of isolation living away from family members and friends (e.g., Abouserie, 1994; Pascolo-Fabrici, de Maria, Corigliano, Aguglia, and Gregori, 2001). Junior and senior level students often face different challenges, including managing multiple responsibilities (e.g., school work, employment, and sometimes family commitments), and apprehension about graduating, finding suitable employment, or applying to graduate school (e.g., Bishop, Bauer, and Becker, 1998; Chandler and Gallagher, 1996). In short, although many people tend to inform students that their college years should be "the best times of their lives," these years are often characterized by considerable stress and vulnerability to stress-related mental health problems.

Many colleges and universities have an infrastructure in place to assist students who experience mental health problems, including counseling centers and personnel who can make referrals to students to specialized mental health providers (e.g., psychiatrists) (Stone and Archer, 1990; Tyrrell, 1997). Unfortunately, however, most mental health services that are offered on college campuses seem treatment-oriented in nature; they are deliberately created to assist students who have already developed at least some level of psychological dysfunction. As is the case elsewhere in the mental health domain (Albee, 1990), the emphasis on the treatment of mental health services on college campuses seems to come at the expense of preventative mental health services that are designed to help students avoid developing mental health problems in the first place (Brown, 2002). In other words, current approaches to dealing with mental health problems in college students tend to be reactive rather than proactive, and as a result, many students may develop mental health problems and other difficulties in functioning because preventative strategies are either not in place or are underdeveloped.

Preventative mental health interventions, by definition, are intended to either inoculate people against ever developing mental health problems (primary prevention) or at the very least to arrest the development of a problem before it reaches pathological proportions and leads to major problems in functioning (secondary prevention) (Duffy and Wong, 2004). Preventative mental health interventions with college students can take many forms, however, any quality intervention should target the factors that have been found to cause, or at least predict, the development of mental health problems. Some of these causes, as discussed earlier, are endemic to the college experience and cannot be prevented or avoided (examples of such causes include moving away from family, friends, and other social supports, and tackling challenging curricular requirements). Other causes may be prevented or at least attenuated. An example of such a cause is stress, which has repeatedly been found to be associated with numerous physical and mental health problems (e.g., Frazier and Schauben, 1994; Zaleski, Levey-Thors, and Schiaffino, 1998). Stress cannot be eliminated from the college experience, however, efforts from prevention-minded faculty, administrators, and mental health professionals may help decrease the impact of it so that college students may avoid some of its troublesome consequences, including academic attrition (i.e., dropping out), the development of mental health problems, and suicide (e.g., Brown, 2002; Crespi and Becker, 1999; Haas, Hendin, and Mann, 2003; Illovsky, 1997).

In this chapter, we propose that preventative interventions can be developed on college and university campuses to help individuals develop proactive behaviors and coping strategies to avoid mental health problems. Specifically, we propose that these preventative interventions can take place at two levels: an institutional level consisting of structural supports sanctioned and supported by college or university administrators and faculty, and an individual level, in which students are provided with information that they could use to succeed in their coursework and protect their own mental health. We discuss these strategies sequentially, beginning with a discussion of how institutions can implement efforts to promote mental wellness, and follow with a discussion of how faculty can assist students in maintaining their own mental health by reducing stress and other negative emotions stemming from poor academic performance. Finally, we offer some concluding comments on the benefits of such preventative approaches relative to standard treatment-oriented approaches, and encourage administrators and faculty to promote psychological wellness rather than simply treat fully manifested psychopathology.

Institutional Strategies

As discussed earlier, many scholars (e.g., Brown, 2002) seem to believe that as institutions, colleges and universities have often not addressed student mental health needs in a preventative fashion—instead relying on retroactive strategies to assist students who have already developed mental health problems. Although a lack of emphasis on prevention is not unique to institutions of higher learning, it is particularly unfortunate in the academic domain, because once students develop mental health problems, they may be less likely to continue pursuing their studies (Illovsky, 1997). Some researchers suggest that academic institutions have failed students with respect to their mental health concerns, by focusing on university goals such as student retention rather than the mental and emotional well being of the students themselves. For example, Shea (2002) reported that many institutions seem to place pressure on students to remedy their own mental health problems, and that instead of profiling students who may experience mental health problems to help them recover from these problems, they instead attempt to profile and attract academically and psychologically successful students, thus potentially eliminating an institution's 'problem students.' If this is true, not only are some academic institutions failing to address an important problem, but they may actually be attempting to avoid the problem altogether.

Some researchers (e.g., Tinto, 1993; Zwerling, 1980) have argued that instead of academic institutions trying to 'fix' problem students, efforts should be made to 'fix' the institutions so that they can become environments that are conducive to the creation and maintenance of happy, healthy, and educationally committed students. It is important to understand how institutions can work to create a healthy environment in which students are less likely to develop mental health problems and to address potential mental health problems before they reach pathological levels. In doing so, we discuss several strategies colleges and universities can take, including expanding the activities of traditional counseling centers, developing peer and faculty mentoring programs, providing adequate advising that addresses academic and psychological concerns, and essentially creating a set of integrated services to promote student well being.

COUNSELING CENTERS

As discussed earlier, many colleges and universities currently have in place counseling centers that offer students opportunities to address psychological and emotional difficulties in a formal environment (Benton, Robertson, Tseng, Newton, and Benton, 2003; Stone and Archer, 1990; Tyrell, 1997). Typically, these counseling centers are staffed by trained personnel who are prepared to address the psychological problems most often experienced by students, including stress, depression, isolation, eating disorders, suicidal feelings, and personality problems that interfere with social and academic functioning (Gallagher, 2001; Haas et al., 2003; Kohn and Frazer, 1986; Lore, 1997; Miller and Rice, 1993; Turner and Berry, 2000). The psychological difficulties faced by students are hardly trivial, and are not only likely to affect the extent to which students succeed in their academic coursework and integration into the academic setting, but also can affect whether or not they survive the university experience; according to the Youth Risk Behavior Survey (1997), some college students suffer from problems so severe that 10% have seriously thought about attempting suicide, 7% have actually made a suicide attempt, and 2% made an attempt serious enough to require medical attention. Psychological problems among students are also pervasive; Shea (2002) reported that 76% of college students report feeling overwhelmed by all that they have to do, and 22% report depression so severe that they cannot function. In sum, although counseling centers may exist on many campuses, psychological problems among students may be so severe and so pervasive that counseling center staff may not be able to meet the demand for their services.

Although we believe that college and university counseling centers are important resources, and that the staff who work at these centers perform extremely valuable work, we maintain that relying solely on these centers to help maintain students' mental health is a poor strategy for at least three reasons. The first reason is that, as noted by Backels and Wheeler (2001) "university counseling centers exist to support the academic mission of universities to educate students" (p. 173); in other words, the provision of mental health services simply to make students more psychologically healthy is not the primary function of many campus counseling centers. The second reason is that not all students who experience mental health problems will use these centers, either because they do not know they exist or because of the well documented stigma about seeking assistance from mental health personnel (Corrigan et al., 2000). The third is that counseling centers are not focused on providing primary prevention (i.e., they are not intended to stop mental health problems from developing in the first place), but rather are focused on providing, at best, secondary prevention intervention (i.e., they are intended to help combat mental health problems that have already begun to manifest themselves; Duffy and Wong, 2004). Waiting for a problem to develop before addressing it is an unsound strategy, we believe, especially in light of research that shows that for every person who develops a mental health problem, an average of 2.6 people experience such stress from that individual's disorder that they too may also need services (Albee, 1990). We argue that it makes much more sense to develop institutional strategies to prevent mental health problems, and we maintain that, by expanding their roles and key functions, college and university counseling centers can help in this regard.

One way that counseling centers can have a greater impact would be to target students who are at risk of developing mental health problems, and provide seamlessly integrated services to decrease the likelihood that they develop such problems. This could potentially be achieved in environments that are not intrusive and do not conjure the stigma associated with visiting the counseling center; counseling center personnel could use validated screening instruments to identify students at risk for depression, suicide, and anxiety in residence halls and in large enrollment introductory courses. Indeed, counseling center personnel at several colleges and universities have done exactly that, and are therefore already engaging in some of the primary prevention activities that we are endorsing here. Furthermore, to facilitate ease of use and to ensure high levels of confidentiality, counseling centers can create and maintain on-line assessments and screenings for students who are concerned that they might be experiencing abnormal levels of disordered thought and feeling. Provided that these on-line materials are well advertised (they would only be helpful if students knew they existed) and include follow up by counseling center staff (particularly for those students who are identified as experiencing problems that could be addressed well by mental health professionals), they would also constitute a primary prevention intervention. They would also likely be successful; Haas, Hendin, and Mann (2003), for example, reported that such an on-line assessment and email follow ups were quite successful for assisting students at risk for suicide.

Another way for counseling centers to reach out to students and to make mental health services available to students before they develop psychological disorders would be for these centers to offer credit courses that specifically address personal, educational, and career development issues. These courses could be well advertised during orientation sessions to help target incoming students who may be most likely to be overwhelmed by the academic and social experience they are about to begin. Counseling centers could also develop their own orientation sessions to provide information to new students on how to adjust to the campus experience and seek assistance for a wide range of academic and personal issues. The Freshman Dialogue Program at the University of Hartford is an example of such an effort (Crespi and Becker, 1999), and other academic institutions could model their own programs on it. Any of these efforts would represent the type of proactive, preventative mental health outreach that we suggest is necessary to help students avoid developing psychological problems in the first place.

Unfortunately, some research suggests that counseling centers—the only option for mental health treatment at many colleges and universities—may be on shaky ground. For example, Lore (1997) expressed concern that due to financial setbacks, administrators at academic institutions may attempt to save money by reducing counseling center budgets. This strategy may not make fiscal sense. Because 20% of students in counseling report that their personal problems are so severe that they are considering dropping out of school (Turner and Berry, 2000), an indirect benefit of counseling is increased retention rates (Bishop and Brenneman, 1986; Bishop and Walker, 1990; Illovsky, 1997; Wilson, Mason, and Ewing, 1997), especially for students who are struggling academically or to adjust to college life (Boyd et al., 1996; Gerdes and Mallinckrodt, 1994; Turner and Berry, 2000). Turner and Berry (2000) report that among students in counseling, 60% reported that counseling was helpful in improving their academic performance and 50% reported that counseling helped them decide to stay in school. Thus, institutions benefit from investing more, not fewer, resources in their counseling programs. Investing some of these additional resources into the development and maintenance of preventative mental health interventions certainly seems to make the most sense, especially in light of continued interest in maximizing both retention and graduation rates.

MENTORING PROGRAMS

Researchers (e.g., Pascarella and Terenzini, 1991) have noted for some time that students feel more integrated into academic institutions when they have frequent, informal contacts with faculty members, and that students who feel that their instructors care about them and their success are likely to remain enrolled and to do well in their coursework (Heverly, 1999; Lamport, 1993). Thus, it is clear that frequent faculty interactions with students may lead to a number of desirable outcomes both for students and for academic institutions. We believe that the establishment of formal mentoring relationships between faculty and students can accomplish more than simply facilitating student success and institutional retention, however; we believe that if colleges and universities develop strong mentoring programs, they may be able to engage in a form of preventative mental health outreach for their students.

As has been discussed elsewhere in this chapter, it is known that stress is a predictor of mental health problems in college students (e.g., Frazier and Shauben, 1994; Zaleski, Levey-Thors, and Schiaffino, 1998). Students who feel isolated due to the lack of relationships with faculty may experience greater stress, as well as a host of other problematic mental health concerns (Blai, 1989). Strong relationships between faculty and students, built through faculty mentoring programs, could potentially reduce the stress and isolation experienced by students. Researchers (e.g., House, 1981; Tinto, 1993) have noted that supportive relationships, such as those developed between faculty and students in a mentoring environment, may prevent and reduce the harmful effects of stress; in a mentoring relationship, faculty may help students develop appropriate coping mechanisms to deal with the stressors encountered in the academic environment. The emotional support that can be provided through mentoring programs may not only reduce the likelihood that students experience pathological levels of stress, but also may lead to many other positive outcomes, such as increasing students' self-esteem and self-efficacy (House, 1981) and overall well being (Sarason, Shearin, Piece, and Sarason, 1987). Mentoring relationships may also allow faculty to persuade students who are experiencing high levels of stress or showing obvious signs of psychological difficulties to visit their campus counseling centers or other appropriate mental health professionals (Brinson and Kottler, 1995).

Although faculty members can be ideal mentors, due to their knowledge of both academic material and campus resources, peer mentors may also be valuable resources for students. Students who have successfully navigated the transition to campus life and are aware of valuable resources may be able to provide mentoring to incoming or at-risk students in an environment less intimidating than a faculty member's office, and the assistance that peer mentors provide may be just as valuable; as reported by Malm (1999), a connection with just one other person on campus may ease the transition to the academic setting and lead to various benefits for a student. We propose that colleges and universities can develop and maintain peer mentoring programs to partner an experienced student with an incoming or at-risk student, and that such programs may be able to promote both student success and positive mental health. Some universities have already begun to create and utilize such programs in the form of social support interventions, which are essentially weekly classes led by peers that cover such important topics as social concerns of incoming students (such as making new friends), residential concerns, and how to balance academic and social demands (Lamothe et al., 1995). Evaluations of these programs suggest that the students involved in them adjust better to university life. Some institutions have also incorporated emotional skills training (e.g., how to understand, regulate, and harness emotions) into their traditional orientation or college transition courses, and evaluation of such training sessions suggest that not only do students develop better emotional skills, but they are also more likely to remain in school and have higher levels of academic achievement (Schutte and Malouff, 2002; Schutte et al., 1998).

Another way that institutions could help build peer mentoring relationships is through the creation of learning communities and cohort groups. Several universities have developed such communities and groups in the past, and they have typically been geared toward students with a common major or living in a common residential area (Tinto, 1999; Wild and Ebbers, 2002). Other institutions have created learning communities based on a philosophy of shared learning (Tinto, 1996). Students in such learning communities take blocks of courses together, which not only allows students to become more familiar with each other, but also creates an automatic peer support system. Tinto, Russo, and Kadel (1994) suggest a type of learning community that may be particularly well suited to developing strong peer supports and enhancing student mental health: Coordinated Studies Programs. In these structured programs, students and faculty meet for specified blocks of time several times each week. During program sessions, a variety of activities are offered, including lectures, discussions, guest speakers, and so forth. Information on student mental health and wellness resources could easily be incorporated into this curriculum. Lastly, Gerdes (1992) suggests targeting freshman in a Freshman Interest Group that organizes students based on common academic interests. The benefits of such a program are numerous, and include facilitating a natural student support system, allowing for informal contact with faculty, and perhaps serving as a gateway for more formal faculty and peer mentoring interaction as well.

ACADEMIC ADVISING

Many people would perhaps not ordinarily consider academic advising an activity that has an impact on student mental health; however, we believe that the connection between the two clearly exists. In fact, we maintain that academic advising can play a critical role in students' psychological well being, campus adjustment, and academic success. However, for academic advising to reach the goal of fostering student overall well being, we agree with Kramer and Spencer (1989) that academic advisors should always strive to identify student needs on multiple levels (including psychological health), rather than simply advising students on what courses to take during the upcoming semester.

In actuality, academic advising sessions are an ideal setting for a preventative mental health intervention, because students who are less stressed about what classes to take to complete their major, what jobs they may be qualified upon graduation, and so forth are likely to feel more prepared for their academic experiences (Kramer and Spencer, 1989; Malm, 1999) and to experience fewer mental health problems. By helping to identify courses that are consistent with students' skill levels and interests, academic advisers can help ensure that students feel they are making progress toward their degrees and that they understand the process (Tinto, 1990). In other words, even the activities that most academic advisors engage in seem related to the mental health of their students. Furthermore, academic advisors, by virtue of their relatively close contact with their students, may be able to refer students who seem abnormally stressed, are at risk of developing psychological disorders, or have other adjustment problems to appropriate campus personnel who can more adequately address these concerns.

In order for academic advisors to be able to provide advice, or to offer the type of preventative mental health outreach that we are advocating, students must have some level of contact with them. In our experiences, many students do not seek the assistance of an academic advisor unless they are required to do so. Therefore, it seems that it would be beneficial for colleges and universities to require at least some contact between academic advisors and students—perhaps through requiring that students meet with an assigned advisor once per term to conduct a degree progress check. Though such a requirement might be seem cumbersome to both students and the faculty members who serve as advisors, and might require additional institutional support for these faculty members (perhaps through periodic course releases for advising), it is highly likely that students would benefit from the arrangement not only academically but psychologically as well.

Individual Strategies

Although we believe, as discussed in the previous portion of this chapter, that it is incumbent on institutions to develop strategies and resources to offer preventative mental health services to college and university students, we also realize that relying solely on institutions to prevent student mental health problems is neither practical nor generally consistent with the principle of empowerment, which is a very important concept in the health promotion and community mental health literatures (Chamberlin, 1997; Duffy and Wong, 2004; Goldstein and Rosselli, 2003). Relying solely on institutions to provide such treatment is impractical because many such institutions may lack the resources to provide the services we maintain are necessary, and such a strategy is inconsistent with the concept of empowerment because the students themselves would not be considered an important actor in safeguarding or promoting their own psychological health. For these reasons, we maintain that, in addition to providing institutionally supported preventative mental health services, institutions and the faculty they employ should offer information on how students can maintain their own mental health and well being.

A number of college and university efforts have been focused on communicating information to students to assist them in their overall wellness (DeStefano and Harger, 1990), including psychological wellness. Many of these efforts have involved communicating information on how such factors as alcohol use, nutrition, and exercise affect well being (e.g., Bates, Cooper, and Wachs, 2001; Mack and Shaddox, 2004; Oleckno and Blacconiere, 1990; Stachula, 2004), and several have also focused on the effects of interpersonal support, stress management, and self-regulation (Bates et al., 2001; Hermon and Hazler, 1999; Newby-Fraser and Schlebusch, 1997). There seems to be little research on efforts to communicate information on how individual study skills can affect psychological overall wellness, however. In this portion of the chapter, we argue that, because students who perform poorly in their studies are likely to experience stress and a variety of undesirable emotions, and because stress and undesirable emotions tend to be associated with the development of mental health problems (Dohrenwend, 1978; Jemmet and Magloire, 1988), teaching students how to do well in their studies is a form of preventative mental health outreach that empowers students to be custodians of their own psychological well being. The key types of individual study skills information that we will discuss include, general study tips, improving reading skills, getting more out of lectures, and improving test-taking strategies. We maintain that if faculty members provide their students with information about these topics, they may be able to help those students minimize academic stress and safeguard their own mental health.

General Study Tips

As many faculty members—particularly those who teach introductory-level courses to students just entering college—understand, many students enter college unprepared or underprepared for the academic challenges ahead. The learning strategies that previously were successful for students in their high school classes may no longer be effective in their college or university courses, and many students probably recognize very quickly that in order to succeed in higher education, they may need different study strategies. Additionally, techniques and strategies that work for one student may not work for another. We maintain that presenting a variety of general study tips to students may enable them to find one or several that work for them, and that by doing so, they will be able to perform better in their coursework and experience less stress as a result. Below, we offer some general study tips for students to consider (Table 1 also contains a Study Skills Checklist developed by McConnell (1998), and this checklist can be given to students to initiate the process of thoughtfully considering effective study strategies). Many of the tips were categorized by Hopper (1998), and are phrased in a way as they would be communicated to a student.

Try not to schedule back-to-back classes. You'll wear yourself out, and you'll miss some of the best times to study—right before and right after class.

Be a student on the first day of class. Don't take the first two weeks of the semester off—even if your classes are off to a slow start. If possible, try to get ahead on reading so you'll be able to keep up later in the semester.

Create a Regular Schedule for Studying. Set aside times during the week that are specifically used for studying (*and only studying*). Choose times when you are at your mental peak—wide-awake and alert. Some people are "morning" people, some are "night" people; choose your time to study accordingly. When scheduling study time, write it down. Many students use appointment books to keep track of classes, assignments, commitments, etc. Get an appointment book that breaks the day into individual hours, and carry the book with you. You can then schedule certain hours for specific activities. Be realistic; don't plan to study for six hours if you know that you can't really do that. Some specific suggestions include (a) set priorities; then do things in priority order, (b) break large tasks into smaller ones, (c) work on one important task at a time, (d) define all tasks specifically (e.g., not "write paper"), and (e) check your progress often.

Table 1 Study Skills Checklist

Yes	No	Items
		1. I spend too much time studying for what I am learning.
		2. I usually spend hours cramming the night before the exam.
		3. If I spend as much time on my social activities as I want to, I don't have enough time left to study, or when I study enough, I don't have time for a social life.
		4. I usually try to study with the radio or TV turned on.
		5. I can't sit and study for long periods of time without becoming tired or distracted.
		6. I go to class, but I usually doodle, daydream, or fall asleep.
		7. My class notes are sometimes difficult to understand later.
		8. I usually seem to get the wrong material into my class notes.
		9. I don't review my class notes periodically throughout the semester in preparation for tests.
		10. When I get to the end of a chapter, I can't remember what I've just read.
		11. I don't know how to pick out what is important in the text.
		12. I can't keep up with my reading assignments, and then I have to cram the night before a test.
		13. I lose a lot of points on essay tests even when I know the material well.
		14. I study enough for my test, but when I get there my mind goes blank.
		15. I often study in a haphazard, disorganized way under the threat of the next test.
		16. I often find myself getting lost in the details of reading and have trouble identifying the main ideas.
		17. I rarely change my reading speed in response to the difficulty level of the selection or my familiarity with the content.
		18. I often wish I could read faster.
		19. When my teachers assign papers, I feel so overwhelmed that I can't get started.
		20. I usually write my papers the night before they are due.
		21. I can't seem to organize my thoughts into a paper that makes sense.

Notes. How to score the results—if you answered yes to two or more questions in any category, you might want to concentrate on these areas: time scheduling (items 1-3), concentration (items 4-6), listening and note-taking (items 7-9), reading (items 10-12), exams (items 13-15), reading (items 16-18), and writing papers (items 19-21).

Establish a routine time to study for each class. Studying means more than just doing your homework. Studying involves general organizational and planning strategies (finishing assignments early, organizing notes), task preparation strategies (literature reviews in library, rereading textbooks), environmental restructuring (finding the right place to study, minimizing distractions), processing/recall ability (remembering), and typical study strategies (taking notes, studying notes) (Garavalia and Gredler, 1998). Prepare for each class as if there will be a pop quiz.

Do as much of your studying in the daytime as you can. Nighttime brings more distractions for adults.

Schedule breaks. Take a brief break after every block of study time. Try to avoid long blocks of studying unless you are sure that is your optimum method of studying. Don't be *unrealistic* in how long you can study—that is, don't schedule an eight-hour study session for Saturday afternoon and evening if that is something that you just won't do when the time comes.

Make use of study resources on campus. Find out about the opportunities for tutoring, study sessions, test review in class, etc. Does your class have teaching assistants that hold office hours? Ask questions in class of your professors.

Find at least one or two students in each class whom you can study with. A fellow student might be able to explain a concept in terms that you can understand better than your professor can. Also, you might feel more comfortable asking questions of another student, and you'll have an opportunity to observe another person's study habits. Try to study with students who are academically equal to, or better than, you; they will stimulate and challenge your abilities.

Study the hardest subject first. Work on the hardest subjects when you are fresh. Putting those subjects off until you're tired compounds their difficulty.

Fight delaying tactics. These are things that you do when you know the task is boring, long, or difficult (Wahlstrom and Williams, 2004). Three strategies for avoiding delaying tactics include (a) face boring assignments with short concentrations of effort, (b) conquer long assignments by breaking them down into smaller tasks, and (c) fight difficult tasks by tackling them first and by making sure you understand them. Delaying tactics differ from procrastination because procrastination is defined as intentionally putting things off. Delaying tactics are typically viewed as unintentional (Wahlstrom and Williams, 2004).

Find a regular place to study where you can concentrate with minimal distractions. Avoid TV or listening to conversations (as in the library). Find your special nook somewhere that is *your* study place.

Reward your studying. Try to reward your *successful* study sessions with something you enjoy (watching TV, a healthy snack, or calling a friend). Many of the traditional rewards of studying (good grades, a college degree) take time, so give yourself some immediate rewards. Take breaks and be realistic about what you can accomplish in one study session.

Be good to yourself. Take care of your other needs—physical, emotional, social, financial, etc. If you can minimize other problems in your life, you can use your efforts to study and understand the subject matter.

Once you develop your basic schedule, add school events (exams, papers, presentations). Sticking to a schedule can help you to avoid cramming and procrastination. Cramming isn't a good study idea, because it strains your memory processes, drains you of energy, and exacerbates test anxiety. When people are faced with a number of tasks, most of us do the easy things first, saving the harder tasks for later. Unfortunately, by the time you get to the harder ones, you're tired and not at your best. To avoid this situation, break difficult tasks into smaller tasks.

One instrument used to assess this complex behavioral pattern is the Learning and Study Strategies Inventory (LASSI) (Weinstein, Palmer, and Schulte, 1987). The following list summarizes the areas of learning and studying that the LASSI measures: (a) attitude and interest; (b) motivation, diligence, self-discipline, and willingness to work hard; (c) use of time management principles for academic tasks; (d) anxiety and worry about school performance; (e) concentration and attention to academic tasks; (f) information processing, acquiring knowledge, and reasoning; (g) selecting main ideas and recognizing important information; (h) use of support techniques and materials; (i) self-testing, reviewing, and preparing for classes; and (j) test strategies and preparing for tests. If you have an interest in taking the LASSI visit your campus Counseling and Testing Center to see if they can administer this inventory to you.

Improving Reading Skills

Most college and university classes assign one or more texts, and as a result, much of the time that students study is probably spent reading. If students do not develop effective reading strategies, they are not likely to be successful in their coursework. To be successful, students need to actively consider and expand upon what they are reading (Craik and Lockhart, 1972). Simply highlighting the boldfaced terms in a required text is not likely to be a particularly effective strategy for deep learning and retention; to help students learn to read effectively and therefore succeed in their classes and reduce course-related stress, faculty can provide important information. A very popular reading system developed by Robinson (1970) is SQ3R, which divides the reading task into these steps: Survey, Question, Read, Recite, and Review. Recommending this system to students may allow faculty to empower their students to succeed in their classes. The steps to following this process are presented below, and again are presented as they might be communicated to a student.

Survey. Before reading the chapter word for word, glance over the topic headings and try to get an overview for the chapter. This will help you know where the chapter is going.

Question. Look at the chapter headings. Turn the headings into questions, questions you want to be able to answer when finished reading. If the heading is "Auditory System," ask yourself, "How does the auditory system work?" If the heading is "Multiple-Personality Disorder," ask, "What are the characteristics of multiple-personality disorder?"

Read. Now you're ready to read the chapter. Your purpose is to answer the questions you just asked. If you finish reading and haven't answered your questions, go back and reread.

Recite. Once you know the answers to your key questions, recite them out loud to yourself *in your own words*. Personalizing these concepts will help you later when you are tested. Once you've said them, write them down.

Review. When you are finished with the entire chapter, test your memory by asking yourself the key questions. Try not to look at the written answers.

Getting More out of Lectures

Students surely know that lectures can occasionally be boring and tedious; however, poor class attendance is associated with poor grades (Landrum and Davis, 2003). Even if the instructor is disorganized, attending class helps students understand how the instructor thinks, which may help with exam questions or assignment expectations. Furthermore, most lectures are coherent and understandable, and accurate note taking is related to better test performance (Landrum and Davis, 2003). Listed below are some for students to improve their note-taking skills, and therefore improve their academic performance. Again, they are presented as they would be communicated to a student.

You need to listen actively to extract what is important. Focus all attention on the speaker, and try to anticipate meanings and what is coming up.

If the lecture material is particularly difficult, review the material ahead of time in the text.

Don't try to be a human tape recorder. Try to write down the lecturer's thoughts *in your own words* (as much as you can). Be organized even if the lecture isn't. Practice determining what is important and what is not (sometimes instructors give verbal or nonverbal cues).

Ask questions during lecture. You can clarify points you missed and catch up in your notes. Most lecturers welcome questions and often wish students weren't so bashful.

If the lecture is fast-paced (or if you are a slow note-taker), try to review your notes right after class if possible. Consult with a fellow classmate or a teaching assistant to make sure you didn't miss anything important. You may want to form a study group to regularly review lecture materials and textbook readings.

Improving Test-Taking Strategies

Many college and university students report that taking exams is a stressful event, and it is likely that most, if not all of these students, hope to do well on their exams. Unfortunately, faculty members know that not all students do well on their exams, and that many of them do quite poorly. Sometimes students fail exams because they have been employing poor test taking strategies (Ellis and Ryan, 2003; Samson, 1985), due to test anxiety (Chapell et al., 2005; Hembree, 1988), or a combination of the two. By helping students to develop and employ solid test-taking strategies, faculty may be able to help them feel less stressed and anxious about taking tests, and may also help them to perform better on these tests (Ellis and Ryan, 2003; Miller, 2000; Samson, 1985; Wachelka and Katz, 1999). Thus, by teaching their students to improve their test-taking strategies, faculty may be helping promote their psychological health as well as facilitating their academic success. Below are some test-taking strategies developed by various researchers and summarized by Landrum and Davis (2003):

- When you first receive your test, "…flip the examination sheet over and simply unload. Unloading means taking two or three minutes to jot down on the back of the exam sheet any key words, concepts, and ideas that are in your mind" (Wahstrom and Williams, 2004, p. 176). This helps to relieve anxiety as well as to prevent forgetting.
- Pace yourself. Make sure that when half the time is up, you're halfway through the test.
- Don't waste a lot of time by pondering difficult questions. If you have no idea, guess (don't leave a question blank). If you think you can answer a question but need more time, skip it and come back later.
- Don't make the test more difficult than it is. Often simple questions are just that—simple.
- Ask a question if you need clarification.
- If you finish all the questions and still have time, review your test. Check for careless mistakes, such as double-checking earlier questions that you may have skipped.
- Here are some tips for multiple-choice exams:
- As you read the question, anticipate the answer without looking. You may recall it on your own.

- Even if you anticipated the answer, read all the options. A choice further down may incorporate your answer. Read each question completely.
- Eliminate implausible options. Often questions have a right answer, a close answer, and two fillers. Eliminating filler items makes for an easier choice.
- Often tests give away relevant information for one question in another question. Be on the lookout.
- Return to questions that are difficult.
- There are exceptions, but alternatives that are detailed tend to be correct. Pay extra attention to options that are extra long.
- Options that create sweeping generalizations tend to be incorrect. Watch out for words such as *always*, *never*, *necessarily*, *only*, *must*, *completely*, and *totally*.
- Items with carefully qualified statements are often correct. Well-qualified statements tend to include words such as *often*, *sometimes*, *perhaps*, *may*, and *generally*.
- Look for opposite choices. One of the two opposites is likely the correct answer.

If you can guess without penalty, then use these options with your multiple choice items: (a) choose between similar sounding options; (b) if options are numbers, pick in the middle; (c) consider that the first option is often not correct; (d) pick a familiar term over an unfamiliar one. Be sure to clarify with the instructor first to make sure there is not a penalty for guessing.

Here are some tips for essay exams:

- Time is usually a critical factor in essay exams. When reviewing questions, consider what you know, the time you think it will take to answer, and the point value. Answer questions that you know first, but don't neglect questions with high point values.
- Organize your thoughts so you can write them down coherently. Take one or two minutes and plan your essay (make an outline). Then make your answer easier to read by numbering your points.
- The challenge with essays is to be both complete and concise. Avoid the "kitchen-sink" method (you don't know the exact answer, so you write all you know hoping the answer is in there somewhere).
- You've probably learned a great deal of jargon and terminology in the course, so demonstrate what you've learned in your essay.

CONCLUSION

In this chapter, we have argued that college and university personnel need to do more to help prevent the development or exacerbation of mental health problems in students of higher education. Although, as noted earlier, the types of stressors that can lead to mental health problems in students may differ as a function of how prepared students are for the college experience and the number of other responsibilities that exist in their lives, psychological problems seem quite pervasive in this population. We have also argued that, although many colleges and universities have some basic infrastructure—in the form of counseling centers—to address existing student mental health concerns, the treatment offered by institutional counseling staff is by nature reactive and intended to help eliminate or at least ameliorate problems that have already developed. Invoking the nursery rhyme of Humpty Dumpty, we maintain that it makes much more sense to engage in preventative efforts to ensure that he remains happily and healthily seated on the wall rather than waiting for him to fall and then attempting to put him back together.

We have presented two general classes of preventative mental health interventions in this chapter. First, we presented efforts that academic institutions can employ to facilitate wellness among their students and to reduce the stressors associated with the development of psychological disorders in this population. We have argued that institutions should not rely simply on the services of counseling centers to keep students psychologically healthy; such centers have a limited scope, restricted resources, and at least to some researchers, may be more focused on retaining students in the institution than on students' psychological health. We maintained that a seamless set of services offered by counseling and wellness center staff, as well as faculty and other students, are necessary for preventative mental health outreach. Second, we have argued that teaching students how to succeed in their classes is a form of preventative mental health outreach, in that students who are empowered to succeed in their classes with ease and enjoyment are less likely to develop mental health problems caused by stress and failure. By presenting these two classes of interventions, we have attempted to demonstrate that there are a multitude of methods for personnel at academic institutions to employ to decrease the likelihood that their students experience mental health problems. We feel that it would be ideal for faculty and administrators at these institutions employ all of the methods, although we realize that this may not be feasible. Employing even a few of them would, however, likely be an improvement over current preventative mental health outreach efforts for many colleges and universities. For any preventative mental health outreach effort to be successful, there must be a commitment by key members of institutions to implement them effectively. Doing so will require considerable resources in time, energy, and financial support. We argue, however, that the benefits of such efforts will be significant for students and the institutions that enroll them.

References

Abouserie, R. (1994). Sources and levels of stress in relation to locus of control and self esteem in university students. *Educational Psychology, 14*, 323-330.

Albee, G. W. (1990). The futility of psychotherapy. *Journal of Mind and Behavior, 11*, 369-384.

Backels, K., and Wheeler, I. (2001). Faculty perceptions of mental health issues among college students. *Journal of College Student Development, 42*, 173-176.

Bates, J. M., Cooper, D. L., and Wachs, P. M. (2001). Assessing wellness in college students: A validation of the Salubrious Lifestyle Scale of the Student Developmental Task and Lifestyle Assessment. *Journal of College Student Development, 42*, 193-203.

Benton, S. A., Robertson, J. M., Tseng, W. C., Newton, F. B., and Benton, S. L. (2003). Changes in counseling center client problems across 13 years. *Professional Psychology: Research and Practice, 34,* 66-72.

Bishop, J. B., and Brenneman, K. A. (1986). An initial assessment of a counseling center's role in retention. *Journal of College Student Personnel, 27,* 461-462.

Bishop, J. B., Bauer, K. W., and Becker, E. T. (1998). A survey of counseling needs of male and female college students. *Journal of College Student Development, 39,* 205-210.

Bishop, J. B., and Walker, S. K. (1990). What role does counseling play in decision relating to retention? *Journal of College Student Development, 31,* 88-89.

Blai, B. (1989). Health consequences of loneliness: A review of the literature. *Journal of American College Health, 37,* 162-167.

Boyd, V., Freisen, F., Hunt, P., Hunt, S., Magoon, T., and Van Brunt, J. (1996). *A summer retention program for students who were academically dismissed and applied for reinstatement.* (Research Report No. 13-96). College Park, MD: University of Maryland Counseling Center. (ERIC Document Reproduction Service No. ED 405 529).

Brinson, J. A., and Kottler, J. A. (1995). Minorities' underutilization of counseling centers' mental health services: A case for outreach and consultation. *Journal of Mental Health Counseling, 17,* 371-385.

Brown, S. L. (2002). Teaching preventive mental health skills to functional college students: A comparison of three classroom-based interventions. *Dissertation Abstracts International: Section B: The Sciences and Engineering, 62,* 3966.

Chamberlin, J. (1997). A working definition of empowerment. *Psychiatric Rehabilitation Journal, 20,* 43-46.

Chandler, L. A., and Gallagher, R. P. (1996). Developing a taxonomy for problems seen at a university counseling center. *Measurement and Evaluation in Counseling and Development, 29,* 4-12.

Chapell, M. S., Blanding, Z. B., Silverstein, M. E., Takahashi, M., Newman, B. Gubi, A., and McCann, N. (2005). Test anxiety and academic performance in undergraduate and graduate students. *Journal of Educational Psychology, 97,* 268-274.

Corrigan, P. W., River, L. P., Lundin, R. K., Uphoff-Wasowski, K., Campion, J., Mathisen, J., Goldstein, H., Bergman, M., Gagnon, C., and Kubiak, M. A. (2000). Stigmatizing attributions about mental illness. *Journal of Community Psychology, 28,* 91-102.

Craik, F. I. M., and Lockhart, R. S. (1972). Levels of processing: A framework for memory research. *Journal of Verbal Learning and Verbal Behavior, 11,* 671-684.

Crespi, T. D., and Becker, J. T. (1999). Mental health interventions for college students: Facing the family treatment crisis. *Family Therapy, 26,* 141-147.

DeStefano, T. J., and Harger, B. (1990). Promoting the wellness life-style on a college campus. *Journal of College Student Development, 31,* 461-462.

Dohrenwend, B. S. (1978). Social stress and community psychology. *American Journal of Community Psychology, 6,* 1-14.

Duffy, K. G., and Wong, F. Y. (2003). *Community Psychology* (3rd ed.). Boston: Allyn and Bacon.

Ellis, A. P. J., and Ryan, A. M. (2003). Race and cognitive-ability test performance: The mediating effects of test preparation, test-taking strategy use, and self-efficacy. *Journal of Applied Social Psychology, 33,* 2607-2629.

Estes, R. (1973). Determinants of differential stress levels among university students. *Journal of the American College Health Association, 21*, 470-476.

Forsyth, D. R. (2003). Managing: Fostering academic integrity, civility, and tolerance. In *The professor's guide to teaching: Psychological principles and practices* (pp. 201-232). Washington, DC: American Psychological Association.

Frazier, P. A., and Schauben, L. J. (1994). Stressful life events and psychological adjustment among female college students. *Measurement and Evaluation in Counseling and Development, 27*, 280-292.

Gallagher, R. P. (2001). National survey of counseling center directors, international campus. *American Journal of Psychiatry, 124*, 303-310.

Garavalia, L. S., and Gredler, M. E. (1998, August). *Planning ahead: Improved academic achievement?* Presented at the American Psychological Association, San Francisco.

Gerdes, H. (1992). A longitudinal retention study: Expectations and reality in college adjustment. *Dissertation Abstracts International, 52*, 3529A.

Gerdes, H., and Mallinckrodt, B. (1994). Emotional, social, and academic adjustment of college students: A longitudinal study of retention. *Journal of Counseling and Development, 72*, 281-288.

Goldstein, B., and Rosselli, F. (2003). Etiological paradigms of depression: The relationship between perceived causes, empowerment, treatment preferences, and stigma. *Journal of Mental Health, 12*, 551-563.

Hass, A. P., Hendin, H., and Mann, J. J. (2003). Suicide in college students. *American Behavioral Scientist, 46*, 1224-1240.

Hembree, R. (1988). Correlates, causes, effects, and treatment of test anxiety. *Review of Educational Research, 58*, 47-77.

Hermon, D. A., and Hazler, R. J. (1999). Adherence to a wellness model and perceptions of psychological well-being. *Journal of Counseling and Development, 77*, 339-343.

Heverly, M. A. (1999). Predicting retention from students' experience with college processes. *Journal of College Student Retention, 1*, 3-11.

Hopper, C. (1998). Ten tips you need to survive college. Retrieved on September 28, 1998, at http://www.mtsu.edu/~studskl/ 10tips.html

House, J. S. (1981). *Work stress and social support.* New York: Random House.

Illovsky, M. E. (1997). Effects of counseling on grades and retention. *Journal of College Student Psychotherapy, 12*, 29-44.

Jemmett, J. B. III, and Magloire, K. (1988). Academic stress, social support, and secretory immuniglobin. *Journal of Personality and Social Psychology, 55*, 803-810.

Kohn, J. P., and Frazer, G. H. (1986). An academic stress scale: Identification and rated importance of academic stressors. *Psychological Reports, 59*, 415-426.

Kramer, G. L., and Spencer, R. W. (1989). Academic advising. In M. Lee Upcraft, John N. Gardner, and Associates, *The freshman year experience: Helping students survive and succeed in college (pp. 95-107).* San Francisco, CA: Jossey Bass.

Kruger, J., Wirtz, D., and Miller, D. T. (2005). Counterfactual thinking and the first instinct fallacy. *Journal of Personality and Social Psychology, 88*, 725-735.

Lamport, M. A. (1993). Student-faculty informal interaction and the effect on college student outcomes: A review of the literature. *Adolescence, 28*, 971-990.

Lamothe, D., Currie, F., Alisat, S., and Sullivan, T. (1995). Impact on a social support intervention on the transition to university. *Canadian Journal of Community Mental Health, 14,* 167-180.

Landrum, R. E., and Davis, S. F. (2003). *The psychology major: Career options and strategies for success* (2nd ed.). Upper Saddle River, NJ: Pearson Education.

Lore, C. J. (1997). Students mental health and funding constraints: A delicate balance. *Journal of American College Health, 46,* 43-47.

Mack, M. G., and Shaddox, L. A. (2004). Changes in short-term attitudes toward physical activity and exercise of university personal wellness students. *College Student Journal, 38,* 587-593.

Malm, N. W. (1999, Summer). Student retention in the community college: The faculty role. *Visions,* 15-19.

McConnell, K. (1998). Study skill checklist. Retrieved September 28, 1998, at http://wwwmc.nhmccd.edu/elc/reading_writing_area/studycl.html

Miller, G. A., and Rice, K. G. (1993). A factor analysis of a university counseling center problem checklist. *Journal of College Student Development, 34,* 98-102.

Miller, P. B. (2000). The effects of anxiety reduction and study skills techniques on achievement and anxiety level of students enrolled in a basic algebra course at a small, private college. *Dissertation Abstracts International Section A: Humanities and Social Sciences, 61,* 497.

Newby-Fraser, E., and Schlebusch, L. (1997). Social support, self-efficacy, and assertiveness as mediators of student stress. *Psychology: A Journal of Human Behavior, 34,* 61-69.

Olnecko, W. A., and Blacconiere, M. J. (1990). Wellness of college students and differences by gender, race, and class standing. *College Student Journal, 24,* 421-429.

Pascarella, E. T., and Terenzini, P. T. (1991). *How college affects students: Findings and insights from twenty years of research.* San Francisco: Jossey-Bass.

Pascolo-Fabrici, E., de Maria, F., Corigliano, N., Aguglia, E., and Gregori, D. (2001). Evaluation of psychoemotional distress in a student population. *New Trends in Experimental and Clinical Psychiatry, 17,* 49-58.

Raab, L., and Adam, A. J. (2005). The University College model: A learning-centered approach to retention and remediation. *New Directions for Institutional Research, 125,* 87-106.

Rayman, J. R., and Garis, J. W. (1989). Counseling. In M. Lee Upcraft, John N. Gardner, and Associates, *The freshman year experience: Helping students survive and succeed in college (pp. 129-141).* San Francisco, CA: Jossey-Bass.

Robinson, F. P. (1970). *Effective study* (4th ed.). New York: Harper and Row.

Samson, G. E. (1985). Effects of training in test-taking skills on achievement test performance: A quantitative synthesis. *Journal of Educational Research, 78,* 261-266.

Sarason, B. R., Shearin, E. N., Pierce, G. R., and Sarason, I. G. (1987). Interrelations of social support measures: Theoretical and practical implications. *Journal of Personality and Social Psychology, 52,* 813-832.

Schutte, N. S., Malouff, J. M. (2002). Incorporating emotional skills content in a college transition course enhances student retention. *Journal of the First-Year Experience, 14(1),* 7-21.

Schutte, N. S., Malouff, J. M., Hall, L. E., Haggerty, D. J., Cooper, J. T., Golden, C. J., and Dornheim, L. (1998). Development and validation of a measure of emotional intelligence. Personality and Individual Differences, 25, 167-177.

Shea, R. H. (2002, February 18). On the edge of campus: The state of college students' mental health continues to decline: What's the solution? *U.S. News and World Report, 132,* 56-57.

Stachula, J. P. (2004). A social norming based proactive intervention for college student alcohol use. *Dissertation Abstracts International: Section B: The Sciences and Engineering, 65,* 3184.

Stone, G. L., and Archer, J. (1990). College and university counseling centers in the 1990s: Challenges and limits. *Counseling Psychologist, 18,* 539-607.

Tinto, V. (1990). Principles of effective retention. *Journal of the Freshman Year Experience, 2,* 35-48.

Tinto, V. (1993). *Leaving college: Rethinking causes and cures of student attrition* (2nd ed.). Chicago: University of Chicago Press.

Tinto, V. (1996). Reconstructing the first year of college. *Planning for Higher Education, 25,* 1-6.

Tinto, V. (1999). Taking retention seriously: Rethinking the first year of college. *NACADA Journal, 19,* 5-9.

Tinto, V., Russo, P., and Kadel, S. (1994). Constructing educational communities: Increasing retention in challenging circumstances. Community College Journal, 64, 26-29.

Turner, A. L., and Berry, T. R. (2000). Counseling center contributions to student retention and graduation: A longitudinal assessment. Journal of College Student Development, 41, 627-636.

Tyrrell, J. (1997). Mental health and student health professionals: A literature review. British Journal of Occupational Therapy, 60, 389-394.

Wachelka, D., and Katz, R. C. (1999). Reducing test anxiety and improving academic self-esteem in high school and college students with learning disabilities. Journal of Behavior Therapy and Experimental Psychiatry, 30, 191-198.

Wahlstrom, C., and Williams, B. K. (2004). College to career: Your road to personal success. Mason, OH: South-Western.

Weinstein, C. E., Palmer, D. R., and Schulte, A. C. (1987). *Learning and study strategiesinventory.* Clearwater, FL: HandH Publishing Co.

Wild, L., and Ebbers, L. (2002). Rethinking student retention in community colleges. *Community College Journal of Research and Practice, 26,* 503-519.

Wilson, S. B., Mason, T. W., and Ewing, M. J. (1997). Evaluating the impact of receiving university-based counseling services on student retention. *Journal of Counseling Psychology, 44,* 316-320.

Youth Risk Behavior Surveillance: National College Health Risk Behavior Survey – United States, 1995. (1997, November 14). *Morbidity and Mortality Weekly Report, CDC Surveillance Summaries, 46,* 1-56.

Zaleski, E. H., Levey-Thors, C., and Schiaffino, K. M. (1998). Coping mechanisms, stress, social support, and mental health problems in college students. *Applied Developmental Science, 2,* 127-137.

Zwerling, L. S. (1980). Reducing attrition at two-year colleges. *Community College Review, 8,* 55-59.

In: Stress and Mental Health of College Students
Editor: Mery V. Landow, pp. 245-260

ISBN 1-59454-839-0
© 2006 Nova Science Publishers, Inc.

Chapter 11

PSYCHOSEMIOTIC MODEL, BODY-MIND CONTINUUM AND PSYCHOTHERAPY

Matti Keinänen
Student Health Service, Turku, Finland

Motto from Plutarchos: the human mind is not a vase to be filled, but a flame to be lit.

ABSTRACT

The aim is to show how the psychosemiosis offers an epistemic key to understand in psychotherapy the dilemma between the human body and mind. The work is essentially based on a series of seven qualitative case studies of the psychoanalytic psychotherapy with university students having borderline personality disorder. The cases were examined by means of the symbolization-reflectiveness model which includes a coding method of signs for the study of therapeutic interaction. Psychotherapy progresses so that the patient internalizes by symbolization-reflectiveness the therapeutic interaction to his/her internal psychic structure: the originally physical observation is transformed into the psychic experience which leads to a functioning coherent body-mind continuum. In psychotherapy adopted proper symbolic function means that the mind disentangles itself from the chains of immediate experience. The healthy functioning mind is essentially a dialogic organ with two dimensions: in horizontal axis with significant others and in vertical axis with the body.

Key words: psychosemiosis, symbolization-reflectiveness, psychoanalytic psychotherapy, body-mind continuum, borderline personality disorder

INTRODUCTION

In spite of the intensive study of connections between the body and mind, their relationship has until now remained a dilemma, although many distinguished articles touch on this issue (e.g. 1-3). There are different theoretical approaches to touch the mind-body problem which are well described in the recent articles (e.g. 1-4). These philosophical positions (4) are substance dualism, property dualism, type identity, token identity, functionalism, eliminative materialism, and explanatory dualism. However, there are no explicit answers to such issues as the origin of intentionality and meaning in the body-mind problem. By the same token, the causality relationships between the body and mind and also the interconnections between the body and mind and psychotherapy have been unsettled.

This work handles in dept the major psychiatric issue, the understanding of the body - mind continuum, and its connection to epistemology and psychotherapy practice from the epistemic viewpoint of psychosemiosis (5,6). Psychosemiosis means that the human mind emerges using a coding method of signs in mutual interaction with the significant others. The four-stage symbolization-reflectiveness model has been developed to study the psychosemiotic process and its evolution in the human mind (5,6).

According to the symbolization-reflectiveness model, if the development of the psychosemiotic process is inhibited and/or disturbed, mental health disorders are the consequence. The correction of the inhibited and/or disturbed psychosemiotic process may be initiated and worked through in psychoanalytic psychotherapy. In this collective study of seven separate journal articles (5 - 11) the development of the stable personality from the borderline personality disorder in psychotherapy is examined.

The aim is to show that:

1. psychosemiosis offers a key to understand the dilemma between the human body and mind
2. the human mind emerges as the development of psychosemiosis which means that the human mind binds the emotionally meaningful interaction with significant others by means of the coding system of signs
3. the four-stage symbolization-reflectiveness model is suitable for the study of the psychosemiotic process and its evolution in the human mind
4. psychoanalytic psychotherapy has a curative effect on the development of the psychosemiotic process in the human mind.

The interconnections between the body-mind problem and psychotherapy have not been thoroughly explored. The aim of this work is to show how the body - mind - continuum develops in psychosemiotic process and further, how to understand psychotherapy´s curative effectiveness. This is clinically important, because the psychotherapeutic treatment is the main treatment method with young adults in order to develop a mature, coherent personality which helps the person as an independent individual to encounter the challenges of the adult life, both in working and private life

In the recent Practice Guideline for the Treatment of Patients with Borderline Personality Disorder psychoanalytic psychotherapy is evaluated by means of the evidence based methods as the treatment of choice (12). Patients with borderline personality disorder will need extended psychotherapy to attain and maintain lasting improvement in their personality, interpersonal problems, and overall functioning (12, p. 4).

APA concludes (p. 43) that the following is one main specific question that need to be addressed by future research: what components of psychodynamic psychotherapy are responsible for its efficiency?

The aim is to show that psychosemiosis creating the body-mind continuum is one relevant component of the efficiency of psychodynamic psychotherapy promoting the capacity for self regulation. The capacities for self regulation and meaning formation are the instruments of human mind which he/she uses to integrate the self experience and the experience from the outer reality, the significant other persons (5,7).

METHOD

The Four-Stage Symbolization-Reflectiveness Model to Describe the Self Regulation and the Meaning Formation in the Human Mind

Every one of us has during his/her psychic development adopted the basic skills of self regulation in relation to our first caregiver (usually the mother [13-15]). The skills described are internalized by means of psychic binding (8,9,16-18). Psychic binding (symbolization) is realized in the human mind by means of symbolic function (by the use of representing signs; 5,7,8,13-15,17).

The word 'symbol' derives from the Greek word 'symbolon', which literally means 'a sign'.

This concept refers to the connection of two initially separate parts (symballein = to throw, bring together, connect) which creates a new entity. By means of a sign we try to describe a certain state of affairs or phenomenon. The sign itself is not related to the before-mentioned phenomenon. It is by nature either a completely private sign or decided by common consent (= i.e. it is conventional) like linguistic signs. By symbolic function we mean the use of symbols, the fact that somebody, by using a symbol, aims at presenting some state of affairs or phenomenon with the help of it. In the presentation of the symbols and of the different forms the symbolic function, the tripartite division of signs is used, the principle originally put forward by semiotician Charles S. Peirce (17). The three types of symbols or representing signs are an index (an indicator or deictic element), icon (a picture) and the symbol per se, i.e. a conventional symbol (e.g. a linguistic verbal or gestural sign). It must be noted here that, while Peirce concentrated on the relation between a sign and its referent in creating his terminology, here is a different point of view, that is, the focus on the psychic use of the signs. The concept 'symbol' is used in a broader sense to cover all three types of signs. The term 'conventional symbol' or 'verbal symbol' is used for the linguistic sign which Peirce called 'symbol'. This division is used because all three types of signs are applied, in symbolic use, parallel in the psychic process. By parallel is here meant that each of the three types of symbols makes up a distinct form of symbolic function which then interact with each other. The three types of symbols are the instruments of the human mind.

1. The first mode of experiencing is *the indexical experience (5,7,9)*. The physical sensation in the body is transformed into an equivalent psychic form which is in parallel with the physical sensation, as smoke is related to fire. The indexical way of experiencing does not differentiate between the self and the object, and it is estimated to have its origin in the first half year of life in the interaction with the mother. Stern (13, ch.3) speaks about generalized interactional experiences, which are, e.g. created when the needs of the infant are repeatedly satisfied in the early interaction between the mother and the child. These generalized

interactional experiences or the indexical experience form the basic substance, the matrix, of the human mind. The indexical way of experiencing is also equivalent to the early body ego functioning of the mind (19), the dream screen described by Lewin (20) and to the emotional tone described by Bucci (21).

2. The second mode of experiencing is *the iconic experience*. This could be described as a continuous flow of pictures in the mind, like a silent film. This way of experiencing is represented, for example, by our dreams (20) in which the prevailing element is the visual-iconic nature of the imagery. An equivalent iconic experience can arise in other sensory areas such as hearing tones of voices (e.g. music) which can then (unconsciously) be integrated into the observation of one´s self and the other, as a symbol for oneself and the other, and as a relational bridge between oneself and the other. This immediate iconic mode of experiencing equally concerns one´s self and the other and their emotional relation.

The iconic mode of experiencing equals the procedural memory described, e.g. by Fonagy (22) and the introjects frequently reviewed in the psychoanalytic literature (e.g. 23, ch.2). Stern (13, ch.3,4) who thinks that the infant has the ability to differentiate experience already at the age of two months, speaks about the sense of a core self. The iconic level of experiencing can also be seen to be equivalent to the visually perceived action in ordinary manifest dream contents, taking place on the dream screen (20).

Iconic experiencing corresponds with Segal´s (16) symbolic equation, the paranoid-schizoid position of Klein (24) and also with the emotional tone described by Bucci (21). Now there is a differentiation between the self and the object in contrast to the earlier undifferentiated indexical experiencing.

3. *The conventional (verbal) symbols* can be integrated into the iconic mode of experiencing. *The conventional (verbal) symbolic experience,* for example, is represented by spoken or sign language; this way of experiencing gives expression to immediate iconic emotional ways of being. Thereafter, these three modes of symbolic experiencing are integrated in the mind to form a representation of oneself and/or the other.

Segal (16) has distinctively separated the immediate symbolization (corresponding to the iconic phase) and the symbolization proper (corresponding to the verbal symbolic phase and the depressive position of Klein (24)) in the psychic development of the child. The symbolic functioning proper (16) is related to the first separation - individuation phase of the child´s psychic development and the achievement of a verbal capacity between 12 and 18 months of life in the interaction with the mother. Stern (13, ch.6) calls this phase of the psychic development the sense of a subjective self, to which the sense of a verbal self is integrated.

The capacity for the full use of verbal symbolization is an important prerequisite for the individualization of the child (7,8,23). The declarative memory function (22) is based on the capacity for verbal symbolic experiencing.

This *psychosemiotic* process takes place *epigenetically*, which means that the development of the previous phase (e.g. iconic experiencing) is a precondition for the development of the following phase (e.g verbal symbolic experiencing). Thus, in *symbolization, all the three described modes of symbolic experiencing are included,* emphasizing the evolving binding process in the body- mind continuum.

The self and object representations and the affective relation between them generate internal object relations in the mind. The abstraction capacity of Bucci (21,25,ch.17) correspond with the conventional (verbal) symbolization.The three types of symbols are the instruments of the human mind, while the continuity of symbolic function is the breathing of the human mind.

The Reflective-Integrative Capacity.

In order to understand how the meaning of symbolic function is manifested in the psyche, *the mind's reflective, observing capacity* (e.g. 7,8) must be considered. During the development, the child adopts the empathic way, in which the mother is relating to him/her and he/she begins to apply this empathic capacity, attained by means of identification, to the introspection of the self and the internal world of the mother. There develops a capacity in the child to observe his/her own fantasy world and the psychic world of the other. Further, the child is able to integrate the representations concerning him/herself into one unity, the self. The separate representations concerned with the other are integrated into a unity, the object, the first representation being of the mother. Integrated images from separate self- and object representations are developed (7,8,15).

The emergence and formulation of the reflective-integrative capacity in the psychic development means that the child becomes able to observe his/her self and the other with his/her feelings and needs. The reflective-integrative experiencing separates him/her from the immediate symbolization (16). The capacity to endure waiting is created, and the ability to reflect oneself (14, ch.2, 26,27) . The capacity to use historical memory becomes possible, which is central for time and history conceptualization. It is generally agreed that these capacities develop from 2 to 2,5 years of age: Stern (13, ch.8) speaks about the domain of verbal and narrative relatedness.

Thus, the reflective-integrative function includes the capacity to observe the indexical, iconic and verbal symbolic ways of experiencing. It integrates them into a unity, forming a symbolic continuity. Its important property is the ability to reflect the different ways of experiencing and the relational mutuality, unlike the indexical way of experiencing, which is only one-sided, deictic. The concept reflective-integrative experiencing aims at an intersubjective, dialogical examination mode, which also Fonagy and his fellow workers (22,26,28-30), Ogden (27,31, ch.5) and Bollas (32, ch.1) have emphasized. The referential activity described by Bucci (21,25,ch.17; pp. 276 -280) corresponds also with reflective-integrative function.

The modes of operating symbolic function, reflective-integrative capacity, and the formed internal object world, remain constant in the mind and are in a continuous dialogue with each other in a normal psychic process. It is the mobility between these three modes of symbolic function and the reflective-integrative way of observing the modes of symbolic function (27, 31,32) which constitute the prerequisite for and the indicator of psychic health. (5).

THE REASON FOR SELECTING UNIVERSITY STUDENTS TO THE STUDY SAMPLE AND THE TREATMENT METHOD OF PSYCHOANALYTIC PSYCHOTHERAPY

Approximately 2% of the population are thought to meet the criteria for borderline personality disorder (BPD), (33). The amount of BPD in clinical psychiatric population is 10% and 15% from hospitalized patients. The part of BPD from personality disorder patients coming to treatment is 30-60%. Thus, BPD is clinically a serious problem. BPD is a typical disorder having a deficiency of self regulation capacity. There is a great need for the adequate psychiatric and psychotherapeutic help in this field, especially when the patients are young having the adult life in front of them. BPD is also an increasing problem among the mental disorders of university students being thus selected as the study group.

All patients selected for the study were diagnosed according to DSM-IV having BPD. In addition, they were also diagnosed according to Kernberg's classification (15) having the borderline personality organization (BPO) which include three main criteria: identity diffusion, primitive defences centering around splitting and the normal reality testing.

In the Practice Guideline for the Treatment of Patients with BPD psychoanalytic psychotherapy is evaluated as the treatment of choice (12). Patients with BPD will need extended psychotherapy to attain and maintain lasting improvement in their personality, interpersonal problems, and overall functioning (12, p 4). Thus, the treatment method for BPD in this study was psychoanalytic psychotherapy.

The treatment frequency was depending on the case 1- 3 times per week and the duration of treatment was in average three years, but also longer treatment was realized (6).

The four-stage symbolization-reflectiveness model was used to evaluate the developmental stage of symbolization-reflectiveness capacity in the various phases of the therapy (6–11). The qualitative case research approach was used; each patient in the study (6-11) was his/her own control: the developmental stage of symbolization-reflectiveness capacity in the various phases of the therapy was compared to that in the initial phase of the therapy concerned. Because the total amount of studied patients was small, no statistical calculations (basing on qualitative methods) were carried out.

After complete description of the study to the subjects, written informed consent was obtained.

RESULTS

The Scientific Basis of Psychotherapy: Qualitative Evidence Based Medicine, Circular Epistemology and Psychotherapy

The linear causality principle is nowadays the epistemological vantage point for the prevailing evidence based medicine (EBM). The background philosophy is the logical empiricism and the basic scientific conception is physical. The research method is according to natural sciences quantitative, using quantitative statistical methods (the qualification preconceives a great amount of objects researched). The influence of the researcher is tried to eliminate with all kind of methods in order to get reliable results with this approach. Prospective randomized controlled double blind studies are carried out.

The empiric-experimental research method is qualified in psychiatry for the research made in biological psychiatry in which causality principle is linear: e.g. in medicine studies.

In psychotherapy research it is not applicable as follows. The human mind and the mental health are understood as a wholeness having psychic, biological and social dimensions. The intrapsychic world constitutes the immediate basic experience which includes the human being's ability to verbal communication. Mental disorders are primarily disorders of experiential world (especially affects) independent on which frame of reference (biological, psychological) is the vantage point in the research.

According to the general systems theory (34) the wholeness of a system is more than the sum of its parts. If one then tries to explain the phenomenon of experiential level merely with localizing it in some disorders in brain functions of metabolism (independent on how excellent the measuring device is, like positron emission tomography), there is an epistemic error (35): it is not possible to assign one part a causal influence vis a vis another, or put any linear markers all. Bateson said: the brain does not think. What thinks, is a brain inside a man who is a part of a larger systems residing in balance within his environment.

New features of systems emerge at higher level of complexity that cannot be predicted from the more basic levels. With these new features come new properties. We need both the brain (the body) and the psychic functions to explain the wholeness of human mind: the mind without brain is brainless and the mind without psyche is mindless.

Bateson takes another example of the difference between kicking a stone and kicking a dog. In the case of the stone, the energy transmitted by the kick will make the stone move a certain distance, which can be predicted by the heaviness of the stone and by the force of the kick. But if a man kicks a dog, the reaction of the dog does not depend wholly on the energy of the man. Because the dog has its own source of energy, the outcome is unpredictable. What is transmitted, is news about a relationship - the relationship between the man and the dog. The dog will respond in one of a number of ways, depending on the relationship and how it interprets the kick. It may cringe, run away, or try to bite the man. And furthermore: the behavior of the dog in turn becomes news for the man, who may modify his own subsequent behavior according to the dog's behavior. If, for instance the man is bitten, he may think twice before kicking that particular dog again.

The communication and the relationship between the human beings become now to a crucial role. Bateson says that we need a new nonlinear grammar, a new language, to depict what is going on in the living world. *This grammar Bateson defined as circular, giving the basis for **circular epistemology.*** In this world the influences are not linear having causality from A derives B. Instead, A may influence on B, but B thereafter may (or may not) influence on A, the influences are interactive, recursive and self -reflective.

These ideas have extraordinary implications for psychotherapy. The therapist can no longer be seen as impacting on the patient and the patient is no longer an object. Both are part of a system in which the therapist and the patient act and react upon each other in often unpredictable ways, because each action and reaction continually changes the nature of the relationship in which the therapeutic system reside. A circular epistemology forces the therapist to take account of the fact that he or she is inevitably part of this system, an inextricable element of that which he attempts to change.

Therefore we cannot do psychotherapy research with linear epistemology of natural sciences when we observe the psychic, lived experience phenomena being outside the direct observations of physical, sense monitored phenomena. *A circular epistemology, having interactive, recursive and reflective nature, is needed, because we observe now the emotional fitting of both parties, the mutuality, the complementarity of feelings and the coevolution in the psychotherapeutic process.*(35).We need reflective consideration both in relational and in intrapsychic dimensions.

The transference- countertransference-dialog of the therapist and the patient now creates the basic structure of the treatment (14,15). The research approach must be hermeneutic which tries to understand the relationship between the patient and the therapist. In this research qualitative research methods must be used, in psychoanalytic psychotherapy case research studies. The scientific conception is humanistic, and the interest of knowledge is hermeneutic- emancipative (36).

Because the nature of experiential phenomena is interactional and unique, we cannot straightly observe large samples, but we must first observe single psychotherapy processes. Then it is possible to gather knowledge from same kind of phenomena. Recurrence of same kind of processes gives inductively knowledge of phenomena which thereafter may be generalized and validated.

Each treated patient is at one and the same time the control patient: the change in the capacity level (the patient´s ability to move in different levels of indexical/iconic/verbal symbolization- reflectiveness) is observed. The gained research knowledge is received through naturalistic research approach.

Linear diagnostics of symptoms (DSM) in psychotherapy is in the same position as pain and fever are in somatic medicine: if we treat the fever with medicine we may get the fever off, but the background disease (the structural pathology) is untreated. That is why it is important to understand the mind ontologically as a dialogic organ: the mind develops by means of psychic binding (symbolization) through the internalization of emotionally significant object relations. The emerged level of internalized object relations (the level of symbolization-reflectiveness capacity) determines the level of personality structure, which in turn is the relevant clinical vantage point for the realization of psychoanalytic psychotherapy.

THE PSYCHOSEMIOTIC DEVELOPMENT: THE DEVELOPMENT OF SYMBOLIZATION-REFLECTIVENESS CAPACITY IN A TYPICAL PSYCHOTHERAPY PROCESS OF BORDERLINE PERSONALITY DISORDER

The First Part of the Therapy - The Indexical and Iconic Symbolic Process

This clinical illustration of a typical treatment process with its consideration from the viewpoint of symbolization-reflectiveness is a modified summary of all treatments in this study (6-11).

At the beginning of the therapy, the borderline patient is in the unstable affective state. He/she is unable to keep in mind and to process his/her own separateness from the therapist in her internal object relationships when he/she is alone (as follows the term she is used from the patient even if the patient might be of course male). This indexical way of experiencing is expressed as an unspecified, overwhelming, oppressive (panic) feeling, which seizes her when she is on her own. The panic feeling is expressed by various bodily symptoms (e.g. shortness of breath, dizziness, palpitation, trembling, sweating, choking, nausea, numbness, flushes, chest pain). To eliminate this feeling, the patient tries to empty her mind, which appear as feelings of emptiness, and often culminate in states of panic prior to the separation from the therapist before a therapy break. Thus, at the beginning of the therapy, she mainly experiences things through indexical symbolization: when the therapist is available and empathic, she has a feeling of well being, but when the therapist is away, she has a feeling of oppression - or she eliminates oppression feeling emptiness.

Being unable to experience her separateness from the therapist, she is lacking a developmentally appropriate self to master the demands of the integrated individual identity. During the development of therapy, a patient may show new symptoms by e.g. throwing up and using suicidal images. By vomiting, and by suicidal images she aims to actively handle the feelings of separation and isolation which seems unbearable. Compared with previous total attacks against her own experiences, her vomiting and suicidal images now include an attempt to process the feelings caused by separation at an iconic level of the symbolic process (6-11). Vomiting seems now to be clearly connected with the handling of separations, and it is not just a random, physical enactment (8,9).

The Transition to Reflective-Integrative Function

The transition to reflective-integrative function is preceded by certain signs. There may be hints of a change in the borderline patient's way of speech, although she still speaks e.g. about suicide as a way of getting rid of her painful feelings anxiety (6-11).

A patient becomes capable of controlling her anguish in a new way. The tone of her voice and her way of using words takes on a new emphasis. They no longer have the same, non-verbally sensed tinge of hopelessness and no alternatives, which was characteristic of her previous manner of speaking. The change in the patient's voice involves a first clear sign of her evolving self experience. These ways of using the voice and speech, which are significant in the therapy process, have been recently considered (31,32).

Where has this crucial change in psychic development originated? In a psychic and psychotherapeutic process, the different levels of the symbolic process are present all the time (5). Each therapy session is stored in the patient's mind through internalizing symbolization and they form the basic matrix of mind (10), including indexical feelings of both pleasure and oppression. The therapist's calm and clear basic attitude as a therapist is stored in patient's mind as an indexical feeling of well-being. The iconic images of herself and the therapist differ from this indexical matrix (7-10). The iconic images are in the therapy relationship bound to the immediate experience of the therapist's presence (good iconic images of the therapist) or absence (bad iconic images of the therapist) during the individuation process (8). During the evolvement of therapy, these images are gradually developed, strengthened and balanced in a new way in the patient's mind.

As a therapist's role in this therapeutic dialogue is to describe the patient's experience as empathically as exactly as possible (23) while keeping the calm attitude all the time. At first, the patient internalizes the therapist's attitude from repeated therapy sessions as an indexical, generalized, tranquilizing experience of interaction (8), which during the evolvement of therapy begins to appear as softer iconic tones in her voice even before any change could be observed e.g. in the contents of her speech and in the development of reflection. The internalization of the therapist's empathic way of imaging (23) is connected to this process and influences on the emergence of the patient's own reflectiveness. Consequently, she may herself grasp and give a name to the previously chaotic, unidentified feelings of oppression.

The above-illustrated internalization, which proceeds epigenetically through a symbolic process, often culminates in a break in the therapy. When the patient may find the therapist sufficiently reliable as a therapist - as a result of his/her return after repeated breaks as agreed and of his/her putting up with her aggressions and despair, while maintaining the role of a therapist (6-11) - she begins herself to reflect her feelings, internal object relations and inner world. This change takes place while the patient is identifying with the therapist's reflective-integrative function (5). Thereafter, she adopts it permanently as her own structure. Since then, the changes achieved are also the result of the verbal interpretations, especially of the patient's fear of abandonment and of fear of non-acceptance in the therapeutic relationship.

The psychic change is impressive in many ways. From that moment on, the patient lives inside herself and is present in the therapeutic relationship as herself. She may be calmer, more considerate and stable. The patient develops an ability to listen to and to study her personality here and now, as well as on a time axis. For example, she begins to explore the origin and history of her depression, which is illustrated by the important findings of her relationship to her mother (8,9).

Symbolization-Reflectiveness Model and the Borderline Personality Organization

In the treatment of BPD the other person (therapist, the caregiver) becomes bound to the patient's mind by means of the symbolic process and her mind stabilizes: the symbol draws to the mind the caregiving other and he (the therapist in this work) is present as a symbolic presentation independent on his physical presence. Symbolic function contains into the mind the presence experience of the other person which may then be recalled. A person becomes capable of waiting for the physical seeing of the significant other without being always physically present. She can by symbolization-reflectiveness transform her bodily needs into psychic desires, wishes and longings for another person. Separation anxiety of a borderline personality patient is from this viewpoint an insufficiency of the internalization of the tranquilizing other by means of symbolic function.

The capacity to self regulation develops so that the mind binds the immediate feeling experience first in the undifferentiated, indexical form (8), then in the iconic, pictographic form, where the self and object are differentiated according to patient's need states. When the patient adopts the capacity to use reflection and verbal symbols for his/her feeling states of neediness, the mind disentangles itself from the chains of immediate experience in the treatment of BPD: now the person can differentiate his/her own immediate experience as his own experience by means of developing reflective function (6-8). This is crucial for the development of self regulation. The person does not need anymore the other person being present all the time: the capacity to be alone develops, when he/she can by means of symbolization call to the mind the absent person and maintain his/her psychic balance (6-9). So we can understand psychoanalytic psychotherapy´s effect as a curative treatment of personality disorders, which offers a possibility to adopt the appropriate symbolization-reflectiveness capacity and therefore the capacity to self regulation and to the integrated identity.

The achieved psychotherapy knowledge can then be a vantage point when we are going to treat a new patient of the same category.

CONCLUSIONS

D. Sackett (37), one of the founders of EBM, hoped that EBM could trace the best possible evidence, by means of which we can ourselves evaluate our treatment practices and then be responsible for the adequacy of treatment methods. The aim of EBM is to connect the best available evidence to the clinical experience so that we can select to our patients the treatment which is most appropriate and need - specific for them.

Thus, the following methodological conclusions from this work are drawn:

1. the descriptive diagnostics of psychiatry (today DSM-IV) describes symptoms, not background factors behind them. Therefore it is problematic to use changes of symptoms´ amount as a substance when one evaluates evidence base in all kind of psychiatric treatments, especially in psychotherapy.

2. using diagnosis according to symptom categorization of DSM EBM today uses the gold principle that one can study the object objectively, without being a part of the observed phenomenon. In the psychotherapy research this is not true, because the observer is always a part of the observation. The therapist (and also the outside observer, if used in the research) always influences to findings obtained with his own action/reaction.

3. we must take into account in psychotherapy research the structure of human mind from the viewpoint of internalized object relations, which means that the mind is ontologically a dialogic organ. The human mind belongs to the area of circular epistemology, separately from natural sciences which often belong to the area of linear epistemology.

4.   due to the difference of epistemology we must use principally qualitatively based methods of evidence in psychotherapy research in contrast to principally quantitatively based methods of evidence in natural sciences. (5-11).

The Four-Stage Symbolization-Reflectiveness Model for the Understanding of the Body-Mind Continuum

Scientific knowledge is based on unification, not on fragmentation of knowledge. The life sciences form two major domains: one extending from molecules to organism, the other from psychology to sociology. The aim of this work has been to present a scientific model to bring together the body and the mind, the body-mind continuum.

Representations in neuroscience (e.g. feature maps of the parts of the body, like the brain) and those in psychotherapy (e.g. body images) are distinctive. Thus, their data coding mechanisms are different. My aim has been to present a new psychosemiotic model to describe, how in the body-mind continuum the information is coded.

How is it possible to understand the body-mind continuum by means of the psychosemiotic model?

At the bottom is biology; the body can be mindless, at least without consciousness, but the mind cannot be without a body, which is the base for the emerging body-mind continuum.

The coding system of three signs (index-icon-conventional symbol) has a central role in the binding of originally physical perceptions into a psychic form: the lived experiences of our relationships with our significant others are stored into memories of mind by means of the epigenetically developing capacity for symbolization- reflectiveness. The aim of this study of symbolization-reflectiveness has been to construct a map to describe the continuum between body and mind: in normally functioning mind there is a body - mind continuum, contrary to mental health disorders where this continuum fails.

SOME IMPLICATIONS OF THE THREE MODES OF EXPERIENCING IN THE BODY-MIND CONTINUUM:

The Indexical Experiencing

The prototype of indexical experiencing is conaesthetic function described by Spitz (38) which collects together the information coming from the inner world (internal tensions through the proprioceptive sense) and from the outer world (through the five senses of sight, hearing, smell, taste and tactile sense).

The example of this elemental experience lived by an infant is the gratification which an infant experiences when being breast fed. The warm milk (from the mother sensed by the tactile sense) transforms the tension of the body (hunger sensed through the proprioceptive sense) into the undifferentiated indexical pleasure experience - creating gratification through the relief of tension.

This same phenomenon has been described by Salonen (39) by means of the concept of primary identification. Primary identification is formed by the mutual identification of infant and mother. This identification is thereafter intensified in parallel with the emergence of the first autonomous self-experience, when the organization of the core self begins to detach itself from the maternal environment. Salonen emphasizes that primary identification can be seen as a threshold phase from undifferentiated towards differentiation, and it forms the step that creates coherence and leads the infant to an integrated personal unity.

Disorders of indexical experience may implicate themselves in specific psychotic disorders. In schizophrenic psychosis the experience of the primary identification (a coherent indexical experience) is broken down and it must be restored in a good relationship between the therapist and the patient.

The Iconic Experiencing

The prototype is the diacritic function (38) which forms the iconic experience and further, by means of conventional symbol (cognition) the conventional (verbal) symbolic experiencing.

The iconic world of experiencing contains the person´s private world of his/her needs and wills and it is immediate, unconscious without proper reflection. When this mode of experience is prevailing, the person acts immediately, impulsively, without a capacity to differentiate his/herself from the experience.

In this work the aim has been to describe that, when there is not yet a fully developed verbal symbolic capacity with the capacity to reflection of iconic mode of experiencing, one consequence is borderline personality organization; then this iconic mode of experiencing is prevailing (including of course epigenetically indexical experience). In the succesful psychotherapeutic process borderline personality disorder is tranformed to a stable personality (6-11) when the patient gradually adopts the symbolization-reflectiveness capacity by means of psychotherapist.

The Conventional (Verbal) Symbolic Mode of Experiencing with Reflective-Integrative Capacity

The capacity for the full use of verbal symbolization is an important prerequisite for the individualization and the capacity for object constancy of the child (5-11). So the continuity of symbolic function is the breathing of the human mind; the essential part of the body-mind continuum.

The reflective-integrative experiencing separates a person from the immediate symbolization. The capacity to endure waiting is created, and the ability to reflect oneself and the other here and now, as well as the changes in oneself and the other in a time dimension. The capacity to use historical memory becomes possible, which is central for time and history conceptualization.

Thus, the reflective-integrative function includes the capacity to observe the indexical, iconic and verbal symbolic ways of experiencing. It integrates them into a unity, forming a symbolic continuity. Its important property is the ability to reflect the different ways of experiencing and the relational mutuality, unlike the indexical way of experiencing, which is only one-sided, deictic.

The classical example of the reflective function is Rene Descartes´ cogito ergo sum - I think, therefore I am. This expression is reflective, but it does not yet take into consideration the other person - the dialogical nature of human mind, which becomes possible in the proper verbal symbolic experiencing. Thus, the problem in cogito ergo sum expression would not be the body-mind dualism but that it does not reflect the reality of significant others.

In the dialectic world of the mind Rene Descartes´ cogito ergo sum can be transformed to a new variation (29):´my caregiver thinks of me as thinking and therefore I exist as a thinker`.

The emphasis, in the concept of the reflective-integrative function is intersubjective, dialogical examination mode. Reflective function may reflect also only iconic experiencing (without words): then the reflection is from inside, like in dreams contents. However, when dreams become verbally reflected, icons become into conscious form contrary to unconscious iconic experiencing (described in the mode of iconic experiencing earlier having no availability to reflection, like in borderline states). Correspondingly, Freud (19) speaks about manifest and latent dreams. In the unconscious mode of iconic experiencing they are in the normally functioning mind out of reflection. As described in this work, in borderline personality organization iconic experiencing may express itself e.g. in an immediate action.

The disorders of the mode of verbal symbolic experiencing with the capacity for reflection include neurotic disorders; there is the developed capacity to symbolization-reflectiveness (including integrated identity), but there are intrapsychic conflicts (19) which inhibit the normal function of the human mind. Then the aim of psychotherapy is by means of symbolization - reflectiveness capacity to get insight into these (often sexual) intrapsychic conflicts and thus to emancipate the function of the human mind by means of insight to these unconscious conflicts.

It is important to remember that the three modes of experiencing described are modes of experiencing; they do not as such tell anything if there is a mental disorder or not. The normal functioning of human mind includes all these three epigenetically developed modes of experiencing as a functional continuum, the body-mind continuum.

In conclusion, the whole body-mind continuum evolves according to the epigenetic emergence principle. We can compare the evolution of the human mind to weaving fabric which metaphor of mind also Enckell (40) has used. The psychic matrix (weave) is woven by means of symbolization like a fabric. The previous mode of the symbolization (like the iconic mode) is a warp to which a weft of words (conventional symbols) are integrated: so the mind (weaver) looms the web and the body-mind continuum is created. By these means the originally physical needs are transformed in the mind into psychical desires and wishes.

The symbolization-reflectiveness capacity, and the internal object world thus formed, remain constant in a normal psychic process. It is the reciprocal mobility between the three modes of symbolic function and the reflective-integrative way of observing the modes of symbolic function which constitute the body-mind continuum and is the prerequisite for and the indicator of psychic health.

This work, which offers the psychosemiotic key, by means of which we may conceptualize and map the bridge between the body and mind, and understand the body-mind continuum as well as its develoment in a succesful psychotherapy, is thoroughly presented in the Book: Psychosemiosis as Key to Body-Mind Continuum. The Reinforcement of Symbolization - Reflectiveness in Psychotherapy (41).

ACKNOWLEDGEMENTS

Grant support: the grants from Finnish Student Health Service and from Finnish Psychiatrist Association.I wish to express my deepest gratitude to Docent Ilpo Lahti, MD, to the chief psychiatrist Kari Pylkkänen, MD, to Prof. Johannes Lehtonen, MD and to Prof. Yrjö Alanen, M.D. They have cooperated, helped and supported my work in many ways and given constructive criticism during the whole study process.

REFERENCES

1. Kandel, E.R. (1998).A new intellectual framework for psychiatry. American Journal of Psychiatry; 155,457-469.

2. Kandel, E.R. (1999). Biology and the future of psychoanalysis: a new intellectual framework revisited. American Journal of Psychiatry,156,505-524.

3. Damasio, A. (1999).The Feeling of What Happens: Body and Emotion in the Making of Consciousness. San Diego: Hartcourt Brace.

4. Kendler, K.S. (2001). A Psychiatric dialogue on the mind-body problem. American Journal of Psychiatry,158, 989-1000.

5. Keinänen, M. (2001). The evolution of the psychosemiosis in the psychic development of the child. Semiotica, 135, 25 – 39.

6. Keinänen, M. (2003). Charles Peirce's sign terminology, psychosemiosis and psychotherapy. A clinical approach. Semiotica, 146, 213 – 236.

7. Keinänen, M. (1997). The meaning of the symbolic function in psychoanalytic psychotherapy. Clinical theory and psychotherapeutic applications. British Journal of Medical Psychology, 70, 325 – 338.

8. Keinänen, M. (1999). The evolution of the internal dialogue during the psychoanalytic psychotherapy process. American Journal of Psychotherapy, 53, 529 – 543.

9. Keinänen, M. (2000). Internalization and symbolization in the process of psychoanalytic psychotherapy: a case study. Nordic Journal of Psychiatry, 54, 347 –354.

10. Keinänen, M. (2001). On symbolic function and its role in psychoanalytic psychotherapy. Psychoanalalytic Psychotherapy, 15, 243 – 264.

11. Keinänen, M. (2002). The transformation of the internal dead mother into the internal living mother in the psychoanalytic psychotherapy of anorexia nervosa. Israel Journal of Psychiatry, 40, 220 –231.

12. American Psychiatric Association: Practice guideline for the treatment of patients with borderline personality disorder. (2001). American Journal of Psychiatry,158, 1 – 52.

13. Stern, D. (1985). The Interpersonal World of the Infant. New York: Basic Books.

14. Ogden, T. (1989). The Primitive Edge of Experience. Northvale, NJ: Jason Aronson.

15. Kernberg, O., Selzer, M., Koenigsberg, H., Carr, A.,and Appelbaum, A. (1989). Psychodynamic Psychotherapy of Borderline Patients. New York: Basic Books.

16. Segal, H. (1957). Notes on symbol formation. International Journal of Psychoanalysis, 38,391-397.

17. Peirce, C.S. (1960). Collected Papers of Charles Sanders Peirce. (ed. A.W. Burks.) Vol. VI. Cambridge, MA: Harvard University Press.

18. Green, A. (1986). The Dead Mother. On Private Madness. London: Hogarth Press.

19. Freud, S. (1961 (1923)). The Ego and the Id. Standard Edition, vol. XIX, pp.1-59. London: Hogarth Press.

20. Lewin, B. (1946). Sleep, the mouth and the dream screen. Psychoanalytic Quarterly,15, 419-434.

21. Bucci, W. (1997). Patterns of discourse in good and troubled hours: a multiple code interpretation. Journal of the American Psychoanalytic Association, 45/1,155-187.

22. Fonagy, P. (1999). Memory and therapeutic action. International Journal of Psychoanalsis, 80,215-223.

23. Tähkä, V. (1993). Mind and its Treatment. Madison, Connecticut: International Universities Press.

24. Klein, M. (1975 (published first1957)). Envy and Gratitude. In: Envy and Gratitude and Other Works, 1946- 1963, pp. 176-235. New York: Delacorte.

25. Bucci, W. (1997). Psychoanalysis and Cognitive Science. A Multiple Code Theory. New York: The Guilford Press.

26. Fonagy, P., Steele M., Moran, G., Steele, H., and Higgitt, A. (1991). The capacity for understanding mental states: The reflective self in parent and child and its significance for security of attachment. Infant Mental Health Journal, 12 (3), 201-218.

27. Ogden, T. (1994). The Analytic third-working with intersubjective clinical facts. International Journal of Psychoanalysis, 75, 3-20.

28. Fonagy, P., Edgcumbe, R., Moran, G. et al. (1993). The roles of mental representation and mental processes in therapeutic action. Psychoanalytic Study of the Child, 48, 9-47.

29. Fonagy, P. (2003). Attachment and borderline personality disorder. Journal of the American Psychoanalytic Association, 48/4, 1129-1146.

30. Fonagy, P., Gergely, G., Jurist, E., and Target. M. (2002). Affect regulation, Mentalization and the Development of the Self. New York: Other Press.

31. Ogden,T. (1994). Subjects of Analysis, ch. 5, 6. Northvale, NJ: Jason Aronson.

32. Bollas, C. (1987). The shadow of the Object. Psychoanalysis of the Unthought Known. New York: Columbia Universities Press.

33. Bateman, A., and Fonagy, P. (2004). Psychotherapy for Borderline Personality Disorder. Mentalization- based treatment. Oxford: Oxford University Press.

34. von Bertalanffy, L. (1968). General Systems Theory, ch. 1, 3. New York: Braziller.

35. Bateson, G. (1979). Mind and Nature New York: E.P. Dutton.

36. Habermas, J. (1971). Knowledge and Human Interest. Boston, Beacon Press.

37. Sackett, D., Richardson, W., Rosenberg, W. (1997). How to practice and teach EBM. London: Chuchill, Livingstone.

38. Spitz, R. (1965). The First Year of Life. New York: International Universities Press.

39. Salonen, S. (1989). The restitution of primary identification in psychoanalysis. Scandinavian Psychoanalytic Review, 12, 102-115.

40. Enckell, H. (2002). Metaphor and the Psychodynamic Functions of the Mind. Kuopio: Kuopio University Publications, Finland.

41. Keinänen, M. (2006). Psychosemiosis as Key to Body-Mind Continuum. The Reinforcement of Symbolization - Reflectiveness in Psychotherapy. New York: Nova Sciences Publishers.

In: Stress and Mental Health of College Students
Editor: Mery V. Landow, pp. 261-305

ISBN 1-59454-839-0
© 2006 Nova Science Publishers, Inc.

Chapter 12

BODY IMAGE ISSUES, EATING DISORDERS AND THEIR PREVENTION IN MALE AND FEMALE COLLEGE STUDENTS

Zali Yager and Jennifer A. O'Dea

Faculty of Education and Social Work, The University of Sydney, Australia

INTRODUCTION

Body dissatisfaction and disordered eating and exercise behaviors are documented among normal weight, non-clinical populations of female (Crawford and Worsley, 1988; Drenowski, Yee, Kurth, and Krahn, 1994; Hill, 2002; Kenardy, Brown, and Vogt, 2001), and male (Drummond, 2002; O'Dea and Abraham, 2002) college students worldwide.

This high prevalence of disordered eating behaviors among college students may be attributed to them being in an age range that is particularly susceptible (Kenardy, et al. 2001). However, the college environment and college experience are consistently found to have common factors that may potentiate or exacerbate eating and exercise problems. It is thought that the competitive nature of the university setting stipulates a need to achieve in professional, personal and romantic arenas (Burkle, 1999; Klemchuck, Hutchinson, and Frank, 1990; Striegel-Moore, Silberstein, Grunberg, and Rodin, 1990). Life changes that may occur due to the transition to university life and study are also reported to affect body image and eating and exercise behaviors (Cooley and Toray, 2001b; Vohs, Heatherton, and Herrin, 2001; Vohs, Voelz et al., 2001). Personality characteristics that may develop during college also include perfectionism (McLaren, Gauvin, and White, 2001) and the ability to cope with stress (Klemchuck et al., 1990); both of which are predisposing factors for eating problems (Stice, 2002a).

Body image issues and eating disorders can have serious and wide ranging effects on the individual. These may include, but are not limited to; depression, suicide attempts, anxiety disorders, secondary health problems, and increased risk of onset of obesity (Johnson, Cohen, Kasen, and Brook, 2002; Pomeroy and Mitchell, 2002; Stice, Cameron, Killen, Hayward, and Taylor, 1999); and substance abuse problems including increased tobacco (Lenz, 2004) and alcohol consumption (Anderson, Martens, and Cimini, 2005). Patients with eating disorders also have the highest rate of suicide attempts and mortality of all psychiatric disorders (Newman et al., 1996)

There is a high reported prevalence of body dissatisfaction, dieting and eating disorders in college and university students, and it has been suggested that one third of women who develop clinical eating disorders do so in college (Winzelberg et al., 2000). However it is still not clear whether body image issues and eating disorders are established before tertiary education (Vohs, Heatherton et al., 2001) or are developed as a result of the transition to college, and the different social and environmental pressures that are associated with the college environment (Compas, Wagner, Slavin, and Vannatta, 1986).

The following chapter will investigate the prevalence of and risk factors for body dissatisfaction, disordered eating behaviors and eating disorders among college males and females. Preventive initiatives are also reviewed.

PREVALENCE OF BODY IMAGE ISSUES AND DISORDERED EATING AMONG COLLEGE MALES AND FEMALES

Reports of the prevalence of body image issues and eating disorders in college students are often varied, and produce some contradictory results. This is largely due to methodological issues of case definition and data collection. Firstly, the majority of samples are composed of convenience samples of lecture or class groups, sororities or athletic teams; or from volunteers recruited through advertising. This fails to create a random sample from the university environment, and limits the generalizability of results. A variety of assessment scales and questionnaires are also used in various studies. Although the majority of the assessment instruments used are standardized, several studies report data using instruments that have been developed specifically by the researcher. Finally, research practices and methods of data collection are largely unreported in research, and this could affect the accuracy of self reported data, and therefore the validity of results.

There are also many inherent methodological issues that have inhibited accurate prevalence statistics in males. These include methods of detection, case definition and diagnosis, response rates and generalizability of samples (Carlat and Carmargo, 1991). The body dissatisfaction and disordered eating instruments used in research have generally been derived from those used for women and may fail to detect cases of eating disorders in men (Turnbull, Freeman, and Barry, 1987). In addition, some of the results of prevalence studies in men must be interpreted with caution due to low response rates, the possibility of selection bias, and the known reluctance of people with body image and eating problems to participate in such studies (Fairburn and Beglin, 1990). This trend is especially pronounced among males (Drummond, 2002). An accurate depiction of the prevalence of these behaviors will be limited while these methodological issues exist.

The overall prevalence of clinical eating disorders in the college population is largely unknown, but estimated to be quite low (Pearson, Goldklang, and Striegel-Moore, 2001). Most reported estimates state that between one and three percent of college students suffer from clinical eating disorders (Beglin and Fairburn, 1992; Fairburn and Beglin, 1990; Kurth, Krahn, Nairn, and Drenowski, 1995; Striegel-Moore et al., 2003). However:

"incidence rates fail to include the considerable proportion of women and girls who do not meet diagnostic criteria, but engage in weight control behaviors which are damaging their health and diminishing their feelings of self worth and wellbeing" (Sanders, Gaskill and Gwynne, 2000, p6).

In a study of young women, Abraham, Mira, Beumont, Sowerbutts and Llewellyn-Jones (1983) found that many young women encounter, or at least "pass through a phase of" (p227), disordered eating. This is supported by statistical evidence of a high occurrence of disordered eating behaviors (Mintz and Betz, 1988; O'Dea and Yager, 2005; Schwitzer, Rodriguez, Thomas, and Salimi, 2001), body dissatisfaction (Drummond, 2002; Grogan, 1999) and dieting (O'Dea and Abraham, 2001, 2002) among college men and women worldwide. These behaviors have been shown to be associated with various negative psychological, physical and physiological effects, some of those being clinical and sub clinical eating disorders (Carlat, Carmargo, and Herzog, 1997; Wertheim, Paxton, Schultz, and Muir, 1997).

BODY DISSATISFACTION

Although many different definitions and understandings of body dissatisfaction exist, it is generally understood to mean some degree of dislike with one's body shape or weight. As we have outlined earlier in this chapter, findings of the prevalence of body dissatisfaction vary greatly, depending on the specific questions or scales used to measure this construct. Body dissatisfaction is a widely recognized risk factor for dieting and disordered eating (Cook-Cottone and Phelps, 2003; Paxton, 2000; Stice, 2002a), as well as having significant negative impacts on self-esteem (O'Dea, 2004; Shisslak, Crago, Renger, and Clark-Wagner, 1998; Tiggemann, 2005). In a longitudinal study of college women, it was found that those who entered college with higher body dissatisfaction generally develop worsening eating disorder pathology over the following three years (Cooley and Toray, 2001a).

University women are often presented as being those who are most dissatisfied with their bodies with 70-80 percent expressing a desire to lose weight (Abraham, Mira, Beumont, Sowerbutts, and Llewellyn-Jones, 1983; Paxton et al., 1991; Vohs, Heatherton et al., 2001) and 13 percent scoring in the range of clinical body dissatisfaction on the EDI-2 (Cook-Cottone and Phelps, 2003). In a large study of 1131 male (n=395) and female (n=735) Australian University students, only 30 percent of the females were satisfied with their body, with 59 percent wanting to be slimmer, and 11 percent wanting to be bigger (O'Dea, 1999). Using a similar questionnaire in a study of clinically underweight (BMI < 20) female university students (n=276), 42 percent of women classified as being underweight reported that they wanted to be slimmer (O'Dea, 1998).

Body dissatisfaction is also now recognized as well entrenched among males. Early studies revealed that males were just as likely as females to be dissatisfied with their body size and shape, with statistics ranging from 78.2 (Silberstein, Striegel-Moore, Timko, and Rodin, 1988) to 95 percent (Mishkind, Rodin, Silberstein, and Striegel-Moore, 1986) of males choosing an ideal figure different from their own; or expressing dissatisfaction with some aspect of their body. Research has consistently agreed and confirmed that males who are dissatisfied with their body are equally as likely to desire weight loss as weight gain (Silberstein et al., 1988). In a large Australian study of 1131 college students, 41 percent of males reported that they were satisfied with their body, while 29 percent wanted to be slimmer, and 30 percent wanted to be bigger (O'Dea, 1999). Males are also commonly reported to be more likely to express dissatisfaction with their chest, upper body, waist and weight (Mishkind et al., 1986) and to have a preference for a "V-shape" (Kearney-Cooke and Steichen-Asch, 1990) with a larger upper body (Thompson and Tantleff, 1992). It is also agreed that muscularity is more important to men's body dissatisfaction than fat (Leit, Gray, and Pope Jr, 2002; Pope Jr, Harrison. et al., 2000). In a cross-cultural study of males in Austria, France and the USA it was found that men chose an ideal body that was an average of 28 pounds more muscular than they actually were (Pope, Harrison et al., 2000).

Body dissatisfaction is not limited to university students in Western countries. In a study of female Taiwanese college students 57.4 percent reported that they thought they were overweight or obese, whereas only 16.2 percent actually were overweight or obese. In addition, over 20 percent of the underweight and severely underweight students wanted to lose weight; and over 60 percent of normal weight participants wanted to lose weight (Wong and Huang, 1999). A comparison of female Japanese and Taiwanese college students found that they had the same mean BMI (20.1), yet the Japanese women tended to rate themselves as heavier and have increased body dissatisfaction; with a very high number of the seriously underweight women still desiring further weight loss (Shih and Kubo, 2005).

DIETING

Although many studies regarding the prevalence of dieting have been undertaken, there is a lack of consistent sampling and surveying techniques that prevents accurate comparison between populations and time frames. Reported dieting behaviors are known to vary significantly, depending on the phrasing of the questions given (Neumark-Sztainer, Jeffery, and French, 1997). General questions (eg, Are you trying to lose weight?) produce a greater affirmative response than the more specific (eg, Are you currently dieting to lose weight?) (Hill, 2002; Neumark-Sztainer et al., 1997). Neumark-Sztainer and colleagues state that "dieting may represent different behaviors for persons of different gender, socio-economic background, and in particular for different weight status" (p448). There is great variation in individual perception of what it means to be on a diet, from a cognitive desire for weight loss with no behavior change, eating less than one would like to, limiting food intake at meals, or skipping meals altogether (Hill, 2002; Neumark-Sztainer et al., 1997).

Dieting to lose weight is known to be common among young women, and has been described as "normative" behavior (Rodin, Silberstein, and Striegel-Moore, 1985). As little as 14 and 33 percent of young women report that they are not currently dieting, and to have "normal" eating behaviors (Drenowski et al., 1994; Mintz and Betz, 1988); with the majority employing some sort of dietary restraint. In a study of Australian University Students, 94 percent wanted to lose weight and 91 percent had successfully dieted at some time (Abraham et al., 1983); while in the USA, 80 percent of women diet during their first year of college (Striegel-Moore et al., 1990). Early reports of dieting report the consumption of low calorie foods (75 percent of dieters) and counting calories (50 percent) to be the most common forms of dieting (Mintz and Betz, 1988).

Current dieting to lose weight was reported by 47 percent of females and 15 percent of male trainee Physical Education teachers in an Australian study (O'Dea and Abraham, 2001). In females, 42 percent of those females who were classified as underweight (BMI<20) still reported currently dieting for weight loss (O'Dea and Abraham, 2001).

Dieting to gain weight has not received equivalent empirical attention. Eating with the aim of weight gain may include behaviors such as excessive consumption of food, excessive consumption of certain types of food, such as protein, or the use of protein powders (O'Dea and Abraham, 2002). In male trainee physical education teachers, 28.9 percent reported currently dieting to gain weight (O'Dea and Abraham, 2001). Other studies have reported 21.1 percent of college athletes (Froiland, Koszewski, Hingst, and Kopecky, 2004) and 45.9 percent of recreational resistance trainers (Williams, Anderson, and Winett, 2004) at college were using protein powders in an effort to bulk up. These behaviors may have equally damaging physical and mental effects as dieting for weight loss, including obsessive behaviors, repeated "failings" and a sense of shame and guilt. In extreme cases, dieting for weight gain and poor body image may lead to muscle dysmorphia (Pope, Gruber, Choi, Olivardia, and Phillips, 1997).

DISORDERED EATING BEHAVIORS

The prevalence of clinical eating disorders is still quite rare, but disordered eating is consistently described as being ubiquitous on the college campus (Forman-Hoffman, 2004; Mann, Nolen-Hoeksema, and Huang, 1997; Pyle, Halvorson, Neuman, and Mitchell, 1986; Stice and Ragan, 2002; Vaughan, King, and Cottrell, 2004; Zuckerman, Colby, Ware, and Lazerson, 1986). Both male and female college students report engaging in disordered eating behaviors, in an attempt to lose or gain weight. These may include starvation, binge eating, vomiting, use of laxatives and diet pills, and the use of creatine and anabolic steroids. Recent reports confirm the use of disordered eating behaviors among college women (Anderson, Martens and Cimini., 2005; Cooley and Toray, 2001b; O'Dea and Abraham, 2001). Males are known to be less likely to engage in typical disordered eating behaviors, such as diet pills and laxatives (Braun, Sunday, Huang, and Halmi, 1999); and more likely to engage in excessive exercise (Garman, Hayduk, Crider, and Hodel, 2004; O'Dea and Abraham, 2002; Zmijewski and Howard, 2003) and creatine use (Froiland et al., 2004).

In addition to the physical and emotional implications of disordered eating and exercise, recent studies have found that frequency of diet pill use and frequency of induced vomiting in women is significantly associated with tobacco use (Lenz, 2004), and that college females who purge also report increased use of alcohol, and more negative consequences of alcohol use (Anderson et al., 2005). Correlations have also been found among college problem gamblers and increased binge eating and weight control efforts (Engwall, Hunter, and Steinberg, 2004).

BINGE EATING

Binge eating is usually defined as eating a large amount of food in a small amount of time. However revisions of DSM IV criteria have narrowed this definition to be "eating a large amount of food in a period of less than two hours at times other than meals" (American Psychiatric Association, 1994; Halmi, Falk, and Schwartz, 1981). Other authors have further classified a binge to be the consumption of foods equal to 1200 calories or more (Abraham and Lovell, 1999; Katzman, Wolchik, and Braver, 1984). Individual definitions of what constitutes binge eating may vary, with females being more likely to inappropriately label consumption of various amounts of food a "binge" (Katzman et al., 1984). For example, in a study of college students, some females described a bowl of ice-cream or four to six cookies as a binge (Zuckerman et al., 1986).

Prevalence studies report that between 30 to 41 percent of college males (Halmi et al., 1981; Katzman et al., 1984; Pyle et al., 1986) and 50 to 63 percent of college females (Abraham et al., 1983; Halmi et al., 1981; Katzman et al., 1984; Striegel-Moore et al., 1990) self report binge eating; with 17 to 23 percent of women (Abraham et al., 1983; Zuckerman et al., 1986) and 14 percent of men self reporting binge eating at least once a week (Zuckerman et al., 1986).

PURGING, VOMITING AND LAXATIVE USE

Self induced vomiting, fasting and diuretic and laxative use are prevalent on the college campus, with 23 percent of college women and nine percent of college men reported using one or more of these harmful weight control behaviors at some time (Zuckerman et al., 1986). In females, 10 percent of freshman and 8 percent of senior women report ever using self-induced vomiting; and two percent of freshman and three percent of senior college students reporting current self-induced vomiting (Zuckerman et al., 1986). Other studies of current vomiting prevalence reveal that between 3.4 and 5.4 percent of female American university students report vomiting or laxative use in the previous 30 days (Anderson et al., 2005; Kurth et al., 1995; Mintz and Betz, 1988).

A large study of American female college students found 25 percent report using diuretics, and 14 percent report laxative use either presently, or in the past (Kurtzman, Yager, Landsverk, Wiesmeier, and Bodurka, 1989). In a study of trainee physical education teachers, 19 percent of the females reported using laxatives (O'Dea and Abraham, 2001)

Studies have found between 3 and 6.1 percent of college males to report self-induced vomiting to lose weight at some time (Connor-Greene, 1988; Halmi et al., 1981; O'Dea and Abraham, 2002; Zuckerman et al., 1986), whereas Zuckerman and colleagues (1986) found no men to report currently inducing vomiting to lose weight. Halmi and colleagues (1981) reported no significant differences between males (6.1 percent) and women (11.9 percent) on a DSM III based survey of vomiting to lose weight.

STARVATION

Skipping meals, fasting and starvation may all be categorized together. An early American study reported that 25 percent of freshman and 16 percent of senior female college students were using starvation as a compensatory behavior for binging. In males, 10 percent of freshman and eight percent of senior college men reported regularly using starvation for weight control (Zuckerman et al., 1986). In addition, other authors found that 20 percent of college females had used fasting at least once per month (Mintz and Betz, 1988). An Australian study found 19 percent of University females, and nine percent of males to use starvation as a form of weight control (O'Dea and Abraham, 2001)

CREATINE AND SUPPLEMENT USE

The socially desirable, hyper-mesomorphic body shape for males is physiologically difficult to obtain without the use of dangerous eating or exercise behaviors, as well as drugs such as anabolic steroids. Professional and recreational participation in sports and physical activity that emphasize or require muscularity is known to predispose athletes to engage in anabolic steroid use. A recent study of college males found that 27 percent reported using over the counter body building supplements such as creatine and ephedrine, and illicit drugs such as anabolic steroids to gain muscle or lose fat (Olivardia, Pope Jr, Borowiecki, and Cohane, 2004). In another study of 148 male recreational resistance trainers at an American college, 47.3 percent reported creatine use (Williams et al., 2004). In that study, 74.3 percent of creatine users were also using protein in an effort to increase muscle bulk (Williams et al., 2004).

High to excessive protein consumption is reported to be prevalent among college males. Recent studies report that 21.1 percent of college athletes and 46 percent of college recreational resistance trainers use protein powders in order to gain muscle or 'bulk up' (Froiland et al., 2004; Williams et al., 2004).

Other supplements are also commonly used, with studies of collegiate athletes revealing that 57 percent report taking vitamin and mineral supplements (Krumbach, Ellis, and Driskell, 1999). More specifically, athletes reported that they regularly (23 percent), occasionally (16 percent) or seldom (22 percent) used nutritional supplements (Froiland et al., 2004). Roughly equal proportions (40 to 42.5 percent) of these athletes report that they use supplements for health, for energy, weight gain and increased strength and power (Froiland et al., 2004).

Very few studies of college students have attempted to determine the Prevalence of anabolic steroid use. Drenowski and colleagues (1995) found a 0.6 percent prevalence of anabolic steroids among 2088 high school graduates during freshman orientation at a large Midwestern University in the USA. Users of anabolic steroids were most likely to be athletes engaging in basketball, weight training, swimming and running. These findings are believed to be underestimates due to fears of legal or personal consequences of using prohibited ergonomic aids.

EATING DISORDERS IN COLLEGE WOMEN

A complete presentation of the etiology of eating disorders among college students is still not available. Attempts to identify the prevalence of eating disorders in a university setting seem to be dependent on the stringency of diagnostic criteria, the response rates and the populations studied. The majority of studies have used the Eating Attitudes Test [EAT] (Garner and Garfinkel, 1979); or the Eating Disorders Inventory [EDI] (Garner, Olmstead, and Polivy, 1983) or other standardized measures to classify the presence of a potential eating problem. Those that use a clinical interview using DSM III or DSM IV criteria are known to produce more accurate (and generally lower) prevalence rates.

The prevalence of Bulimia Nervosa in college women is reported to range from one to 19 percent using DSM-III criteria (Coric and Murstein, 1993; Fairburn and Beglin, 1990; Halmi et al., 1981; Katzman et al., 1984; Pope Jr, Hudson, Yurgelun-Todd, and Hudson, 1984; Pyle et al., 1986). However, it has been suggested that those studies reporting a low prevalence of bulimia nervosa also had a low response rate (Coric and Murstein, 1993). In regard to the current prevalence of Bulimia Nervosa using DSM III criteria, Kurth and colleagues (1995) reported a two percent prevalence with a 66 percent response rate; Zuckerman and colleagues (1986) reported an eight percent prevalence with a 75 percent response rate; while Coric and Murstein (1993) reported an 11.3 percent prevalence with a 94.1 percent response rate. It is known that women with eating disorders are less likely to respond to surveys about eating disorders (Beglin and Fairburn, 1992). Therefore, prevalence findings from studies receiving low response rates may be underestimates.

Anorexia Nervosa has received less empirical attention. The prevalence of Anorexia Nervosa among college women has been observed to be between one and 4.2 percent in college females (Fairburn and Beglin, 1990; Kurtzman et al., 1989; Pope et al., 1984). Mintz and Betz (1988) describe 1.2 percent of college females to have a body weight that may be classified as anorexic.

Mintz and Betz (1988) described 61 percent of American college women to have some sort of sub clinical eating problem, including chronic dieting, binge/purging and sub clinical Bulimia Nervosa. More recently, Drenowski and colleagues (1994) identified 10 percent of college women to be dieters "at risk", meaning that they met the diagnostic criteria for Bulimia Nervosa except for binge eating frequency. Similarly, other studies have reported a high prevalence of cases where participants experienced most, but not all symptoms of Bulimia Nervosa. For example, Krahn and colleagues (1992) found that 16 percent of females fulfilled most, but only two percent fulfilled all criteria for Bulimia Nervosa.

Using an EAT cutoff score of 20, between 11 and 17 percent (Prouty, Protinsky, and Canady, 2002; Thome and Espelage, 2004) of American college women scored high enough on the EAT scale to indicate an eating disorder. When 30 was used as the cutoff score, between nine and 13.8 percent (Evers, 1987; Garner and Garfinkel, 1980; Palmquist-Fredenberg, Berglund, and Dieken, 1996) of women were considered to be classified as having an eating disorder. In a study of 1482 Norwegian University students, it was found that 7.2 percent of males and 20.2 percent of females scored 40 or above on the Eating Disorders Inventory [EDI], which is indicative of an eating disorder (Kjelsas and Augestad, 2004).

EATING DISORDERS IN COLLEGE MALES

Reports of the clinical prevalence of eating disorders among males present various findings, with a general agreement that 5-10 percent of all individuals who experience eating disorders are male (Carlat and Carmargo, 1991; Lucas, Beard, O'Fallon, and Kurland, 1991). Prevalence statistics among males are believed to be underestimates due to the reluctance of male patients to seek diagnosis and treatment (Anderson and Holman, 1997) and methodological limitations exist in the detection of eating disorders in males, as the criteria and scales used were originally developed for females. Participation numbers of males in typical studies are also generally quite low, reducing the possibility for statistical analysis. In addition, males also fail to attract attention to their disordered eating or exercise behaviors as they may not appear to lose large amounts of weight. Excessive exercise behaviors may go unnoticed, as a dedication to an exercise program has become highly socially accepted and valued. Finally, males are difficult to diagnose, and may be excluded from clinical diagnosis, as they do not experience amenorrhea.

In an Australian study of college men using the Eating and Exercise Examination – Computerized [EEE-C] (Abraham and Lovell, 1999), 21 percent of males displayed eating attitudes and behaviors characteristic of eating disorders and disordered eating (O'Dea and Abraham, 2002). Nine percent of these men actually self reported suffering from disordered eating; 18 percent reported weight control problems, and two percent met criteria to be diagnosed with clinical Bulimia Nervosa (O'Dea and Abraham, 2002).

EXERCISE DISORDERS

Many college students engage in exercise, however, for some, exercise may become excessive, or obligatory in terms of dedication to or quantity of exercise (Bamber, Cockerill, Rodgers, and Carroll, 2003). Although some authors have reported that exercise dependence is more prevalent among males (Garman, Hayduk, Crider, and Hodel, 2004); females are known to be more likely to exercise for aesthetic (as apposed to health related) reasons, which is linked to exercise disorders (McDonald and Thompson, 1992; Silberstein et al., 1988; Strelan, Mehaffey, and Tiggemann, 2003).

At present there are no DSM criteria for exercise disorders. Criteria have been proposed from as early as 1987 (De Coverly Veale, 1987); but have yet to have been accepted by the American Psychiatric Association. Some researchers have defined dependent exercisers as engaging in more than six hours of exercise per week (Garman, Hayduk, Crider, and Hodel, 2004), others use the duration of each session, with "greater than two hours per day not related to professional career or training" used to indicate an exercise disorder (Abraham and Lovell, 1999; O'Dea and Abraham, 2002). Other authors argue that it is the psychological commitment, and withdrawal symptoms experienced that indicate obsessive exercise behaviors (Pasman and Thompson, 1988). Issues of definition therefore preclude comparable analysis of the prevalence of exercise disorders.

Using the Eating and Exercise Examination- Computerized [EEE-C] (Abraham and Lovell, 1999), 22 percent of college males met the behavioral criteria for excessive exercise; and eight percent were able to be diagnosed with a clinical eating disorder (O'Dea and

Abraham, 2002). Using an unvalidated scale, (Garman, Hayduk, Crider, and Hodel, 2004) reported that 21.8 percent of 257 male and female college students met criteria for excessive or dependent exercise, 52.7 percent being male, and 47.3 percent female. Zmijewski and Howard (2003) found that 45.9 percent of college students (47.5 percent of males and 44.2 percent of females) exhibited three or more symptoms of exercise dependence using the Exercise Dependence Criteria [EDC] (Howard, 2002), based on the DSM-IV criteria for substance abuse and dependence.

It has been reported that people who exercise for health and fitness reasons gain high body satisfaction and self esteem (Strelan et al., 2003); while those pursuing aesthetic goals are more likely to develop exercise disorders (McDonald and Thompson, 1992; Silberstein et al., 1988; Strelan et al., 2003). Women are presumed and reported to be more likely than men to exercise for aesthetic reasons (Davis and Cowles, 1991; Strelan et al., 2003); however in a group of Australian college men, equal proportions of men (33 percent) reported exercising to feel good, and exercising for shape and weight (O'Dea and Abraham, 2002). Thome and Espelage (2004) also found that exercise was significantly associated with negative affect among women with eating disorders, but with positive affect and coping among non eating disordered women. In addition, a dedication to exercise is known to be a prominent and prevalent feature in the development and maintenance of eating disorders among men and women (Brewerton, Stellefson, Hibbs, Hodges, and Cochrane, 1995; Calogero and Pedrotty, 2004; Davis, 1997).

Men are known to see physical activity as a masculine and effective method of weight loss (Drummond, 2002; Yates, 1991) and it appears to be the primary method of weight loss and weight control in males (Drenowski and Yee, 1987; Yates, 1991). These complicates the diagnosis of eating and exercise disorders in males, as they are likely to gain muscle (and therefore weight) and so, are unlikely to attract attention to their behavior. A dedication to exercise has also become socially acceptable and highly admired, as well as being equated with health and fitness.

In some cases, an extreme dedication toward weight gain, in particular muscularity, may lead to the development of muscle dysmorphia This is a form of body dysmorphic disorder involving a pathological fear of being too small, and a persistent desire for, and engagement in activity to achieve a more muscular body that interferes with an individual's social and occupational functioning due to the long periods of time spent thinking about, planning, and actually exercising (Pope et al., 1997). Men with muscle dysmorphia differ from other men who train with weights in that they aspire to unrealistic levels of muscularity and body size, have increased rates of body dissatisfaction, may abuse anabolic steroids, consume excessive amounts of protein and creatine supplements, engage in dieting and disordered eating practices and have increased levels of anxiety and mood disorders.

CHANGE IN PREVALENCE OVER TIME

Although some authors report the prevalence of dieting and disordered eating behaviors (Klemchuck et al., 1990; Pyle et al., 1986; Theander, 2002) and eating disorders (Reinstein, Koszewski, Chamberlain, and Smith-Johnson, 1992) to be increasing over time, others suggest that this is not the case (Cash, Morrow, Hrabosky, and Perry, 2004; Heatherton et al.,

1995). Cash and colleagues (2004) used the Multidimensional Body-Self Relations Questionnaire [MBSRQ] in 22 studies between 1983 and 2001 at the same university, including 3242 male and female college students in total. They found that female body image improved over this time frame despite increases in body weight; and that there was no observable change among male students. It was also reported that there was an increased preoccupation with weight and shape from the 1980s to early-mid 1990s, but a decline in body dissatisfaction in the late 1990s-2000s (Cash et al., 2004).

Heatherton and colleagues (1995) assessed the body image of 1300 male and female university students in total, using the EDI in 1982 and then again in 1992. They found that, although more participants were classed as overweight in the second study, a lesser proportion of participants classified themselves as being overweight. Subsequently, a significantly lower number of women reported wanting to lose at least 10 pounds. There was also a significant decline in Bulimia Nervosa scores on the EDI. Authors commented that although body dissatisfaction had declined, it was still quite high, with body dissatisfaction and a desire to lose weight being the norm for 70 percent of women, and 10 percent scoring in the range of clinically significant eating disorders (Heatherton et al., 1995).

Research is once again divided as to whether the prevalence of eating disorders has increased (Reinstein et al., 1992) or decreased (Heatherton et al., 1995) over time. One study of the incidence of Bulimia Nervosa from 1982-1992 showed a decrease among both males and females from 7.2 percent to 5.1 percent in females and 1.1 percent to 0.4 percent in males (Heatherton et al., 1995). Reports of vomiting and diuretic pill use also decreased among females (Heatherton et al., 1995). However, the authors of this report also argued that a greater media focus and increased availability of information about eating disorders may be affecting the subsequent reporting of behaviors among sufferers.

RECENT RESEARCH AMONG AUSTRALIAN UNIVERSITY STUDENTS

We have conducted a number of research studies among Australian university students between 1999- 2005. The cumulative results of body image and self reported eating disorders from these five separate studies are given in table 1.

In general, one fifth to one third of the young female college students perceived themselves as "too fat", yet nearly 80 percent reported wanting to lose weight and half of all females were actively trying to lose weight. A concerning and consistent finding of our studies among young female college students was the use of dangerous and unhealthy methods of weight control such as starvation, vomiting, laxative abuse and slimming pills. The use of cigarette smoking for weight control and appetite suppression among college women remained constant at 7-18 percent in earlier studies (O'Dea and Abraham, 2001) and in more recent data collected in 2004 (Yager and O'Dea, Unpublished). This is a very serious health concern which shows no sign of abating.

Self reported eating disorders among college women exists in around 15 percent in keeping with other studies among this population group (Drenowski et al, 1994; Garner and Garfinkel, 1980; Prouty et al. 2002; Thome and Espelage 2004).

Table 1. Body image and eating disorders in the authors' studies of Male and female Australian University Students

	Males n = 46[a]	n = 93[b]	n = 383[c]	n=182[d]	Females n=169[a]	n = 721[c]	n = 320[d]
	% (n)	% (n)	% (n)	% (n)	% (n)	% (n)	% (n)
Body Image							
"Too Thin"	19.6 (9)	-	-	13.6 (25)	3.5 (6)	-	1.6 (4)
"About right"	73.9 (34)	-	-	69.2 (126)	62.7(106)	-	70.3 (225)
"Too fat"	6.5 (3)	-	-	12.0 (22)	31.4 (53)	-	21.8 (70)
Desired Body Weight							
A lot heavier	6.5 (3)	-	-	4.9 (9)	4.7 (8)	-	0 (0)
A little heavier	47.8 (22)	-	30 (114)	39.6 (72)	4.1(7)	11 (80)	1.8 (6)
Present weight	28.3 (13)	-	41 (157)	19.1 (35)	10.6 (18)	30 (216)	15.3 (49)
A little lighter	13.1 (6)	-	29 (111)	25.8 (47)	66.3 (112)	59 (425)	69.1 (221)
A lot lighter	4.3 (2)	-	-	1.65 (3)	14.7 (25)	-	7.5 (24)
Current weight loss/gain							
Currently trying to lose weight	15.2 (7)	20 (19)	-	17.1 (31)	47.3 (80)	-	49.4 (158)
Currently trying to gain weight	28.3 (13)	-	-	16.2 (30)	2.4 (4)	-	2.2 (7)
Dangerous/ unhealthy weight loss methods							
Starvation	9 (4)	-	-	5.1 (9)	32.1 (19)	-	15.2 (49)
Vomiting/ attempted vomiting	0	3.2 (3)	-	2.2 (4)	22 (37.1)	-	10.8 (35)
Laxative abuse	0	-	-	2.2 (4)	32.1 (19)	-	5.7 (18)
Slimming pills	0	-	-	3.9 (7)	13.5 (8)	-	5.7 (18)
Smoking for weight loss	6 (3)	-	-	3.9 (7)	11.83 (7)	-	7.9 (25)
Excessive exercise	22 (10)	22.6 (21)	-	11.8 (21)	49.0(29)	-	16.5 (52)
Current eating disorder diagnoses	%(n)	%(n)					
Anorexia Nervosa	2.1(1)	0(0)	-	1.7 (3)	.6 (1)	-	0.3 (1)
Bulimia Nervosa	0(0)	1.1(1)	-	1.7 (3)	1.9 (2)	-	0
Eating disorder not otherwise specified (EDNOS)	-	20(19)	-	1.1 (2)	3 (5)	15.9 (115)	0.3 (1)
Exercise disorder	-	7(7)	-	1.1(2)	-	-	0.3 (1)
Believe currently have an eating disorder	2.1(1)	8.6(8)	-	1.7 (3)	14 (18)	-	3.2 (10)

(a) O'Dea and Abraham, 2001 (b) O'Dea and Abraham, 2002 (c) O'Dea, 1999 (d) Yager, Unpublished

Body image problems and eating disorders are certainly not confined to the female college population. As outlined in Table 1, male students are concerned about being "too fat" but are also concerned about being "too thin". This dual problem places a huge amount of pressure on college males to work towards developing the "perfect" mesomorphic male body, and consequently places them at risk of eating problems, drug and steroid usage, and injuries caused by weight lifting or excessive exercise. The prevalence of diagnosed anorexia nervosa was 1.7 to 2.1 percent in males and for bulimia nervosa, the prevalence was 1.1 to1.7 percent. In some cases the prevalence of these eating disorders in males was higher than the females (Yager and O'Dea, Unpublished).

Clearly, body image concerns and eating disorders are problems that affect a significant proportion of both male and female college students.

RISK FACTORS SPECIFIC TO COLLEGE STUDENTS

Stice (2002a) defines a risk factor as a variable that has been shown to prospectively predict some pathological outcome. The unique combination of academic, social, and environmental changes and pressures that occur in the college environment may put students at risk for body image issues and eating problems (Vohs, Heatherton., and Herrin, 2001). Risk factors may be described as sociocultural or developmental.

There are many risk factors for body dissatisfaction and disordered eating that are specific to university students, including the increased prevalence of dieting, the transition to college, being enrolled in a college major that is linked with food, exercise or appearance, collegiate athlete programs and sororities, and possessing certain personality characteristics. These will now be discussed.

DEVELOPMENTAL RISK FACTORS

The inheritability of eating disorders has recently become an important research focus. Twin studies suggest that over half of the risk of developing an eating disorder may be attributed to genetics (Bulik, Sullivan, and Kendler, 1998; Klump, Miller, Keel, McGue, and Iacono, 2001; Wade et al., 2000). A study of 4667 Finnish twins (2545 male and 2122 female) found that inheritability of eating disorders differed among the sexes. In women, eating disorders had a moderate to high heritability; whereas for men, disordered eating behaviors appeared to be purely environmental (Keski-Rahkonen et al., 2005).

Early onset of puberty is considered to foster body dissatisfaction, dieting and disordered eating (Rierdan and Koff, 1991). This is said to be due to the fact that menarche leads to increased adiposity and therefore takes the young woman further away from the highly praised thin ideal. This increases body dissatisfaction and therefore increases attempts at dieting. Although early pubertal development has been found to increase eating pathology among college (Cooley and Toray, 2001b) and adolescent (Hayward et al., 1997) females. In the study of 4667 male and female Finnish twins, it was found that there was a statistically significant indication that early onset of puberty, early initiation of sexual activity and increased number of sexual partners were risk factors for the development of eating disorders (Keski-Rahkonen et al., 2005). Alternatively, Stice (2002a) found little support for a strong relationship between early pubertal development and disordered eating in his meta- analysis of risk factors for eating pathology.

Self esteem is known to be a protective factor for body dissatisfaction, dieting and disordered eating among college women (Killen et al., 1994; Phelps, Dempsey, Sapia, and Nelson, 1999). Low self esteem is consistently identified as being a risk factor for the development of eating problems and women with eating disorders are known to have a significantly lower self esteem (Geller, Zaitsoff, and Srikameswaran, 2002; Wilksh and Wade, 2004).

SOCIOCULTURAL RISK FACTORS

Sociocultural influences impact on eating attitudes and behavior through social reinforcement and modeling (Stice, 2002b). Social pressure to be thin promotes an internalization of the thin ideal, and social reinforcement of this ideal may lead individuals to become dissatisfied with their own body (Stice, 2002a; Thompson and Stice, 2001). This body dissatisfaction may then foster dieting and disordered eating behaviors to reduce the perceived difference between an individual's actual and ideal body shape or weight (Killen et al., 1994; Striegel-Moore, Silberstein, and Rodin, 1986) and attempt to obtain an unrealistic body shape (Graff Low et al., 2003; Stice, Schupak-Neuberg, Shaw, and Stein, 1994; Thompson and Stice, 2001). Internalization of the thin ideal is positively correlated with body image disturbances and eating pathology among female college students (Stice et al., 1994); and as a risk factor for eating disorders (Graff Low et al., 2003; McCarthy, 1990; Thompson and Stice, 2001). Targeting the internalization of the thin ideal has been theorized (Graff Low et al., 2003; Striegel-Moore et al., 1986) and shown (Stice, Chase, Stormer, and Appel, 2001; Stice, Mazotti, Weibel, and Agras, 2000) to reduce body dissatisfaction, dieting and disordered eating behaviors among female college students.

Modeling refers to the process whereby individuals observe the attitudes and behaviors of others, and begin to emulate them (Stice, 2002b). In addition to the direct modeling effects of watching someone engage in disordered eating behaviors and then going on to perform them; these observations may lead to the belief that these behaviors are more normal and safe than they actually are.

Sociocultural influences may come from the media, family and from peers. Following is an exploration of risk factors for body dissatisfaction and disordered eating that are specific to college students.

DIETING

In this chapter, we have previously outlined that the majority (80 to 91 percent) of female college students are dieting to lose weight (Abraham, 2003; Abraham et al., 1983; Mintz and Betz, 1988; Striegel-Moore et al., 1990). Despite the paucity of research among males, dieting to gain weight has been reported to be common among college men (O'Dea and Abraham, 2001). However, very little research has been conducted about dieting to gain weight. For the purposes of this section of the review, 'dieting' will refer to dietary restraint with the intention of weight loss.

Stice (2002a) reports that dieting "theoretically fosters eating pathology because individuals may binge eat to counteract the effects of caloric deprivation" (p. 833). Dieting is known to have biological, cognitive and effective consequences that may lead an individual to disordered eating. Short term dieting results in a reduction in tryptophan (carbohydrate) levels, to which the biological response is to consume energy-rich foods (Kaye, Gendall, and Strober, 1998). Dieting may also promote binge eating due to the body's inherent tendency to defend a set point in terms of body weight or body fat levels (Keesey, 1986). The transfer to a cognitive control over eating that occurs in the dieting process is also known to leave the individual vulnerable to disinhibited eating due to the all-or-nothing mindset (Brownell,

1991; Brownell and Rodin, 1994; French and Jeffery, 1994; Polivy and Herman, 1985). Finally, the appeal of "forbidden" foods may increase due to nutritional preference conditioning, which may lead to binge-eating (Wilson, 2002).

Eating pathology may develop from apparently 'normal' attempts at dieting, or dieting behaviors (Beaumont, 2002). Prospective studies of dieting have found that High School girls defined as severe dieters were 18 times more likely to develop an eating disorder within six months (Patton, 1988). Dietary restraint and eating pathology levels remained stable over three years in a longitudinal study of 118 women entering college (Cooley and Toray, 2001a).

In his meta-analysis of risk factors for disordered eating, Stice (2002a) concludes that dieting is not actually a risk factor for eating pathology, but that it "attenuates overeating tendencies" (p 836). This assumption was made as self-reported dieting was found to be a risk and maintenance factor for Bulimia Nervosa pathology; however experiments with manipulated caloric deprivation did not concur with this finding.

TRANSITION TO COLLEGE

One third of women who develop clinical eating disorders are reported to do so in college (Winzelberg et al., 2000). The college environment is one that may increase the risk of development of an eating disorder in those who already display risk factors (Compas et al., 1986; Striegel-Moore et al., 1986). It is suggested that the competitive focus of the university environment creates a desire to achieve in professional, personal and romantic arenas (Burkle, 1999; Klemchuck et al., 1990).

The effects of the transition to college were investigated by Vohs and colleagues (2001) in a longitudinal study, following 342 American female students from high school to college. The participants reported less dieting in their first year of college, and disordered eating behaviors remained stable. Although the women reported themselves to be heavier in college, and to have increased body dissatisfaction, this did not appear to result in actual behavioral change (Vohs, Heatherton et al., 2001). Cooley and Toray (2001b) also found disordered eating behavior to remain relatively stable throughout out the first year of college in American freshman women.

In order to study the college environment retrospectively, Heatherton and colleagues (1997) also conducted a longitudinal study assessing the dieting and eating disorder symptoms of college men and women while they were at university, and then 10 years later. They found that the percentage of women who could be classified as having some sort of eating problem declined from over 40 percent in college, to just over 15 percent 10 years later. The women were also significantly less likely to identify themselves as overweight, and less likely to report wanting to lose weight. In addition, there was a strong trend for less frequent dieting among the women (Heatherton, Mahamedi, Striepe, Field, and Keel, 1997). A converse relationship was found in men, with significantly more men reporting body image concerns, and an increased desire to lose weight, as well as significantly more men reporting that they were on a diet (Heatherton et al., 1997).

The authors suggested that the decline in dieting and disordered eating behavior in women may have been due to a reluctance of disclosure, and an increased tolerance for and acceptance of behaviors; so women would be less likely to self report them as being present.

However the main findings revealed that for women, leaving the college environment allows them to develop a greater sense of self, and to experience success independent of aesthetics and body weight. This in turn is said to decrease their inclination to diet and engage in disordered eating behaviors (Heatherton et al., 1997).

These studies suggest that the college environment may be a major influence in the initiation and perpetuation of disordered eating behaviors. There is also evidence to show that the effects of the college environment may vary, and that individuals in specific degree programs may be more susceptible to body image and eating problems.

DEGREE PROGRAM

In general, the research literature to date suggests that individuals in food and exercise related career paths have been observed to engage in disordered dieting and exercise behaviors to the same or higher extent than the general population (Barbarich, 2002; Kinzl, Traweger, Trefalt, Mangweth, and Biebl, 1999; O'Dea and Abraham, 2001; Palmquist-Fredenberg et al., 1996; Pope et al., 1984; Worobey and Schoenfeld, 1999). Increased attention to or an emphasis on body weight and shape for professional competence (either explicit or implicit), has been suggested to increase the use of disordered eating and exercise behaviors, and the risk of developing eating disorders (Dross and Silverman, 1979; Garner, Garfinkel, Schwartz, and Thompson, 1980; Schulken, Pinciaro, Sawyer, Jensen, and Hoban, 1997; Striegel-Moore et al., 1986).

Employment in the health and fitness industry is unique in that the knowledge and competence of staff is intentionally or subconsciously judged by their appearance. Studies have found an increased prevalence of disordered eating pathology and symptomatology among models, actors, and athletes (Dross and Silverman, 1979; Joseph, Wood, and Goldberg, 1982). Research tends to link this increased preoccupation with weight and shape to the perceived importance and emphasis of physical attractiveness in their environment (Connor-Greene, Striegel-Moore, and Cronan, 1994).

Other reasoning for the higher prevalence of disordered eating behaviors among individuals in food and exercise related career paths argue that, although they are exposed to similar socio-cultural pressures as other adults, their career path is highly involved with food, eating and weight control. As a preoccupation with food and exercise is known to be characteristic of individuals with eating disorders (Larson, 1989; Worobey and Schoenfeld, 1999); it has been suggested that this personal preoccupation with food and exercise may cause individuals to gravitate towards careers that are food and exercise related (Crockett and Littrell, 1985; Reinstein et al., 1992; Sours, 1980). This is especially evident in a study of Austrian dietitians, where 14 percent of participants reported that they had chosen their career path partly due to their own preoccupation with food and exercise (Kinzl et al., 1999).

Professionals in careers closely linked to eating disorders are known to be those who report personal or family experience with these eating problems. The personal lifetime prevalence of eating disorders among eating disorder treatment professionals has been self reported from 27.3 percent to 31 percent (Barbarich, 2002; Bloomgarden, Gerstein, and Moss, 2003). This proportion reflects prevalence significantly higher than that of the general population, which is estimated at between 0.5 and three percent (Drenowski et al., 1994;

Fairburn and Beglin, 1990). These findings were accompanied by evidence that not all professionals had received treatment, and that 24 percent had experienced a relapse after entering the eating disorder field (Barbarich, 2002).

Dietetics majors are another population who exhibit concerning levels of disordered eating pathology, behaviors and symptoms (Crockett and Littrell, 1985; Drake, 1989; Johnston and Christopher, 1991; Joseph et al., 1982; Kinzl et al., 1999; McArthur and Howard, 2001; Palmquist- Fredenberg et al., 1996; Reinstein et al., 1992; Worobey and Schoenfeld, 1999). Approximately 24 percent of dietetics majors in the USA (Drake, 1989) and 25 percent in Austria (Drake, 1989; Kinzl et al., 1999) exhibit characteristics of Anorexia Nervosa. Dangerous weight loss techniques such as fasting, vomiting, laxatives and skipping meals were also reported by trainee dietitians, even though they would not recommend these techniques to clients, and some dietitians reported that they continued to use the techniques even though they did not find them useful (McArthur and Howard, 2001).

Professionals in nutrition, health, and fitness related careers are therefore subjected to additional pressures to achieve the coveted lean, muscular appearance. In order to adhere to this idealistic and often unattainable goal, extreme forms of weight control may be employed. This may lead them to engage in exercise behaviors and other dangerous weight loss techniques to achieve this goal (Brownell, Rodin, and Wilmore, 1992; Phillips and Drummond, 2001).

Physical education teachers are presumed and expected to be slim, physically fit, and to embody the lean, muscular ideal body shape (Clark, Blair, and Culan, 1988; Davis, 1999; Jenkins and Olsen, 1994; Kirk and Tinning, 1994; Melville and Cardinal, 1997; Melville and Maddalozzo, 1988). The only major study of trainee home economics and physical education teachers, found the females use excessive exercise (29 percent), starvation (19 percent), inducing vomiting (22 percent), laxatives (19 percent) and smoking (7 percent) to control their weight (O'Dea and Abraham, 2001). Among male teachers, 29 percent desired weight gain to "bulk up" their muscles and reported disordered eating behaviors such as excessive exercise (22 percent), starvation (9 percent) and smoking (6 percent) for weight control (O'Dea and Abraham, 2001).

Professionals in nutrition, health, and fitness related careers; as well as college students training to fulfill these positions have been found to have a high prevalence of disordered eating. The susceptibility of professionals involved in the prevention and treatment of eating disorders and obesity to eating and weight issues themselves may present serious issues in terms of their own health. Furthermore, attitudes and behaviors may be inadvertently modeled or intentionally transferred to students, patients or clients (O'Dea, 2000; Rutz, 1993). It may then be the responsibility of tertiary training programs to recognize the potential vulnerability of these students, and to include screening and interventions during these courses.

COLLEGE ATHLETES

College athletes have a comparable or higher prevalence of eating disorders than non-athlete college students and the general population, and are therefore described as being at an increased risk (Garner and Garfinkel, 1980; Johnson, Powers, and Dick, 1999; Sundgot-Borgen, 1993; Thompson and Sherman, 1993). College athletes are thought to be susceptible as they are subjected to both the general sociocultural pressure to conform to an ideal body shape; and the specific pressure to achieve an ideal body for performance reasons (Striegel-Moore et al., 1986). This may be due to intrinsic motivation from within, or external pressure from coaches or trainers. Athletes are also known to possess personality characteristics such as perfectionism, competitiveness and narcissism that are common to individuals with eating disorders (Brownell et al., 1992; Byrne and McLean, 2001; Davis, 1992; Davis and Scott-Robertson, 2000; Striegel-Moore et al., 1990). Furthermore, it has been suggested that athletes may be able to rationalize their disordered eating behaviors according to the norms and expectations that exist in their athletic community, for example, that it is normal for gymnasts and wrestlers to use starvation in order to maintain a low body weight (Thompson and Sherman, 1993).

As we have outlined earlier in this chapter, the prevalence of body dissatisfaction and disordered eating behaviors varies according to methodological procedure, and this methodological limitation also extends to eating disorder research among college athletes. Using strict criteria, Johnson and colleagues (1999) conducted a large prevalence study of 1445 National Collegiate Athletic Association [NCAA] athletes. Only 1.1 percent of females were diagnosed with clinical Bulimia nervosa (using DSM IV criteria) with no other diagnoses being made (Johnson et al., 1999).

Although this clinical prevalence was found to be quite low, a far higher prevalence rate was found for sub-clinical eating problems. Johnson and colleagues reported that 13 percent of the NCAA athletes could be diagnosed with a clinically significant eating disorder; and that 34.7 percent of females and 9.5 percent of males could be considered at risk for Anorexia Nervosa; and 38 percent of females and 38 percent of males for Bulimia Nervosa according to their scores on relevant EDI-2 scales. These estimates of athletes at risk are significantly higher than those of the non-athlete college population (Kjelsas and Augestad, 2004; Kurth et al., 1995; Mintz and Betz, 1988) as outlined earlier in this chapter. In terms of disordered eating behaviors, 22.7 percent of females and 11.9 percent of males met full binge eating criteria; while 23.9 percent of females and 5.9 percent of males reported ever vomiting; and 1.7 percent of females and 5 percent of males reported ever using laxatives (Johnson et al., 1999). Similarly, in a study of 182 female university athletes across 10 different sports, 32 percent were found to be currently using at least one unhealthy method of weight control (Rosen, McKeag, Hough, and Curly, 1986).

A meta-analysis of female college athletes found the difference between the EDI and EAT scores of athletes and non athletes to be statistically significant. Controlled studies comparing college dancers with other students have also reported significant differences between the groups (Evers, 1987; Garner and Garfinkel, 1980; Joseph et al., 1982). Evers (1987) reported that 33.3 percent of university dancers and 13.8 percent of the control group scored in the anorexic range on the EAT, and that this difference was statistically significant. Garner and Garfinkel (1980) concluded that Anorexia Nervosa and excessive dietary concerns were over represented among dance students compared to other university students. Joseph, Wood and Goldberg found that 27 percent of dance and 20 percent of drama students scored in the anorexic range on the EAT; and were at a higher risk than English (eight percent) and physical education (seven percent) students. However, these results must be observed with caution, as the methodology of these studies, including control group selection, using athletes of varying discipline and level and small sample sizes, were clearly limited.

Despite problems with measurement, participation in certain collegiate sports are known to be more susceptible to disordered eating and exercise problems; with risk being dependent on the level of competition and type of sport (Brownell et al., 1992; Smolak, Murnen, and Ruble, 2000). Research has yet to conclusively determine whether it is the recreational (Hopkinson and Lock, 2004), or elite (Byrne and McLean, 2002; Sundgot-Borgen, 1993) athletes who are at a greater risk of developing an eating disorder. Athletes who perceive themselves to be at increased pressure to be thin have been found to exhibit a higher occurrence of eating problems (Byrne and McLean, 2002). Athletes in sports with a weight requirement or an aesthetic component are also reported to be at a greater risk of developing full clinical eating disorders (Byrne and McLean, 2002; Petrie, 1996; Picard, 1999; Smolak et al., 2000). Therefore, Byrne and McLean (2002) concluded that being an athlete doesn't necessarily put you at risk of developing an eating disorder, but being involved in an aesthetic, thin build or weight classified sport does.

Athletes competing in sports with either an aesthetic component or weight classifications are assumed to be more susceptible to disordered eating and exercise behaviors due to the norms and expectations of their sport. Sports with an aesthetic component, such as gymnastics, dance, and diving require an individual to conform to very specific appearance in order to succeed (Smolak et al., 2000). Therefore, in order to do well, athletes will use any method to gain or maintain that figure. Athletes in sports that use weight classifications, such as rowing, boxing and wrestling are able to gain a competitive advantage by participating in the lowest possible weight class (Kiningham and Gorenflo, 2001). Therefore there is intense pressure to "cut" a relatively large amount of weight in a small time (Kiningham and Gorenflo, 2001). In addition to the internal pressures of the sport, there is also indirect pressure from judges, coaches and parents to obtain a certain body weight to compete in a weight class, or appeal aesthetically.

Recent reports have begun to question whether athletes suffer the true psychopathology of eating disorders, or that they display the behavioral characteristics of disordered eating behaviors in order to achieve performance goals (Byrne and McLean, 2002). For example, many athletes in sports with weight criteria report engaging in dangerous weight loss behaviors (such as severe caloric restriction, fasting, saunas and dehydration) only when they are in season (Anderson, Barlett, Morgan, and Brownell, 1995). Davis and Robertson (2002) also found that although female Anorexia Nervosa patients and male competitive bodybuilders shared higher scores of obsessive, perfectionist, anhedonic and narcissistic personality traits; the bodybuilders reported very positive perceptions of their self worth and body image, whereas the women with eating disorders did not. Byrne and McLean (2002) also found that athletes had a higher drive for thinness than non-athletes, but that they did not differ in terms of body dissatisfaction. The authors suggested that this might be due to the fact that these athletes wish to control their weight for performance reasons, yet they still realize that they are indeed thinner than others in the population; and therefore do not necessarily dislike their appearance. Although anecdotal and empirical reports of disordered eating and exercise behaviors among athletes suggest that they are at risk; it may also be possible that athletes are using disordered eating behaviors in order to succeed, without experiencing the psychological correlates.

To summarize, prevalence statistics show that college athletes are engaging in disordered eating and exercise behaviors to the same, or higher level than other university students. It has been suggested that they may assess the body in terms of athleticism rather than aesthetics, and be using disordered eating behaviors to achieve their sporting goals (Smolak et al., 2000). Regardless of intention, individuals will experience physical consequences of disordered eating; and it is a possibility that they may develop a clinical eating disorder. It is important for coaches, trainers and athletes to be aware of healthy weight control behaviors; and the consequences of disordered eating and exercise.

PERSONALITY TRAITS

Personality variables are considered to be important in the development of disordered eating behaviors. Prospective studies have highlighted the fact that personality factors may play a causal role, but they may also interact with other variables to increase risk (Cooley and Toray, 2001b; Vohs, Bardone, Joiner, Abrahmson, and Heatherton, 1999). The caliber of students that are inclined to go on to university tend to be high achievers. College students are also known to be under internal and external pressure to excel academically and socially (Burkle, 1999; Klemchuck et al., 1990). It is therefore not surprising then, that university students would exhibit perfectionism.

Perfectionism and eating disorders are known to be related (Franco-Paradedes, Mancilla-Diaz, Vazquez-Arevalo, Lopez-Aguilar, and Alvarez-Rayon, 2005; Lilenfeld et al., 2000). In his meta-analysis of risk factors for disordered eating, Stice (2002a) reported that perfectionism was a risk factor for eating disorder pathology and maintenance. It has been reported that perfectionism predicts (Bulik et al., 2003) and is a maintenance factor for Bulimia Nervosa (Fairburn, 1997); and eating disorder symptomatology (Holsten and Cashwell, 2000). Other studies report that the correlation between perfectionism and eating disorders is stronger for Anorexia Nervosa than Bulimia Nervosa (Halmi et al., 2000); and that perfectionism is necessary for the development of Anorexia Nervosa (Slade, 1982) . In addition, some authors have specified that perfectionism only predicts eating disorders when individuals perceive themselves as overweight (Joiner, Heatherton, Rudd, and Schmidt, 1997).

A unique Italian study investigated the effect of academic stress on body dissatisfaction and drive for thinness (Ruggiero, Levi, Ciuna, and Sassaroli, 2003). Participants (42 female high school students) were given the EDI and a specialized measure of perfectionism on a normal day, on the day of an exam, and on the day the examination results would be returned to them. It was found that body dissatisfaction was associated with perfectionism on all three occasions, but that drive for thinness was only associated with perfectionism on the day that the students received their results. This suggests that anticipating academic failure may prompt disordered eating in individuals with a perfectionistic personality (McGee, Hewitt, Sherry, Parkin, and Flett, 2005; Ruggiero et al., 2003).

Eating disorders are also known to be ineffective coping mechanisms used to manage stressful situations and uncomfortable emotions. Use of certain maladaptive coping strategies to deal with stress is said to contribute to the onset or progression of eating pathology (Ball and Lee, 2002). Ball and Lee (2002) found that in the short term, high EDI scores were associated with perceived stress, coping and disordered eating. However, their longitudinal study revealed that there was an association between disordered eating, stress and coping over time, but that it was in the opposite direction to what was expected; disordered eating predicted later stress (Ball and Lee, 2002).

COLLEGE STUDENTS WHO ARE MEMBERS OF SORORITIES

Sorority women have been anecdotally and empirically observed to have a preoccupation with their appearance and to engage in disordered eating (Alexander, 1998; Allison and Park, 2004; Schulken et al., 1997). Research has yet to report whether sorority women develop these problems prior to, or as a result of being a part of a sorority. Regardless of causation, this may represent a group of women who are particularly susceptible to disordered eating; and may also be easily targeted for interventions.

The majority of controlled prevalence studies report a trend towards (Alexander, 1998; Allison and Park, 2004) or statistically significant (Schulken et al., 1997) difference in prevalence, with a greater proportion of sorority women experiencing body dissatisfaction and disordered eating problems. In a study of 627 sorority women, those in sororities had significantly higher scores on drive for thinness and body dissatisfaction than the non-sorority college women in five previous studies (Schulken et al., 1997). Alexander (1998) studied 239 college women, 103 of whom were in sororities. A trend towards greater reported eating disorders and disordered eating behaviors on the EDI, BULIT and EAT among sorority women was identified; but the results were not statistically significant (Alexander, 1998). Meilman, Von Hippel and Galor (1991) found that a significantly higher percentage of the 229 college women studied who purged belonged to a sorority. Of the 28 participants who reported purging behaviors, 72.2 percent were sorority members (Meilman, von Hippel, and Galor, 1991). In addition, 80 percent of the 21 participants who were classified as high frequency purgers (at least four times per month) belonged to a sorority (Meilman et al., 1991).

Palmquist-Fredenberg and colleagues (1996) reported that there were no statistically significant differences in EAT scores between the five subgroups used, including dietetics and home economics majors and athletes (Palmquist-Fredenberg et al., 1996). However these results should be interpreted with caution due to low numbers in each subgroup (n = 30-35).

Although it has been reported that women who belong to sororities are more attractive, have a higher family income, higher use of alcohol, and are more willing to try and fit in at parties (Atlas and Morier, 1994); other studies have found there is no significant difference in eating disorders between college women who join or do not join a sorority in their first year (Allison and Park, 2004). In a longitudinal study of 49 sorority and 156 psychology women, Allison and Park (2004) measured the body image, weight control and disordered eating behaviors in the first, second and third year of university. They found that results were similar when the women entered college, but that over time, non-sorority women's scores on the EDI decreased; while sorority women remained much the same. Therefore, there was a significant difference on EDI scores of body dissatisfaction, bulimia and drive for thinness between sorority and non-sorority women at time 3 (third year at college). It was found that sorority women gained an average of three pounds during that time. (Allison and Park, 2004).

Sorority women are believed to be particularly susceptible to body dissatisfaction and disordered eating due to the norms and pressures of the social group. As sorority women live and socialize together, peers can have a great effect on the thoughts and actions of each other; and sorority membership can become an important part of the college woman's identity (Allison and Park, 2004). Social pressure among groups such as dance, sorority or cheerleading sports is said to develop social norms in relation to dieting, and weight control (Festinger, 1954). Crandall (1988) argues that "social pressures in friendship groups are important mechanisms by which binge eating is acquired and spread" (p590). So that if binge eating, dieting or exercise are important to a social group, then over time, it's member's beliefs tend to unite, leading to the adoption of dieting and disordered eating by some members (Crandall, 1988). In order to demonstrate this theory, Crandall studied sorority women's social groups and disordered eating behaviors. By the end of the year, members with friends who were binge eaters adopted this behavior to the same extent; and that as the sorority group grew to be closer, so did the levels of their binge eating.

This powerful example of the extent of social pressures and modeling of disordered eating behavior demonstrates the importance of eating disorder prevention and interventions in social situations similar to sororities; in order to target women at risk.

PREVENTION IN THE COLLEGE SETTING

College students are known to be at risk for body dissatisfaction and disordered eating behaviors, due to the developmental, environmental and social transitions they are undertaking and the significance of this time period in developing established lifestyle behaviors. It is therefore important that prevention initiatives are implemented in the university setting.

There are several types of prevention initiatives. Primary prevention is where individuals in the target population do not necessarily show signs or symptoms of a problem. This type of prevention is designed to stop or delay the onset of the problem behavior. Secondary prevention of eating disorders is targeted toward those who are at risk of but have not yet developed an eating disorder. The target group may be engaging in disordered eating behaviors. Finally, tertiary prevention is aimed at those who have been treated for an eating disorder, in order to prevent a relapse. For the purposes of this review, all prevention initiatives have been included. The majority could be classified as primary or secondary prevention, however in most cases this has not been specified in the published articles.

In general, prevention programs in the college setting have been limited by small sample sizes that are either targeted or self selected which reduces the ability to generalize results to the whole college population, or the general, non-college community. In addition, many studies did not include a true control group. Finally, there has been a paucity of longitudinal studies that are methodologically sound, with the follow-up period being brief in the majority of studies.

A summary of all controlled, college-based body image and disordered eating interventions over the past 20 years is presented in Table 2. In order to thoroughly examine the literature to date, all relevant studies have been included. The table includes all published intervention reports, including those that were clinically-based trials and studies that were non-randomized.

Table 2. Chronological review of body image and disordered eating interventions with college students

Authors	Sample	Description of program	Results	Comments/ limitations
(Butters and Cash, 1987)	31 female undergraduates Mean age= 21.3 (SD= 5.0)	Participants were randomly assigned to a Cognitive Behavioral Therapy [CBT] program (n=15), or a wait list control group (n = 16). CBT intervention consisted of six, one-hour individual counseling sessions that applied CBT techniques to body dissatisfaction [BD]	- CBT intervention significantly improved body dissatisfaction [BD] and negative affect at post test	- Small numbers severely limits generalizability - No follow up
(Dworkin and Kerr, 1987)	79 college women experiencing body image problems Mean age not available Most were education majors	Participants were randomly divided into a cognitive therapy (CT), cognitive-behavioral therapy (CBT), or reflective therapy (RT) group for three 30-minute individual counseling sessions; or to the wait list control (WL). - CT- Aimed to change automatic negative thoughts to positive ones. - CBT- CT with the addition of behavioral exercises eg. Fantasy - RT-Explored feelings and beliefs about body image at various life stages	All 3 therapies were more effective than the control - CT, CBT and RT able to improve body image and self esteem - CT most effective in improving body image	- Self-referred participants - Authors suggested that the unexpected results of CT being more effective than CBT may be due to fantasy exercise which included participants imagining themselves getting larger. Authors caution about the content of fantasy exercises - No follow up
(Rosen, Saltzberg, and Srebnik, 1989)	23 female undergraduates with body image concerns Mean age = 19.0 (SD= 1.15)	Targeted body image improvement program using CBT (Butters and Cash, 1987) in small groups for 6 sessions. "Minimal treatment" control program of the same length and duration, and with similar content but without CBT.	CBT achieved clinically and statistically significant reduction in body size overestimation and BD	- Very small numbers in intervention (n = 13) - Inadequate control condition
(Wiese, Wilson, Jones, and Neises, 1992)	75 male (n =54) and female (n =21) undergraduate medical students Mean age = 23.7 years (SD = 2.1)	All participants were enrolled in "Communication and Interviewing", a required first- year course. They were randomly assigned to a single session, 2 hour educational intervention aimed at decreasing negative attitudes towards overweight and obesity (n =32) or to the control group (n = 43).	- Intervention group achieved statistically significant change on six out of eight measures of attitudes towards obesity - Effects still present at one year follow up.	- Lack of standardized measures of attitudes as questionnaires were developed specifically for the study. - Possibility of a Hawthorne effect due to participants realizing the intent of the intervention

Table 2. Chronological review of body image and disordered eating interventions with college students (cont.)

(Mann et al., 1997)	113 freshman females Mean age = 17.9 years	Half of the participants attended a universal intervention aimed at both the primary and secondary prevention of eating disorders in a single (90 minute), didactic, psycho-educational presentation in groups of 10-20. Intervention was presented by two students who had histories of disordered eating. Content included information about eating disorders and personal stories about experiences with eating disorders.	- No effects for BD or disordered eating behaviors at post-test or 1-month or 3-month follow-up - Intervention participants reported more symptoms of eating disorders at post-test	- The program was deemed unsuccessful as primary or secondary prevention, - The authors conclude that primary and secondary prevention of eating disorders cannot be combined in a universal program; and that this approach may inadvertently encourage the behaviors they are trying to prevent.
(Franko, 1998)	23 female college students. Recruited to attend an "Introductory workshop about eating habits".	Participants were assigned to either eight, 90 minute sessions of a psycho educational prevention program (n = 12) which included didactic presentations, group discussion and exercises about the thin ideal, healthy and dysfunctional attitudes and behaviors; or to the assessment only control group (n = 11) according to convenience and availability.	- Significant improvement in body image - No effects for disordered eating behaviors	- $10 payment for survey completion - Very small sample size - Non randomized assignment of groups - Although two males registered for the study, they were turned away due to low numbers.
(Rabak-Wagener, Eickhoff-Shemek, and Kelly-Vance, 1998)	105 male and female undergraduate students who elected to take a "healthful living" class Mean age not available	Intervention group (n = 60) received a psycho educational media literacy program aiming to improve body image attitudes and behaviors. Four, 1 ½ hour, consecutive weekly classes included: Video presentation "Slim hopes", fashion advertisement critique, construction of magazine collages and discussion of stereotypes of thin ideal promoted by the media.	- Intervention group women improved significantly in their overall perceptions of body image. - No significant changes in behaviors - In men there was no change	- Authors concluded that this intervention was more effective with the women than the men - Although males were included in the intervention, there was no focus on the muscular ideal, and the video presentation was specifically designed to target women.

Table 2. Chronological review of body image and disordered eating interventions with college students (cont.)

(Winzelberg et al., 1998)	57 undergraduate female, recruited to participate through on -campus advertisement. Mean age not available	Participants were randomly assigned to either the "student bodies" program (n= 27); an online psycho-educational eating disorder prevention program that includes audio and video presentations about eating disorders, healthy weight regulation, and nutrition. Participants also communicated through email support groups. The other participants formed the wait-list control group (n = 30).	- There was a Significant improvement in body image by intervention group participants - No other significant differences on Eating Disorder Inventory [EDI] or Eating Disorder Examination-Q [EDE-Q]	- Participants were paid $10 for their involvement in the study - Very few (53%) of participants completed the whole program. They did some parts of the online program, but not others - 21% attrition rate may indicate lack of motivation for self-paced prevention programs
(Martz and Bazzini, 1999)	Study one: 114 females in general psychology courses who signed up for a "healthy habits study". Mean age = 19 Study Two: 77 female college students Mean age = 19	Participants were randomly assigned to intervention or control groups. Study one: Intervention group (n = 73) participants attended a one- hour, didactic psycho-educational information session addressing body image, eating disorders and healthful eating and exercise. Study Two: Intervention identical to study one, but with the addition of an imagery exercise.	- Study One Intervention had no significant effects for thin ideal internalization, body dissatisfaction, dieting at evaluation or one-month follow-up. - Study two was not found to have any stronger intervention effects than the previous study	- Self Selection of participants may have affected results - Authors conclude that one session of an intervention program may be insufficient to achieve attitudinal and behavioral change
(Celio et al., 2000)	76 college women recruited for study that was advertised to help women with body image concerns. Mean age = 19.6 (SD= 2.2)	Participants were randomly assigned to either "Student Bodies"(n=27), an internet- delivered program described earlier in this review (Winzelberg et al., 1998); the "Body Traps" program (Springer, Winzelberg, Perkins, and Taylor, 1999) (n = 25) a classroom delivered program using a purely educational approach that utilized lecture and group discussions; with no emphasis on participant's personal change; or to a wait-list control group (n = 24).	Student bodies: Significant reduction in BD and disordered eating attitudes and behaviors compared to control - Results remained and were stronger at follow up. - Significantly higher effect on high risk participants Body traps: No significant results compared to the control group.	-Higher compliance (71% of participants completed the entire program) than the original study program) was noted, due to changes made to update the Student Bodies software - Body Traps participants' compliance rate was lower, with statistically higher number of students dropping out of the Body Traps program

Table 2. Chronological review of body image and disordered eating interventions with college students (cont.)

(Stice, Mazotti et al., 2000)	30 female undergraduate students with elevated body image concerns. Mean age not available.	The first ten participants to respond were allocated to the thin-ideal dissonance program, while the remaining 20 made up the control group. The intervention consisted of one hour small group sessions, conducted each week for three weeks. The intervention included group discussion and role play exercises designed for participants to counter the thin-ideal	- Statistically significant decreases in thin- ideal internalization that led to a subsequent decline in BD, dieting and bulimic symptoms. - Decreases in thin-ideal internalization, BD and dieting were still significant at one-month follow-up.	- Subjects were paid $10 for questionnaire completion - Very small number in intervention program (N = 10) - Non-randomized group allocation
(Winzelberg et al., 2000)	60 female undergraduates with a desire to improve body image. Mean age not available.	Participants were randomly assigned to the intervention group (n = 31) who participated in the "Student Bodies" program, which has been previously described (Celio et al., 2000; Winzelberg et al., 1998); or to the control condition (n = 29).	- No significant results at post-intervention - Significant differences were found at follow-up between intervention and control groups for BD and Drive for thinness.	- Participants were paid $25 for their involvement in the study
(Irving and Berel, 2001)	110 female college students. Mean age = 18.93 (SD= 2.07)	Participants were randomly assigned to one 45 minute session of : - ExML- An externally oriented media literacy intervention (n = 27). "Slim Hopes" video; discussion and class exercises focusing on critical analysis of advertising and media; and activism against the thin ideal at a personal, interpersonal and societal level. - InML- Internally oriented media literacy intervention (n = 31). "Slim Hopes" video, psycho education and CBT for body image distortion. - VO- Video only intervention (n = 28). "Slim Hopes" video presentation. - No-intervention control (n = 24) received "About Face" Postcards	- ExML, InML and VO interventions were found to have similar effects in terms of increasing critical appraisal of thin-ideal images presented in the media - No intervention had significant effects on body dissatisfaction - InML did not achieve a reduction in BD or reduction of the thin ideal, even though it was specifically designed to impact these variables.	- Authors mention that the length of intervention was quite brief compared to the cumulative impact of many years of media exposure
(Nicolino, Martz, and Curtin, 2001)	85 college women in undergraduate psychology courses. Mean age = 18.9 years (SD= 2.5)	Participants were randomly assigned to either the control (n=40) or the intervention group (n = 45); who received a two-hour, CBT body image therapy session in small groups.	- No significant effects	- Authors suggest that 'normal' student population used may have had little scope for improvement on baseline measures; or the participants may not have found the program to be relevant.

Table 2. Chronological review of body image and disordered eating interventions with college students (cont.)

Citation	Sample	Intervention	Results	Notes
(Zabinski et al., 2001)	62 college women in an introductory psychology course with elevated BD. Mean age= 19.3 (SD= 1.4)	Participants were randomly assigned to either the intervention group (n = 31) who received the "Student Bodies" program, described earlier (Winzelberg et al., 1998) and were contacted on a weekly basis to remind them of assignments to be completed. Others assigned to wait-list control group (n = 31).	Control and intervention groups decreased BD and improved disordered eating behaviors at post-test. With no significant differences between intervention and control.	-Authors attribute the increase by both groups to the dynamic nature of body image; the small sample sizes; and the variability of what is considered to be "high risk".
(Mutterperl and Sanderson, 2002)	107 first year university females. Mean age = 18.08 (SD = 0.57)	Participants were randomly assigned to read either the norm misperception brochure aimed at revealing the truth about how much college women eat and exercise in order to reduce misconceptions about the perceived norms and adherence to high standards and levels of eating and exercise behavior; or the general healthy behavior control brochure.	-Participants reported the healthy behaviours brochure to be significantly more personally relevant - No significant effects of brochure condition on thin ideal internalization or disordered eating.	- Participants were paid $10 for their participation in the study.
(Stice and Ragan, 2002)	66 female college students, Mean age not available	Participants who had enrolled in a class called "eating disorders" became the intervention group (n = 17). This group met twice weekly for 1 ½ hours over the 15 week semester for didactic presentations and group discussion about eating disorder pathology, etiology and epidemiology; as well as options for prevention and treatment Up to three control participants (enrolled in other upper-division psychology courses) were matched to each intervention participant to form the control group (n = 49).	- Intervention participants showed significant decreases in thin-ideal internalization, eating disorder symptoms, BD and dieting	- Intervention group reported significantly greater dieting and eating disorder symptoms at pre-test. May have enrolled in course seeking treatment. - Small sample size limits generalizability and statistical power.
(Matusek, Wendt, and Wiseman, 2004)	84 undergraduate college women with elevated body image concerns. Mean age = 19.86 (SD= 1.55)	Participants were randomly assigned to a thin-ideal, dissonance based [DTI; n = 26]; psycho educational, healthy behavior [HB; n = 24] workshop or wait-list control group [WL, n = 34]; as a replication of (Stice et al., 2001).	- Significant improvement in thin-ideal internalization for DTI and HB groups - Significant improvement in disordered eating behaviors for DTI. -No significant effects: drive for thinnessm BD or self esteem in DTI or HB.	Participants in the DTI condition did not experience greater improvement than the HB group on the dependent variables

The findings presented in Table 2 provide an overview of controlled body image and eating disorder prevention programs conducted among college students. It may be observed that 89 percent of these programs were restricted to women, and that 40 percent were conducted among self-selected participants, who responded to advertisements for women with body image concerns. Of the programs that did include males, one focused on decreasing negative attitudes toward overweight; and the other aimed to improve body image attitudes and behaviors through a psycho-educational, media literacy intervention that did not report any significant effects among the males (Rabak-Wagener et al., 1998). The lack of intervention effects among males is likely to be due to the program being designed for women, and although it included males, it was not adapted to their specific body image concerns.

Early prevention programs in the college setting tended to use single lecture sessions providing information about eating disorders, including symptoms and medical complications in an attempt to motivate those with eating disorders to seek treatment (Koszewski, Newell, and Higgins, 1990). These initiatives have been consistently unsuccessful, and some are thought to potentially promote disordered eating (Mann et al., 1997); yet knowledge based programs remain the most popular method of "prevention". Even longer attempts incorporating didactic, cognitive behavioral or psycho educational methods of prevention have reported very little change, either at a universal (Becker, Franko, Nussbaum, and Herzog, 2004; Irving and Berel, 2001) or targeted (Huon, 1994; Rosen et al., 1989) level.

Recent success in prevention among college students and adolescents has been achieved using self-esteem and dissonance based approaches. These will now be briefly discussed

DISSONANCE BASED APPROACHES

Cognitive Dissonance Theory (Festinger, 1957) operates on the notion that when there is an inconsistency or dissonance between an individual's beliefs and behaviors, the resulting psychological discomfort will motivate them to change their attitude or behaviors in order to reduce this inconsistency (Festinger, 1957; Stice, Mazotti et al., 2000). This approach has been used successfully in influencing health behaviors such as smoking cessation (Killen, 1985) and condom use (Stone, Aronson, Crain, Winslow, and Fried, 1994). Dissonance programs have also targeted the internalization of the thin female ideal among young women in order to reduce body dissatisfaction, and disordered eating practices (Green, Scott, Diyankova, Gasser, and Pederson, 2005; Matusek et al., 2004; Stice et al., 2001; Stice, Mazotti et al., 2000; Stice, Trost, and Chase, 2003).

The socio-cultural model of eating pathology proposes that social pressure to be thin promotes an internalization of the thin ideal, which may lead individuals to become dissatisfied with their own body. Targeting the internalization of the thin ideal has been theorized (Graff Low et al., 2003; Striegel-Moore et al., 1986) and shown (Stice et al., 2001; Stice, Mazotti et al., 2000) to reduce body dissatisfaction, dieting and disordered eating behaviors among female college students. Thin-ideal dissonance interventions for the prevention of eating disorders posit that by providing appropriate information and stimuli, participants will voluntarily take a stance against the thin –ideal, which will induce cognitive dissonance (Stice, Hayward, Cameron, Killen, and Taylor, 2000). Therefore, in order to reduce the cognitive distress induced by this dissonance, participants will have to alter their own body dissatisfaction, weight control, and disordered eating attitudes and behaviors in order to reduce the discrepancy between their thoughts and actions (Stice, Hayward et al., 2000).

This thin-ideal eating disorder prevention approach has demonstrated consistent positive results and evaluation among adolescent and young women. The first was a non-controlled study among 30 college women with elevated body concerns who attended three thin-ideal dissonance-based sessions (Stice, Mazotti et al., 2000). This same randomized, controlled methodological approach and dissonance based or healthy weight intervention has since been conducted in two separate studies of 148, 13-18 year old females with elevated body concerns in high schools and universities (Stice et al., 2003). Stice's thin- ideal dissonance program has achieved a reduction in thin ideal internalization and consequent decline in body dissatisfaction, dietary restraint, negative effect and bulimic symptomatology in young women at post-test and one –month followup (Stice et al., 2001; Stice, Hayward et al., 2000).

A similar dissonance-based approach to prevention was implemented by Matusek and colleagues (2004) among 84 college women with body image concerns. These women were assigned to either a single session thin-ideal dissonance based workshop, a single session healthy weight control behavior workshop that used a psycho-educational approach, or to a wait list control group. Results reported a significant reduction in body dissatisfaction, thin ideal internalization and improved eating behaviors for both intervention groups from baseline to follow-up. The thin- ideal dissonance group rated the session more highly than the women in the healthy behavior intervention (Matusek et al., 2004).

The most recent empirical investigation of a dissonance approach to eating disorder prevention and intervention was conducted by Green and colleagues (2005). In this study, 155 randomly selected college women enrolled in psychology courses were invited to participate. Participants were classified as symptomatic (n=78) or asymptomatic (n=77) according to their responses to a self-reported eating disorder questionnaire. Participants were then assigned to two sessions of a low level dissonance intervention, a high level dissonance intervention (both two hours in duration) or a no-treatment control. Although the content of both programs was the same, the high level dissonance group were involved in activities and discussion that they perceived to be voluntary, and that required high effort expenditure and public expression of their attitudes in accordance with known requirements for high levels of dissonance (Aronson and Mills, 1959; Axsom and Cooper, 1985; Green et al., 2005; Thibodeau and Aronson, 1992; Wicklund and Brehm, 1976). The low dissonance intervention required a low level of effort expenditure and participants were led to believe that their participation was less voluntary, and that their attitudes were confidential (Green et al., 2005).

Results of this study are limited by the absence of baseline measurements. In contrast to results of previous dissonance interventions (Matusek et al., 2004; Stice et al., 2001; Stice, Mazotti et al., 2000), neither the high or low dissonance program was reported to be superior to the no-treatment control (Green et al., 2005). However, it was found that the high-level dissonance intervention achieved significantly greater reductions in EDE-Q scores than those in the low-level dissonance intervention at post-intervention and four week follow up (Green et al., 2005).

Thin-ideal dissonance based approaches have achieved consistent success in reducing thin-ideal internalization, body dissatisfaction, dieting and disordered eating behaviors among college women (Green et al., 2005; Matusek et al., 2004; Stice et al., 2001; Stice, Mazotti et al., 2000; Stice et al., 2003). The findings suggest that the dissonance approach would be similarly useful for preventing the muscular body ideal in males.

THE SELF ESTEEM APPROACH

The self-esteem approach, based on the self efficacy component of Bandura's Social Learning Theory (Bandura, 1986) postulates that in order to change behavior, it is necessary to first change the factors that contribute to these behaviors, including environmental influences such as the media; personal factors such as values and attitudes; and self perceptions, for example self concept, including body image. It is known that low self esteem is a risk factor for body dissatisfaction, dieting, eating disorders and obesity among men and women of all ages (Button, Loan, Davies, and Sonuga-Barke, 1997; Croll, Neumark-Sztainer, Story, and Ireland, 2002; Stice, 2002a) as well as being related to the broad spectrum of mental health (Mann, Hosman, Schaalma, and de Vries, 2004). Many authors have suggested that improving self esteem will reduce risk factors such as body dissatisfaction and internalization of the thin ideal that may lead to body image and weight problems (Bayer, 1984; Mann et al., 2004; Shisslak, Crago, and Neal, 1990). Prevention programs that have been based on the improvement of self esteem have achieved success in the reduction of body dissatisfaction, dietary restraint and disordered eating (McVey, Davis, Tweed, and Shaw, 2004; Neumark-Sztainer, Sherwood, Coller, and Hannan, 2000; Neumark-Sztainer, Sherwood, Coller, and Hannan, 2000; O'Dea, 1995; O'Dea and Abraham, 2000; Stewart, Carter, Drinkwater, Hainsworth, and Fairburn, 2001).

The Everybody's Different program (O'Dea, 1995) was the first self-esteem based prevention program that achieved a significant decline in beliefs and attitudes at post-intervention and follow-up among adolescent males and females (O'Dea and Abraham, 2000). This program promotes themes of promoting self acceptance, tolerance, diversity, uniqueness and rejection of cultural stereotypes in order to improve the self identity and self worth of adolescents, and therefore reduce the emphasis and importance on physical appearance (O'Dea, 1995). The program was designed so that both the student centered, cooperative, interactive teaching style and the content free curriculum and activities complemented each other to build student self-esteem. Promising results have been received by both this intervention, and others involving self esteem (McVey et al., 2004; McVey, Lieberman, Voorberg, Wardrope, and Blackmore, 2003; Neumark-Sztainer et al., 2000; Phelps, Sapia, Nathanson, and Nelson, 2000; Steiner-Adair et al., 2001; Stewart et al., 2001).

A CURRENT PREVENTION PROGRAM AIMED AT COLLEGE MALES AND FEMALES

In order to investigate the effectiveness of a self-esteem and dissonance based prevention program among college males and females, we designed a longitudinal, controlled intervention study. We hypothesize that increased self-esteem and dissonance aimed at reducing the slim and muscular ideals can enhance body image, reduce shape and weight concerns and reduce internalization of media stereotypes and of the thin and muscular ideals.

This in turn is expected to decrease the attitudes, beliefs and behaviors related to body dissatisfaction, weight control disordered eating and exercise disorders.

The participants in this program are trainee physical education teachers. Despite physical education teachers receiving increased training about nutrition, body image and disordered eating behaviors, it is unclear as to whether this is enough to prevent body dissatisfaction, and harmful weight control behaviors in those responsible for the prevention of dieting, body dissatisfaction and eating disorders in schools (O'Dea and Abraham, 2001).

Our current study involves a control and intervention group of third year trainee physical education teachers enrolled in their undergraduate coursework. Control participants will be given a pretest survey, and will then undergo the previous curriculum for that unit of study. A post test survey will be given at the end of the subject, and a follow up will be conducted four to six months later. Intervention participants will be given the pretest survey, and will then be given similar course content, but it will incorporate self esteem and dissonance-based activities that aim to reduce body dissatisfaction through a reduction in the internalization of the stereotypical thin and muscular ideals. In addition to the dissonance and self-esteem basis for the study, the methods of teaching used will take an interactive, student centered approach. This has been found to increase self esteem and body image in adolescents (O'Dea, 1995; O'Dea, 2004; O'Dea and Abraham, 2000), and has also been found to be more effective in achieving attitudinal and behavioral change relevant to body dissatisfaction, dieting and eating disorders (Becker, Smith, and Ciao, 2004; Franko and Orosan-Weine, 1998; Striegel-Moore and Steiner-Adair, 1998). A four to six month follow up will then be carried out to determine the effects of the intervention over time.

No study to date has tested the efficacy of this combined dissonance and self-esteem approach, and none have implemented this approach among both genders.

CONCLUSION

Male and Female college students are a population at risk of sub clinical body dissatisfaction, disordered eating and exercise behaviors, and clinical eating disorders. Due to the community setting and academic atmosphere of the college, prevention initiatives and interventions could be implemented. These should take a cognitive dissonance or self esteem based approach to the prevention of body image and eating problems in order to gain attitudinal and behavioral change.

REFERENCE LIST

Abraham, S. (2003). Dieting, body weight, body image and self esteem in young women: Doctors' dilemmas. *The Medical Journal of Australia, 178*(12), 607-611.

Abraham, S., and Lovell, N. H. (1999). Eating and Exercise Examination- Computerized. Melbourne: Ashwood Medical.

Abraham, S. F., Mira, M., Beumont, P. J. V., Sowerbutts, T., and Llewellyn-Jones, D. (1983). Eating behaviors among young women. *Medical Journal of Australia, 2*, 225-228.

Alexander, L. A. (1998). The prevalence of eating disorders and eating disordered behaviors in sororities. *College Student Journal, 32*, 66-75.

Allison, K. C., and Park, C. L. (2004a). A prospective study of disordered eating among sorority and non sorority women. *International Journal of Eating Disorders, 35*, 354-358.

American Psychiatric Association. (1994). *Diagnostic and Statistical Manual of Mental Disorders : DSM IV.* Washington, DC: American Psychiatric Association.

Anderson, A. E., Barlett, S. J., Morgan, G. D., and Brownell, K. D. (1995). Weight loss, psychological and nutritional patterns in competitive male body builders. *International Journal of Eating Disorders, 18*(1), 49-57.

Anderson, A. E., and Holman, J. E. (1997). Males with eating disorders: Challenges for treatment and research. *Psychopharmacology bulletin, 33*(3), 391-397.

Anderson, D. A., Martens, M., and Cimini, M. D. (2005). Do female college students who purge report greater alcohol use and negative alcohol-related consequences? *International Journal of Eating Disorders, 37*, 65-68.

Aronson, E., and Mills, J. (1959). The effect of severity of initiation on liking for a group. *Journal of Abnormal and Social Psychology, 59*, 177-181.

Atlas, G., and Morier, D. (1994). The sorority rush process: Self-selection, acceptance criteria, and the effect of rejection. *Journal of College Student Development, 35*, 346-353.

Axsom, D., and Cooper, J. (1985). Cognitive dissonance and psychotherapy: The role of effort justification in inducing weight loss. *Journal of Experimental Social Psychology, 21*, 149-160.

Ball, K., and Lee, C. (2002). Psychological stress, coping, and symptoms of disordered eating in a community sample of young Australian women. *International Journal of Eating Disorders, 31*, 71-81.

Bamber, D. J., Cockerill, I. M., Rodgers, S., and Carroll, D. (2003). Diagnostic criteria for exercise dependence in women. *British Journal of Sports Medicine, 37*(5), 393-400.

Bandura, A. (1986). *Social foundations of thought and action: A social cognitive theory.* Englewood Cliffs: Prentice Hall.

Barbarich, N. (2002). Lifetime prevalence of eating disorders among professionals in the field. *Eating Disorders, 10*, 305-312.

Bayer, A. E. (1984). Eating out of control: Anorexia and bulimia in adolescents. *Child Today, Nov/Dec*, 7-11.

Beaumont, P. J. V. (2002). Clinical Presentation of Anorexia Nervosa and Bulimia Nervosa. In C. Fairburn and K. D. Brownell (Eds.), *Eating Disorders and Obesity (p 209-243).* New York: The Guilford Press.

Becker, A., Franko, D., Nussbaum, K., and Herzog, D. (2004). Secondary prevention for eating disorders: the impact of education, screening, and referral in a college-based screening program. *International Journal of Eating Disorders, 36*, 157-162.

Becker, C. B., Smith, L. M., and Ciao, A. C. (2004). Eating disorder prevention in sororities. *Behavior therapy, in press.*

Beglin, S., and Fairburn, C. (1992). Women who choose not to participate in surveys on eating disorders. *International Journal of Eating Disorders, 12*, 113-116.

Bloomgarden, A., Gerstein, F., and Moss, C. (2003). The last word: A "recovered enough" therapist. *Eating Disorders, 11*, 163-167.

Braun, D. L., Sunday, S. R., Huang, A., and Halmi, K. A. (1999). More males seek treatment for eating disorders. *International Journal of Eating Disorders, 25*, 415-424.

Brewerton, T. D., Stellefson, E. J., Hibbs, N., Hodges, E. L., and Cochrane, C. (1995). Comparison of eating disorder patients with and without compulsive exercising. *International Journal of Eating Disorders, 17*(4), 413-416.

Brownell, K. D. (1991). Dieting and the search for the perfect body: Where physiology and culture collide. *Behaviour Therapy, 22*(1-12).

Brownell, K. D., and Rodin, J. (1994). The dieting maelstrom: Is it possible and advisable to lose weight? *American Psychologist, 49*(9), 781-791.

Brownell, K. D., Rodin, J., and Wilmore, J. H. (1992). Eating, body weight and performance in athletes: An introduction. In K. D. Brownell, J. Rodin and J. H. Wilmore (Eds.), *Eating, body weight and performance in athletes: Disorders of modern society* (pp. 3-16). Philadelphia: Lea and Fabinger.

Bulik, C., Sullivan, P. F., and Kendler, K. S. (1998). Heritability of binge-eating and boradly defined bulimia nervosa. *Biological Psychiatry, 44*, 1210-1218.

Bulik, C., Tozzi, F., Anderson, C., Mazzeo, S., Aggen, S., and Sullivan, P. (2003). The relation between eating disorders and components of perfectionism. *The American Journal of Psychiatry, 160*(2), 366-368.

Burkle, M. (1999). Forms of competitive attitude and achievement orientation in relation to disordered eating. *Sex roles: A journal of research, 40*(853-870).

Butters, J. W., and Cash, T. F. (1987). Cognitive-behavioural treatment of women's body-image dissatisfaction. *Journal of Consulting and Clinical Psychology, 55*(6), 889-897.

Button, E. J., Loan, P., Davies, J., and Sonuga-Barke, E. J. (1997). Self esteem, eating problems and psychological well-being in a cohort of schoolgirls aged 15-16. A questionnaire and interview study. *International Journal of Eating Disorders, 21*, 39-47.

Byrne, S., and McLean, N. (2001). Eating disorders in athletes: A review of the literature. *Journal of science and medicine in sport, 4*(2), 145-159.

Byrne, S., and McLean, N. (2002). Elite Athletes: effects of the pressure to be thin. *Journal of Science and Medicine in Sport, 5*(2), 80-94.

Calogero, R. M., and Pedrotty, K. N. (2004). The practice and process of healthy exercise: An investigation of the treatment of exercise abuse in women with eating disorders. *Eating Disorders, 12*, 273-291.

Carlat, D. J., and Carmargo, C. A. (1991). Review of Bulimia Nervosa in males. *American Journal of Psychiatry, 148*, 831-843.

Carlat, D. J., Carmargo, C. A., and Herzog, D. B. (1997). Eating disorders in males: A report on 135 patients. *American Journal of Psychiatry, 154*, 1127-1132.

Cash, T. F., Morrow, J. A., Hrabosky, J., and Perry, A. (2004). How has body image changed? A cross-sectional investigation of college women and men from 1983 to 2001. *Journal of Consulting and Clinical Psychology, 72*(6), 1081-1089.

Celio, A., Winzelberg, A., Wilfley, D., Eppstein-Herald, D., Springer, E., Dev, P., et al. (2000). Reducing risk factors for eating disorders: Comparison of an internet and a classroom delivered psychoeducational program. *Journal of Consulting and Clinical Psychology, 68*(4), 650-657.

Clark, D., Blair, S., and Culan, M. (1988). Are HPE teachers good role models? *Journal of Physical Education, Recreation and Dance, 54*, 76-80.

Compas, B. E., Wagner, B. M., Slavin, L. A., and Vannatta, K. (1986). A prospective study of life events, social support, and psychological symptomatology during the transition from high school to college. American Journal of Community Psychology, 14, 241-257. *American Journal of Community Psychology, 14.*

Connor-Greene, P., Striegel-Moore, R., and Cronan, S. (1994). Perceived social climate and weight preoccupation in college women. *Eating Disorders, 2*(2), 126-134.

Connor-Greene, P. A. (1988). Gender differences in body weight perception and weight-loss strategies of college students. *Women and Health, 14*(2), 27-43.

Cook-Cottone, C., and Phelps, L. (2003). Body dissatisfaction in college women: Identification of risk and protective factors to guide college counseling practices. *Journal of College Counseling, 6*, 80-88.

Cooley, E., and Toray, T. (2001a). Body image and personality predictors of eating disorder symptoms during the college years. *International Journal of Eating Disorders, 30*, 28-36.

Cooley, E., and Toray, T. (2001b). Disordered eating in college freshman women: A prospective study. *Journal of American College Health, 49*(5), 229-235.

Coric, D., and Murstein, B. (1993). Bulimia nervosa: Prevalence and psychological correlates in a college community. *Eating Disorders, 1*(1), 39-51.

Crandall, C. S. (1988). Social contagion of binge eating. *Journal of Personal and Social Psychology, 55*, 588-598.

Crawford, D. A., and Worsley, A. (1988). Dieting and slimming practices of South Australian women. *Medical Journal of Australia, 148*, 325-331.

Crockett, S. J., and Littrell, J. M. (1985). Comparison of eating patterns between dietetic and other college students. *Journal of Nutrition Education, 17*, 47-50.

Croll, J., Neumark-Sztainer, D., Story, M., and Ireland, M. (2002). Prevalence and risk and protective factors related to disordered eating behaviors among adolescents: Relationship to gender and ethnicity. *Journal of Adolescent Health, 31*, 166-175.

Davis, C. (1992). Body image, dieting behaviours and personality factors: A study of high performance female athletes. *International Journal of Sport Psychology, 23*, 179-192.

Davis, C. (1997). Normal and neurotic perfectionism in eating disorders: An interactive model. *International Journal of Eating Disorders, 22*, 421-426.

Davis, C., and Cowles, M. (1991). Body image and exercise: A study of relationships and comparisons between physically active men and women. *Sex Roles: A journal of Research, 25*, 33-44.

Davis, C., and Scott-Robertson, L. (2000). A psychological comparison of females with anorexia nervosa and competitive male bodybuilders: Body shape ideals in the extreme. *Eating Behaviors, 1*, 33-46.

Davis, T. (1999). Health educators as positive role models. *Journal of Health Eudcation, 30*, 60-61.

De Coverly Veale, D. M. W. (1987). Exercise Dependence. *British Journal of Addiction, 82*, 735-740.

Drake, M. A. (1989). Symptoms of anorexia nervosa in female university dietetic majors. *Journal of the American Dietetic Association, 89*(1), 97-99.

Drenowski, A., and Yee, D. K. (1987). Men and body image: Are males satisfied with their body weight? *Psychosomatic Medicine, 49*, 626-634.

Drenowski, A., Yee, D. K., Kurth, C. L., and Krahn, D. D. (1994). Eating Pathology and DSM-III-R Bulimia Nervosa: A continuum of behavior. *American Journal of Psychiatry, 151*(8), 1217-1219.

Dross, R. G., and Silverman, J. A. (1979). Body image and perfectionism in ballerinas: Comparison and contrast with anorexia nervosa. *General Hospital Psychiatry, 1*, 115-121.

Drummond, M. (2002). Men, body image and eating disorders. *International Journal of Men's Health, 1*, 79-93.

Dworkin, S., and Kerr, B. (1987). Comparison of interventions for women experiencing body image problems. *Journal of Counseling Psychology, 34*, 136-140.

Engwall, D., Hunter, R., and Steinberg, M. (2004). Gambling and other risk behaviors on university campuses. *Journal of American College Health, 52*(6), 245-256.

Evers, C. L. (1987). Dietary intake and symptoms of anorexia nervosa in female university dancers. *Journal of the American Dietetic Association, 87*(1), 66-68.

Fairburn, C. (1997). Eating Disorders (pp209-243). In D. M. Clark and C. Fairburn (Eds.), *Science and practice of cognitive behavior therapy*. Oxford: Oxford University Press.

Fairburn, C. G., and Beglin, S. J. (1990). Studies of the epidemiology of bulimia nervosa. *American Journal of Psychiatry, 147*, 401-408.

Festinger, L. (1954). A theory of social comparison process. *Human Relations, 7*, 117-140.

Festinger, L. (1957). *A theory of cognitive dissonance*. Stanford: Stanford University Press.

Forman-Hoffman, V. (2004). High prevalence of abnormal eating and weight control practices among U.S. high school students. *Eating Behaviors, 5*, 325-336.

Franco-Paradedes, K., Mancilla-Diaz, J. M., Vazquez-Arevalo, R., Lopez-Aguilar, X., and Alvarez-Rayon, G. (2005). Perfectionism and eating disorders: A review of the literature. *European Eating Disorder Review, 13*, 61-70.

Franko, D. L. (1998). Secondary prevention of eating disorders in college women at risk. *Eating Disorders, 6*, 24-40.

Franko, D. L., and Orosan- Weine, P. (1998). The prevention of eating disorders: Empirical, methodological and conceptual considerations. *Clinical Psychology science and practice, 5*, 549-477.

French, S., and Jeffery, R. (1994). Consequences of dieting to lose weight: Effects on physical and mental health. *Health Psychology, 13*, 195-212.

Froiland, K., Koszewski, W., Hingst, J., and Kopecky, L. (2004). Nutritional supplement use among college athletes and their sources of information. *International journal of Sport Nutrition and Exercise Metabolism, 14*, 104-120.

Garman, J. F., Hayduk, D. M., Crider, D. A., and Hodel, M. M. (2004). occurrence of exercise dependence in a college-aged population. *Journal of American College Health, 52*(5), 221-228.

Garner, D. M., and Garfinkel, P. E. (1979). The eating attitudes test: An index of the symptoms of anorexia nervosa. *Psychological Medicine, 9*, 273-279.

Garner, D. M., and Garfinkel, P. E. (1980). Socio-cultural factors in the development of anorexia nervosa. *Psychological Medicine, 10*, 647-656.

Garner, D. M., Garfinkel, P. E., Schwartz, D., and Thompson, M. (1980). Cultural expectations of thinness in women. *Psychological Reports, 47*, 483-491.

Garner, D. M., Olmstead, M. P., and Polivy, J. (1983). The eating disorder inventory: A measure of cognitive-behavioural dimensions of anorexia nervosa and bulimia. In A/Liss (Ed.), *Anorexia Nervosa: Recent developments in research*. New York: LEA.

Geller, J., Zaitsoff, S., and Srikameswaran, S. (2002). Beyond shape and weight: Exploring the relationship between nonbody determinants of self-esteem and eating disorder symptoms in adolescent females. *International Journal of Eating Disorders, 32*, 344-351.

Graff Low, K., Charanasomboon, S., Brown, C., Hiltunen, G., Long, K., and Reinhalter, K. (2003). Internalization of the thin ideal, weight and body image concerns. *Social Behavior and Personality, 31*(1), 81-90.

Green, M., Scott, N., Diyankova, I., Gasser, C., and Pederson, E. (2005). Eating Disorder Prevention: An experimental comparison of high level dissonance, low level dissonance and no-treatment control. *Eating Disorders, 13*, 157-169.

Grogan, S. (1999). *Body Image: Understanding body dissatisfaction in men, women and children*. New York: Routlege.

Halmi, A. K., Sunday, R. S., Strober, M., Kaplan, A., Woodside, B. D., Fichter, M., et al. (2000). Perfectionism in anorexia nervosa: Variation by clinical subtype, obsessionality, and pathological eating behavior. *American Journal of Psychiatry, 157*(11), 1799-1805.

Halmi, K. A., Falk, J. R., and Schwartz, E. (1981). Binge eating and vomiting: A survey of a college population. *Psychological Medicine, 11*, 697-706.

Hayward, C., Killen, J., Wilson, D., Hammer, L., Litt, I., and Kraemer, H. (1997). Psychiatric risk associated with early puberty in adolescent girls. *Journal of the American Academy of Child and Adolescent Psychiatry, 36*, 255-262.

Heatherton, T. F., Mahamedi, F., Striepe, M., Field, A. E., and Keel, P. K. (1997). A 10-year longitudinal study of body weight, dieting, and eating disorder symptoms. *Journal of Abnormal Psychology, 106*(1), 117-125.

Heatherton, T. F., Nichols, P., Mahamedi, F., and Keel, P. (1995). Body weight, dieting, and eating disorders symptoms among college students. *American Journal of Psychiatry, 152*(11), 1623-1629.

Hill, A. (Ed.). (2002). *Prevalence and demographics of dieting*. New York: The Guilford Press.

Holsten, J. L., and Cashwell, C. S. (2000). Family functioning and eating disorders among college women: A model of prediction. *Journal of College Counseling, 3*, 5-16.

Hopkinson, R. A., and Lock, J. (2004). Athletes, perfectionism, and disordered eating. *Eating and Weight Disorders, 9*, 99-106.

Howard, M. O. (2002). *The Exercise Dependence Criteria*. St Louis: Washington University.

Huon, G. F. (1994). Towards the prevention of dieting-induced disorders: Modifying negative food-and-body-related attitudes. *International Journal of Eating Disorders, 16*(4), 395-399.

Irving, L. M., and Berel, S. R. (2001). Comparison of media-literacy programs to strengthen college women's resistance to media images. *Psychology of Women Quarterly, 25*, 103-111.

Jenkins, A., and Olsen, L. (1994). Health behaviours of health educators: A national survey. *Journal of Health Education, 25*, 324-332.

Johnson, C., Powers, P. S., and Dick, R. (1999). Athletes and eating disorders: The National Collegiate Athletic Association Study. *International Journal of Eating Disorders, 26*, 179-188.

Johnson, J. G., Cohen, P., Kasen, S., and Brook, J. S. (2002). Eating disorders during adolescence and the risk for physical and mental disorders during early adulthood. *Archives of General Psychiatry, 59*, 545-552.

Johnston, C. S., and Christopher, F. S. (1991). Anorexic-like behaviours in dietetics majors and other student populations. *Journal of Nutrition Education, 23*, 148-153.

Joiner, T. E., Jr., Heatherton, T. F., Rudd, M. D., and Schmidt, N. (1997). Perfectionism, percieved weight status, and bulimic symptoms: Two studies testing a diathesis-stress model. *Journal of Abnormal Psychology, 106*, 145-153.

Joseph, A., Wood, I. K., and Goldberg, S. C. (1982). Determining populations at risk for developing anorexia nervosa based on selection of college major. *Psychiatry Research, 7*, 53-58.

Katzman, M. A., Wolchik, S. A., and Braver, S. L. (1984). The prevalence of frequent binge eating and bulimia in a nonclinical college sample. *International Journal of Eating Disorders, 3*(3), 53-62.

Kaye, W. H., Gendall, K., and Strober, M. (1998). Serotonin neuronal function and selective serotonin reuptake inhibitor treatment in anorexia and bulimia nervosa. *Biological Psychiatry, 44*, 825-838.

Kearney-Cooke, A., and Steichen-Asch, P. (1990). Men, body image and eating disorders. In A. E. Anderson (Ed.), *Males with eating disorders* (pp. 54-74). New York: Brunner/Mazel.

Keesey, R. E. (1986). A set-point theory of obesity. In K. D. Brownell and J. P. Foreyt (Eds.), *Handbook of eating disorders: Physiology, psychology and treatment of obesity, anorexia and bulimia (pp63-87)*. New York: Basic Books.

Kenardy, J., Brown, W., and Vogt, E. (2001). Dieting and health in young Australian women. *European Eating Disorders Review, 9*, 242-254.

Keski-Rahkonen, A., Bulik, C., Neale, B., Rose, R., Rissanen, A., and Kaprio, J. (2005). Body dissatisfaction and drive for thinness in young adult twins. *International Journal of Eating Disorders, 37*(3), 188-199.

Killen, J. (1985). Prevention of adolescent tobacco smoking: The social pressure resistance training approach. *Journal of Child Psychology and Psychiatry, 26*, 7-15.

Killen, J., Taylor, C. B., Hayward, C., Wilson, D., Haydel, K., and Hammer, L. (1994). Pursuit of thinness and onset of eating disorder symptoms in a community sample of adolescent girls: A three year prospective analysis. *International Journal of Eating Disorders, 16*, 227-238.

Kiningham, R. B., and Gorenflo, D. W. (2001). Weight loss methods of high school wrestlers. *Medicine and Science in Sports and Exercise*, 810-813.

Kinzl, J., Traweger, C., Trefalt, E., Mangweth, B., and Biebl, W. (1999). Dieticians: Are they a risk group for eating disorders? *European Eating Disorders Review, 7*, 62-67.

Kirk, D., and Tinning, R. (1994). Embodied self-identity, healthy lifestyles and school physical education. *Sociology of health and illness, 16*(5), 601-624.

Kjelsas, E., and Augestad, L. B. (2004). Gender, eating behavior and personality characteristics in physically active students. *Scandinavian Journal of Medicine and Science in Sport, 14*, 258-268.

Klemchuck, H. P., Hutchinson, C. B., and Frank, R. I. (1990). Body dissatisfaction and eating problems on the college campus: Usefulness of the eating disorder inventory with a non-clinical population. *Journal of Counselling Psychology, 37*, 297-305.

Klump, K. L., Miller, K. B., Keel, P. K., McGue, M., and Iacono, W. G. (2001). Genetic and environmental influences on anorexia nervosa syndromes in a population-based twin sample. *Psychological Medicine, 31*, 737-740.

Koszewski, W., Newell, G. K., and Higgins, J. J. (1990). Effect of a nutrition education program on the eating attitudes and behaviors of college women. *Journal of College Student Development, 31*, 203-210.

Krumbach, C. J., Ellis, D. R., and Driskell, J. A. (1999). A report of vitamin and mineral supplement use among university athletes in a Division 1 institution. *International Journal of Sport Nutrition, 9*, 416-425.

Kurth, C. L., Krahn, D. D., Nairn, K., and Drenowski, A. (1995). The severity of dieting and bingeing behaviors in college women: Interview validation of survey data. *Journal of Psychiatric Research, 29*(3), 211-225.

Kurtzman, F. D., Yager, J., Landsverk, J., Wiesmeier, E., and Bodurka, D. C. (1989). Eating disorders among selected female populations at UCLA. *Journal of the American Dietetic Association, 89*(1), 45-52.

Larson, B. (1989). The new epidemic: Ethical implications for nutrition educators. *Journal of Nutrition Education, 21*, 101-103.

Leit, R. A., Gray, J. J., and Pope Jr, H. G. (2002). The media's representation of the ideal male body: A cause for muscle dysmorphia? *International Journal of Eating Disorders, 31*, 334-338.

Lenz, B. (2004). Tobacco, depression, and lifestyle choices in the pivotal early college years. *Journal of American College Health, 52*(5), 213-219.

Lilenfeld, L. R., Stein, D., Bulik, C., Strober, M., Plotnicov, K., Pollice, C., et al. (2000). Personality traits among currently eating disordered, recovered, and never ill first-degree female relatives of bulimic and control women. *Psychological Medicine, 30*(6), 1399-1410.

Lucas, A. R., Beard, M., O'Fallon, W. M., and Kurland, L. T. (1991). 50-year trends in the incidence of Anorexia Nervosa in Rochester, Minn: A population-based study. *American Journal of Psychiatry, 148*, 917-922.

Mann, M., Hosman, C., Schaalma, H., and de Vries, N. K. (2004). Self-esteem in a broad-spectrum approach for mental health promotion. *Health Education Research, 19*(4), 357-372.

Mann, T., Nolen-Hoeksema, S., and Huang, K. (1997). Are two interventions worse than none? Joint primary and secondary prevention of eating disorders in college females. *Health Psychology, 16*, 215-225.

Martz, D. M., and Bazzini, D. G. (1999). Eating disorders prevention programming may be failing: Evaluation of 2 one-shot programs. *Journal of College Student Development, 40*(1), 32-42.

Matusek, J. A., Wendt, S. J., and Wiseman, C. (2004). Dissonance thin-ideal and didactic healthy behavior eating disorder prevention programs: Results from a controlled trial. *International Journal of Clinical Practice, 36*, 376-388.

McArthur, A., and Howard, A. (2001). Dietetics majors' weight-reduction beliefs, behaviours, and information sources. *Journal of American College Health, 49*, 175-184.

McCarthy, M. (1990). The thin ideal, depression and eating disorders in women. *Behavioural Research Therapy, 28*, 205-215.

McDonald, K., and Thompson, J. K. (1992). Eating disturbance, body image dissatisfaction, and reasons for exercising: Gender differences and correlational findings. *International Journal of Eating Disorders, 11*(3), 289-292.

McGee, B. J., Hewitt, P. L., Sherry, S. B., Parkin, M., and Flett, G. L. (2005). Perfectionistic self-presentation, body image, and eating disorder symptoms. *Body Image, 2,* 29-40.

McLaren, L., Gauvin, L., and White, D. (2001). The role of perfectionism and excessive commitment to exercise in explaining dietary restraint: Replication and extension. *International Journal of Eating Disorders, 29,* 307-313.

McVey, G. L., Davis, R., Tweed, S., and Shaw, B. F. (2004). Evaluation of a school-based program designed to improve body image satisfaction, global self-esteem, and eating attitudes and behaviors: A replication study. *International Journal of Eating Disorders, 36,* 1-11.

McVey, G. L., Lieberman, M., Voorberg, N., Wardrope, D., and Blackmore, E. (2003). School-based support groups: A new approach to the prevention of disordered eating. *Eating Disorders, 11,* 169-185.

Meilman, P. W., von Hippel, F. A., and Galor, M. S. (1991). Self-induced vomiting in college women: Its relation to eating, alcohol use, and Greek life. *Journal of American College Health, 40,* 39-41.

Melville, D. S., and Cardinal, B. J. (1997). Are overweight physical educators at a disadvantage in the labor market? A random survey of hiring personnel. *The Physical Educator, 54,* 216-221.

Melville, D. S., and Maddalozzo, J. G. F. (1988). The effects of a physical educator's appearance of body fatness on communicating exercise concepts to high school students. *Journal of Teaching in Physical Education, 7,* 343-352.

Mintz, L., and Betz, N. (1988). Prevalence and correlates of eating disordered behaviors among undergraduate women. *Journal of Counseling Psychology, 35*(4), 463-471.

Mishkind, M. E., Rodin, J., Silberstein, L. R., and Striegel-Moore, R. (1986). The embodiment of masculinity. *American Behavioral Scientist, 29*(5), 545-562.

Mutterperl, J. A., and Sanderson, C. A. (2002). Mind over matter: Internalization of thinness norm as a moderator of responsiveness to norm misperception education in college women. *Health Psychology, 21,* 519-523.

Neumark-Sztainer, D., Jeffery, R. W., and French, S. A. (1997). Self-reported dieting: How should we ask? What does it mean? Associations between dieting and reported energy intake. *International Journal of Eating Disorders, 22,* 437-449.

Neumark-Sztainer, D., Sherwood, N., Coller, T., and Hannan, P. J. (2000). Primary prevention of disordered eating among preadolescent girls: Feasibility and short term effect of a community-based intervention. *Journal of the American Dietetic Association, 100*(12), 1466-1473.

Newman, D. L., Moffitt, T. E., Caspi, A., Magdol, L., Silva, P. A., and Stanton, W. R. (1996). Psychiatric disorder in a birth cohort of young adults: Prevalence, comorbidity, clinical significance, and new case incidence from ages 11-21. *Journal of Consulting and Clinical Psychology, 64,* 552-562.

Nicolino, J. C., Martz, D. M., and Curtin, L. (2001). Evaluation of a cognitive-behavioral therapy intervention to improve body image and decrease dieting in college women. *Eating Behaviors, 2,* 353-362.

O'Dea, J. (1995). *Everybody's Different: A self esteem program for young adolescents.* Sydney: University of Sydney Press.

O'Dea, J. (1998). The body size preferences of underweight young women from different cultural backgrounds. *Australian Journal of Nutrition and Dietetics, 55*, 75-80.

O'Dea, J. (1999). Cross-cultural, body weight and gender differences in the body size perceptions and body ideals of university students. *Australian Journal of Nutrition and Dietetics, 56*, 144-150.

O'Dea, J. (2000). School based interventions to prevent eating problems: First do no harm. *Eating Disorders, 8*, 123-130.

O'Dea, J. (2004). Evidence for a self-esteem apprroach in the prevention of body image and eating problems among children and adolescents. *Eating Disorders, 12*, 225-239.

O'Dea, J., and Abraham, S. F. (2000). Improving the body image, eating attitudes, and behaviours of young male and female adolescents: A new educational approach that focuses on self esteem. *International Journal of Eating Disorders, 28*, 43-57.

O'Dea, J., and Abraham, S. F. (2001). Knowledge, beliefs, attitudes and behaviours related to weight control, eating disorders, and body image in Australian trainee home economics and physical education teachers. *Journal of Nutrition Education, 33*, 332-340.

O'Dea, J., and Abraham, S. F. (2002). Eating and Exercise Disorders in Young College men. *Journal of American College Health, 50*, 273-278.

O'Dea, J., and Yager, Z. (2005). Body image and eating disorders in male adolescents and young men. In P. Swain (Ed.), *New Developments in Eating Disorders Research.* New York: Nova Science Publishers.

Olivardia, R., Pope Jr, H. G., Borowiecki, J. J., and Cohane, G. (2004). Biceps and body image: The relationship between muscularity and self-esteem, depression, and eating disorder symptoms. *Psychology of Men and Masculinity, 5*(2), 112-120.

Palmquist- Fredenberg, J., Berglund, P., and Dieken, H. (1996). Incidence of eating disorders among selected female university students. *Journal of the American Dietetic association, 96*, 64-66.

Pasman, L., and Thompson, K. J. (1988). Body image and eating disturbance in obligatory runners, obligatory weightlifters, and sedentary individuals. *International Journal of Eating Disorders, 7*, 759-769.

Patton, G. C. (1988). The spectrum of eating disorders in adolescence. *Journal of Psychosomatic research, 32*, 579-584.

Paxton, S. (2000). Body image dissatisfaction, extreme weight loss behaviours: Suitable targets for public health concern? *Health Promotion Journal of Australia, 10*, 15-19.

Paxton, S. J., Wertheim, E. H., Gibbons, K., Szmukler, G. I., Hillier, L., and Petrovich, J. C. (1991). Body image satisfaction, dieting beliefs and weight loss behaviours in adolescent girls and boys. *Journal of Youth and Adolescence, 20*, 361-379.

Pearson, J., Goldklang, D., and Striegel-Moore, R. (2001). Prevention of eating disorders: Challenges and opportunities. *International Journal of Eating Disorders, 31*, 233-239.

Petrie, T. A. (1996). Differences between male and female college lean sport athletes, nonlean sport athletes, and nonathletes on behavioral and psychological indices of eating disorders. *Journal of Applied Sport Psychology, 8*, 219-230.

Phelps, L., Dempsey, M., Sapia, J. L., and Nelson, L. (1999). The efficacy of a school-based eating disorder prevention program: Building physical self esteem and personal competencies. In N. Piran, M. Levine and C. Steiner-Adair (Eds.), *Preventing eating disorders: A handbook of interventions and special challenges (pp 163-174).* Philadelphia: Brunner/Mazel.

Phelps, L., Sapia, J. L., Nathanson, D., and Nelson, L. (2000). An empirically supported eating disorder prevention program. *Psychology in Schools, 37*(5), 443-452.

Phillips, J., and Drummond, M. (2001). An investigation into the body image perception, body satisfaction and exercise expectations of male fitness leaders: implications for professional practice. *Leisure Studies, 20*, 95-105.

Picard, C. L. (1999). The level of competition as a factor for the development of eating disorders in female college athletes. *Journal of Youth and Adolescence, 28*(5), 583-591.

Polivy, J., and Herman, C. P. (1985). Dieting and Binging: A causal analysis. *American Psychologist, 40*(193-201).

Pomeroy, C., and Mitchell, J. (2002). Medical complications of anorexia nervosa and bulimia nervosa. In C. Fairburn and K. D. Brownell (Eds.), *Eating Disorders and Obesity: A comprehensive handbook* (2nd Edition., pp. 278-285). New York: The Guilford Press.

Pope, H. G., Gruber, A. J., Choi, P., Olivardia, R., and Phillips, K. (1997). Muscle Dysmorphia: An underrecognized form of body dysmorphic disorder. *Psychosomatics, 38*, 548-557.

Pope, H. G., Hudson, J. I., Yurgelun-Todd, D., and Hudson, M. S. (1984). Prevalence of Anorexia Nervosa and Bulimia in three student populations. *International Journal of Eating Disorders, 3*(3), 45--51.

Pope, j., Harrison G., Gruber, A. J., Mangweth, B., Bureau, B., deCol, C., Jouvent, R., et al. (2000). Body image perception among men in three countries. *The American Journal of Psychiatry, 157*(8), 1297-1301.

Prouty, A., Protinsky, H., and Canady, D. (2002). College women: Eating behaviors and help seeking preferences. *Adolescence, 37*(146), 353-363.

Pyle, R. L., Halvorson, P. A., Neuman, P. A., and Mitchell, J. E. (1986). The increasing prevalence of bulimia in freshman college students. *International Journal of Eating Disorders, 5*(631-647).

Rabak-Wagener, J., Eickhoff-Shemek, J., and Kelly-Vance, L. (1998). The effect of media analysis on attitudes and behaviors regarding body image among college students. *Journal of American College Health, 47*(1), 29-35.

Reinstein, N., Koszewski, W., Chamberlain, B., and Smith-Johnson, C. (1992). Prevalence of eating disorders among dietetics students: Does nutrition education make a difference? *Journal of the American dietetic association, 92*, 949-954.

Rierdan, J., and Koff, E. (1991). Depressive symptomatology among very early maturing girls. *Journal of Youth and Adolescence, 20*, 219-225.

Rodin, J., Silberstein, L. P., and Striegel-Moore, R. H. (Eds.). (1985). *Women and weight: A normative discontent.* Lincoln: University of Nebraska Press.

Rosen, J. C., Saltzberg, E., and Srebnik, D. (1989). Cognitive behavior therapy for negative body image. *Behavior therapy, 20*, 393-404.

Rosen, L. W., McKeag, D. B., Hough, D. O., and Curly, V. (1986). Pathogenic weight-control behavior in female athletes. *The Physician and Sports Medicine, 14*(1), 79-86.

Ruggiero, G., Levi, D., Ciuna, A., and Sassaroli, S. (2003). Stress situation reveals an association between perfectionism and drive for thinness. *International Journal of Eating Disorders, 34*, 220-226.

Rutz, S. (1993). Nutrition educators should practice what they teach. *Journal of Nutrition Education, 25*(2), 87-88.

Sanders, F., Gaskill, D., and Gwynne, E. (2000). An overview of issues related to eating disorders. In D. Gaskill and F. Sanders (Eds.), *The encultured body: Policy implications for healthy body image and disordered eating behaviors* (pp. 6-21). QLD: Queensland University of Technology.

Schulken, E. D., Pinciaro, P. J., Sawyer, R. G., Jensen, J. G., and Hoban, M. T. (1997). Sorority women's body size perceptions and their weight related attitudes and behaviors. *Journal of American College Health, 46*(2), 69-74.

Schwitzer, A. M., Rodriguez, L. E., Thomas, C., and Salimi, L. (2001). The eating disorders NOS diagnostic profile among college women. *Journal of American College Health, 49*, 157-173.

Shih, M.-Y., and Kubo, C. (2005). Body shape preference and body satisfaction of Taiwanese and Japanese female college students. *Psychiatry Research, 113*, 263-271.

Shisslak, C., Crago, M., Renger, R., and Clark-Wagner, A. (1998). Self-Esteem and the prevention of eating disorders. *Eating Disorders, 6*, 105-117.

Shisslak, C. M., Crago, M., and Neal, M. E. (1990). Prevention of eating disorders among adolescents. *American Journal of Health Promotion, 5*, 100-106.

Silberstein, L. R., Striegel-Moore, R., Timko, C., and Rodin, J. (1988). Behavioural and psychological implications of body dissatisfaction: Do men and women differ? *Sex Roles: A Journal of Research, 19*(3/4), 219-232.

Slade, P. D. (1982). Towards a functional analysis of anorexia nervosa and bulimia nervosa. *British Journal of Clinical Psychology, 21*, 167-179.

Smolak, L., Murnen, S. K., and Ruble, A. (2000). Female athletes and eating problems: A meta-analysis. *International Journal of Eating Disorders, 27*, 371-380.

Sours, J. (1980). *Starving to death in a sea of objects: The anorexia nervosa syndrome.* New York: J Aronson.

Springer, E., Winzelberg, A., Perkins, R., and Taylor, C.B (1999). Effects of a body image curriculum for college students on improved body image. *International Journal of Eating Disorders, 26*, 13-20.

Steiner-Adair, C., Sjostrom, L., Franko, D., Seeta, P., Tucker, R., Becker, A., et al. (2001). Primary prevention of risk factors for eating disorders in adolescent girls: Learning from practice. *International Journal of Eating Disorders, 32*, 401-441.

Stewart, D. A., Carter, J. C., Drinkwater, J., Hainsworth, J., and Fairburn, C. (2001). Modification of eating attitudes and behaviour in adolescent girls: A controlled study. *International Journal of Eating Disorders, 29*(2), 107-118.

Stice, E. (2002a). Risk and maintenance factors for eating pathology: A meta-analytic review. *Psychological Bulletin, 128*(5), 825-848.

Stice, E. (2002b). Sociocultural influences on body image and eating distubance. In C. Fairburn and K. D. Brownell (Eds.), *Eating Disorders and Obesity* (pp. 103-107). New York: The Guilford Press.

Stice, E., Cameron, R. P., Killen, J., Hayward, C., and Taylor, C.B. (1999). Naturalistic weight-reduction efforts prospectively predict growth in relative weight and onset of obesity among female adolescents. *Journal of Consulting and Clinical Psychology, 67*(6), 967-974.

Stice, E., Chase, A., Stormer, S., and Appel, A. (2001). A randomized trial of a dissonance-based eating disorder prevention program. *International Journal of Eating Disorders, 29*, 247-262.

Stice, E., Hayward, C., Cameron, R. P., Killen, J. D., and Taylor, C.B (2000). Body-image and eating distrubances predict onset of depression among female adolescents: A longitudinal study. *Journal of Abnormal Psychology, 109*(3), 438-444.

Stice, E., Mazotti, L., Weibel, D., and Agras, S.W. (2000). Dissonance prevention program decreases thin-ideal internalization, body dissatisfaction, dieting, negative affect, and bulimic symptoms: A preliminary experiment. *International Journal of Eating Disorders, 27*, 206-217.

Stice, E., and Ragan, J. (2002). A preliminary controlled evaluation of an eating disturbance psychoeducational intervention for college students. *International Journal of Eating Disorders, 31*, 159-171.

Stice, E., Schupak-Neuberg, E., Shaw, H. E., and Stein, R. I. (1994). Relation of media exposure to eating disorder symptomatology: An examination of mediating mechanisms. *Journal of Abnormal Psychology, 103*, 836-840.

Stice, E., Trost, A., and Chase, A. (2003). Healthy weight control and dissonance-based eating disorder prevention programs: Results from a controlled trial. *International Journal of Eating Disorders, 33*, 10-21.

Stone, J., Aronson, E., Crain, A. L., Winslow, M. P., and Fried, C. B. (1994). Inducing hypocrisy as a means of encouraging young adults to use condoms. *Personality and Social Psychology Bulletin, 20*, 116-128.

Strelan, P., Mehaffey, S. J., and Tiggemann, M. (2003). Self-objectification and esteem in young women: The mediating role of reasons for exercise. *Sex Roles: A Journal of Research, 89*(7), 89-96.

Striegel-Moore, R., Dohm, F., Kraemer, H., Taylor, C.B, Daniels, S., Crawford, P., et al. (2003). Eating disorders in black and white women. *American Journal of Psychiatry, 160*, 1326-1331.

Striegel-Moore, R., Silberstein, L., and Rodin, J. (1986). Toward an understanding of risk factors for bulimia. *American Psychologist, 41*, 246-263.

Striegel-Moore, R., and Steiner-Adair, C. (1998). Primary Prevention of Eating Disorders: Further considerations from a feminist perspective. In W. Vandereycken and G. Noordenbos (Eds.), *The Prevention of Eating Disorders* (pp. 1-22). London: The Athlone Press.

Striegel-Moore, R. H., Silberstein, L. R., Grunberg, N. E., and Rodin, J. (1990). Competing on all fronts: Achievement orientation and disordered eating. *Sex Roles: A Journal of Research, 23*, 697-702.

Sundgot-Borgen, J. (1993). Prevalence of eating disorders in elite female athletes. *International journal of sport nutrition, 3*, 29-40.

Theander, S. (2002). Literature on Eating Disorders during 40 Years: Increasing Number of Papers, Emergence of Bulimia Nervosa. *European Eating Disorder Review, 10*, 386-398.

Thibodeau, R., and Aronson, E. (1992). Taking a closer look: Reasserting the role of self-concept in dissonance theory. *Personality and Social Psychology Bulletin, 18*, 591-602.

Thome, J., and Espelage, D. L. (2004). Relations among exercise, coping, disordered eating, and psychological health among college students. *Eating Behaviors, 5*, 337-351.

Thompson, J. K., and Tantleff, S. (1992). Female and male ratings of upper torso: Actual, ideal and stereotypical conceptions. *Journal of Social Behaviour and Personality, 7*, 342-354.

Thompson, K. J., and Stice, E. (2001). Thin-ideal internalization: Mounting evidence for a new risk factor for body-image disturbance and eating pathology. *Current directions in psychological science, 10*(5), 181-183.

Thompson, R. A., and Sherman, R. T. (1993). Reducing the risk of eating disorders in athletics. *Eating Disorders, 1*(1), 65-78.

Tiggemann, M. (2005). Body Dissatisfaction and adolescent self esteem: Prospective findings. *Body Image, 2*, 129-135.

Turnbull, J. D., Freeman, C., and Barry, F. (1987). Physical and psychological characteristics of five male bulimics. *British Journal of Psychiatry, 150*, 25-29.

Vaughan, J. L., King, K., and Cottrell, R. R. (2004). Collegiate athletic trainers' confidence in helping female athletes with eating disorders. *Journal of Athletic Training, 39*(1), 71-76.

Vohs, K. D., Bardone, A. M., Joiner, T. E., Abrahmson, L. Y., and Heatherton, T. F. (1999). Perfectionism, perceived weight status, and self esteem interact to predict bulimic symptoms: A model of bulimic symptom development. *Journal of Abnormal Psychology, 108*, 695-700.

Vohs, K. D., Heatherton, T. F., and Herrin, M. (2001). Disordered eating and the transition to college: A prospective study. *International Journal of Eating Disorders, 29*, 280-288.

Vohs, K. D., Voelz, Z. R., Pettit, J., Bardone, A. M., Katz, J., Abramson, L. Y., et al. (2001). Perfectionism, body dissatisfaction, and self esteem: An interactive model of bulimic symptom development. *Journal of Social and Clinical Psychology, 20*(4), 476-497.

Wade, T. D., Martin, N. G., Tiggemann, M., Abraham, S., Treloar, S. A., and Heath, A. C. (2000). Genetic and environmental risk factors shared between disordered eating, psychological and family variables. *Personality and Individual Differences, 28*, 729-740.

Wertheim, E., Paxton, S., Schultz, H., and Muir, S. (1997). Why do adolescent girls watch their weight? An interview study examining sociocultural pressures to be thin. *Journal of Psychosomatic research, 42*, 345-355.

Wicklund, R. A., and Brehm, J. (1976). *Perspectives on cognitive dissonance*. Hillsdale: Erlbaum.

Wiese, H. J., Wilson, J. F., Jones, R., and Neises, M. (1992). Obesity stigma reduction in medical students. *International Journal of Obesity, 16*, 859-868.

Wilksh, S., and Wade, T. D. (2004). Differences between women with anorexia nervosa and restrained eaters on shape and weight concerns, self-esteem and depression. *International Journal of Eating Disorders, 35*, 571-578.

Williams, D. M., Anderson, E. S., and Winett, R. A. (2004). Social cognitive predictors of creatine use versus non-use among male, undergraduate, recreational resistance trainers. *Journal of sport behavior, 27*(2), 170-183.

Wilson, G. T. (2002). The controversy over dieting. In C. Fairburn and K. D. Brownell (Eds.), *Eating Disorders and Obesity* (pp. 93-97). New York: The Guilford Press.

Winzelberg, A., Taylor, C.B, Sharpe, T., Eldredge, K., Dev, P., and Constantinou, P. S. (1998). Evaluation of a computer-mediated eating disorder intervention program. *International Journal of Eating Disorders, 24*, 339-349.

Winzelberg, A., Eppstein, D., Eldredge, K., Wilfley, D., Dasmahapatra, R., Dev, P., et al. (2000). Effectiveness of an internet -based program for reducing risk factors for eating disorders. *Journal of Consulting and Clinical Psychology, 68*, 346-350.

Wong, Y., and Huang, Y. C. (1999). Obesity concerns, weight satisfaction and characteristics of female dieters: A study on female Taiwanese college students. *Journal of the American College of Nutrition, 18*, 194-200.

Worobey, J., and Schoenfeld, D. (1999). Eating disordered behaviour in dietetics students and students in other majors. *Journal of the American Dietetic Association, 99*, 100-104.

Yager, Z., (2004). Unpublished Thesis Data.

Yates, A. (1991). *Compulsive exercise and the eating disorders : toward an integrated theory of activity*. New York, N.Y.: Brunner/Mazel.

Zabinski, M. F., Pung, M. A., Wilfley, D. E., Eppstein, D. L., Winzelberg, A. J., Celio, A., et al. (2001). Reducing risk factors for eating disorders: Targeting at-risk women with a computerised psychoeducational program. *International Journal of Eating Disorders, 29*, 401-408.

Zmijewski, C. F., and Howard, M. O. (2003). Exercise dependence and attitudes toward eating among young adults. *Eating Behaviors, 4*, 181-195.

Zuckerman, D. M., Colby, A., Ware, N. C., and Lazerson, J. S. (1986). The prevalence of bulimia among college students. *American Journal of Public Health, 76*(9), 1135-1137.

INDEX

B

C

E

F

N

Q

R

T

Y